──────────Cambridge──────────
THE COMPLETE SLIM CUISINE

Also by Sue Kreitzman

CAMBRIDGE SLIM CUISINE

CAMBRIDGE SLIM CUISINE: A SECOND HELPING

SUE KREITZMAN

Cambridge

The Complete Slim Cuisine

BANTAM PRESS

LONDON · NEW YORK · TORONTO · SYDNEY · AUCKLAND

To my family: more comforting than chicken soup,
more fun than chocolate soufflé,
much nicer than banana brûlée

TRANSWORLD PUBLISHERS LTD
61–63 Uxbridge Road, London W5 5SA

TRANSWORLD PUBLISHERS (AUSTRALIA) PTY LTD
15–23 Helles Avenue, Moorebank, NSW 2170

TRANSWORLD PUBLISHERS (NZ) LTD
Cnr Moselle and Waipareira Aves,
Henderson, Auckland

Published 1990 by Bantam Press
a division of Transworld Publishers Ltd
Copyright © Sue Kreitzman 1990

Originally published as *Cambridge Slim Cuisine*,
© Sue Kreitzman 1988 and
Cambridge Slim Cuisine: A Second Helping,
© Sue Kreitzman 1989

The right of Sue Kreitzman to be identified
as author of this work has been asserted in accordance
with sections 77 and 78 of the Copyright, Designs and
Patents Act 1988.

British Library Cataloguing in Publication Data

Kreitzman, Sue
The complete slim cuisine.
1. Food: Low fat dishes. Recipes
I. Title
641.5

ISBN 0-593-01874-5

Printed in Great Britain by
Mackays of Chatham plc, Chatham, Kent

Contents

List of Illustrations

gratin (page 272): meltingly tender potato slices in a creamy sauce under a crusty top.

Salad delights: clockwise from top right: greens with creamy herbed dressing (page 284); ripe tomatoes and Mozzarella cheese with shredded basil (page 289); fennel-pepper salad with mushrooms and capers (page 288).

Between pages 146–147

Mexican baked beans with tiny Mexican meatballs (page 156) and chilaquiles (tortilla pieces and chicken in a piquant sauce) (page 184).

Clockwise from lower right: spinach-stuffed goose skirt steak with wine sauce (page 136) and stock-sautéed root vegetables (page 24); chick pea-potato salad (page 293); pasta with terracotta sauce (page 234); fresh mango sorbet with berries (page 316).

Between pages 178–179

Tortilla chips (page 307). A tempting array of open sandwiches, from pizza (page 306) to smoked salmon with tzatziki and dill (page 304).

Mixed summer fruits are delicious topped with fromage frais and caramelized brown sugar.

Between pages 210–211

What would life be without pudding? Indulge your sweet tooth without widening your waistline: orange jelly in a meringue nest; fudgy chocolate torte; black and white meringue cookies; and cherries in honeyed cream.

A traditional English 'fry'-up breakfast (page 59), minus the grease.

Between pages 242–243

An elegant picnic (page 58), worthy of Glyndebourne or Henley; gazpacho; stuffed mushrooms; smoked chicken pesto potato salad; and strawberries with raspberry sauce.

Couscous with curried vegetables and spicy lamb meatballs (pages 203 and 160) make a festive party meal.

A luxurious dinner party: chicken liver pâté (page 80); meltingly tender veal shanks with wild mushrooms (page 166); polenta with aubergine (page 215); poached pears in honeyed red wine (page 326).

California-style cioppino (page 120) is an exhilarating fish and shellfish soup/stew. Serve it with croûtons topped with red pepper-garlic spread.

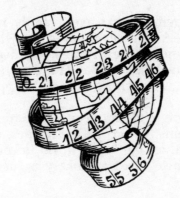

Acknowledgements

Sandie Perry and Rosemarie Espley, my kitchen assistant and my secretary, make my working life a great pleasure. Besides working hard in the kitchen and at the word processor, they are both ready at all times to drop everything and rush madly around the country, helping me cook, teach and lecture. We have shared many food adventures together, from cooking for foreign royalty to feeding 180 scientists in the dining hall of one of the Cambridge colleges. They are fun to be with, look terrific and I can never thank them enough.

Mary Hardy acts as our housemother, and – as always – helps in many ways. She is an important part of my life in England, and I thank her too.

Thank you also to Sue Atkinson, who understands Slim Cuisine very well and photographs it with great sensitivity, to her home economist Elaine Andrews, to my agent David Grossman, who has a warm heart and an infectious laugh, to Lizzie Laczynska and Oriol Bath, who helped make both *Slim Cuisines* such handsome volumes, to Ursula Mackenzie and Mark Barty-King, who conceived the idea of a *Slim Cuisine* compendium, to Heidi Lascelles and Clarissa Dickson Wright at Books for Cooks, who are always ready to answer questions and give advice, to Dr Ann Coxon, whose support of and enthusiasm for Slim Cuisine is greatly appreciated, to Mary Clarke, who makes working with British Gas such a pleasure, and to my mentor, Dr Alan N. Howard. And thanks to Robert Parsons for working so hard to make a low-fat cocoa powder available to British chocoholics.

Warm and grateful thanks to the BBC's Mary Clyne and Vicky Kimm, who have become valued friends as well as colleagues, and to all the rest of the *Daytime Live* folks.

Unlimited and loving thanks to my family: to my son Shawm, whose surreal conversation never bores me, whose horn-playing always moves me, and whose writing ability has far out-stripped that of his parents; and to my husband Steve, who has taught me to think like a scientist, and whose love and support are the mainstays of my life.

Finally, thank you to all the people who took Slim Cuisine to their collective bosoms, who cook the recipes, send me wonderful letters, and have let me know in no uncertain terms that a hedonistic approach to low-fat cookery is just what the world needs.

Preface to

'The Complete Slim Cuisine'

Isn't food wonderful? When life turns sour, food is there to console us; when fortune smiles, food is there to help us celebrate. It nourishes, comforts and provides sensuality and fun in equal measure. Alas, food can also make us fat and ill, and cause us to lead anguished pendulum lives as we yo-yo between near-normal weight and obesity, between guilty enjoyment and despairing aversion.

My love of food in all its social, sensual, physiological and cultural guises, and my own desperate struggle with obesity and the 'yo-yo' syndrome led me to develop Slim Cuisine, a very low-fat style of cookery that provides the comfort, the celebration and the sensuality without the usual accompaniments of guilt and overweight. I depend on Slim Cuisine to help me maintain both my physical and my mental health. This compendium of *Slim Cuisine* and *Slim Cuisine: A Second Helping* encompasses a complete guide to my particular philosophy of low-fat lifestyle and cookery.

It is meant to be a safe harbour for those who struggle with obesity and a guilt-ridden relationship with food. Revel in food in all its delicious aspects, and never be fat again.

Enjoy!

Sue Kreitzman
Cambridgeshire, 1989

Preface

'They had lunched, as was their wont, on sugar, starches, oils and butter-fats. Usually they ate sandwiches of spongy new white bread greased with butter and mayonnaise . . . thick wedges of cake lying wetly beneath ice cream and whipped cream and melted chocolate gritty with nuts . . . patties sweating beads of inferior oils containing bits of bland meat bogged in pale, stiffening sauce . . . pastries limber under rigid icing filled with indeterminate sweet stuff, not yet solid, not yet liquid, like salve that has been left out in the sun. They chose no other sort of food, nor did they consider it.'

Dorothy Parker, *The Standard of Living*

The concept of Slim Cuisine is a direct result of my own personal battle with obesity, and my attempt to achieve, after a 6½ stone weight loss since 1982, a beautifully balanced state of slim happiness, nutritional well-being and gastronomic satisfaction. Tasteless food, compulsive Calorie counting and grim dietetics are anathema to me, yet I *never* want to weigh 15-plus stone again, and I never want to hop on to that bleak and self-defeating see-saw of gluttony/starvation.

Maintaining a large weight loss is a lifetime affair. I feel those 6½ lost stones of quivering schmaltz haunting me. They hover, waiting for the first slip, the first heedless slide into the fat-filled abyss that surrounds every ex-fatty. I have learned how to shun added dietary fat, yet enjoy good food. I have learned to ignore the blaring commands of a fat-crazed world, a world dedicated, it

1

sometimes seems, to making ex-fatties fat again. If I, the mother of all food-lovers, can do it, you can too. Stick with me through *Slim Cuisine*. Learn to eat pastries, soufflés, chocolate cream sauce and bread puddings. Learn how to prepare a full-dress Sunday lunch, an epic Christmas dinner, a full English breakfast. Learn to do this while maintaining a radiant and healthy slimness, in fact, learn to *lose* weight with Slim Cuisine, if you need to. And most important, learn how to experience the *therapeutic binge* – specially developed for those who find an occasional bout of over-eating good for the soul. Be happy, be slim, be well-fed – in short, be the master – or mistress – of your own destiny.

Never Trust a Skinny Cook?!

'Cookery writers are these days expected, I fear, to save the contemporary soul, which now inhabits the waistline.'

Jane Grigson, *Observer* Sunday Magazine

'Never Trust a Skinny Cook.' The words were embroidered on my aprons and emblazoned on my soul. There I was, 215 pounds (15-plus stone) of rotund, bursting-at-the-seams womanhood, cooking up a storm of goodies all absolutely delicious and utterly fattening. When I saw the light and shed 5½ stone on the Cambridge Diet I threw out all my aprons with their obsolete embroideries, but I was left with a problem. Both the 15-plus stone and my profession of food writer were a result of my passion for food. The passion was still there along with a new one – the burning desire to remain slim. Can one indulge both such passions simultaneously? Is it possible to satisfy a hunger for deep, rich and complex flavours and still maintain a newly sylphlike figure? I am here to tell you that it can be done. All my professional (and passionate) skill has been devoted to developing this new maintenance cuisine. A cuisine that utilizes techniques enabling the cook to produce tantalizing and delicious dishes that are low in Calories (especially empty Calories and fat Calories), high in nutrition, yet eminently satisfying. These cookery methods can be used for all the family, even family members with no weight problems. My methods comprise a healthier way of preparing food that benefits everyone, even those who do not have to watch every Calorie, and the food is so good that no one will feel deprived.

2

I think of myself as a 215-pound woman in a size 10 body. Since I have begun cooking Slim Cuisine exclusively, those looming lost pounds have been kept at bay. What joy it is to be able to feast heartily, to enjoy large satisfying portions of my favourite foods, without suffering that all-too-familiar, inexorable, and demoralizing weight regain. For the first time in my life, I'm off the dieter's classic see-saw.

The basic premise of Slim Cuisine is that Dietary Fat is a villain. At more than twice the number of Calories per gram as carbohydrate and protein, it is a significant contributor to obesity. Even worse, it is considered to be one of the biggest cardiac risks. And, in addition to heart and blood vessel disease, it has been linked to several kinds of cancer. Not just the saturated animal fats. There are health problems with monounsaturated fats and polyunsaturated fats too. And it doesn't matter if you're cooking with butter, margarine, sunflower oil, yak fat or blubber – it still has a dense 9 Calories per gram – and these Calories go straight to your hips with deadly efficiency.

The NACNE Report in the UK and the American Heart Association in the USA recommend a dietary fat level of no more than 30 percent of total Calories. Slim Cuisine brings the fat levels down to below that point, yet it avoids the stultifying boredom that will engulf the desperate foodie who may gamely try to eat his or her way through other low-fat diets. Why will this regime succeed where others have caused terminal boredom and eventual failure? Because it pioneers the use of a whole battery of cookery techniques that enable the cook to eliminate added cooking fat altogether, yet retain the ravishing richness that foodies crave. The techniques save hundreds, sometimes thousands of Calories in a day's eating, yet they enable the cook to prepare compelling, rich-tasting, satisfying food, even though the added fat is missing. The techniques are simple and they form the basis of a whole lifetime of healthy eating.

It must be stressed that this maintenance programme, although an incredible boon to chronic dieters (no matter what their chosen weight-loss diet), is not for those dieters alone. Everyone will benefit significantly from eating this way. The recipes are Calorie and fat shy, yet nutrient dense. Sugar and salt have been drastically reduced too, yet there is enough taste, and texture to knock your socks off. Some recipes are for family-type meals, others are for elegant entertaining. There is plenty of 'junk-food': hamburgers, chips, pizza and icecream, and there is even a clutch of curries. How delightful and comforting to know that one can feast on pesto, mashed potatoes, lasagne, even mince pies, without a qualm.

'Sam, we can't starve the boy,' Ethel protested. 'If he wants pie, let him have some. You're carrying this reducing fetish too far.'

Robert Silverberg, The Iron Chancellor

Join the Revolution

'The philosophy of this kitchen rests on deep resources of eggs, cream and butter, shinbone marrow, boiled pig skins, and polysaturated pâtés of rich country meat. "Deny yourself nothing" is the motto . . .'

John McPhee, Brigande De Cuisine

Once upon a time, fat was necessary for survival. Dwelling places were not well heated and clothes and fabrics were not nearly as efficient as they are now at keeping out the cold. Labour-saving devices were unknown. People in every walk of life expended much more energy from day to day, whether they were farmers, labourers, housewives, secretaries . . . Fat-Calorie dense foods were vital for warmth, for work and to make some stored fat for the inevitable lean times ahead. But here we are in the last years of the twentieth century, bombarded with newer and more efficient ways of lightening our workload every day. Tractors and cars have power steering; the manual typewriter gave way to the electric version which in turn fell prey to the word processor. Telephones dial themselves, food processors chop the vegetables, washing machines clean the clothes, and escalators and lifts whisk us upstairs and down. Galloping technology and an ample food supply have drastically decreased our bodies' needs for fat-Calories, yet the culinary arts and sciences have stayed blindly in the past. Recipes still insist on the need to sauté in quantities of butter, stir-fry in oil, lard and bard with animal fat, enrich with cream, sprinkle with high-fat cheese and, in general, pile on the fat in frightening and prodigious quantity. Think of the dollops of clotted cream and whipped cream, the lashings of butter and margarine, the turgid lakes of oil and drippings, the hunks of Cheddar and Brie, the fistfuls of nuts, the greasy mountains of fish and chips and hamburgers and crisps you have consumed in your lifetime. These fat-laden foods doggedly continue to pile on stored fat that you do not need; indeed, that you hate with all your heart and soul. Why cling tenaciously to outmoded and dangerous traditions? If your typewriter and lawn mower are electric, your car is power-steered and your laundry is automatically washed and spun dry, then you must bring the revolution into the kitchen too, or you will be caught in a headlong and inevitable spiral into obesity. Many people have already faced this problem and use drastic dieting to periodically stop the fat binge, and to temporarily reduce the unattractive and unhealthy excess body fat. But crash dieting can't go on for ever. Continually alternating such diets with periods of high-fat foods results in a way of life that is both physically and mentally unhealthy.

> 'The bonds linking us were compulsory starvation, the dreams of food, and the drastic measures required to maintain our diets.'
>
> Gelsey Kirkland, *Dancing on My Grave*

It's time to beat the tradition. Stop depending on fat-based cookery methods. You may save your life. You will certainly hold obesity at bay.

But, alas, tradition is hard to undo. Fat has been the basis of the world's cuisines for countless centuries. In fact, the classic way to identify a particular cuisine is through its flavour principle: a particular fat plus characteristic seasonings. Lard, paprika, marjoram and sour cream immediately identify a dish as Hungarian; olive oil, garlic and herbs place a dish firmly in the Mediterranean; butter, cream and tarragon are indisputably classic French; olive oil, lemon and oregano, Greek; and so on. Thus the fat imparts an identifying flavour to a cuisine, and is inextricably identified with that cuisine.

My purpose in developing Slim Cuisine is finally to beat the system and eliminate the added fat once and for all. All sorts of new techniques and tricks have been substituted for the old fat-based ones. As a result, the food – although extremely low in fat – is quite delicious, and *large portions* will not add to the fat stores. It would be wrong to think it acceptable to add *tiny* bits of fat here and there. Perhaps you think that a mere teaspoon of butter, margarine, or oil used to sauté the onions won't hurt. Avoid that teaspoon of fat like the plague. Don't spread even a sliver of margarine on your bread. And avoid low-fat spreads as well. They are *lower* in fat than butter and margarine, but they are a long way from being no-fat. We are a nation, indeed a world, of fatoholics. The only way to recover from such an addiction is to avoid the noxious substance entirely. An alcoholic does not take a few drops of brandy or whisky each day;

so must you not ingest even half a teaspoon of oil a day. Don't keep the stuff in the house or you will find yourself having a drizzle here, a dollop there, and soon your ugly fat stores will be filling up hatefully again.

We *do* have a need for a certain amount of fat in our diets, but the generous variety of meat, fish, poultry, whole grains and vegetables you will be consuming on the Slim Cuisine regime will provide more than enough of the essential fats needed. There is no need for *added* fat. This is not just a guess or wishful conjecture. All Slim Cuisine recipes have been computer-analysed. Further checking was done by sending samples of many cooked recipes to an independent laboratory for analysis. The fatty acids necessary for good health were shown to be present in ample quantity.

Slim Cuisine is not a difficult or arduous way of kitchen life. It is no harder than any sort of everyday cookery. Practise its simple precepts, and your cookery will catch up with the rest of your life-style. Remember, this is the late twentieth century, even in the kitchen.

'He is the fat cook not only because of his personal avoirdupois but also because he writes his signature with butter on a dish already heavy with suet and cream.'

John Thorne, *Simple Cooking*

Weight Maintenance

'Many people who love to eat, constantly think about food – they daydream about places where mountains are made of fudge, rivers of flowing chocolate, and so on.'

Isaac Asimov, *The Science Fiction Weight-Loss Book*

Pitfalls of Weight Maintenance

Foodies are fascinated, delighted and comforted by food. They expect cuisine to be rich, compelling and delicious and they want portions to be generous. Even FFFs (formerly fat foodies) like me want food to conform to these standards. Although we long to stay slim we still crave plenty of good things to eat. I mean *really* good things. A leaf of lettuce, a naked morsel of broiled fish and a steamed vegetable do little to assuage our cravings. We want sauces, we want creamy textures, we want glamour, we even want, occasionally, junk food. What to do? Periods of abstinence followed by periods of indulgence are unhealthy and frustrating. Tiny portions of luscious things cause agony. Calorie counting and continuous deprivation in the name of slimness is sheer hell, and difficult as well. Yet a return to blimphood is too hideous to contemplate. Don't let this problem compromise your physical and mental health, *or* your sensual enjoyment of food. Be very careful. Don't fall into the three major weight maintenance traps.

> 'My soul is dark with stormy riot
> Directly traceable to Diet.'
>
> Samuel Hoffenstein, *Out of the Everywhere into the Here*

Trap No. 1 is Food Obsession

Food obsession occurs when one is constantly worried about what one eats, counts every Calorie, and checks the scale several times a day for added pounds. Pleasure in food becomes forbidden: feared and longed for at the same time. Occasional lapses occur. Fraught with guilt, the diner gorges on unsuitable, unhealthy and fattening foods, only to diet austerely for several days afterwards to make up for the digression. This behaviour results in an extremely unhealthy and nutritionally unbalanced diet and a dicey mental state.

Trap No. 2 is the Maths Major Syndrome

If you are determined to eat nutritious food, to balance your diet properly and to ingest every Calorie, every micro and macro nutrient in perfect harmony according to your needs, you may find yourself a slave to your calculator and to nutritional tables. Every meal becomes an intricate maths exercise as you work out protein levels, vitamins, minerals and trace minerals . . . Mealtimes are grim accounting sessions, and soon become so boring that you fling your calculator away, and yourself into bad old eating habits again, in reaction to the tedium of endless calculations.

Trap No. 3 is the See-Saw Syndrome

I'm sure this is all too familiar to many of you. The initial joy and novelty of newly lost weight slowly wears off as food's siren song becomes louder and louder. It's so easy to fall back into the bad old habits. After all, if you eat that gooey chocolate-cream gateau, devour a jumbo order of greasy fish and chips, succumb to oceans of hollandaise, mountains of fudge, cream-slathered scones, why, you can always go back on your diet for a few days, can't you? Soon you find yourself eating mindlessly again, no thought at all for nutrition and Calories, until your clothes are embarrassingly tight and you can't stand the sight of your puffy face in the mirror any more. Then the struggle starts again to begin dieting, to stay on it through the first difficult days, to go through the exercise of dredging up the same old discipline and will-power. 'Losing weight on Cambridge is so easy,' you say, 'I did it once, I can always begin again tomorrow.' Sometimes tomorrow never comes, or it comes far too late. And if you *do* it again, lose the weight all over again, what happens? You're back to the maintenance point, face to face once more with those dreadful traps. It's a vicious circle!

Well – do I have the answer? Yes, of course I do. It's Slim Cuisine. I invented it, I live by it, I love it, and I want you to do the same. I believe in food that is scrumptious, glorious, fun to eat – but I also believe in a lifetime of good health and slimness. That's what Slim Cuisine is all about.

> 'Yet no sooner has a man achieved a one-pound loss,
> Than he gains two through the application to an old
>   familiar dish or a new irresistible sauce.'
>
> Ogden Nash, 'In the Diet Kitchen'

Food As Comfort

'The further I travel in search of the ideal slimming method, the more I am convinced that food is one of the oldest and greatest comforters. If this comforter – this secret return to the womb – is suddenly taken away from me, I begin to feel anxiety, depression, tension.'

Roy Andries de Groot, *Esquire* Magazine

During Cambridge sole source or any stringent diet, daydreams of glorious food fill many waking moments. 'Soon, soon,' you promise yourself, 'I will reach my target weight, and then I can return to the comfort of real food.'

Comfort food encompasses a huge culinary spectrum. There are, of course, the rice puddings and creamy potato dishes of the nursery, but there are also the gorgeous sauces and rich desserts of classic cookery, the cold comfort of icecream, the steam-wreathed comfort of thick soups, and the nightmare-chasing solace of a post-midnight fridge forage. Unexpected contrasts of taste and texture give comfort too, as well as rustic, ethnic feasts and juvenile junk food like hamburgers, pizza and fried fish.

Alas, most of us separate the food that nourishes the soul from that which nourishes the body. We tend to indulge in comfort when we are deeply – psychically as well as physically – hungry, and then, in the name of slimness, return to spartan eating until the deep hunger strikes again. But why should this be? Why can't we nourish both body and soul at the same time?

This book is the result of my determination to achieve such double nourishment.

I want to eat food that satisfies in the deep recesses of the soul that only rich and delicious Comfort Food can reach, but I also regard a return to my old excessive weight with fear and trembling. It's foolish to compromise by dieting half the time and eating high-fat, high-Calorie disasters the other half. If you share my passions for slimness and health, and for Comfort Food, you can now indulge them both. The new techniques you will be using will change your life. For the first time in your adult life, you may find yourself enjoying your food body *and* soul, with none of the shadows of guilt or dissatisfaction that haunt so many of our mealtimes.

The Slim Cuisine Regime

Use Slim Cuisine as follows to achieve a perfect balance: *slim happiness*, *nutritional well-being* and *gastronomic satisfaction*.

An Overview of Slim Cuisine Basics

Yes, there is culinary life after achieving your target weight. A culinary life that does not result in a depressing and unhealthy regain of all your lost poundage. The new techniques described in this book will enable you to produce rich, satisfying and comforting food without the excess Calories and fat. All Slim Cuisine recipes are nutrient dense, Calorie shy and exceedingly palatable. Here is a brief overview of the basic rules.

> 'Poor old Pyecraft! Great, uneasy jelly of substance! The fattest clubman in London. He sits at one of the little club tables in the huge bay of the fire, stuffing. What is he stuffing? I glance judiciously, and catch him biting at a round of hot buttered teacake.'
>
> H. G. Wells, *The Truth About Pyecraft*

9

1   Except for seasoning your non-stick cookware (see page 53) dispense with all cooking fats and oils. It doesn't matter if the fats are unsaturated (monounsaturated or polyunsaturated) or saturated; dump them all, and forget about them for the rest of your life. The no-no list includes:
** Butter
** Margarine
** Drippings, lard, suet, poultry fats
** Poultry skin
** All oils: sunflower, olive, peanut, corn, soybean, etc.
** Solid, hydrogenated shortenings
** Mayonnaise and salad dressings
** All dairy products *not* made from skimmed milk, with the exception of a few medium-fat cheeses: Parmesan, semi-skimmed Mozzarella, Bruder Basil, Jarlsberg, medium-fat chèvres (French goat cheeses), which may be used *occasionally* in *small* quantities.
** High-fat meats
** Nuts, except for a *very small* amount here and there for flavouring and garnishing.
** Baked goods and prepared foods containing any of the above fats, or high-fat ingredients

'Stop!' I hear you cry. 'How can I manage to cook anything even vaguely delicious, hampered by such rules?' Read on.

2   Use the following as substitutes for the forbidden fats:
** Skimmed milk yoghurt. Use it as is or drain it to make a substitute for cream cheese or a base for Slim mayonnaise and salad dressings. (See page 40.)
** Skimmed milk fromage blanc or fromage frais. Use as described for yoghurt, above, also in place of soured cream and crème fraîche.
** Buttermilk cultured from skimmed milk
** Skimmed milk quark
** Skimmed milk and skimmed milk powder
** Chicken, beef and vegetable stocks. (See page 21.) Use very good-quality stock in place of butter and oil to sauté-flavour vegetables. (See page 24.)
** *Lean* meats, poultry trimmed of skin and fat

'Things are seldom what they seem,
Skimmed milk masquerades as cream.'

W. S. Gilbert, *H.M.S. Pinafore*

3   Use vegetables that have been baked and then puréed to give body to sauces, casseroles, stews, soups and gratins. (See pages 32 to 39.) The best vegetables for this purpose are garlic, onions, carrots, potatoes, parsnips, swedes and turnips.
4   Use baked, puréed aubergine as a filler in meatballs, hamburgers, and bolognese sauce. It gives body and moisture, cuts down on the amount of meat used and adds *no* aubergine taste. Purée grilled and peeled peppers, season and use as a no-fat, delicious sauce for pasta, meats, fish or poultry.
5   Don't give up desserts, only those that are laden with fat and excessive sugar. For instance, icecream, that high-fat, sugary disaster, becomes low-fat, low-Calorie and highly nutritious made the Slim Cuisine way. (See page 314.)

'The hour of grim decision is the first Monday after the New Year of any year. And this day should have a name: All Fat Souls' Day, maybe.'

Miriam Ungerer, *Country Food*

6   If you love red meat, eat lean meat 3–4 times a week.
7   Egg yolks contain fat, but eggs are a high-protein, vitamin- and mineral-filled food. If you like eggs, eat up to 3 cooked whole eggs a week if you wish. (When counting your whole egg total, make sure that you include eggs contained in recipes such as Bread Pudding, page 330, as well.) If your blood cholesterol levels are high, however, eat no egg yolks at all. In any case, you may use as many egg *whites* as you wish.
8   Eat a large variety of foods.
9   Eat plenty of whole grains.
10 Eat plenty of potatoes.
11 Eat plenty of fish.
12 Be greedy with vegetables. Eat all you want, cooked any way you want them, as long as the cooking techniques are Slim Cuisine ones. This collection contains many sumptuous all-vegetable recipes (pages 197–223). Indulge frequently and lavishly, especially those marked ♡ (Very Low Fat, see page 16) and ✤ (Therapeutic Binge, see page 16). Raw vegetables make great snacks, especially when dunked in Slim Cuisine spreads and dips. Remember two things about raw vegetables, however.
    (a) A little bit of cooking breaks down some of the cell walls in vegetable matter and actually makes some vegetables *more* nutritious, so don't depend on raw vegetables only.

11

(b) Raw carrot sticks and red and yellow pepper strips are sweet, crisp and juicy – they make extremely satisfying snacks. What's more, they are rich in beta carotene (your body uses beta carotene to make vitamin A, one of the fat-soluble vitamins), so it's a good idea for people on fat-free regimes to munch away on these particular vegetables. (Spinach, peas, broccoli, tomatoes, sprouts and apricots are also rich sources of beta carotene – indulge freely.) And to make them even more attractive, many scientists feel that beta carotene is a protector against some types of cancer. One word of advice: if the palms of your hands turn a startling orange, or you develop orange splotches on your skin, you may be indulging a little too freely. Large doses of beta carotene can produce such skin changes. It is not dangerous, but if you want it to fade to your normal colour, cut down on the raw vegetable snacks.

13 Use salt, sugar and artificial sweeteners sparingly. They are seasonings, meant to enhance – not to overpower. They will not harm you in small quantities, but don't get carried away.

14 Alcohol contains 7 empty Calories per gram. I know this is not everyone's happiest news, but if you want to stay slim and healthy, you have a better chance of doing so *without* alcohol. And, if you want to lose weight, you *must* do without it. Use it as a cooking ingredient (heat dissipates the alcohol and thus the alcohol Calories), but stop there.

The Food Day

'Everywhere you turn, food awaits you in huge wondrous quantities. Giant neon burgers dance in circles above your head. A chocolate chip cookie calls your name.'

David Hoffman, *The Joy of Pigging Out*

The food happenings of the day are not confined to mealtimes. Snacking, in-between munching and 'picking' all play an important role in a food-lover's passage through life. Whether that life is an unhealthy one of miserable obesity or one of robust and well-nourished slimness is up to you. You *must* be the master of your own destiny. It seems as if the world is out to make you fat; indeed, it sometimes seems that the world is out to kill you. The media – television, radio, billboards, newspaper and magazine ads – blare loud and persuasive messages. The pictures, sounds and smells of fatty, sugary, salty, ridiculously calorific foods are *everywhere*. The food and drink itself – sugar-coated, salt-sprinkled and dripping mega-fat – is everywhere, too; at eye level and brilliantly packaged in the supermarket, sending forth seductive vapours from fast-food and fish-and-chip emporia, patiently waiting in fizzy anticipation inside soft-drink machines. Because it is there, because you are being inundated with commands to drown yourself mindlessly in it, does not mean that you have to comply.

It can be difficult. I remember standing in the snackbar of a British Rail station, ravenous and exhausted. I was desperate for something to tide me through the long journey home, but there was *nothing* that looked remotely edible by my fat-shunning standards. The girl behind the counter reacted with astonishment when I asked for a sandwich without butter or mayonnaise. 'Madame,' she said, her voice dripping with contempt, 'We can't bother to make things that people *like*, you know.' All through the long train ride I comforted myself with visions of the huge bowlful of mashed potatoes, garnished with all sorts of beguiling things, that I would have as soon as I reached home.

The advantage of the Slim Cuisine regime is that after a few months, high-fat, over-sugared foods lose their charm, indeed they become downright disgusting. Resisting them becomes a pleasure rather than a chore, and mastering your own destiny becomes easy. The media's siren songs become grotesque to your ears, and the foods that you crave are those waiting at home in your fridge, freezer and pantry.

Snack Advice

'Off and on the sign went. It was a distant neon arrow pointing down through the night to JACK'S GOLDEN DOME TURNPIKE DINER, EAT . . . EAT . . . EAT . . . EAT . . . it endlessly intoned . . . EAT . . . EAT . . . EAT . . . And so we did.'

Jean Shepherd, *A Fistful of Fig Newtons*

When the world of sweet bars, confectionery, crisps, and so on, is shut to you, what do you do about between-meal nibbles and treats? Here are some suggestions. They all contribute to the day's overall nutrition and provide fun eating as well.

1 **Raw Vegetables** ⚛ ♡ (see page 11) with quark or Slim Cuisine dips. They are crisp (a good snack should crunch),

13

colourful, and many are *sweet*, and so are very satisfying to a sweet tooth.

2 **Fresh Fruit** ♡ . I swoon over greengrocers' displays: tart, snappy apples; green, purple, or red grapes; oranges, blood and otherwise; mangoes; pears; bananas; pineapples; cherries and berries in season; lychees. Why would anyone want to settle for a horrible packaged piece of flabby pastry or an artificially flavoured sweet bar coated with inferior, vegetable-fat injected chocolate, when such a panoply of juicy delight is available at any supermarket? Keep your fridge well stocked, and carry a good supply with you, or learn to stop in the supermarket's fresh produce section when the snack attack hits. Many markets now carry vegetables (and sometimes fruits) all peeled, sliced and ready to eat. This fills my heart with joy and thankfulness.

'Sometimes there would be tangerines, and he would peel off the pock marked orange skin for her and the spongy white threads that laced over the fruit. She would eat the sections one by one, the juice spurting sweet and sharp into her mouth.'

Sylvia Plath, *Among the Bumblebees*

3 **Dried Fruits.** Dried fruits are very concentrated in sweetness and flavour. They make a power-packed snack, because they are low in fat, yet rich in vitamins, minerals and fibre. But be warned. Because they are so concentrated, so delicious, so easy to eat, they can pile on the sugar Calories at top speed. One pound (480 grams) of dried apricots weighs in at approximately 1,179 Calories. That's only about 14 Calories per apricot, but you'd be surprised at how quickly a pound disappears down a snack-loving gullet – especially during relaxed circumstances; watching the telly, reading a good book, and so on. If you are going to snack mindlessly, turn to raw vegetables, tortilla chips and popcorn. If you feel willing to exercise a certain amount of discretion, enjoy dried fruits in sensible amounts. Use them in puddings as well, but don't feel that you can polish off the whole recipe all by yourself. Share it, or hide the leftovers for another day.

4 **Popcorn** ♡ . Make your own in the microwave with *no* fat or oil. A full pint (600 ml) of popcorn contains only 66 Calories, and practically no fat at all. A pint (600 ml) or so of popcorn and a good movie on the video make a very cosy combination.

5 **Tortilla Chips** ♡ (page 307). Make these every once in a while in huge batches, and store them in airtight tins. Eat them plain, or with Mock Guacamole (page 81) or Red Pepper and Garlic Spread (page 303).

6 **Icecream** ♡ (page 312). Whip up a batch of Slim Cuisine Instant Icecream any time you get the urge. It takes minutes to make and contributes plenty of good things (calcium, protein, vitamins and minerals) to your daily nutrition. And what it does for your daily well-being is immeasurable.

7 **Breakfast Cereals** ♡ . These are the unsung heroes of the snack world. Read the labels and buy those that have no added sugar, salt, or fat. If a brand is fortified with vitamins and minerals, so much the better. Cereals are an excellent source of fibre, and those made with wholemeal grains are a good source of vitamin E, one of the fat-soluble vitamins. When you douse these cereals in milk they turn into a soggy mess, but eaten out of the hand they are crispy and delicious. Perfect snack food, especially for children, who need all the fat-free and sugar-free nutrition they can get. And small shredded wheat, dabbled in Slim Cuisine Chocolate Cream Sauce (page 335), make a very classy sweet bar substitute.

'It was Scott Fitzgerald who ordered shredded wheat at Voisin's.'

Mrs E.C.N., in a letter

8 **Bread** ♡ . I get so irked when people turn away from bread because they are trying to watch their weight. Don't be guilty of such nonsense. Snack on bread when you want something delicious, filling and satisfying – don't think of shunning such excellent food. Learn to be a connoisseur; try a variety from different bakeries so that you can see what diversity of choice there is. My favourite breads have a crust that is tough and chewy, or so crisp that it showers the table with a storm of shards as you eat it. I like a fairly dense crumb, too, with a high percentage of whole grain and rye flours. A good slice of bread needs no greasing with butter and margarine; the very thought makes my tastebuds cringe. But if you want something voluptuously creamy on a slice of bread, try a good 'schmeer' (forgive the New Yorkese) of quark, the perfect no-fat spread. Learn to read labels and to quiz the baker. Don't buy breads that have fat or an excess of sugar in their formulation.

15

'Butter was not rolled into marbles during the 1870s.
Well, we should say not!
It was lifted in half-pound gobs and those who smeared it
    never felt improvident.'

George Ade, *Fables in Slang*

How To Use This Book

'You have fed me wretched food, vegetables boiled to
extinction, fistfuls of white sugar, slabs of fat, mucousy
casseroles made with gobs of cream of mushroom, until it's
amazing that my heart still beats.'

Garrison Keillor, *Lake Wobegon Days*

Symbols

Several symbols appear regularly throughout the book, marking
various recipes as useful in a particular way. Here is a guide to
symbol interpretation.

1   ♡   (Heart Symbol). These are *very* low fat recipes, and very
    low sugar as well. If you wish to *lose* weight, yet stay well-
    nourished, confine yourself to these recipes.

2   🐻   (Teddy Bear Symbol). Everyone needs an occasional
    therapeutic binge – an opportunity to eat all they want of some-
    thing delicious without fear of dire consequences (galloping fat,
    burgeoning flab, high blood pressure, clogged arteries . . .). If a
    recipe is marked with a teddy bear, it is suitable for therapeutic
    bingeing; eat *all you want* of that particular dish. If at the end of
    your 'binge' your waistband feels too tight and you appear to
    have developed a definite paunch, fear not. That full feeling
    and pot belly will disappear in a few hours – in the morning you
    will feel as slim as ever. Do plan to have therapeutic binges
    every once in a while. They fill you up beautifully with the best
    vegetables – very important to your vitamin, mineral and fibre
    levels – and they give you a marvellous sense of gastronomic
    freedom.

'The reason diet books don't work for me is that they use
terminology I don't begin to understand. "Eat one portion
of chicken" they say. As far as I'm concerned, a portion of
chicken is a chicken. A portion of beef is a cow. A portion of
ice cream is whatever container it happens to come in.'

Peter Feibleman, *Lear's Magazine*

16

3   ⊕ (Clock symbol). A clock indicates a fast recipe, perfect for those days when you come home late, there is nothing prepared in the freezer, and you want something wonderful to eat. Some of the ⊕ recipes are elegant enough for guests. Some are homely, family-type recipes.

4   ❄ (Snowflake symbol). Snowflaked recipes are suitable for freezing. Directions for thawing and reheating (with the microwave and by conventional methods) will be contained in the body of the recipe.

5   ⊠ (Microwave symbol). Many recipes in this book call for a microwave oven. Some recipes are followed by microwave adaptations. Such recipes and footnotes are marked with ⊠ .

6   ⑤ (Food processor symbol). This symbol indicates a recipe that calls for the use of a food processor.

Techniques

'A diet's a very delicate thing.
You have to keep your momentum going.
You have to stick to your routine.'

Ellen Gilchrist, *Victory Over Japan*

Some Slim Cuisine techniques – the ones you will use over and over again – are detailed in this section. Other more specific techniques – stir-frying without oil, for instance, or ridding meat of fat – are outlined in the appropriate chapters.

I hope that these techniques will enable you to think about cookery in an entirely new way. Make them part of your culinary life, substitute them for the old high-fat methods, and you will be cutting hundreds, even thousands of Calories out of your day's intake. One of the most exciting results of this kitchen revolution is that you will be able to increase the *amount* of food you ingest each day. Small portions of delicious things cause anguish. With these new techniques, food will still be delicious and you can enjoy large, satisfying portions. Your total nutrition intake will be high, but fat and Calories will be low.

Use these techniques to your own taste. Once they are mastered, adapt them to your own recipes; recipes that please you and those you feed.

A Note on Technique and Planning

For those who work full time and then come home to cook, weekday meals *must* be quick. It is a terrible shame, though, to

18

succumb to the lure of high-fat packaged and frozen foods because of limited time. And it is even more of a shame to fall back on old familiar techniques – sautéing in butter, margarine, or oil, deep frying, and so on – because you are afraid that the new techniques of Slim Cuisine might be difficult and time-consuming. If you want to stay slim, well-nourished and comforted, make a commitment to a personal kitchen revolution, even if you don't have unlimited kitchen time.

Changing over to Slim Cuisine means learning some new techniques and habits. It takes no longer to do Slim Cuisine than any other kind of cookery, especially if you plan ahead. Here are some planning tips to make life easier and cooking a joy.

1 The Slim Cuisine method of sautéing in stock is easy; don't let it make you nervous. Because it is new, it may seem daunting or difficult as you read each recipe, but once you have actually tried it, you will see how quick and simple it is.

2 Use your freezer to store home-made stocks in small portions, and batches of sautéed onions and mushrooms. And why not, on leisurely days or evenings, make large batches of your favourite recipes. Freeze in small portions. What luxury to just pop a container in the microwave at the end of a hard day. Instant comfort!

3 Home-made stocks are marvellous but time-consuming. If you just don't want to put in the effort, don't worry. Search your local wholefood, health, or speciality food store for good vegetable stock powder or paste, such as Friggs Vegetale (a powder) or Healthrite vegetable stock paste. Although many stock cubes and powders have a characteristic harsh, artificial taste, and contain far too much fat and salt, these two products are excellent. If your local small store does not carry them, ask that they be ordered. Friggs Vegetale is labelled as a low-Calorie vegetable *drink* but – trust me – it makes an excellent vegetable stock for sauté purposes, and it contains no fat. It is not necessary to reconstitute the powder first. Simply combine whatever you want to sauté with the amount of water given in the recipe, sprinkle in a bit of the powder, and proceed.

Most Chinese take-aways and restaurants have huge quantities of good quality chicken stock on hand. In many cases, salt and monosodium glutamate are not added until the moment the stock is transformed into a soup or added to a cooked dish. If you are a regular customer at a friendly local take-away, ask the owner if you can occasionally buy some. Often, if you bring a container, the proprietors of many such places (if they know you) will cheerfully fill it for a very modest price. When you get

19

the stock home, it needs to be chilled so that the fat can be skimmed off. Quick chill, if necessary by placing the stock in the freezer for a few minutes or by dropping a few ice cubes into the stock.

4 Always have quark and fromage frais in the fridge, so that you can make gorgeous spreads and salad dressings when you get the urge. Also have on hand at all times: buttermilk, very low fat yoghurt, skimmed milk, medium-fat Mozzarella cheese and Parmesan cheese.

Kitchen Sense

There is an art to following a recipe and everyone – novice or old kitchen hand – should practise that art if they want to avoid chaos, wasted time and culinary disaster. The rules are simple.

1 First, read the recipe through completely.
2 Then have all the ingredients chopped, sliced, diced, poured, measured, and so on. Set the prepared ingredients out on your work surface.
3 Also set out on your work area any equipment needed. Heed the directions in the recipe. If it calls for a frying pan and a wooden spoon, don't assume that you can get good results by substituting a saucepan and a stainless steel fork. A ▨ or ⑤ indicate the need for a microwave or food processor in a particular recipe. The recipes are well thought out and carefully worded. Don't sabotage them.

Only when these three steps have been carried out should you begin the actual cooking.

Measurement Note

All ingredients are given in imperial and in metric measurements. Use one or the other, but do not mix measurements in any one recipe.

'[Maria Callas's] close friend Marlene Dietrich
feared that the loss of weight might have weakened her,
and, becoming anxious during the rehearsals,
spent several hours boiling down eight pounds of
the best beef to a quart of the very finest broth.
"It's wonderful!" Maria declared. "How kind! Do tell me –

what brand of beef cubes did you use?"'

Charles Neilson Gattey, *Foie Gras and Trumpets*

Stock

Good stock is one of the most important components of Slim Cuisine. It does much to make up for the lack of cooking fats and oils. Stock acts as a superb sautéing medium, and contributes flavour and body. Recipes follow for several basic stocks. If you can fit their making into your kitchen rhythm, your cookery will have a wonderful dimension of depth and vibrancy. (See page 19 for shortcuts, if you don't have time to brew home-made stock.)

BASIC CHICKEN STOCK

Makes approximately 4 pts/2.5 l

Order chicken wings from your butcher. They are very inexpensive and make a wonderfully full-bodied stock. It is so rich that it jells when chilled. In my kitchen, my assistant Sandie Perry and I get double our money's worth out of chicken wings by using them twice. After we've drained the solids from a batch of stock, we pick out the wings, combine them with fresh vegetables and do the whole thing over again. As far as I'm concerned, chicken stock is the best sautéing medium there is. Make it regularly in large batches, and freeze it in small batches. Thaw (in the microwave, if you have one) when needed.

2½–3½ lb/1¼–1½ kg chicken wings, plus backs, necks and carcasses if you have them	2 carrots 1 small onion A few garlic cloves, unpeeled
3 celery stalks 2 parsnips	Several sprigs of parsley Salt

1   Wash the chicken pieces well. Scrub the celery, parsnips and carrots, leaving the carrots and parsnips unpeeled. Peel the onion. Cut the celery, carrots, parsnips and onion into chunks.

2   Boil the chicken parts in 6½ pts/4 l of water. After 10 minutes, skim all foam and scum from the top. Add the garlic and vegetables. Reduce the heat so that the liquid stays at a steady simmer. Simmer, partially covered, for 2½–3 hours. Cool.

3   Carefully strain the stock through a fine sieve or strainer. Press down on the solids to extract all their goodness. Pour the stock into clean jars, cover tightly and refrigerate overnight.

4   By the next day the fat will have risen to the top of each jar of stock and solidified. Meticulously scrape away every speck of fat and discard it. Pour the de-fatted stock into freezer containers, label with the date and store in the freezer until needed.

♡ ✿ ❄   **VEGETABLE STOCK**

Vegetable stock is quicker and less expensive than chicken stock. There are many versions, one of which follows. Vegetable stock is a boon for vegetarians, orthodox Jews who want to cook with stock for a dairy meal, or for anyone else who for one reason or another does not want a meaty stock. Again, as with chicken stock, make it in large quantities and freeze it in small containers or in ice cube bags or trays.

4 leeks	*2–3 fresh bay leaves or one dried*
5 stalks of celery with leaves	*bay leaf*
2 large onions	*3–4 sprigs fresh thyme*
4 oz/120 g mushrooms	*Handful of fresh parsley*
4 white turnips	*1 large potato*
5 carrots	*Salt and freshly ground pepper*
4 parsnips	

1   Trim the vegetables and clean them well, but leave them unpeeled. Cut them into large chunks. Place them in a deep pot and cover generously with cold water. Bring to the boil.

2   Skim off foam. Partially cover the pot. Lower the heat and simmer for approximately 1 hour.

3   Season with just a bit of salt and some freshly ground pepper. Strain the broth through a fine sieve or strainer (discard the solids). Cool and refrigerate. Use the stock within 3 days or store in the freezer.

♡ ✿ ⊕ ❄   **FISH STOCK**

Makes 4 pts/2.5 l

You can usually pick up fish scraps free from your fishmonger. Fish stock is a snap to prepare; it needs to simmer for 30 minutes only. Use it for any of the fish dishes in this collection.

4 lb/1.8 kg fish bones and heads (use lean white fish only; halibut, cod, etc.)	3 stalks celery, coarsely chopped
	½ pt/300 ml dry white wine
	4 pts/2.5 l water
2 large onions, coarsely chopped	Several sprigs parsley
4 carrots, peeled and coarsely chopped	A few peppercorns
	½ bay leaf

1 Rinse fish bones and heads well under cold running water.
2 Combine the chopped vegetables, 2 fl oz/60 ml of wine and ½ pt/300 ml water in a non-reactive pot. Cover and bring to the boil. Boil for 5 minutes. Uncover, lower the heat a bit and simmer until the vegetables are almost tender but not browning, and the liquid is almost gone.
3 Add fish bones and heads and all remaining ingredients. Bring to the boil, reduce heat and simmer, partially covered, for 20–30 minutes. Strain, discard solids, cool and then refrigerate, or freeze in small portions.

♡ ☆ ⊕ ❄ COURT BOUILLON

Makes 1½ pts/900 ml

Court bouillon is often used for poaching fish and shellfish. Because it takes only 10 minutes to prepare, and has a nice depth of flavour despite that short time, it makes a dandy stock substitute when you have nothing else at hand.

1 large onion, peeled and coarsely diced	1 bay leaf
	2–3 sprigs parsley
1 large carrot, scraped and coarsely diced	1-inch/2.5-cm piece lemon zest
	½ pint/300 ml dry white wine
1 large celery stalk, coarsely diced	2 pts/1.2 l water

1 In a large non-reactive saucepan combine all ingredients except water. Bring to the boil for 2 minutes. Add water. Cover and boil for 10 minutes. Drain. Discard solids.

♡ ☆ ⊕ DESPERATION STOCK

When all else has failed – you are out of home-made stuff, there is no more vegetable stock powder left in the larder, you are tired and hungry and you want to be ready to sauté right *now* – put onions in a heavy non-reactive frying pan with a combination of half water and half dry white wine or dry white vermouth. Sauté as directed (see page 24 or individual recipes).

Sautéing in Stock

Think about the way many recipes begin: 'Sauté onions and/or garlic in 4 (or more) tablespoons oil or butter.' Follow such directions and immediately, without even thinking, you add at least 400 fat Calories to the meal. Of course, it is usually much more than 400. Other recipes in the same meal may begin with similar directions. Add to this the recipes prepared for the other meals of the day – butter or margarine spread on bread, fried foods, high-fat snacks, melted butter on vegetables, mayonnaise on sandwiches, etc. etc. – and the day's fat-Calories intake can easily mount to well over 1,000, without any effort at all. Begin your Slim Cuisine kitchen revolution by changing the sauté method from a fat-based one to a stock-based one.

It is important to realize that merely boiling or simmering onions in stock result in *flabby* vegetables, not *sautéed* vegetables. My technique combines onions and/or other vegetables with stock in a way that achieves a true, deeply flavoured *sauté* effect.

> 'All that oil? What is this, oil soup?' Picket . . . picked the book up and took a look at the cover, on which was a picture of a startlingly fat man with a pudding face, grinning out across an appalling lot of sausages. "You're cooking out of this man's book?"'
>
> James P. Blaylock, *The Last Coin*

♡ 🧸 🕐 ❄ SAUTÉED ONIONS

61 Calories per 1 large sautéed onion
0.2 g fat
(Traditional sautéed onions: 250 Calories per 1 large sautéed onion, 24 g fat)

This is the basic technique. Chopped carrots and celery can be added. The best pot to use is an 8-inch/20-cm enamelled cast-iron frying pan. Do *not* use a non-stick frying pan. The intense flavour that results from this method depends upon a little judicious and controlled burning, occurring toward the end of the recipe. Don't even think about substituting a bouillon cube for homemade stock. The cube is loaded with salt, monosodium glutamate and other undesirables and has no place in Slim Cuisine. (See page 21 for recipes for and hints about stock.)

1 large onion, chopped	Splash of dry vermouth, dry red or
1 clove garlic, minced	white wine, dry sherry, wine
6 fl oz/180 ml stock	vinegar or additional stock

1   Combine all ingredients except the final splash in an 8-inch/20-cm frying pan. Cover and bring to the boil.
2   Uncover. Boil for approximately 5 minutes until most of the liquid has cooked away. Reduce heat and simmer until just about dry and beginning to stick a little bit.
3   Lower the heat. Toss and stir constantly with a wooden spoon until you smell a lovely, toasty, oniony aroma and the bottom of the pan is beginning to brown just a bit. Pour in a splash of dry wine or additional stock and turn the heat up again. Stir with the wooden spoon, scraping up all the browned bits. When the liquid is gone, the onions should be meltingly tender and amber-coloured and the tantalizing smell should be driving all members of the household mad. Remove from heat. Use in a recipe at once or refrigerate for later use.

♡ 🐻 ⊕ ❄   'FRIED' ONIONS

Makes 1 pt/600 ml

'Fried' onions are the pride and joy of Slim Cuisine, and a good illustration of the no-fat stock sauté method. Who would guess that this mass of meltingly tender, syrupy, amber brown, tantalizingly odorous 'fried' onions is *diet* food!? My son eats these regularly, heaped on to a Slim Cuisine hamburger (see page 154), enclosed in a bap spread with ketchup on its lower half and New York Deli Mustard (page 305) on its upper. I eat the same thing, without the hamburger. Fried onion sandwiches! What bliss. If you wish, the onions may be chopped or sliced, instead of being cut into wedges. Please note that the onions should be cooked in an enamelled cast iron frying pan, *not* a non-stick one.

2–3 large Spanish onions	10–15 fl oz/300–450 ml chicken stock

1   Peel the onions and cut them into wedges: eighths or sixteenths. Separate the pieces.
2   Combine the onions and 10–12 fl oz/300–360 ml of stock in a *heavy-bottomed*, large frying pan (enamelled cast iron is best) that can be covered. Cover and bring to the boil. Let

boil, covered, for 5–10 minutes, uncovering to stir very occasionally.

3   Uncover and reduce heat just a bit. When the onions are beginning to stick, pour in a splash of stock and stir and scrape well to loosen any browned bits on the bottom of the frying pan. Continue cooking and stirring for another minute or two, adding a splash of stock, and scraping to loosen the browned bits as necessary. When the onions are meltingly tender, amber brown and syrupy, they are ready.

'"Scheherazade! Scheherazade!" the king was calling. "Where shall I begin? I will peel the onions. We shall need hundreds and hundreds . . ."'

Wadeeha Atiyah, *Scheherazade Cooks*

♡ 🧸 ❄   **BROWNED ONIONS**

Makes about ¾ pt/450 ml

This makes the most delicious concoction imaginable. It is what the French call onion jam or onion marmalade. This Slim Cuisine version can save you many Calories, yet the final result is just as good as the sinful versions, if not more so.

6 large onions, peeled and trimmed	*Splash of additional stock, dry*
16 fl oz/480 ml stock	*vermouth, dry red or white*
	wine, dry sherry or wine vinegar

1   Cut onions in half. Slice into thin half-moons. Combine onions and 16 fl oz/480 ml of stock in a deep, 10-inch/25-cm, enamelled cast-iron frying pan. Cover and bring to the boil. Reduce heat a bit and simmer briskly for 10 minutes.

2   Uncover. Simmer for 35–40 minutes, stirring occasionally. After this period of time the onions will be turning amber brown and the liquid will be almost gone. Stir constantly and allow to cook for a few more minutes. The onions will begin to stick just a bit. Keep stirring for approximately 10 minutes more until the onions are just about dry and browned deposits are forming on the bottom of the frying pan. As you stir with your wooden spoon, keep scraping up the browned deposits.

3   Turn up the heat a tiny bit and let the onions start to burn just a *little* – that's what makes the ravishing flavour. Be very careful not to allow wholesale burning and blackening – that way lies ruin.

26

4   Splash in 3–4 tablespoons of dry wine, wine vinegar or additional stock. Boil until just about dry, vigorously stirring and scraping up the browned bits on the bottom of the frying pan. Immediately remove from heat. Use a rubber spatula to scrape the mass of browned onions into a storage container. Use as a garnish for lean meats, use as a base for stews, sauces and soups, or serve as a vegetable accompaniment.

'One of the most satisfying properties of the onion . . . is its grace . . . in bringing out the flavour of anything with which it is combined.'

Jean Bothwell, *Onions Without Tears*

 ## ONION-HERB INFUSION

This is another way of using onions and stock (spring onions or shallots this time) to make an intensely flavoured base for many recipes. Please note that in this method and the previous one the wine is boiled dry so no alcohol (and no alcohol Calories) are left. The herb you choose for the infusion will depend upon how you wish to use it. Tarragon, oregano, thyme all work beautifully with this method.

8 oz/250 g sliced spring onions (both the green and white portions), or finely chopped shallots or finely chopped onion	*Pinch or two cayenne pepper (to taste)*
4 fl oz/120 ml stock	*2½ tablespoons chopped fresh herbs or ½ tablespoon dried herbs*
4 fl oz/120 ml dry vermouth or dry red or white wine	*1 tablespoon chopped fresh parsley*

Combine all ingredients in a small, heavy frying pan. Bring to the boil, reduce heat and simmer briskly, uncovered, until almost all the liquid has evaporated. Use at once in a recipe or refrigerate for later use.

 ## SAUTÉED ONIONS FOR CURRIES

Curries present a challenge. Indian cookery depends very heavily on ghee (clarified butter) or oil. The myriad spices and herbs that make up the flavouring mix for each curry must be gently cooked in the fat or oil. Sometimes herbs or spices are whole, sometimes ground, or sometimes pounded to a paste with garlic, ginger and onions, but in whatever form they are always gently fried early in the recipe. It is this important step that gives Indian food its distinctive taste and texture. Just adding the appropriate spice mix to a fatless version of the recipe results in a finished dish with a sandy, gritty texture and a harsh, raw-spice taste: unpleasant to eat, and very un-Indian as well. Frying the spices dry in a non-stick pan scorches them. I've finally worked out a way to 'fry' the spices with onions, ginger and garlic in such a way that produces a smooth, gentle effect, with no scorching, and in which all the seasonings blend well, and leave no harshness. As is typical in Indian cookery, each curry recipe in this book has its own spice mix. The sauce base that results from this technique can be used to make meat, poultry, fish or vegetable curries.

---

3 onions, chopped, sliced or cut into eighths
10 fl oz/300 ml stock

Spice mixture (see individual curry recipes for specifics)

---

1 Separate the segments of the chopped onion pieces and spread them in a heavy, non-stick frying pan. Add *no* liquid or fat. Heat the frying pan gently. Cook at moderate heat, without stirring, for 7–10 minutes, until the onions are sizzling, speckled with dark amber, and beginning to stick to the pan.

2 Stir in 10 fl oz/300 ml of stock and let it bubble up, stirring up the browned deposits in the pan with a wooden spoon as it bubbles. Stir in the spices and garlic. Turn the heat down a bit and simmer, stirring frequently, until the mixture is very thick (not at all soupy), and the onions and spices are 'frying' in their own juices. Don't rush this step, it is essential that the spices should not have a raw harsh taste. Taste. Cook very gently for a few more minutes if necessary.

3 If you wish, for a thick sauce, purée half of the mixture in a liquidizer or food processor, then combine the puréed mixture with the unpuréed portion.

To this basic onion-curry mixture add more stock, or chopped tomatoes, or tomato paste. Stir in cubed meat, poultry, vegetables, prawns or fish and simmer until done. At the very end, yoghurt may be added to the sauce. (See index for specific curry recipes.)

Note: This basic method is correct for chilli con carne, goulashes and other dishes made with paprika, as well as curry.

'Reading them [Indian cookery books] is a great adventure: Roast this or that mystery spice for 1.75 minutes, grind it to ½ mm pieces, fry for 17 seconds in jumping-bean fat at 316° F then add it to another mystery spice. Soak in hokum-cokum water for 2 days then blanch in the midday sun at 81° F.'

Pat Chapman, Indian Restaurant Cookbook

SWEET AND SOUR ONIONS

These rich onions are perfect as a topping for meats – braised liver, grilled steak, hamburgers etc. – but they are very good on their own as well. (See page 123 for the lowest-fat steaks.)

6 large onions, peeled	1 tablespoon sugar
4 fl oz/120 ml stock	2 cloves garlic, crushed
½ teaspoon Dijon mustard	1 dried bay leaf, broken in half
1½ tablespoons red wine vinegar	Salt to taste

1   Slice onion into ½-inch/1.5-cm thick rings. Place in a non-reactive frying pan with the remaining ingredients.
2   Bring to a boil, reduce heat, cover and simmer for 30 minutes, uncovering to stir occasionally.
3   Remove the cover and simmer, stirring until the onions are beautifully browned and the liquid has greatly reduced. Remove bay leaf before serving.

 SAUTÉED MUSHROOMS

I didn't think I would be able to produce acceptable 'sautéed' mushrooms without butter or, at the very least, a bit of oil. I was wrong.

The Slim Cuisine fat-free mushroom sauté method results in mushrooms that are so vivid with mushroom flavour, they are an almost supernatural fungi essence. The more types of mushroom you use, the better. See page 219 for a mushroom ragoût that adds dried mushrooms as well, for even more mushroominess.

Leave button mushrooms whole if desired – larger mushrooms may be sliced or cut into quarters or eighths. It is fun to use a variety of fresh mushrooms: field, chestnut, shiitake, oyster, etc. Sauté them in the 'Holy Trinity' of mushroom cookery: stock, dry sherry and soy sauce (or teriyaki sauce). Sometimes I add a splash of balsamic vinegar as well. Spread the mushrooms out in a heavy-bottomed pan, and pour in 2–3 fl oz/60–90 ml of each liquid, and a splash of balsamic vinegar, if you are using it. Cook over high heat, stirring. The mushrooms will release a great deal of liquid. Keep on cooking, stirring occasionally, until the liquid has been absorbed, and the mushrooms are 'frying' in their own juices. *Never* let the mushrooms scorch, burn, or stick to the pan. Season with freshly ground pepper. These mushrooms may be prepared ahead of time and stored in the fridge. They also freeze well. They may be cooked in a non-stick frying pan, or a heavy enamelled cast iron one.

These mushrooms are not only good – they are addictive. Use them as a garnish, stir them into soups and sauces, or eat them right out of the pan, if you are as wild about mushrooms as I am.

'After an hour or so in the woods, looking for mushrooms, Dad said "Well, we can always go to the store and buy some real ones."'

John Cage, *A Year from Monday*

Peppers

Because of their flavour, deep colour and luscious texture, yellow and red peppers are Slim Cuisine staples. To make the most of peppers, they must be peeled with a swivel-bladed vegetable peeler. Simply cut the peppers into their natural sections or cut them into strips and then peel each piece. The bonus of this peeling is that the peppers will become much more digestible as well as much more delicious and texturally interesting.

My secretary Rosemarie Espley – who is as adept at kitchen drill as at word processing – always gets the pepper-peeling detail when we are involved in demonstrations, and feeding large groups of people. She has peeled hundreds at a time. She advises that pepper peeling is a wonderful skin treatment; the pepper juices leave your hands soft and lovely. (Eat your heart out, Estée Lauder.)

Peppers may be peeled by two other methods as well: micro-waving and grilling.

1   **To microwave.**   ⊠ Cut peppers in half, remove stems, seeds and ribs. Place 4 halves at a time, skin side down, on a paper towel

on the microwave carousel. Microwave at full power for 3 minutes (yellow peppers) or 4 minutes (red peppers). Remove and let stand for 2 minutes. Strip the skins away with your fingers. Microwaved peppers are no longer raw, so use this method when you do not mind the loss of crispness. It will not work, for instance, for Marinated Peppers (page 290).

2   **To grill peppers.** Cut peppers in half. Remove core, ribs and seeds. Preheat the grill to high. Line the grill pan with foil, shiny side up. Place the peppers on the foil, skin side up. Push down to flatten slightly. Grill, until the peppers are blackened. Close the charred peppers in a bag. (Save any juices that have collected in the pan.) After 10 minutes, remove the peppers. Strip off the burnt skins and discard. This method produces *cooked* peppers. It has the added bonus of a pleasantly smoky taste.

Note: If you have a gas cooker, to grill the peppers place them directly on the flame of the plate on the gas stove. As the peppers blacken and char, turn them with tongs. Or they may be cut in half and grilled, cut side down, until they blacken and char. When they are blackened and charred, continue as above.

Time-Saving Tip: Good news – you can buy peeled red peppers in tins. They are labelled 'sweet red peppers' or 'pimientos'. Some brands of tinned peppers have been grilled. When you are in a hurry you may substitute these for fresh peppers in any recipe that calls for the peppers to be cooked.

♡ 🐻 ❄   **STIR-'FRIED' PEPPERS**

When I serve these at dinner parties, I get startled reactions. 'How *did* you prepare these peppers?', guests ask suspiciously as they gobble them down. They suspect the worst, that I have succumbed to the lure of butter and added a knob or two during the sautéing. I always offer these beauties as part of a Vegetable Selection (page 250). Eat as much as you like; despite the rich taste, the Calories are minimal, the fat is nil and the vitamins are just what you need.

3 red peppers	6 fl oz/180 ml stock
3 yellow peppers	Freshly ground pepper to taste

1   Cut the peppers in half, lengthwise. Remove the stem, the seeds and the ribs. Cut the halves into their natural sections.
2   Peel each pepper piece with a swivel-bladed vegetable peeler. Cut each piece into strips about ½ inch/1.25 cm wide.

31

3   Combine the peppers and the stock in a heavy frying pan. Grind in some black pepper and bring to the boil. When boiling, use two wooden spoons to toss and turn the peppers in the hot stock until the liquid has cooked down considerably. Turn down the heat a bit and 'fry' them for a few minutes in their own juices, until they are very tender, and the pepper juices have formed a thick sauce. Serve at once with their delicious juices. This dish may be made in advance and rewarmed later or the next day.

Baked Vegetables

Everyone knows that potatoes can be baked with delicious effect. But did you ever think of baking a whole head of garlic? (Yes, I said garlic!) or a large sweet onion? It can be done, and the results will delight you, both for immediate eating and for use in thickening soups, stews and sauces.

Glorious Garlic

I am trying to bring about a garlic revolution in the UK. Fresh, firm, large heads of garlic (never pathetic old withered and sprouting ones) can be baked in the oven so that the meat of each garlic clove turns soft, buttery and *mild*. The garlic purée that results from such baking is one of the most valuable of Slim Cuisine ingredients. It provides mellowness and gorgeous mild flavour, and increases perceived richness in sauces, stews and soups.

'Garlic is as good as ten mothers.'

Teluga proverb

 ## BAKED GARLIC FOR GARLIC PURÉE

When garlic bakes in the oven for an hour or so, it loses its strong assertiveness and becomes mellow, sweet and vaguely nut-like. The texture changes too; the meat of each clove softens into a purée. The purée is excellent as a thickening agent for soups, sauces and stews. It imparts body and a mysterious and gentle flavour boost without adding salt, fat or excess Calories. The whole baked heads of garlic also make a dandy starter for a dinner party. It is fun to watch each guest fidget nervously in their chairs as you place the garlic in front of them. 'A garlic allergy, perhaps?', they desperately think. 'A mad dash home to check on the children?' Quickly demonstrate the proper method of spreading the garlic on toast and take a bite yourself. When your guests see that you survive that first taste, they will be emboldened to try. And once they have had that first taste, they will be garlic fans for life. Be sure to use the largest, firmest, freshest heads of garlic you can find for this procedure.

Keep a supply of the purée in the refrigerator and use it to liven up all kinds of dishes. Stir it into soups and stews by the spoonful; use it to thicken sauces, and to spread on bread (mixed with quark or Slim Cuisine cream cheese if you wish). Garlic popcorn – freshly popped popcorn with a good dollop of garlic purée – makes a simple, unbelievably savoury snack. No salt is needed; the garlic flavour is sufficient.

Whole heads of garlic

---

1   Preheat oven to 375° F, 190° C, Gas Mark 4.
2   Remove the papery outer covering of the whole garlic heads, but do not separate the cloves or peel them. Place each whole head of garlic on a square of foil (shiny side of the foil in). Fold up the foil and crimp so that the head is completely wrapped.
3   Bake in the preheated oven for approximately 1 hour 15 minutes (depending upon size of garlic bulb).
4   Remove from the oven, unwrap and cool for at least 5 minutes. Gently separate the cloves and squeeze each one over a fine-meshed sieve so that the softened garlic pops into the sieve.
5   With a wooden spatula or spoon rub the garlic through the sieve into a small container or bowl. (If you are in a hurry, forget the sieve. Simply squeeze the garlic into the bowl.) Cover tightly with plastic wrap and refrigerate until the purée is needed.

 # BAKED GARLIC AS A STARTER

Whole heads of garlic
Toasted rounds of wholemeal bread

---

1   Preheat oven to 375° F, 190° C, Gas Mark 4.
2   Remove the papery outer covering of the whole garlic heads,

but do not separate the cloves or peel them. Place as many whole heads of garlic on a large square of foil (shiny side of the foil in) as there are people to be served. Fold up the foil so that the cloves are completely wrapped.

3   Bake in a preheated oven for approximately 1 hour 15 minutes (depending upon size of garlic bulb).

4   Serve each diner a head of garlic and some bread. Separate the cloves. Hold a clove over a piece of bread and squeeze. The garlic purée will pop out, like toothpaste from a tube.

♡ 🧸 🕐 ⊠   **MICROWAVE VERSION OF BAKED GARLIC**

If you try to put a whole head of garlic into the microwave to bake, you will end up with something quite horrid. The cloves become tough and the taste becomes acrid and revolting. There *is* a way, however, to achieve a melting, mellow and sweetly delicious garlic purée in the microwave. Be *very careful* when you remove the cling film. Follow the directions meticulously, or you may get scalded by the steam.

1   Remove the papery outer covering from 2–3 large, firm heads of garlic, but do not peel them. Separate the cloves. Scatter them, in one layer, in an 8-inch/20-cm square, 1–2 inch/2.5–5-cm deep glass baking dish. Pour in water to a depth of a little more than ½ inch/1.25 cm. Cover *tightly* with microwave cling film.

2   Microwave on high for 10 minutes. Carefully remove from the oven (do not remove or loosen cling film) and let stand for 10 minutes.

3   With tongs peel away a corner of the cling film on the side *away from you*, to allow steam to escape. Be very careful: the steam is hot, and you don't want to get burned. With the tongs, remove the cling film.

4   When the garlic is cool enough to handle, remove the skins (they will slip right off). Drain the garlic and place in a bowl. Mash with a fork or a wooden pestle. If desired, push through a sieve to make a very fine purée.

Glorious Garlic

Glorious Garlic

It's no secret that I love garlic, particularly in quantity. While some people add a clove or two to a sauce, wondering nervously all the while if they are erring on the side of excess, I throw the cloves in by the double handful. In my view, garlic is much more than a seasoning to be used with discretion. The glorious bulb is a vegetable, meant to be used in exhilarating quantity. The fascinating thing about garlic is that the whole cloves, cooked in quantity, gently and slowly, become soft, buttery, mild and sweet – so unlike garlic's usual sharp pungency. Such gentle cooking also renders garlic much more digestible.

The really exciting news is that garlic (like onion), consumed in quantity, is now recognized as a significant health food. Research from both the US National Cancer Institute and the Chinese Institute for Cancer Research suggests that high consumption of garlic and onions may lessen susceptibility to stomach cancer. And many researchers also believe that high consumption of glorious garlic may help bring high blood pressure and blood cholesterol levels down. So if you needed the perfect excuse to have an unbridled allium wallow, you've got it now!

'Some people are allergic to garlic. They may or may not be vampires.'

Lloyd John Harris, *The Garlic Lover's Handbook*

Garlic Breath and Onion Tears

I'm always amazed at the variations in the personal chemistry of people. Some individuals can chop, slice, dice and purée garlic and onions with abandon and never breathe a hint of it or shed the smallest tear. Others merely touch a clove or a bulb of the pungent vegetables and immediately weep buckets while they light up the vicinity with an incandescent allium glow. For those who are sensitive to the volatile chemicals in both onions and garlic, here are a few helpful hints.

1   **Garlic on the Hands.** For some, soap and water work fine. If not, try rubbing your hands with lemon juice or a little salt. If your hands still reek, here is the ultimate foolproof method. It sounds strange, but it really works:

After handling garlic, rub your fingers thoroughly with the

bowl of a stainless steel spoon (it *must* be stainless steel), under cold running water, then wash your hands with soap. The metal neutralizes the garlic, and the lingering odour will be gone.

2　**Onion Tears.** There are many folk remedies offered to cure onion tears: chill the onions, freeze them, peel them under cold running water, peel them with a wooden match clenched between your teeth, handle them near an open window, an extractor fan, an open flame. If you are prone to onion tears and you try one of these methods, you will exclaim 'This method (sob, sniff) does not work!' Wear swimming goggles or a gas mask. It's the only way.

3　**Garlic Breath.** Alas, there are no easy remedies for this. Breath mints and mouth washes and all the folk remedies (parsley, a raw coffee bean, anise seeds) sweeten the mouth, but the problem is not in the mouth; it is in the lungs and in the very pores of the skin. My favourite old remedy is the one that suggests eating vast quantities of garlic every day for a week. Garlic breath, claims Ford Madox Ford in a famous excerpt from *Provence*, 'attends only those timorous creatures who have not the courage as it were to wallow in that vegetable'. Wrong. If you wallow in garlic you will smell of it.

　　There is only a partial solution to the problem.

(a) If the garlic is baked, or otherwise gently cooked in a way that makes it mellow, the subsequent odour will be mellow.

(b) See that your family, friends and associates eat as much garlic as (or more than) you do. Then they will all have that allium glow, but no one will notice it. Just remember this: it's chic to reek.

'Now there is no good cooking except wth garlic . . .'

　　　　　　　　　　Ludwig Bemelmans, *Father Dear Father*

Aubergine Purée

Aubergine purée discreetly stretches meat. Used in hamburgers, sausages, and mince sauces such as Bolognese sauce, it allows you to use less meat without affecting the taste. *Lean* meat can be very dry and 'bitty' – aubergine restores moistness and smoothness; it adds lightness, and cuts the Calories without adding any taste of its own. Even if you hate aubergine, you will love what it does to minced meat. And for a delicious Middle Eastern dip, try the baked flesh, puréed or mashed with baked garlic, baked onion and baked pepper purées, yoghurt, chopped tomatoes, herbs and spices (cumin, coriander leaves, cayenne). Serve with pitta bread triangles, or crudités (raw vegetable dippers).

 ## BAKED AUBERGINE

Whole aubergines

1 Preheat oven to 400° F, 200° C, Gas Mark 7.
2 Pierce the aubergines in several places with a fork or thin skewer. Bake directly on the oven rack for 30–40 minutes, until soft and collapsed. Cool.
3 Cut away the stem, strip off and discard the skins, and chop finely or mash. (If the clumps of seeds are large and tough they may be discarded.)

MICROWAVE VERSION OF BAKED AUBERGINE

Aubergines must be pierced before they are microwaved, or they may explode. To make aubergine purée to use as a filler that provides moistness in meatballs, hamburgers and sausages, they must be steamed, in ½ inch/1.25 cm of water. Again, be very careful not to scald yourself with the steam. To roast the aubergine in the microwave so that it can be sliced into deeply flavoured, good-textured pieces, suitable for casseroles, see page 215.

1 Place 1 aubergine (½ lb/240 g) in an 8-inch/20-cm square, 1–2 inch/2.5–5 cm deep glass baking dish. Pour in ½ inch/1.25 cm water. Cover tightly with microwave cling film. Microwave on high for 6 minutes. Remove from the oven. Do not uncover. Let rest for 5 minutes.
2 With tongs, very carefully peel away one corner of the cling film on the side away from you to allow steam to escape. It is very hot, so use caution, you do not want to scald your hand or face. With the tongs, remove cling film. When the aubergine is cool enough to handle, strip off the skin with a dull knife. Chop the pulp very finely with a chef's knife.

BAKED ONION

A baked onion served whole, sprinkled with fresh pepper and lemon juice, makes a lovely vegetable accompaniment to a meal. It can also be puréed in a liquidizer and used as garlic purée can be used: to thicken sauces, soups and stews and to give them a low-fat, low-Calorie and low-salt flavour and texture boost.

Large Spanish onions

---

1   Preheat the oven to 425° F, 220° C, Gas Mark 6.
2   Put the onions on a double sheet of foil, shiny side out, but do not wrap them. Bake for 1¼ hours, or until very soft and almost collapsed.
3   With a sharp knife, cut off the stem and root ends of the onions. Remove and discard the blackened skin and first layer. Serve as they are with pepper and lemon juice, or put the onions into a liquidizer and purée for use in other recipes.

Microwave version of baked onion:

Wrap a large Spanish onion in microwave cling film. Place a sheet of kitchen paper towelling on the carousel. Put the wrapped onion on the towelling.

Microwave on high for 3 minutes, turn over and microwave on high for an additional 3 minutes. Let stand for a minute or two.

BAKED TURNIPS, CARROTS, SWEDES AND PARSNIPS

Why condemn turnips, carrots and parsnips to a watery, vitamin-stripped death? Forget boiling. Bake them so that they steam in their own juices. Instead of poor flabby things, they will be tender and succulent. When mashed or puréed, these baked vegetables are very useful for thickening and giving body to soups and stews. They may also be eaten as they are, or mashed with a bit of buttermilk and Parmesan cheese. Or they may be baked into a crusty gratin. (See pages 261–263.)

Turnips	*Carrots*
Parsnips	*Swedes*

---

1   Preheat the oven to 425° F, 220° C, Gas Mark 6.
2   Peel the turnips. Scrub the carrots, parsnips and swedes.

Leave them unpeeled if they are to be eaten whole, peel them if they are to be mashed. Quarter the swedes.

3   Wrap the turnips loosely in foil, shiny side in. Crimp well so that no steam escapes. Do the same with the parsnips, carrots, and swedes. Bake for 1–1¼ hours, until tender.

'But yesterday I caught him in her dairy, eating fresh butter with a tablespoon. Today he is not well.'

W. S. Gilbert, *Patience*

♡ DRAINING YOGHURT OR FROMAGE FRAIS TO MAKE CREAM CHEESE AND MAYONNAISE

This 'cream' cheese is thick and creamy, perfect for spreading on bread or toast or dolloping into jacket potatoes in place of high-fat soured cream, cream cheese or butter. Use it, too, as a base for 'mayonnaise' or creamy salad dressing. Yoghurt cheese and fromage frais cheese are very easy to make and so versatile that it pays to have some on hand in the fridge at all times. Fromage frais results in a milder cheese than yoghurt.

1   Line a sieve or colander with a long piece of doubled damp cheesecloth. (Rinse it first in cold water, then wring it out well.) Place the lined sieve over a large bowl. Dump in the yoghurt or fromage frais, fold the cheesecloth over to cover well and leave in a cool part of the kitchen for 24 hours. Every once in a while, pour off the liquid that accumulates in the bowl.

2   At the end of the 24-hour period unwrap the cheese and scrape it into a bowl or crock. Refrigerate. If desired, interesting ingredients can be added to the cheese to produce a delicious spread. Try one of these:

Crushed garlic marinated in wine vinegar	Shredded smoked fish
Chopped fresh chives	Minced, mixed vegetables (radishes, celery, carrots, red and yellow peppers)
Chopped fresh dill	

♡ MAYONNAISE

Makes approximately 8 fl oz/240 ml

Forget real mayonnaise, yummy though it may be. The wicked stuff is made from egg yolks and a whole lot of oil, with a little mustard and wine vinegar thrown in. Pure, unadulterated fat, with no redeeming value whatsoever. Slim Cuisine 'mayonnaise' is low-fat and low-Calorie. Use it in salad recipes or as a sandwich spread. (See the Salad chapter for more ideas.) You may feel as smug as you please as you eat your salad and sandwiches: real mayo has 99 Calories and 11 grams of fat per tablespoon; this version only 7 Calories, and 0.03 grams of fat.

4 fl oz/120 ml yoghurt cheese or fromage frais cheese, or a combination	*3–4 tablespoons buttermilk*
	1–2 tablespoons wine vinegar
1–2 teaspoons Dijon mustard (to taste)	*Salt and freshly ground pepper to taste*

Whisk all the ingredients together, adding the buttermilk and vinegar gradually, tasting as you go, until a mayonnaise-like consistency is achieved, and until the flavour pleases you. Season to taste. Refrigerate overnight for flavours to blend.

Note: Add any one of the following to your mayonnaise, if desired:

Crushed garlic	*Red pepper purée (see page 30)*
Chilli powder, hot or mild	*Tomato paste*
Hungarian paprika, hot or mild	*Chopped fresh herbs*
Curry spices	

'Mayonnaise: One of the sauces which serve the French in place of a State Religion.'

Ambrose Bierce, *The Devil's Dictionary*

Ingredients

Dairy Products

♡ QUARK

It sounds like the cry of a drunken duck, a physicist will tell you that it is a sub-atomic particle, but food-lovers know that quark is a smooth, creamy, skimmed milk curd cheese. Several brands of quark are available throughout food stores in the UK; avoid those that list modified food starch in the ingredients. Quark is a superb cooking ingredient, and it is very good indeed spread on bread and toast in place of butter. Its bland creaminess makes it perfect for use in recipes that call for cream cheese, soured cream or even whipped cream. Quark can also be used for cooking in many sauces that call for cream. 3½ oz/100 g of the versatile stuff contains 77 Calories.

♡ SKIMMED MILK YOGHURT

Yoghurt is an extremely valuable and useful product (3½ oz/100 g is 55 Calories, 0.2 g fat). Use it in place of soured cream and crème fraîche (3½ oz/100 g is 212 Calories, 20 g fat). Or drain it to form a delightful cream cheese (see page 39). Yoghurt cream cheese can be turned into a fat-free, low-Calorie mayonnaise (see page 40).

Undrained yoghurt can also be used in cooking in place of cream. If the yoghurt is to be simmered in a sauce or cooked dish, it must be stabilized to prevent curdling (see below).

41

The Magic of Yoghurt

Ilya Metchnikoff was obsessed with *Lactobacillus Bulgaris*. Metchnikoff, a Nobel Laureate and the sub-director of the Pasteur Institute in Paris, believed the human ageing process to be tragic and premature. He was convinced that a regular diet of yoghurt (the result of the bacteria *Lactobacillus Bulgaris* on milk) would significantly prolong life, and hold senility and physical degeneration at bay. Secure in his belief, Metchnikoff wrote a book, *The Prolongation of Life,* and fed himself lavish amounts of yoghurt until the end of his life. That end, alas, came at the age of 71 – a decent enough span, but not the century-plus length of years he was so sure he would achieve.

Today, almost seventy years after the publication of Metchnikoff's book, yoghurt is a supermarket staple. Although it won't help you to live forever, it is a magnificent cooking ingredient – tangy, custardy and smooth – and the low-fat version is one of the standbys of Slim Cuisine. Thank you, Monsieur Metchnikoff: how lovely it is to indulge in mayonnaise and creamy salad dressings without indulging in fat and excess Calories as well.

♡ ## STABILIZED YOGHURT

Heat applied to yoghurt causes it to curdle. Very low-fat yoghurt seems to be more prone to curdling than that with higher fat levels. Cornflour stabilizes the yoghurt so that it can be used in soups and hot sauces, but even stabilized yoghurt must be simmered only gently. Boiling will cause it to 'break' or become grainy.

2 teaspoons cornflour blended with 1 tablespoon water	*1 pt/600 ml skimmed milk yoghurt at room temperature*

1   Whisk together the cornflour, water and yoghurt. Dump into a non-reactive, heavy saucepan. Gently bring to a simmer, stirring.
2   Simmer gently for 5 minutes, stirring often.

♡ ## FROMAGE FRAIS

Fromage frais is not as dense as quark. The texture is similar to that of soured cream or crème fraîche. Although it is called fromage – cheese – it is not particularly cheese-like. When you crave something creamy and rich, consider eating this exemplary dairy product right out of its container. Read the label – make sure you are buying fromage frais with less than 1% fat. How can anyone be depressed about a low-fat regime, with products like this to soothe and satisfy one's cravings?

It contains only 44 Calories per 3½ oz/100 g, 0.1 g fat. Soured cream and crème fraîche contain 18 per cent fat and 212 Calories, 20 g fat per 3½ oz/100 g. Use fromage frais in sauces, jacket potatoes, sweets and anywhere else you would use soured cream. Like sour cream, it will separate when overheated, so never allow it to simmer or boil.

♡ **BUTTERMILK**

Cultured from skimmed milk, buttermilk is thick, creamy, only slightly tangy and a mere 35 Calories per 3½ oz/100 g, 0.1 g fat. It gives a lovely flavour and texture to sweets and to low fat 'mayonnaise'-type salad dressings. It is worth searching for. Many large supermarkets carry buttermilk, as do many small delicatessens and whole food shops. Strawberries, buttermilk and a light sprinkling of brown sugar make a heavenly finish to a meal. Buttermilk is also an important component of Slim Cuisine icecreams (see pages 312–315).

> 'Well, I worked for him on that 101 inch aluminium line that he laid from Pennsylvania to California. We laid it to pipe buttermilk out to his camp out there. Paul [Bunyan] likes buttermilk so well himself that he had a twenty-four inch petcock running wide open all the time to catch enough for him to drink.'
>
> Acel Garland, *Foller de Drinkin' Gou'd*

♡ **SKIMMED MILK**

> 'There's warmth, comfort, cooing, eye contact, bonding, all those good things associated with nurturing and love, which then all get associated with the taste of milk.'
>
> Dr Stephen Locke quoted in
> *The International Herald Tribune*

If you think you hate skimmed milk don't despair. Eventually your palate will adjust to the thinner texture, and you will (if you like milk in the first place) find it perfectly acceptable. In fact, those who use skimmed milk regularly find whole milk quite revolting. It coats the tongue, and feels thick and unpleasantly fatty in the mouth. Forget whole milk, semi-skimmed milk and cream, whether it's double, single, half or one of those new ones that has been relieved of butterfat and filled with polyunsaturates (it will still be chock-full of fat Calories). Do check with your doctor, however, before you switch young children from whole to skimmed. You will find skimmed milk quite useful as a cooking ingredient. Keep powdered skimmed milk in the larder for emergencies.

PARMESAN CHEESE

Parmesan cheese is a *medium*-fat classic grating cheese with a deep cheese taste. A little bit of Parmesan goes a very long way. One tablespoon of this medium-fat cheese adds approximately 25 Calories (1.8 g fat) to a recipe. If possible, buy real Italian *Parmiggiano reggiano* and grate it yourself as follows:

Cut the cheese into smallish chunks. Put them in the liquidizer. Blend until finely grated. Store in the refrigerator or the freezer. *Save the rind:* Parmesan rind is one of the magic ingredients of Slim Cuisine. Use a piece of it when simmering certain sauces, soups and ragoûts. When the dish is finished, discard the rind. It will have imparted a good Parmesan flavour but very little in the way of Calories and fat.

> 'And in the evening . . . I did dig another [pit in the garden] and put our wine in it and my parmazan cheese . . . and some other things.'
>
> Samuel Pepys, *On the Great Fire of London*

MOZZARELLA CHEESE

Another Italian classic. This one melts into a bland, gooey, creamy, pully mass – quite wonderful. Buy real Italian Mozzarella cheese, found in the dairy case of many supermarkets. It will be labelled 'part-skim' or 'medium fat', and will be packed in a liquid-filled pouch. Italian Mozzarella has a fresh, mild, milky taste.

Other medium-fat cheeses to be used in small quantities

Jarlsberg – A Swiss-type cheese from Denmark
Bruder Basil – A delicately smoked cheese
Feta – A creamy, Greek, ewe's milk cheese. Read the label to be sure you are not buying a full fat Feta. It's very salty; rinse it before using it.

Chèvre – There are several of these creamy French goat's milk cheeses that are medium fat. Chèvres are a personal favourite of mine in cooking. Again read the label and buy medium or low fat only.

SMOKED CHICKEN

There are very good smoked chickens available in some speciality shops and delicatessens. I regularly buy the Galina brand from Greenstage in Newmarket, producers of the famous Musk's Sausage. A smoked chicken is ready to eat so needs no further cooking other than a brief warming, but it's good cold too. It can be stored in the freezer for months, with no appreciable loss of quality. Use smoked chicken in sandwiches (for suggestions see page 298) or to give a wonderful smoky accent to pasta dishes (see page 228 for an example). If you can, freeze your smoked chicken in pieces, because you will only need a little bit at a time. *Never* throw away the smoked chicken bones and scraps. Save them in the freezer until you have enough to make stock. The stock will have a haunting and lovely smoky edge, making it perfect for split pea and bean soups, chestnut soup, some sauces – anywhere you want a smoky taste without resorting to high-fat smoked bacon, ham and so on.

Seasonings

'Wheat and beef, rice and fish are the prose of food, herbs and spices are its poetry.'

Waverly Root, *Herbs and Spices*

GARLIC

Don't be afraid of garlic. It is an important part of Slim Cuisine, and adds a wonderful depth of flavour and richness to many preparations. You will find that there are no strong garlicky tastes in any of the recipes in this book that involve cooking, even those that use quantities of the bulb. Slim Cuisine cooking techniques involve steaming, poaching, baking, simmering and boiling; no frying or sautéing in oils or fats. It is these latter techniques that bring out garlic's pungent qualities. On the other hand in salads and dressings that call for raw garlic, the taste will be stronger. By all means in these cases leave out the garlic if you wish.

When shopping, choose your garlic carefully. Lift the bulbs and squeeze them. They should be heavy and firm. Never buy heads that have shrivelled or bruised cloves. (Remember, a clove is one section, a bulb or head is the whole thing.) And never buy garlic that is visibly sprouting. If, when peeling and mincing the cloves, you find that each contains a greenish sprout in the centre, split the clove, remove the sprout and discard it. Store garlic bulbs in a cool well-ventilated part of the kitchen. They should not be tightly wrapped – a basket is the ideal receptacle. Never refrigerate them. Do *not* use garlic salt, garlic powder, or other processed garlic products. They will impart a harsh, rancid and unpleasant taste to your cookery.

When crushing garlic, use a mallet, not a garlic press. The press is an infamous utensil that releases all of garlic's strong, indigestible qualities. The mallet is handy for peeling the cloves as well as crushing them. Hit the clove with the mallet, remove the loosened skin, and proceed.

GINGER

Fresh ginger root has become a supermarket staple. Once you try it, you will be delighted with its clean, bracing flavour. Always peel it first with a paring knife or a swivel-bladed peeler, and then grate it or mince it. If you cannot find the fresh root, substitute ground ginger. It won't be the same as fresh, but it will do.

BLACK PEPPER

Use whole peppercorns cracked in a peppermill, as needed, instead of packaged pre-ground pepper. The taste it imparts to your recipes will be flavourful, not merely sharp. White peppercorns are the same berry as the black ones, at a different stage of ripeness. White pepper is the mature berry with the outer husk removed. Black pepper is slightly underripe. If you abhor black specks in your food, keep a mill filled with white peppercorns for light-coloured food.

SALT

Somehow we have become accustomed to quantities of salt in our food. Try cutting down gradually and learn to savour the taste of good fresh ingredients without their usual cloak of saltiness. Salt is invaluable as a flavour enhancer, and a sprinkle here and there brings out natural flavour in a wonderful way. But those who use it by the handful, who sit down and salt their food liberally before they even taste it, are connoisseurs of salt only, not of food. For the sake of your health, and for the sake of good taste, wean yourself from the excess salt habit. 'Salt to taste', specify the instructions in recipes in this book. Try to make it a sprinkle, not an avalanche.

Canned beans (chick peas, kidney beans, borlotti and cannellini beans, etc.) are excellent larder staples, as is canned tuna, but they contain masses of salt. Wash most of it away by emptying the contents of the can into a colander, and then rinsing well under cold water.

'An overturned Salt-Cellar is to be feared only when it is overturned in a good dish.'

Grimod de la Reyniere, *Almanach des Gourmands*

SOY SAUCE

An excellent Chinese condiment, very useful with mushrooms. Simmer the fungi in a mixture of stock and wine, with a dash of soy sauce and you won't miss the butter or oil. Read the labels, and buy a brand of soy sauce that does *not* contain monosodium glutamate. All soy sauces contain salt, so wield the salt shaker sparingly when you use the sauce. People who must confine themselves to a low-salt regime will find balsamic vinegar (page 50) an excellent substitute.

SUGAR

Like salt, sugar is very much a matter of taste. And, like salt, sugar is an amazingly good flavour enhancer. It helps bring out natural flavours and put them into balance. Unfortunately, most people do not think of sugar as another seasoning. They think of the sweet stuff as a major ingredient, and consume an enormous amount of it each day. The goal should not be to experience an overwhelming sweetness, but to experience sweetness in concert with other flavours. Learn to orchestrate ingredients, and to use them with finesse, so that the overall effect is harmonious. Sugar is just one part of the orchestra; fight the urge to make it a soloist.

CHILLI PEPPERS

Fresh chillies have found their way into the supermarkets, and welcome they are, to lovers of incendiary cuisine. There are thousands of kinds of chilli peppers in the world; out of the profusion only a few find their way here. You will need to experiment with what your local market has to offer, but if you love edible fire, as I do, you will find such experimentation pure pleasure. Fresh chillies can be searingly hot; exercise caution when working with them.

To those who are sensitive to the volatile oils, preparing chillies can be a painful and even dangerous exercise. You *must* wear rubber gloves while handling chillies; it is the only safe protection. *Never* touch your eyes or any other sensitive area (men, for instance, should not attempt to go to the loo) until the gloves are safely stripped off and stowed away, and your hands are thoroughly washed. Should your eyes or other mucous membranes become burnt or irritated, flush at once with cold water. And if you burn your mouth with a bite of chilli-ridden curry or other too-spicy food, don't attempt to quench the burn with floods of cold drink. Cold drinks exacerbate the problem. Try a bite of bread or banana or a spoonful of honey.

Two kinds of canned chillies are convenient to have in the larder. Green chillies (fairly mild) and jalapeños (very hot). Look for them on the supermarket or delicatessen shelf that houses Mexican-style foods.

In any recipe in this book containing chilli peppers, reduce or omit them if you don't like piquant food.

CHILLI POWDER, CAYENNE PEPPER, ETC.

Recipes calling for chilli powder have been tested with Schwartz chilli powder. Use mild, hot, or a combination, according to your taste and discretion. Feel free to cut down on the amounts called for, or even to cut them out, if you do not possess an asbestos palate.

'One bite, and your tongue dials the fire department.'

N. Steinberg and D. Palumbo, *My Favourite Year*

♡ **TOMATOES**

At certain times of the year there are no tomatoes in the shops, only a bewildering array of pulpy, pale-pink, tennis-ball-like imposters. Tomato lovers treat these objects with the scorn they deserve, and depend upon canned Italian tomatoes until summer comes along, bringing its ripe bursting-with-flavour, ruby beauties. In the winter, if you long for fresh tomatoes, search for tomatoes from the Canary Islands and store them at room temperature, in a closed paper bag. In a few days to a week they will have ripened and may even taste vaguely like tomatoes, although not like fully-fledged summer beauties. To peel a fresh tomato, immerse it in boiling water for 10 seconds, then cut out the stem and slip off the skins. The seeds may be removed with your finger. Tomato skins and seeds pass right through the human digestive system untouched, so you won't be losing valuable nutrients. If canned tomatoes seem particularly acidic, add a pinch of sugar when you cook them.

♡ 🐻 SUN-DRIED TOMATOES

In America, they say that sun-dried tomatoes are the ketchup of the eighties. Wait until you taste them! Leathery, with a dark, intense, over-the-top ripe tomato flavour, they are quite irresistible, and add wonderful depth to sauces, soups and stews. Sun-dried tomatoes are now available dry pack (no oil), so you can eat yourself silly on them, and use them freely in recipes. The ones from Italy are slightly salty, the ones from the United States are not. They are not budget food, but why not count up the money you are saving by *not* buying butter, crisps, cigarettes, sweet bars, fish-and-chip takeaways, vegetable oil, and so on. Invest some of those healthy savings on sybaritic, healthy treats. Sun-dried tomatoes and balsamic vinegar help to make a low-fat lifestyle a culinary dream.

♡ 🐻 HERBS

> 'You are trying to find out not what this or that herb is in itself but what it is to you. If something reminds you of new-mown grass – or a paint factory on an off day, Nana's pantry, Uncle Joe's tobacco pouch, the first restaurant where you met your last love, or the last restaurant in which you saw your first – then that is what it is.'
>
> Robert Farrar Capon, *Food for Thought*

I am delighted to see fresh herbs available in many supermarkets throughout the country. They bring a dimension of freshness and clear flavour that is never realized with the dried variety. A good rule of thumb: use three times the amount of fresh herbs as dried. Do taste as you go, though, and be flexible. Too much of a dried herb will give unpleasant results. And watch the quality of your dried herbs. They become old and musty all too easily. Buy them in small amounts, and store them, tightly covered, in a cool, dark place. To release the flavour components in dried herbs, crumble them between your fingers as you scatter them into the pot.

SPICES

Spices are a collection of aromatic barks, seeds, roots and buds that are used to season foods. Buy them in small quantities, store them, tightly covered, in a cool, dark spot, and try not to keep them beyond 6 months. When their oils turn rancid, they are unusable. Through kitchen experiment, learn the tastes of various spices, and learn the way they harmonize or clash with other spices and with various foodstuffs. Soon you will be seasoning food to please your own palate.

WINE

Dry red and white wine, dry sherry and dry vermouth are important Slim Cuisine ingredients. Don't worry about the alcohol (and the alcohol Calories) in such wines. As they cook in your sauces, soups and sautés, the alcohol evaporates away. You are left with an intense and delicious flavour but it won't make anyone drunk, and it won't cause anyone to consume empty alcohol Calories. There is no need to invest in vintage wines for your cookery, but don't use a wine you wouldn't drink on its own. What is bad in the glass is worse in the pot.

♡ ## WINE VINEGARS

Here is another area for splurging, or try dropping hints here and there, before Christmas or your birthday. 'Designer' vinegars – those elegant ones such as sherry, raspberry, etc. – are expensive but they add an exciting dimension to food, especially to fat-free salad dressings and sauces.

♡ ## BALSAMIC VINEGAR

A magic ingredient if ever there was one. Balsamic vinegar is produced by boiling the must of Trebbiano di Spagno grapes until it thickens and caramelizes, then culturing it in wooden barrels. The flavour intensity, colour and quality of the vinegar is deter-

mined by the type of wood, the size of the barrel and the length of curing time. Good balsamic vinegar bears no resemblance to any other wine vinegar; the heady liquid is sweet-tasting, intense and mouth-filling. As it is, it makes a superb salad dressing, or a sauce for steamed vegetables, potatoes, fish, or meats. Because I don't eat salad dressing or sauces in restaurants (they contain too much fat), I depend on the pocket flask of balsamic vinegar that I carry with me all the time. My husband (brilliant and considerate man that he is) gave me the flask for my birthday, and keeps it topped up with a good balsamic vinegar. I get odd looks in restaurants when I pull out my flask and flourish it over naked salads and vegetables, but it makes low-fat restaurant meals positively luxurious. And – of course – it's a great conversation piece. Orso's, one of my favourite London restaurants, uses balsamic vinegar in several dishes, and – if you ask – will actually put a large bottle of the nectar on your table, so that you can pour at will. How tempted I have been to pull out my flask and a siphon, or even to pour it into my wine glass and quaff it down. But civilized behaviour always wins in the end and I confine myself to pouring it liberally over everything in sight.

♡ DRIED MUSHROOMS

Dried *Boletus edulis* mushrooms (called porcini in Italy, cèpes in France) and dried Chinese or Japanese mushrooms (shiitakes) are available in delicatessens, speciality food halls and some super-markets. An ounce/30 grams of dried mushrooms goes a long way, and can give low-fat cookery an enormous flavour boost. When reconstituted, dried mushrooms plump up to at least five times their dried weight. The flavour, then, will be up to twenty times as intense as that of an ounce/30 grams of the same mushroom in its undried (fresh) state.

Dried mushrooms harbour quantities of sand and grit in their nooks and crannies. Always rinse them well in *cold* water before reconstituting. After soaking ½–1 hour, rinse them again and strain the soaking water through a coffee filter, or doubled cheese cloth. *Never* discard the strained soaking water; it is a rich essence of mushroom and should be used in the dish being prepared, or frozen to enrich future soups, stews and sauces.

Larder and Freezer Staples

Frozen Vegetables and Fruit. Commercially frozen vegetables can be terrific. Not all of them. Frozen asparagus is a travesty of the real

51

thing, frozen broccoli and frozen potatoes are pretty grim, frozen courgettes, mushrooms and cauliflower are terrible. But frozen sweetcorn, peas, button sprouts, diced swedes: it's hard to imagine doing without them. Frozen fruits, too, make one's cooking life so much easier. They are incredibly useful in all sorts of recipes, and their taste and quality involve *no* compromise. One of the best kitchen investments you can make is a big chest freezer. If you keep your eye on the classifieds in your local paper, you may find a good bargain in a used freezer. Security is having a freezer full of high-quality staples, so that when a cooking frenzy strikes, the raw ingredients are there, waiting in suspended animation.

Tinned Vegetables. There are several tinned vegetables that are so useful and good tasting that you should never be without them.

Artichoke hearts
Sweet red peppers (pimientos)
Italian tomatoes
Broad beans
Red kidney beans and white ones (cannellini)
Borlotti beans and black-eyed beans
Chick peas
Chillies (jalapeños and green chillies)

> 'One of my chief pleasures in life was dealing with store bought food – all so virginally packaged yet bursting to be opened.'
>
> Lucy Ellman, *Sweet Desserts*

Equipment

'Except for a few ancient, lethally sharp carbon steel knives, my mother's kitchenware made a mockery of all recipes calling for well insulated pots and enamelled exteriors. As they grew older (they) became so dented on the bottom that they could not stand upright when empty.'

Mimi Sheraton, *From My Mother's Kitchen*

Non-Reactive Cookware

Cast iron, tin and aluminium cookware will react with acid ingredients such as tomatoes, wine and spinach to produce off flavours and discolorations. To avoid these problems, use *non-reactive* cookware, such as *enamelled* cast iron, stainless steel, flame-proof glass and ceramic, and non-stick coatings such as Tefal and Silverstone. Because no added fat is used in Slim Cuisine, you will find the non-stick cookware invaluable. When choosing such equipment, go for weight. Hefty, heavy-bottomed pots and pans cook evenly and will ensure success. Read the directions that come with your cookware. Many non-stick pots and pans must be seasoned, sometimes by rubbing the non-stick finish with oil (this is the only time you will be using oil in your kitchen), sometimes by simmering milk in the pan.

An enamelled cast-iron frying pan is handy for sautéing – for those times when you want a non-reactive pot, but not a non-stick one (see Sautéed Onions, page 24). If you plan to do a lot of stir-frying (easy to do without fat – see page 258), you might want to invest in a wok. Big ones with cover, steamer rack and non-stick interior are available in cookware departments throughout the country. They work with both gas and electric cookers.

A steamer is an absolute necessity for vegetables. It can be used for fish, chicken breasts and rice as well. Buy a folding one that fits into a large saucepan or, better still, a stock pot with a perforated steamer-basket which fits inside. If necessary, improvise a steamer with a colander set in a saucepan. If you live near a Chinese food shop, consider acquiring a Chinese bamboo steamer that fits in a wok. Such a steamer is fairly inexpensive, easy and versatile to use, and wonderful looking.

For straining, puréeing and draining yoghurt and fromage frais, have several non-reactive sieves or strainers on hand. Nylon mesh sieves are perfect. Cheesecloth or butter muslin is essential to line the sieve when you use it to make cream cheese (see page 39). If you want to make fat-free icecreams, purées, dips and so on, both a food processor and a liquidizer are invaluable tools. You will use them again and again. A microwave oven, of course, makes a busy cook's life so much easier. And don't forget a fat bouquet of wooden spoons and wire whisks standing in a jar by your work area, and a faithful set of measuring utensils, both spoons and jugs.

Meals for Special Occasions

'Each succeeding course must lead to new ecstasy, else will the dinner turn out the worst of failures.'

Elizabeth Robins Pennell, *A Guide for the Greedy by a Greedy Woman*

Liberated Sunday Lunch

Where I come from, people eat brunch on Sunday. It begins at 12-ish with Mimosas (champagne mixed with fresh orange juice) or Bloody Mary Soup (vodka mixed with piquant tomato juice, served up in a soup plate with a generous sprinkling of fresh herbs, chopped chillies and a *large* soup spoon). The liquid refreshment is usually followed by poached or scrambled eggs, and bagels thickly spread with cream cheese, draped with smoked salmon, and topped with ruby red slices of ripe tomato and slivers of sweet onion. Coleslaw, potato salad, Greek black olives, Danish pastry and cup after cup of strong black coffee complete the New York Sunday ritual. It's a casual and very relaxed meal – someone runs out for the Sunday papers (someone strong – the Sunday *New York Times* is bigger than all the English Sunday papers *put together!*), someone else nips out to the corner deli to pick up the bagels, salads, smoked salmon and Danish pastry, and everyone lazes around in comfortable old clothes.

When we arrived in England, invitations flooded in from new friends for Sunday lunch. Sunday after Sunday, we sat at formal tables, in our good clothes, and consumed roast leg of lamb, roast potatoes, huge plates of vegetables and profound puddings, only to stagger home in the evening replete and bemused by our sudden departure from our old Sunday brunch habits.

I must say that the traditional English Sunday lunch is festive and tasty, but its major flaw, other than its ridiculously high fat and Calorie count, is that it reduces the cook (usually the woman of the house) – the poor slave responsible for the orchestration of the epic production – to the status of a drudge, madly trying to organize a complicated and labour-intensive meal on what should be a relaxing day off. For the one who prepares it, Sunday lunch can be nightmarishly exhausting. The elaborate several-course meal turns mother into a whirling dervish in the centre of a hysterical flurry of flashing knives, roaring kitchen machines and blasting cookers. When the food – painstakingly choreographed so that each component is done at the same time – is finally prepared, the cook slumps at the table, almost too tired to lift fork to mouth, but the slump doesn't last long. She must bounce up and down like a manic yo-yo, replenishing plates with extra servings, filling glasses, clearing dishes away, rushing in the pudding, pouring coffee . . . and when it's all over, and the relaxed family nod off over the paper and the telly, she must face the shambolic kitchen.

Do yourself a favour and rethink Sunday lunch. I'm offering suggestions on two points: (1) how to cut down on the frightening fat and Calorie count, and (2) how to cut down on the drudgery. Enjoy the ritual and delicious Sunday family food, but make it healthy, relaxing and festive for *all*, even the cook.

SUNDAY LUNCH MENU

Braised Brisket of Beef (page 125) *or* Pot Roast Lamb (page 170)
Roast Potatoes (page 277)
Braised Carrots (page 251)
Whipped Swedes (page 260)
Fruit Compôte (page 325) *or* Bread Pudding (page 330)

'Every Sunday, everyone got stoned on dinner except the women who cooked it and thereby lost their appetites – the rest of us did our duty and ate ourselves into a gaseous stupor and sat around in a trance and mumbled like a bunch of beefheads.'

Garrison Keillor, *Lake Wobegon Days*

DRUDGERY BEGONE!

My liberated Sunday lunch gives a choice of two joints: a brisket of beef or a leg of lamb.

Brisket is a remarkable cut of beef. Boned and mercilessly trimmed of fat (see page 124 for specific instructions), it cooks for hours unattended, and emerges from the oven buttery tender. The gravy is spectacularly rich and deeply flavoured, although virtually fat-free after you've skimmed it. The brisket may be completely prepared as much as 3 days before you plan to serve it. Indeed, it tastes even better when it has mellowed in the refrigerator for a day or so. The leg of lamb is marinated first in a mixture of wine, tomatoes and spices. This marination can be done as early as two days ahead of time. On Sunday morning, once the joint is put into the oven, it is unattended except for basting after the first hour.

The whipped swedes can be prepared days ahead of time, and refrigerated or frozen. They reheat from frozen in the microwave with no loss of quality. If your oven has a grill compartment that doubles as an extra oven, use it to roast the carrots and potatoes while the joint cooks. Once they are in the oven, they need not be fussed over. If you have no extra oven compartment, roast them along with the joint. Because the oven temperature will be lower than what is called for in the recipe, leave them in for longer than specified. The carrots can be trimmed and peeled and arranged in a baking dish the night before, or early in the morning. The stock in the potato recipe can be poured into a baking dish and refrigerated the night before or early morning as well. Cut and add the potatoes on Sunday just before roasting.

All these things can roast happily together with minimal interference from the cook, and they fill the house with delicious Sunday smells.

Both puddings are do-ahead ones: the compôte can be made days ahead – the longer it mellows the better it tastes. The bread pudding can be assembled on the day before, and then cooked while the family eat the joint and vegetables, or it can be assembled the morning before, baked in the evening, and cooled and refrigerated. Bring it out of the fridge early enough on Sunday for it to be at room temperature when served.

Barbecues and Picnics

Picnics during daylight hours have a nutritional importance that goes beyond the food. There are four 'fat-soluble' vitamins, vitamin A, E, K and D. These vitamins are generally found associated with fatty or oily foods. People existing on very low fat diets have no problem with vitamin A if they eat food rich in beta-carotene (see page 12); our bodies can use the beta-carotene to manufacture plenty of the vitamin.

Our bodies' need for vitamin E is tied to the amount of unsaturated fat we ingest. The less fat consumed, the less vitamin E needed. And vitamin E, along with K and A, is readily available in whole grains, meat and leafy greens – important components of Slim Cuisine, so no problem exists. But vitamin D is another story. In fact, it may not be a vitamin at all, since it is not readily available in natural foods but can be manufactured in the body. In England, butter and margarine are artificially fortified with D. When you cut these foods out, you also cut out your dietary source of the vitamin. Of course, to get the full daily requirement of D it would be necessary to eat more than 1,200 Calories of margarine a day, or 9,000 Calories of butter – not a desirable or healthy practice. But expose yourself to sunlight, and your body, that exquisite organic machine, manufactures plenty of vitamin D, and you never have to give butter or margarine another thought. That doesn't mean that you have to strip naked and fling yourself on the ground to grill for hours under a relentless, blazing sun. Normal exposure in every day clothing is fine, even in a country like England, that feels so grey most of the time. People who compulsively cover themselves – arms, faces and all – and never venture out of doors may develop vitamin D deficiency, but these cases are rare.

How pleasant to bolster your vitamin D by eating out of doors every once in a while, even on partly cloudy days. Just remember, when holidaying in sunny climates, or enjoying a rare English heatwave, there is no need to overdo it. *Over*exposure to sunlight results in wrinkles and possible skin cancer.

BARBECUE MENU

Beetroot Borscht (page 107)
Vegetable Canapés (page 73)
Grilled Goose Skirt Steak (page 133)
Spicy Potato Salad (page 292)
Oranges with Orange Brandy (page 324)

PICNIC MENU

Gazpacho (page 106)
Stuffed Mushrooms (page 73)
Chicken Pesto Potato Salad (page 189)
Strawberries with Raspberry Purée (page 319)

Breakfast

There is something appealing about a large breakfast; huge platters of steaming food, ending the long fast of the preceding night, and stoking the body and brain for the onslaught of a new and vigorous work day. But the traditional English breakfast carries things too far. Sausages, potatoes, eggs, mushrooms, and so on, are undoubtedly marvellous, but oh! the rivulets of grease, the sputtering fat, the lashings of butter, the downright lardiness of it all. Why not enjoy the wonderfully strength-giving glories of an English breakfast minus the fat dimension? The tastes of the good ingredients, without their usual blunting veil of grease, will delight you.

What a lovely way to start the day!

'Today's the day I'm gonna do it. Today's the day I'm gonna go on a diet . . . I gotta have will power – I gotta be strong . . . So make me a big breakfast 'cause I got to have a lot of strength to go with this diet.'

Sid Caesar, a monologue from *Your Show of Shows*

SLIM CUISINE VERSION OF TRADITIONAL ENGLISH 'FRY-UP' BREAKFAST

Poached Egg (Eat eggs only occasionally – the yolks contain fat. And if your blood cholesterol levels are high, avoid them altogether.)

Pan-'Fried' Potatoes (page 276)
Pan-'Fried' Mushrooms (page 29, use whole button mushrooms)
Grilled Tomatoes (halve tomatoes and cook under the grill)
Baked Beans (use the kind that are made with no sugar or fat)
Breakfast Sausage Patties (page 165)
Toasted Wholemeal Bread with Plum Jam (page 343)

Although I have specifically decided that I would *not* normally include Calorie and fat counts in this book (see page 70), I could not resist hauling out the tables and computing levels for the good old English breakfast. The following chart is a dramatic example of Calorie and fat savings possible using Slim Cuisine techniques. A full Slim Cuisine breakfast instead of a traditional one will save you 666 Calories and 56.1 grams of fat.

Total Calories and Fat

Slim Cuisine Style			**Traditional Style**	
Calories	*fat (g)*		*Calories*	*fat (g)*
78	5.5	Poached/Fried Egg	210	20.2
171	0.5	Pan-'Fried' Potatoes	450	20.0
7	0.0	Mushrooms	20	2.0
20	0.0	Grilled Tomatoes	20	0.0
54	0.0	Baked Beans	72	0.0
20	0.2	Breakfast Sausage	94	8.8
55	0.7	Wholemeal Toast	55	0.7
00	0.0	Butter per tablespoon	102	11.3
11	0.0	Plum Jam per tablespoon	59	0.0
416	6.9		1082	63.0

'She says that she will be his if he renounces his lust for treasure and saturated fats.'

Tom Weller, *Cvltvre made Stvpid*

QUICK BREAKFASTS

Not everyone can face a heaped plate of hot food early in the day. And many people lack the time even to consider a labour-intensive kitchen production at the start of a work day. What a shame though, to forgo breakfast entirely because of such restriction. Try one of the following quickies to give your day a good nutritional and psychological boost.

Traditional New York Breakfast

Bagels halved, and then each half spread with quark or Chive Spread (page 303). Lay on each a slice of smoked salmon, a slice of ripe tomato and a few slivers of Spanish onion.

Cereal

Small shredded wheats or other cereal that has no added fat or sugar, mixed with berries or sliced fruit, dribbled with skimmed milk.

Cheese-Lover's Breakfast

Toasted rye or wholemeal bread with a thin slice or two of low-fat Italian Mozzarella cheese. Grill until the Cheese is melted, bubbly and lightly speckled with brown.

Fish-Lover's Breakfast ⑤

Quark or fromage frais and flaked smoked mackerel blended until smooth in a food processor. If you wish, blend in some chopped chives and a drop or two of lemon juice. Serve spread on toasted rye, granary, or wholemeal bread.

Christmas

In January, every women's magazine devotes itself to low-Calorie cookery advice, every publisher releases the newest crop of weight loss books, every newspaper offers wisdom on healthy eating, and almost everyone gets down to some serious dieting. Why? Because December is the month in which *everyone*, even reformed fatoholics, succumb to temptation. All the fat-lined pitfalls are there to ensnare you: over-the-top family dinners; office parties and cocktail gatherings with unlimited supplies of free booze and fatty, sugary nibbles; traditional eggnogs; stuffed geese and turkeys; fruit cakes; suet puddings; mince pies; brandy butter; potatoes roasted in dripping; butter-bathed vegetables; oil-drenched salads. Mayonnaise – lard – chicken fat – olive oil. Clotted cream – whipped cream – double cream – soured cream. It's enough to drive one literally insane with fat overkill.

> 'Near the Eastern Horizon the sky was the colour of chicken livers simmering in butter. Flocks of birds melted against the sunrise in chocolate tones.'
>
> Scott Sanders, *The Artist of Hunger*

I am one thin voice calling out in the December fat jungle. Please listen. *You don't have to succumb.* The police will not show up at your door to haul you away to the clink if you refuse to bake the traditional mince pies this year. Nowhere in the Bible is it commanded that you glut yourself or your family with fat on the day set aside to honour Christ's birth. If you eschew the salted nuts, the brandy butter, the fruit cake, the chipolatas, a bolt of lightning will not plunge through your roof to scorch you to cinders. If you play down the Dickensian excess, your citizenship will not be snatched from you. Chances are you do not want to fall into the fat-lined pit, in fact you probably long – with all your heart – to avoid it. *Do* so. Be the master of your own destiny. If the booze and fattening food are undulating and pulsating all around you, *you don't have to consume it.*

I have learned this over the years, but it can be difficult. At a gala banquet at one of the Cambridge colleges an eminent nutrition professor seated on my left accused me of anorexia because I refused the rack of lamb (nestled as it was in half an inch of its own fat), took only the vegetables that were not swimming in butter and cream sauce, passed on the salad dressing, quaffed mineral water and ended my meal with naked raspberries. This is not anorexia, Professor; this is common sense, good taste and self-protection. Let them call you anorexic, heartless, a goody-goody, or an ascetic – it doesn't matter. You are the master of your own destiny, and January will find you beautifully slim, healthy and laughing up your perfectly fitting sleeve at the rest of the chubby population.

SLIM CUISINE CHRISTMAS MENU

There is nothing spartan or dietetic-tasting about this menu. You will need to make no apologies. Everyone will feel beautifully and festively fed, but they will not hate themselves in the morning.

Vegetable Canapés (page 73)
Chicken Liver Pâté (page 80)
Roast Turkey (page 193)
Chestnut Stuffing (page 194)
Sausage Patties (page 165)
Spicy Sprouts (page 257)
Purée of Swede, Turnip and White Beans (page 261)
Cauliflower and Peppers (page 255)
Roast Potatoes (page 277)
Mince Pies (page 333) or Mincemeat Bread Pudding with Lemon
   Cream Sauce (page 325)
Black and White Meringues (page 337)
Oranges in Orange Brandy (page 324)

Menu Planning

'For supper Jill cooks a filet of sole, lemony, light, simmered in sunshine, skin flaky brown. Nelson gets a hamburger with wheatgerm sprinkled on it to remind him of a Nutburger. Wheatgerm, zucchini, water chestnuts, celery salt, Familia: these are some of the exotic items Jill's shopping brings into the house.'

John Updike, *Rabbit Redux*

Changing over to Slim Cuisine means learning some new techniques and habits. It takes no longer to do Slim Cuisine than any other kind of everyday cookery, especially if you plan ahead. Always keep a supply of baked aubergine and baked garlic purée in the fridge, for instance. Then, if you want to make meatballs or pesto, you don't have to begin first baking the aubergine and the garlic before getting down to the business of the recipe itself. And Slim Cuisine icecream is the fastest pudding imaginable if the freezer is well stocked with frozen fruit and berries. You must keep these things on board as well: stock or a good stock powder, and drained yoghurt and/or drained fromage frais. Plan ahead, keep these things on hand, and cooking will be a breeze.

Dinner Parties

All too often, dinner parties are excuses for total culinary depravity. Creamed sauces, roasts with thick layers of fat, rich gravies, vegetables swimming in butter, sugary puddings drowning in oceans of double cream: it is almost as if the hostess/cook says: 'The Robinsons are coming to dinner. Let's *kill* them!' As a devotee of Slim Cuisine, you know that culinary mayhem is obsolete, even at dinner parties. It is possible to entertain lavishly and deliciously without Calorie and fat overkill. Herewith a few suggestions:

Turkey and melon with mint pesto	(page 73)
Wild mushroom soup	(page 93)
Stuffed rolled skirt steak	(page 136)
Potato gratin	(page 272)
Stir-'fried' courgettes	(page 258)
Mango sorbet	(page 316)
Mushroom ravioli with green sauce	(page 75)
Jellied gazpacho	(page 106)
Grilled plaice with mustard	(page 116)
Braised fennel	(page 253)
Steamed broccoli	(page 246)
Blackberry gratin	(page 323)
Steamed asparagus on yellow pepper sauce	(page 245)
Herbed tomato soup	(page 86)
Pork medallions Esterhazy	(page 168)
Roast potatoes	(page 277)
Strawberries on red and white sauce	(page 318)
Poached mushrooms stuffed with mint raita and beet purée	(page 74)
Soup of baked vegetables	(page 94)
Steak with garlic wine sauce	(page 136)
Stir-'fried' cauliflower	(page 255)
Stuffed potatoes	(page 270)
Blueberry icecream	(page 315)
Tuna mousse	(page 83)
Onion soup	(page 91)
Chicken with yellow pepper sauce	(page 172)
Creamed spinach	(page 247)
Potato cases filled with mushroom ragoût	(page 271)
Tropical fruit jelly	(page 321)
Shashi's parma aloo on a bed of mint raita	(page 79)
Turnip soup	(page 88)
Breast of duck à l'orange	(page 195)
Onion-tomato relish	(page 294)
Stir-'fried' yellow and red peppers	(page 256)

Vegetarian Dinner Parties

Ethnic Feasts

For a wonderful dinner party, try a buffet of ethnic delicacies. The ethnic recipes in Slim Cuisine are all based on authentic ones, but they have been redesigned to eliminate fat. Even though the identifying fat of a particular cuisine is gone (lard for Mexico, olive oil for Italy, etc.) the remaining flavour principles are unchanged.

Mexican

65

| Raita | (page 286) |
| Ginger lime mousse | (page 322) |

Everyday and Family Meals

Everyday cooking needn't be elaborate; in fact, it shouldn't be. A hearty main dish and perhaps a salad or a vegetable and a good pudding should be more than enough. I'm particularly fond of family-type dishes that fill the house with heavenly aromas as they bubble happily away, in the oven or on the hob.

Italian sausage soup	(page 98)
Tomato-basil salad	(page 289)
Strawberry icecream	(page 314)

Shepherd's pie	(page 148)
Creamed spinach or	(page 247)
Cole slaw	(page 287)
Crunchy bananas	(page 320)

Carrot soup	(page 88)
Baked potatoes with a choice of fillings	(page 268)
Raspberry icecream	(page 313)

Hamburgers with browned onions and red pepper sauce	(page 154)
Cole slaw	(page 287)
Apple icecream	(page 314)

Oven-'fried' fish	(page 117)
Oven chips	(page 274)
Selected greens with creamy salad dressing	(page 284)
Banana icecream	(page 313)

Vegetarian Family Meals

Larder lasagne	(page 242)
Tomato salad with creamy dressing	(page 284)
Blueberry icecream	(page 315)

Rajmaa (bean casserole)	(page 199)
Tabouli	(page 295)
Blackberry gratin	(page 323)

Quick Meals

For those who work full time, and then come home to cook, weekday meals *must* be quick. There are a wealth of quick, delicious and deeply satisfying dishes to choose from. It seems a shame to have to succumb to the lure of packaged and frozen foods because of limited time. Try the following suggestions or make your own prepared meals by freezing small portions of chilli con carne, beef in red wine, shepherd's pie, bolognese sauce, lasagne, etc. to be microwaved when needed.

Steak and onions   (page 136)
Steamed broccoli   (page 246)
Strawberry-orange icecream   (page 314)

Pizza   (page 306)
Sweet and sour courgettes   (page 259)
Pineapple sorbet   (page 315)

Plaice en papillote   (page 114)
Steamed new potatoes
Fresh berry gratin   (page 323)

Spaghetti bolognese   (page 143)
Wholemeal toast and garlic spread   (page 300)
Strawberries with raspberry sauce   (page 319)

Vegetarian Quick Meals

Pasta with terracotta sauce   (page 234)
Steamed cauliflower
Apple icecream   (page 314)

Farmer's omelette   (page 222)
Beets (use cooked beets from the market)
   in mustard cream   (page 263)
Sliced bananas or peaches with a
   sprinkle of brown sugar

Pasta shells Alfredo   (page 226)
Poached mushroom caps (unfilled)   (page 74)
Raspberry icecream   (page 313)

Recipes

'Food imaginatively and lovingly prepared, and eaten in good company, warms the being with something more than mere intake of Calories.'

Marjorie Kinnan Rawlings, *Cross Creek Cookery*

Adapting Recipes

These recipes are meant to guide you through the new techniques of Slim Cuisine. After a while, I hope you will be making up your own, based on the precepts set forth here. The comforting thing about Slim Cuisine is the flexibility it gives to your everyday cooking. You can use many of your old recipes; in fact you can try new ones from intriguing new cookbooks. Just apply Slim Cuisine techniques in place of traditional ones and you will be safe from the fat demons that lurk in conventional cookery. If a recipe calls for onions sautéed in butter or oil for instance, substitute Slim Cuisine sautéed onions. Use baked garlic purée instead of minced garlic sautéed in oil, fromage frais or yoghurt cheese in place of sweet or sour cream, Slim Cuisine 'mayonnaise' in place of the very wicked real thing. You will save thousands of Calories, yet eating and exploring the world of cuisine will continue to be a joyous activity.

A Note on Calorie and Fat Counts

I have decided that I would *not* label all recipes for fat and Calorie values. Nutrition tables used to compute such values give numbers that are only approximate. Nutrient levels in food change with the time of the year, the geographical origin of the food and many other factors. Besides, Calorie counting is boring and self-defeating. When you worry too much about such things, you ruin your eating pleasure, and you may find yourself cutting down too much out of fear of Calories. Because Slim Cuisine cuts out so much fat, the Calorie levels in my recipes are very low in general; in fact, you will save even more Calories than standardized charts would have you think. For a long time it was believed that fat weighed in at 9 Calories per gram. Recent reports from a major research facility in the US suggest that fat may actually be 11 Calories per gram. (Compare that to 4 Calories per gram for carbohydrate and protein!)

It *is* fun, though, occasionally to contrast the Calorie and fat levels in the traditional version of a recipe and the Slim Cuisine version. But remember, compulsive Calorie counting is self-defeating and horribly tedious. If you eliminate high-fat ingredients and high-fat cookery methods, Calories take care of themselves.

It is important to eat lavishly to keep your nutrients and morale high. Use Slim Cuisine techniques religiously, do not succumb to wicked outside temptations, use your common sense, and there will be no need to compute every Calorie. And don't hop on and off the scales every hour, or even every day. There is no need to be obsessive. Check your weight every week or two. If you establish good, steady Slim Cuisine habits, nature will take its course and your weight will be stable. And if you stick to the ♡ recipes for a while, you will *lose* weight in a very well fed manner.

'I am the ringleader of the faction that says, yes, we must diet. We must go to bed hungry and fit back into our clothes and never give in to inertia and complacence.

'So I dieted all summer and in three months I had gained three pounds. Needless to say I do not think this is funny. I think it is very cruel and unfair.'

Ellen Gilchrist, *Falling through Space*

Starters and Dips

'Alice tempers her rigidity on the meals-per-day issue by having a broad view of what constitutes an hors d'oeuvre.'

Calvin Trillin, *Alice, Let's Eat*

Starters should tease the palate, amuse the eyes, and launch the diner into the adventure of a meal. Serve a nibble or two with sherry or sparkling water in the lounge, or serve a beautifully arranged first course at the dining table, but don't overwhelm the diner with an embarrassment of riches or the rest of the meal will be an anticlimax. Many of these starters would work well on a buffet table.

VEGETABLE CANAPÉS

An array of chicory leaves, mushroom caps and varying-coloured pepper boats, filled with vivid (in flavour as well as hue) stuffings, makes a stunning first course for a special dinner party or buffet. It provides an almost over-the-top feast for the eyes, titillates the palate with fresh and exhilarating tastes, and gives the diners something to talk about. If you don't want to fiddle about with teaspoons ('Life is too short to stuff a mushroom', and all that), pile each filling into a separate glass bowl, place on a platter, and surround with lavish heaps of multi-coloured pepper pieces, mushroom caps and chicory leaves. It will still be delicious, visually beautiful and a conversation starter. Along with the fillings suggested below, you might want to add Beetroot Purée and Jellied

Gazpacho (double the amount of gelatine called for) from pages 263, and 106.

½ lb/240 g small button
    mushrooms
3 fl oz/90 ml vegetable stock
3 fl oz/90 ml dry white wine or dry
    white vermouth
2 dashes soy sauce
Chicory heads

Peppers (a combination of red,
    green, yellow, purple – whatever
    you can find)
Herb Fillings (see below)
Pesto (see page 231)
Red Pepper and Garlic Spread (see
    page 303)
Mock Guacamole (see page 81)

---

1   Carefully remove the stems from the mushroom caps. Save the stems for another use. With a teaspoon, gently even out the mushroom cap opening so it will hold a filling nicely.
2   Pour the stock, vermouth and soy sauce into a non-stick frying pan that will hold the mushroom caps in one layer. Bring the liquid to the boil. Add the mushroom caps in one layer, stem side up, reduce heat, and simmer for 2–3 minutes. Raise heat and cook, tossing the mushrooms in the pan for a few minutes, until the caps are cooked but still quite firm, and the liquid is reduced and syrupy. Remove from the pan, drain upside down on paper towels.
3   Slice off the core of the chicory heads and separate the leaves. Rinse and dry.
4   Stem and seed peppers and derib. Cut into 'boats' about 1 inch/2.5 cm long.
5   With a teaspoon, fill each mushroom cap. Put a teaspoonful of filling at the base of each chicory leaf. Fill each pepper boat. Arrange on a beautiful plate.

♡ 🧸 ⊕   HERB FILLINGS

---

1 pt/600 ml very low fat yoghurt
Chopped fresh mint
Chopped fresh basil

Chopped fresh parsley or fresh
    coriander

Divide the yoghurt into three parts. Stir the mint into one, the basil into the second and the parsley or coriander into the third. Refrigerate until needed.

♡ ❄ MUSHROOM RAVIOLI

Makes 50 ravioli

Won Ton wrappers (squares of noodle dough) are available in Chinese groceries. These delicate, mushroom-stuffed triangles are very special. Do not overwhelm them with sauce or the intense mushroom taste will not come through.

2 packages Won Ton wrappers	*1 pt/600 ml Duxelles (see page 247)*
(about 50 wrappers)	*Fresh, washed spinach leaves*

1   Sprinkle your work surface with flour. Have 2 clean teatowels at hand. Have a small bowl filled with water on your work surface.

2   Put 1 Won Ton wrapper flat on the work surface (keep the remainder covered with a clean teatowel). Place a teaspoon of Duxelles in the centre of the wrapper. Dip your finger in the water and moisten the edge of the wrapper all around. Fold over to form a triangle and press the edges together so they adhere. Put the wrapper on the floured surface and cover with the second clean teatowel. Repeat until all the wrappers and Duxelles are used up. (The ravioli may be frozen at this point. Dust two baking sheets with flour. Place the ravioli on the sheets in one layer, cover with cling film and freeze. When they are frozen solid, put them in a plastic bag and store in the freezer until needed. Do not thaw before cooking.)

3   Bring water to the boil in the bottom of the steamer. Line the steamer basket with spinach or lettuce leaves. Place the ravioli in one layer, on the greens. You will need to do this in several batches. Steam, covered, for 6–8 minutes, until tender. If they were frozen, steam for 10–12 minutes. Serve with Smooth Tomato Sauce (see page 236), or with Hungarian Green Sauce (see page 231). Ladle a bit of sauce over each serving, but do not swamp them.

4   Alternatively, do as my housekeeper Mary Hardy suggests: serve these mushroom-filled morsels as dumplings on beef stew. (See pages 126–127 for beef stew recipes.)

Filo Pastry

Filo (sometimes spelt 'phyllo') or strudel, tissue-thin sheets of delicate pastry, are available frozen from some supermarkets and delicatessens. Some brands contain no fat at all, one brand contains a very small percentage of corn oil – not enough to preclude your using the versatile stuff when you suffer pastry cravings. The traditional method of handling this dough involves layering the thin sheets, and brushing each layer with butter or oil, thus forming a many-layered, crispy finished pastry. I've substituted egg white for the butter and oil. As a result the nature of the pastry changes; it is more like a tender yeast dough than a brittle strudel or a mille-feuille.

Filo is fun, and easy to work with; just follow the directions exactly, and you should have no problems. If not cosseted, the sheets dry out quickly and turn into a parchment-like, brittle substance that disintegrates at a touch, hence the instructions for covering with waxed paper and a damp cloth. Many people have asked me how they can have pastry on the Slim Cuisine regime. Here is the answer. Enjoy it to your heart's content. (See also the Mince Pie recipe on page 333.)

❄ LAMB SAMOSA

1 box of filo makes 12 samosas

The lamb mixture is also good as a pâté; a sort of spiced lamb rillettes. Chill it in ceramic ramekins, and serve with wedges of split, toasted pitta bread. Leftover lamb filling freezes very well.

Lamb Filling

2 medium onions, chopped	1 teaspoon cinnamon
2 cloves garlic, minced	½ teaspoon cardamom
1 thin slice peeled ginger, minced	½ teaspoon allspice
2 lb/960 g lean minced lamb	4 fl oz/120 ml stock
Salt to taste	2 tablespoons tomato paste
1 teaspoon turmeric	1 Baked Aubergine, peeled and
1½ teaspoons ground coriander	chopped (see page 37)
¼ teaspoon red pepper flakes	1 tablespoon garam masala
Pinch of cayenne pepper	

1   Combine onions, garlic, ginger and lamb in a wide heavy frying pan. Cook slowly until the lamb is thoroughly cooked.

Break up the meat with a wooden spoon as it cooks. Drain in a colander over a bowl to drain away all fat. Blot the meat with paper towels to eliminate even more fat. Blot the frying pan. Return meat and onion mixture to the frying pan.

2   Add the spices from salt through allspice to the meat. Cook and stir over low heat until the meat is coated with the spices. Stir in stock, tomato paste, aubergine and garam masala. Simmer, partially covered, for about 30 minutes, until thick. Set aside. (At this point it can be refrigerated for 2–3 days.)

Pastry

1 package frozen filo pastry

Place the filo pastry in the refrigerator to thaw the night before you want to use it. It can stay in the refrigerator for up to 2 days.

To Assemble

Thawed filo   *Lamb filling*
2–3 egg whites, lightly beaten

1   Preheat oven to 375° F, 190° C, Gas Mark 5.
2   Put a barely damp tea towel on your work surface. Cover it with a sheet of waxed paper. Unwrap the filo, unfold it and place it on the paper. From top to bottom, with a sharp knife, cut the stack of pastry down the centre. Immediately cover the stack with another sheet of waxed paper and then with another barely damp tea towel.
3   Take one piece of filo from the stack. Keep the rest well covered. Spread the sheet out on a clean surface. With a pastry brush, lightly coat it with egg white. Fold the top third down and then the bottom third up as if folding a business letter. Place a generous tablespoon of filling on the lower right-hand corner. Fold down to form a triangle. Brush with egg white. Fold back up to form a new triangle. Brush with egg white. Continue folding and brushing lightly until you have formed a compact, many-layered triangle. (See diagram below.) Brush the finished triangle lightly with egg white and place on a *non-stick* baking dish. (At this point, the samosas may be refrigerated for a day or two, or frozen for months.)
4   Bake the samosas in the oven for 20–30 minutes, or until puffed up and golden. If baking from frozen, add an extra 5 minutes to the baking time. Serve at once.

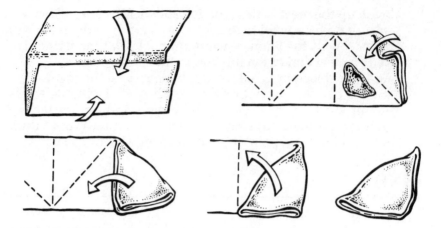

Variation: Vegetable Samosa ♡ ❄

Follow directions above, substituting Couscous Vegetables (page 203) or Vegetable Curry (page 264) for the lamb mix.

TURKEY AND MELON WITH MINT PESTO

This is a colourful starter and the combination of tastes and textures is unusual and pleasing. The plates may be arranged an hour or so before serving. The Pesto may be made days in advance.

Ripe melon	*Slim Cuisine Pesto made with fresh*
Thinly sliced smoked turkey breast	*mint leaves (see page 231)*
(available in delicatessens)	*Fresh mint leaves*

1   Slice melon thinly. Cut off rind. Wrap each slice in a slice of turkey breast.
2   Arrange 3 wrapped slices on each plate. Place a blob of Pesto on the base of the plate. Garnish with fresh mint leaves and serve.
♡   Substitute Remoulade Sauce (page 304) or Russian Dressing (page 119) for the Pesto.

ARTICHOKE TOASTS

Makes approximately 15 pieces

A crisp bread base with a rich creamy topping laced with artichoke pieces. Artichoke toasts are ridiculously easy to prepare, but they make an impressive party nibble.

4 fl oz/120 ml fromage frais	Dash or two Tabasco sauce
½ tablespoon Dijon mustard	1 medium baguette, about 10
1 tin artichoke hearts, drained and	inches/25 cm long, split
chopped	Freshly ground pepper
1 tablespoon grated Parmesan	
cheese	

1   Preheat grill.
2   Whisk together fromage frais and mustard in a bowl. Stir in the chopped artichoke hearts, Parmesan cheese and Tabasco sauce.
3   Spread this mixture on the cut sides of the two baguette halves. Grill, 3 inches/8 cm from the heat, until browned, approximately 3 minutes. Cut into 1 inch/2.5 cm slices, place on a plate, and serve.
♡   Omit cheese.

♡ ⊕ ALOO CHAT

Serves 4

Potatoes, coriander and chilli make up my favourite Indian starter. It is sour, spicy and stimulating.

2 small, fresh green chillies,	4 tablespoons thinly sliced spring
stemmed, seeded and minced	onions
8 medium new potatoes, steamed	Salt to taste
until tender and diced	4 tablespoons lemon juice
4 tablespoons coarsely chopped fresh	
coriander	

Gently toss all ingredients together. Allow to sit at room temperature for at least ½ hour before serving.

♡ SHASHI'S PARMA ALOO (STUFFED POTATOES, INDIAN STYLE)

Makes 8 pieces

This glorious dish is an old family recipe of Shashi Rattan's. I have omitted the oil and substituted lemon juice for hard-to-find mango powder. As the potatoes bake, the spicy coating blackens in places and forms a delicious crust. Parma Aloo are good served hot or cold. I think they taste best eaten with the fingers.

½ teaspoon ground turmeric	Juice of ½ small lemon
½ teaspoon garam masala	1 tablespoon tomato paste
¼ teaspoon ground cumin	8 small new potatoes

1 Preheat oven to 350° F, 180° C, Gas Mark 4.
2 Combine everything except potatoes in a bowl. Mix to a paste.
3 Peel potatoes. Pierce in several places with skewer or a fork. Cut a lengthwise wedge (½ inch/1.25 cm wide) out of each potato. Rub the hole with spice paste and insert the wedge back in. Rub the potatoes all over with the remaining paste.
4 Place a rack on a baking tray and arrange the potatoes on the rack. Bake for 30–40 minutes, turning every 10 minutes, until tender. Serve at once.

Ⓢ CHICKEN LIVER PÂTÉ

My favourite piece of ill-conceived menu prose comes from somewhere in the hinterlands of the American South: 'Chef's own Liver Pâté'. Talk about throwing oneself into one's work! This recipe should by rights be called 'Annie's own Liver Pâté', because I've adapted it from a recipe developed by my friend Dr Ann Coxon.

The pâté has a silken texture. As you feel it roll voluptuously over your tongue, you'll also feel pangs of guilt; it tastes wickedly fattening. But have no fear. High nutrition, minimal fat – isn't life wonderful?

1¼ lb/600 g chicken livers, trimmed	Juice and zest of 1–2 large lemons
Approximately 8 fl oz/240 ml stock	14 fl oz/420 ml fromage frais
1 onion, chopped	Salt and freshly ground pepper to taste
3 tablespoons brandy	Pinch or two of allspice
30 pitted prunes, soaked in water for an hour or so and drained	

1 Film a non-stick frying pan with a tiny bit of stock. Sauté chicken livers in one layer in the pan until they are *just* cooked through. (Use tongs to turn them.) Set aside. Pour out liquid.
2 Put chopped onion in the pan with the brandy and 4 fl oz/120 ml of stock. Boil for 1 minute, stirring and scraping the browned bits on the bottom of the frying pan. Turn the heat down, cover and simmer briskly until the onions are tender and amber brown. Add more stock if needed, but there should

be no liquid left when the onions are done. Scrape the onions into the food processor container along with the livers.

3   Add the prunes, juice and zest from 1 lemon, fromage frais, salt and pepper to taste and a pinch of allspice. Blend until very smooth.
4   Taste and add more seasonings, lemon juice and zest if desired. Blend again.
5   Pour into ceramic pots, cover and leave overnight in the refrigerator to set and for the flavours to blend.

Note: Chicken livers are high in vitamins and minerals, but high in cholesterol as well. If your blood cholesterol levels are high, do not eat liver of any kind.

♡ 🧸 ⏱ MOCK GUACAMOLE (MONTEZUMA'S MUSHY PEAS)

Makes 1 pt/600 ml

I wish I had invented this brilliant recipe. I've adapted it from *Secret Ingredients* by Michael Roberts, an enthusiastic and innovative (to say the least) American chef. Guacamole is an ancient Mexican classic: ripe avocados, chillies and onions ground to a rough purée in a *molcajete* (a mortar carved from volcanic rock). Modern city-bred Mexican cooks use electric liquidizers to make the rough green paste (they affectionately refer to the *molcajete*, still in use in rural areas, as the 'liquidora Azteca'), but the resulting guacamole is the same as it has been for many centuries. I once served guacamole to an ethnobotanist who had earned his graduate degree in Mexico. 'Montezuma would have recognized this,' he mused, as he scooped a bit more of the vivid and spicy mixture on to a tortilla chip. His comment gave me a giddy feeling of timelessness, as if I were about to trade recipes with Montezuma himself. But times change. Avocados are very high in fat Calories, and have no place in Slim Cuisine, hence my devotion to this odd recipe, a kind of cross between guacamole and mushy peas. Odd it may be (Montezuma would laugh me out of the kitchen), but it is also absolutely splendid; one of the freshest, zingiest mixtures imaginable.

1 tablespoon fresh coriander leaves	1 lb/480 g defrosted frozen peas
2 tablespoons lime juice	¼ teaspoon ground cumin
1 fresh chilli pepper, seeded and coarsely diced	Salt to taste
	¼ medium red onion, diced

1   Place coriander, lime juice and chilli in the jar of the liquidizer or food processor. Process until coarsely chopped.
2   Add peas, cumin and salt and blend to a rough purée. Scrape into a bowl and stir in the onion. Serve with tortilla chips, toasted split pitta bread wedges, or motzah crackers.

❄ Ⓢ   SMOKED FISH PÂTÉ

Makes ½ pt/300 ml

Twin Marks, a loyal fan of Slim Cuisine, made this for a buffet, and the murmur went round, 'Have you tasted the fish pâté? It's fabulous!' This is a great people-pleaser.

6–8 oz/240 g smoked trout or mackerel fillets, flaked *8 fl oz/240 ml yoghurt cream cheese, fromage frais, cream cheese (see page 39) or quark*	*2 tablespoons chopped fresh chives*

1   Combine all ingredients in the bowl of a food processor.
2   Process until very smooth. Scrape into a crock and refrigerate overnight for the flavours to blend.
3   Serve with thin slices of wholemeal bread, toasted or not, as you prefer.

DILLED SMOKED SALMON SALAD

Makes ¾ pt/480 ml

This tastes exactly as if it were made with crème fraîche. If you wish, pack it into a fish-shaped mould and refrigerate it overnight. The next day, unmould it onto a sea of greens.

2 tablespoons drained yoghurt *2 tablespoons buttermilk* *⅓ pt/200 ml skimmed milk quark* *4 oz/120 g chopped fresh parsley*	*4 tablespoons chopped fresh dill* *½ lb/240 g smoked salmon, shredded* *Freshly ground pepper to taste*

1   Combine all ingredients. Mix gently with a wooden spoon.
2   Scrape the mixture into a crock. Refrigerate overnight for flavours to blend.
3   Serve with chicory leaves and radicchio leaves. Each diner spoons a bit of the mixture into a leaf.

KATHLEEN EDWARDS'S
TUNA MOUSSE

Serves 8

This creamy mousse is attractive in a fish-shaped mould. Decorate it beautifully for a buffet table.

---

3 teaspoons gelatine
2 tablespoons white wine vinegar
½ pt/300 ml boiling chicken or vegetable stock
½ small onion, finely chopped
1 clove garlic
¼ teaspoon dried tarragon

Salt and freshly ground pepper to taste
8 oz/240 g tuna in brine, very well drained
4 tablespoons fromage frais
Garnish (cucumber, parsley, watercress, fresh tarragon, etc. as desired)

---

1   Place gelatine and vinegar in the liquidizer container and let stand for one minute.
2   Add the chicken or vegetable stock and blend.
3   Add all remaining ingredients except fromage frais and garnish. Blend until perfectly smooth, about 1 minute.
4   Pour the tuna mixture into a bowl and let sit at room temperature until thickened but not set.
5   Stir the fromage frais into the tuna mixture. Pour into a mould and refrigerate until set.
6   To serve, unmould onto a serving plate and decorate with fresh herbs, watercress, etc. Serve with Melba toast or motzah crackers if you wish.

Soups

'"Have some soup", Lizzie said. "Soup is good for stress."'

Marsha Norman, *The Fortune Teller*

Asteam-wreathed tureen of soup, emitting delectable and tantalizing whiffs of comfort, never fails to delight even the grumpiest diner. Soup nourishes the soul as well as the body. It evokes memories of cosy evenings by the hearth, while the cruel winter elements rage outside. Soup slides down soothingly – smooth and easy – making the diner feel loved and indulged. I am happy to tell you that Slim Cuisine soups are nutrient-dense but not Calorie-dense; you can wallow in that lovely, cosseted feeling without wallowing in fat as well. Several Slim Cuisine techniques make this splendid state of affairs possible; use them to reduce the fat and Calorie levels of any soup recipe you might come across:

1   Never use oil, butter or margarine to sauté the vegetables that form the flavour base of a soup. Use the stock-sauté method, or the onion infusion.

2   The classic way of enriching many soups is with butter, egg yolk and cream. Don't do it! The best way to enrich a creamy vegetable purée soup is with the vegetable itself. Use more of the vegetable than called for in a traditional recipe. When cooked, purée the soup in a liquidizer or processor, or put it through a food mill. It will be rich and creamy. In some cases, you might want to purée half of the soup, then combine

the puréed and unpuréed portions. This makes a lovely, interesting texture.

3   Substitute low-fat fromage frais, yoghurt, quark or skimmed milk, for sour cream, crème fraîche or cream.

4   Use potato for body and thickening. It adds plenty of nutrients but few Calories and no fat.

5   Baked vegetables, especially baked garlic, give wonderful depth to low-fat soups. One of the soups in this section is made up entirely of baked vegetables. It is satisfying enough to be a main dish, yet it has only 98 Calories per 8 fl oz/240 ml serving! Experiment with adding various puréed baked vegetables to soup for flavour and body.

6   Splash wine and spirits generously into your soups. In the simmering, the alcohol (and alcohol Calories) evaporate but the flavour remains. For instance, red wine and cognac combine to add richness to French Onion Soup (see page 91). Without them, this extremely low-fat soup would have a somewhat anaemic taste.

Soup Savvy

Do you love to begin a meal with a nice hearty bowlful of steaming soup? If you do, you will be pleased to know that soup has been shown to be a splendid diet food. Recent research studies at several American universities have suggested that soup, eaten in large quantities before a meal, results in fewer total Calories ingested in that meal. In fact the more soup, the fewer total Calories. Furthermore, the study suggests that enthusiastic soup eaters who eat the hot, soothing stuff regularly, are much more likely to keep to their target weight over the long term than non-soup eaters.

The liquidizer is used to purée many soups. Never fill the liquidizer jar with hot soup. When the machine is switched on, the hot liquid will surge up, blow off the cover, splash and burn the cook, and make a spectacular mess on the ceiling. Let the soup cool somewhat first, then fill the jar less than halfway.

♡ ⚛ ⊕ HERBED TOMATO SOUP

Makes 3 pts/2 l

This soup, adapted from Barbara Kafka's *Food for Friends*, is so easy that it is almost embarrassing. 'How did you make this?' your friends will exclaim as they savour every sip. Remain smugly silent. Fresh herbs are on sale all year round in many supermarkets. As for the tomato liquid, it is almost *free!* When using tinned tomatoes *never* throw the precious liquid away. Save it for ambrosial concoctions like this. If the juice is too acidic for your taste, add a pinch of sugar. (Step 1 may be done in advance. Complete Step 2 just before serving.) And note the method of measuring the herbs in a graduated measuring jug. It's easy and exact.

2 pts/1.25 l chicken or vegetable stock	2 tablespoons fresh parsley, finely chopped
2 pts/1.25 l tomato liquid (drained from tinned Italian tomatoes)	Pinch sugar (optional)
2 tablespoons fresh basil, finely shredded	3 cloves garlic, crushed or minced
2 tablespoons fresh dill, snipped	Salt and freshly ground pepper to taste
	½ teaspoon Tabasco sauce
	Pinch cayenne pepper
	Juice of 1 lemon

1   Combine the stock, tomato liquid and herbs in a non-reactive pot. Simmer for 15 minutes.
2   Stir in remaining ingredients. Serve at once.

♡ ✿ ⊕ LETTUCE AND FENNEL SOUP

Makes 1½ pts/900 ml

This recipe was given to me by Tony Smith, the proprietor of the Mange Tout Bistro in Norwich. The soup's creamy richness comes from the eponymous vegetables.

1 large iceberg (crisphead) lettuce	16 fl oz/480 ml stock
3 bulbs fennel, trimmed (save the feathery leaves) and coarsely chopped	Salt and freshly ground pepper to taste
	Fromage frais

1   Chop the head of lettuce into chunks. Cook it slowly in a heavy-bottomed pot. When juices begin to form, add the fennel.
2   Let the vegetables sauté in their own juices until tender, about 20 minutes, stirring occasionally.
3   Stir in the stock and season to taste. Simmer for 5 minutes more.
4   Purée the soup in the liquidizer. Serve hot, with a dollop of fromage frais and a sprig of fennel leaves on each serving.

♡ 🐻 ⊕ ❄️   **TURNIP SOUP**

Makes 3 pts/2 l

The garlic may seem excessive, but (if the garlic is fresh) there is *no* vulgar garlicky taste in this soup, just a gentle, nutty sweetness. Although there is no cream, only a few ounces of skimmed milk, the texture is velvety and creamy. Those who overdosed on turnips at boarding school may want to skip this one, but I feel that the humble root reaches exquisite heights in this soup. This also works well with parsnips, swedes or a combination of root vegetables.

2½ lbs/1 kg peeled, coarsely-diced small white turnips	1 orange
15 large cloves garlic, peeled	4 fl oz/120 ml skimmed milk
1⅗ pts/960 ml stock	Salt and freshly ground pepper to taste

1   Combine turnips, garlic and stock in a non-reactive soup pot. Bring to the boil. Skim off scum.
2   Reduce heat and simmer partially covered until the turnips and garlic are tender, 15–20 minutes. Cool slightly.
3   Purée the soup in a liquidizer and return to the pot. The texture should be very smooth and velvety.
4   With a citrus zester, zest the orange rind right over the pot so that the rind goes in and orange oil as well. Save the orange for another use (a private nibble, perhaps). Stir in the milk and seasonings to taste. Reheat gently, stirring occasionally. Serve piping hot. (This soup may be made in advance and refrigerated for several days.)

Variation:

Omit the orange rind. Prepare red pepper purée from baked or grilled red peppers (see page 31). Swirl a blob of red pepper purée decoratively onto the surface of each serving of soup.

♡ 🐻 ⊕ ❄️   **CARROT SOUP**

Makes 3 pts/2 l

This burnt-orange soup has two versions: the first elegant, smooth and piquant; the second chunky, homely and mild.

1½ lb/720 g carrots, peeled and coarsely chopped	½ teaspoon ground nutmeg
2 stalks celery, coarsely chopped	Freshly ground pepper
5 cloves garlic, peeled	2 pts/1.2 l stock
1 large onion, coarsely chopped	Salt to taste
3 fl oz/90 ml stock	3 tablespoons non-fat fromage frais, at room temperature
3 fl oz/90 ml dry sherry	1 rounded tablespoon Dijon mustard
1 baking potato, peeled and coarsely diced	1 tablespoon snipped fresh dill

1   Combine carrots, celery, garlic, onion, 3 fl oz/90 ml of stock and 2 fl oz/60 ml of sherry in a non-reactive soup pot. Cover and bring to the boil. Allow to boil, uncovering to stir occasionally, until almost dry.

2   Uncover. Let cook for a few moments more until the mixture begins to burn just a bit and to stick to the bottom of the pot. Splash in 1 fl oz/30 ml of sherry and boil, scraping up the brown bits on the bottom of the pan with a wooden spoon.

3   Toss in the potato. Cook over medium heat for a minute or two, stirring. Stir in the nutmeg and pepper and toss to coat the vegetables with the spices.

4   Stir in the stock and salt. Cover and bring to the boil. Reduce heat and simmer, partially covered, until the vegetables are tender, 20–30 minutes. Cool slightly.

5   Put the soup into the liquidizer in batches. Purée to a smooth, velvety consistency. (The soup may be made in advance to this point. Cool and refrigerate until needed.) Return to the soup pot and bring to a simmer.

6   Remove the soup from the heat. Whisk together the fromage frais and the mustard. Gradually stir some of the soup into the mustard mixture. Then, slowly, stir the mustard-soup mixture into the soup, along with the dill.

Variation:

Instead of puréeing the soup to a velvety smoothness, pulse the liquidizer on and off a few times, so that the soup is chunky. Omit the fromage frais and the mustard. Stir in the dill.

♡ 🐻 ❄ RED PEPPER SOUP

Makes 3½ pts/2.1 l

Red peppers are fleshy, sweet and brilliantly coloured. They give all three properties to this gentle soup. Potatoes add additional substance and fromage frais gives a touch of creaminess with no added fat.

---

2 medium onions, chopped	8 large red peppers, trimmed,
2½ pts/1.5 l stock	ribbed and coarsely diced
2 fl oz/60 ml dry white wine	1 teaspoon dried thyme, crumbled
1 medium baking potato, peeled and	Cayenne pepper to taste
coarsely diced	Non-fat fromage frais
Salt and freshly ground pepper to	
taste	

---

1   Combine onions and 4 fl oz/120 ml of the stock in a soup pot. Cover and bring to the boil. Reduce heat and allow to steam for 5 minutes.

2   Uncover and continue cooking for another few minutes until the mixture begins to brown and stick to the bottom of the pan. Splash in the wine, and boil, scraping the browned bits off the bottom of the pot.

3   Stir in the potato and 4 more fl oz/120 ml of stock. Cover and cook over medium heat for 5 minutes. Uncover and stir once or twice during this time. After 5 minutes, splash in a bit more stock and again scrape any browned bits from the bottom of the pot. Season the mixture with a bit of salt and a generous grinding of pepper.

4   Toss in the peppers, the thyme and a bit of cayenne. Pour in the remaining stock and simmer, partially covered, until the vegetables are tender, about ½ hour. Cool.

5   In batches, purée the soup in a liquidizer. Pour it through a fine sieve into the soup pot. Rub the solids through with a wooden spoon or a rubber spatula. The tough pepper skins will be left behind in the sieve. Discard them. (The soup may be cooled at this point, and refrigerated for a few days.)

6   Gently heat the soup. Add more salt, black pepper and cayenne pepper to taste. Crumble in a touch more dried thyme if you feel that it is needed.

7   Serve with a dollop of fromage frais on each serving.

♡ 🐻 ❄ RED CABBAGE SOUP

Makes 2½ pts/1.5 l

A dazzlingly purple soup with a homely, comforting taste. Perfect cold-weather fare.

¼ pt/150 ml chopped shallots	1 large tart apple, peeled, cored and
3 pts/1.8 l chicken stock	coarsely chopped
1 medium baking potato, peeled and	Salt and freshly ground pepper to
coarsely chopped	taste
1 medium red cabbage, cored and	Freshly ground nutmeg
shredded	4–6 tablespoons low fat yoghurt at
	room temperature

---

1. Combine shallots and 4 fl oz/120 ml of the stock in a non-reactive soup pot. Cover and bring to the boil.
2. Uncover. Reduce heat slightly and simmer briskly until the liquid has evaporated and the shallots are beginning to stick to the pan.
3. Toss in the potatoes and an additional splash of stock. Toss, stirring and scraping up the browned bits on the bottom of the pot.
4. When the potatoes begin to brown slightly, toss in the cabbage and the apple. Toss and cook over medium heat for 2–3 minutes.
5. Pour in the remaining stock. Season to taste. Bring to the boil, reduce heat and simmer, partially covered, for 15 minutes, until the cabbage and potatoes are tender but not mushy. Season to taste and cool slightly.
6. In a liquidizer, purée the soup. Do this in several batches. (The soup may be made in advance to this point and refrigerated for a day or two.)
7. At serving time, heat the soup until it is piping hot. Serve it in clear glass bowls, to show off its gorgeous purple colour. Swirl one tablespoon of yoghurt decoratively over the surface of each serving, and sprinkle on some freshly grated nutmeg.

♡ 🐻 ❄ ONION SOUP

Makes 3½ pts/2.1 l
69 Calories per 10 fl oz/300 ml
0.2 g fat
(Traditional onion soup 263 Calories, 13 g fat)

French onion soup without butter or oil? Yes, if you utilize two Slim

Cuisine techniques: browned onions and spring onion/shallot infusion. A good portion of the long cooking time is untended simmering, so you need not feel tied to the cooker for the whole time.

---

6 large Spanish onions, thinly sliced	1 piece of Parmesan rind
	4 fl oz/120 ml cognac
5 leeks, cleaned, trimmed and thinly sliced	1 bunch spring onions, trimmed and thinly sliced
16 fl oz/480 ml stock	3 shallots, chopped
3 fl oz/180 ml dry red wine	3 fl oz/90 ml dry red wine
1 tablespoon plain white flour	Salt and pepper to taste
3½ pts/2 l stock, brought to the boil	

---

1 Combine onions, leeks and 16 fl oz/480 ml stock in a deep soup pot. Cover and bring to the boil. Reduce heat a bit and simmer briskly for 10 minutes.
2 Uncover. Simmer for 35–40 minutes, stirring occasionally. At this point, the onions will be turning amber brown and dry. Stir constantly as they cook a few minutes more. They will soon begin to stick and burn. Keep stirring over low heat for about 10 minutes more. As you stir, scrape up the browned deposits on the bottom of the pot. Turn up the heat a bit. Splash in 3 fl oz red wine. Boil until dry, stirring and scraping like mad.
3 Turn the heat to low, and stir in the flour. Stir for about 3 minutes over low heat.
4 Gradually add the hot stock, and 3 fl oz/90 ml red wine, stirring all the while. Add the Parmesan rind. Partially cover the pot and simmer for 40 minutes, skimming and stirring occasionally.
5 During the last 20 minutes, stir the cognac into the soup. Then combine the spring onions, shallots and 3 fl oz/90 ml red wine in a small saucepan or frying pan. Bring to the boil, reduce heat, and simmer briskly until almost all liquid has evaporated. Stir this mixture into the simmering soup.
6 When the soup has simmered for 40 minutes, remove from the heat. Season to taste. Remove the Parmesan rind. Serve piping hot.

♡ 🧸 ❄ WILD MUSHROOM SOUP

Makes 2½ pts/1.5 l

The dried mushrooms are available in delicatessens and speciality food shops. Chinese and Japanese dried mushrooms may be substituted if necessary. The soup may be made a few days in advance. If fresh oyster mushrooms are available, use them as part of the measure of fresh mushrooms. They will impart a lovely, buttery quality to the soup.

---

1 oz/30 g dried Boletus edulis
  (cèpes)
½ oz/15 g dried morels
2 lb/960 g fresh mushrooms,
  cleaned and quartered
Approx. ½ pt/300 ml medium
  sherry
Dash or two of soy sauce

4 oz/120 g chopped shallots
2 cloves garlic, minced
1 teaspoon dried tarragon,
  crumbled
2½ pts/1.5 l stock
Salt and pepper to taste
Piece of Parmesan cheese rind

---

1   Rinse dried mushrooms well under cold running water. Put them in a bowl with hot water to cover generously. Let soak for 1 hour.
2   In a heavy, large, non-stick frying pan, combine the fresh mushrooms with the sherry and soy sauce. If your frying pan is too small, do this step in several batches. Simmer briskly until the mixture is almost dry. Stir frequently and do not let them scorch or brown. Scrape the mixture into a large pot.
3   Strain the soaking water from the dried mushrooms through a sieve lined with cheesecloth or a coffee filter to eliminate grit and sand. Rinse the mushrooms well under cold running water. Discard any tough stems and chop the mushrooms coarsely.
4   Add the soaked mushrooms and their filtered water to the fresh mushrooms in the pot.
5   In a small frying pan, combine the shallots, garlic, tarragon, 4 fl oz/120 ml stock and a splash of sherry. Boil until almost dry. Add to the pot.
6   Add the remaining stock, a bit of salt and pepper, and the Parmesan rind. Bring to the boil, reduce heat and simmer, partially covered, for 1 hour. Discard the cheese rind. Taste and add more salt and pepper if necessary. Cool. In batches, put the soup in the liquidizer. Flick the motor on and off once or twice (you want a rough chopped effect, *not* a smooth purée). Serve piping hot. The soup will keep in the refrigerator for several days and may be frozen.

SOUP OF BAKED VEGETABLES

Makes 2½ pts/1.5 l

Do not be daunted by the number of steps in this recipe. It is *very* easy and makes one of the richest most deliciously satisfying soups you have ever eaten. Serve it with crusty bread spread with low-fat quark, and you have a meal.

---

4 small aubergines, about ½ pound/240 g each	32 fl oz/960 ml stock
1 large Spanish onion	Salt and freshly ground pepper to taste
2 heads garlic	½ teaspoon dried thyme, crumbled
2 red peppers	½ teaspoon dried tarragon, crumbled
1 tin (1 lb 12 oz/840 g) Italian tomatoes, well drained	⅛ teaspoon allspice
1 tablespoon tomato paste	2 fl oz/60 ml cognac

---

1 Preheat the oven to 425° F, 220° C, Gas Mark 7. Prick the aubergines in several places with a skewer or the prongs of a fork.

2 Spread the aubergines, onion, garlic and red peppers on a large baking sheet. Bake for 1 hour. Turn the peppers once or twice during this time.

3 After 1 hour, remove all vegetables except onion from the oven and allow to cool. The peppers should be quite black. If so, close them up in a paper bag for a few minutes. (If they are not charred all over, place them under the grill first, turning frequently, until they are thoroughly blackened. Then, remove from grill and close up in a paper bag.)

4 Place the drained tomatoes in the liquidizer. Cut the stems from the aubergines and strip off the skins. Place the pulp in the liquidizer. Purée. Push through a fine sieve into a soup pot so that all the tomato and aubergine seeds are left behind. Discard the seeds.

5 Squeeze the garlic cloves so that the softened garlic purée pops from the skins. Add the purée to the pot.

6 Remove the peppers from the bag and strip off the charred skins. Discard the skins and the seeds. Purée the peppers in the liquidizer and add to the pot.

7 By this time, the onion will be soft. Remove it from the oven. (Work with an oven glove; the onion will be hot!) Cut off the stem and root ends and strip off the first two layers. Cut, into quarters, place in the liquidizer and purée. Add to the pot.

8 Stir in the tomato paste, the stock and all the seasoning. Simmer, partially covered, for 30 minutes, stirring occasionally.
9 Stir in the cognac and simmer for 5 minutes more. Serve piping hot. This soup may be prepared two days ahead and refrigerated. The flavour will improve each day.

⊕ ⊠ Prepare aubergines, garlic and onion in the microwave. Use tinned peppers.

♡ ❄ ## ROOT VEGETABLE SOUP

Makes approx 3 pts/2 l

Root vegetables, mellow sweet garlic, fennel, and a mustard, wine, soy sauce flavour base, combine to make a deeply satisfying, hearty soup. It is almost a stew, and would make a delicious winter main dish, accompanied by a loaf of crusty wholemeal bread.

1 head garlic, each clove peeled but left whole	2 pts/1,200 ml stock
1 Spanish onion, peeled, cut in half, then into ½-inch/1.25-cm wedges	½ teaspoon dried tarragon, crumbled
	1 tablespoon Dijon mustard
1 bulb fennel, trimmed and cut into ½-inch/1.25-cm wedges	2 tablespoons tomato paste
	3–4 dashes soy sauce
1 small swede, peeled and cut into ½-inch/1.25-cm pieces	4 fl oz/120 ml red wine
	Juice of ½ large lemon
1 large parsnip, peeled and cut into ½-inch/1.25-cm pieces	Salt and freshly ground pepper to taste
2 carrots, peeled and sliced into ½-inch/1.25-cm slices	1 piece Parmesan rind
	1 tin (14 oz/420 g) white beans, drained and rinsed
2 stalks celery, sliced into ½-inch/1.25-cm pieces	

1 Put vegetables into a large, heavy, non-reactive pot with 4 fl oz/120 ml stock. Cover and simmer for approximately 5 minutes. Uncover and simmer for 5 minutes more, stirring occasionally.
2 Pour in the remaining stock. Stir together remaining ingredients except the Parmesan rind and the beans. Add the mixture to the soup. Add the Parmesan rind. Season to taste.
3 Simmer, partially covered, for 40 minutes.
4 Stir in the beans. Taste and adjust seasoning. Simmer for 10–15 minutes more, until the ingredients are very tender.

🐻 Omit the white beans.

'One day I did not sing at all. The major sent for me.
"Why do you not sing today, Caruso?"
"I cannot sing on greasy soup."
Next day my soup was strong and there was no grease on
it.'

Enrico Caruso, in a newspaper interview

♡ ❄ VEGETABLE SOUP

Makes 5½ pts/3.3 l

This recipe is purposely designed to make a large quantity
of soup. It really doesn't pay to embark on the chore of
slicing, dicing, peeling, washing, etc., for a measly amount.
Make it and freeze it in small containers. What luxury, at
the end of a long, exhausting, aggravating day, to be able to
conjure a feast like this from the freezer.

---

10 oz/300 g fresh spinach	3-inch/8-cm piece orange zest
2 large onions, cut in half and sliced into thin half-moons	1 bay leaf
3 cloves garlic, crushed	½ teaspoon dried oregano, crumbled
3 pts/1.8 l stock	½ teaspoon dried basil, crumbled
3 large carrots, peeled and thickly sliced	4 fl oz/120 ml tiny pasta
1 white turnip, peeled and diced	1 tin (14 oz/420 g) black-eyed beans, drained and rinsed
½ small swede, peeled and diced	Salt and freshly ground pepper to taste
1 large tin (1 lb 12 oz/840 g) plum tomatoes, undrained and crushed with the hands	4 oz/120 g frozen runner beans, thawed and thickly sliced
4 fl oz/120 ml dry red wine	2 tablespoons chopped parsley

---

1   Wash the spinach well. Strip the leaves off the stems. Shred
the leaves. Reserve the stems.
2   Combine the onions, garlic and 8 fl oz/240 ml stock in a large
pot that can be covered. Cover and boil for 5–7 minutes.
Uncover, and simmer briskly until the onions are tender and
beginning to stick to the pan, and the stock is almost gone.
Splash in a bit more stock. Stir and scrape the browned bits on
the bottom of the pan. When the onions are browned and
syrupy, stir in the carrots, turnip and swede. Stir and cook
over low heat for 2–3 minutes.
3   Stir in the tomatoes and their juices, the wine, the remaining
stock, the orange peel, bay leaf, oregano and basil. Bring to the
boil, partially cover and reduce heat. Simmer for 1–1½ hours
until the vegetables are tender. Skim off scum occasionally.

4   Stir in the spinach stems, pasta, black-eyed beans, salt, pepper, and runner beans. Simmer for 5–10 minutes more until the pasta is cooked.
5   Stir in the parsley and spinach leaves. Season to taste.

Note: The soup may be prepared in advance up to and including step 4. To serve, slowly bring to the boil. Stir in the parsley and spinach leaves. If you plan to freeze the soup, prepare it right through to step 5. Cool, then freeze in small containers.

Omit the black-eyed beans and the pasta. Substitute diced all-purpose potato.

♡ CHESTNUT SOUP

Serves 8

This is a soup for special occasions, a rich starter for a gala meal. The use of tinned chestnuts (available in delicatessens and many supermarkets) makes it very easy to prepare. Happily, chestnuts, unlike other nuts, are very low in fat.

---

6 shallots, chopped
¾ lb/360 g carrots, peeled and
*   chopped*
1 large celery stalk, chopped
3 pts/1.8 l stock
8 fl oz/240 ml dry red wine

32 fl oz/960 ml tinned unsweetened
*   chestnuts, drained*
Salt and freshly ground pepper to
*   taste*
¼ teaspoon freshly grated nutmeg
8 fl oz/240 ml skimmed milk

---

1   Combine the shallots, carrots, celery, 4 fl oz/120 ml of stock and 4 fl oz/120 ml of wine in a soup pot. Cover, bring to the boil, and boil until almost all the liquid is cooked away.
2   Add chestnuts, remaining stock and seasonings. Simmer, covered, for 45 minutes to 1 hour, until the chestnuts and vegetables are very tender. Cool slightly.
3   Purée in a liquidizer. Return to the soup pot and stir in the milk. Bring back to a simmer and simmer for 10 minutes. The soup may be served at once, or cooled and refrigerated for serving up to 3 days later.
4   To serve, bring to a simmer. Stir in remaining wine and simmer for a few minutes.

'There were great, round, pot-bellied baskets of chestnuts, shaped like the waistcoats of jolly old gentlemen.'

Charles Dickens, *A Christmas Carol*

ITALIAN SAUSAGE SOUP

Serves 8

This one-pot meal is more of a stew than a soup. It provides lavish comfort on a cold, wintery evening. Eat it in front of the fire. Serve a crusty rustic wholegrain loaf with it. The soup reheats very well – in fact it improves in flavour if made a day or so ahead.

2 large onions, coarsely chopped
3 cloves garlic, crushed
2½ pts/1.5 l stock
1 tin (1 lb 12 oz/280 g) plum tomatoes, drained and crushed with the hands
12 fl oz/360 ml dry red wine
1 teaspoon dried basil, crumbled
1 teaspoon dried oregano, crumbled
1 piece Parmesan cheese rind
1 small red pepper, seeded, ribbed and coarsely diced

3 small courgettes, trimmed and sliced ½ in/1.25 cm thick
2½ oz/75 g tiny pasta shells
Salt and freshly ground pepper to taste
4 tablespoons fresh parsley, chopped
25 Italian Sausage Balls, cooked (see page 163)
1 tin (15 oz/450 g) cannellini beans, drained
Grated Parmesan cheese

1   Sauté onions and garlic in 6 fl oz/180 ml stock according to the Slim Cuisine technique (see page 24) until amber brown and tender. Stir in tomatoes, wine, remaining stock, herbs, and Parmesan rind. Simmer briskly, uncovered, for 15 minutes.
2   Add red pepper, courgettes, pasta, salt and pepper. Cover. Simmer for 10 minutes, or until the pasta and vegetables are tender. Stir occasionally.
3   Add parsley, sausage balls and beans. Heat through. Discard the Parmesan rind. Serve piping hot. Pass round Parmesan cheese at the table.

❄ GOULASH SOUP

Makes 3½ pts/2.1 l

I discovered Hungarian food the week of my honeymoon, almost thirty years ago, and I've been fascinated by the subtle and complex cuisine ever since. In 1972 I prepared a Hungarian dinner party for a group of influential people, and as a result (one influential person wrote to her editor about me) I was invited to write my first cook book. So you might say that Hungarian gastronomy looms large in my life. The Hungarians have a predilection for lard, cream and sour cream; converting this richness to Slim

Cuisine without losing the underlying splendid Hungarian character has been a labour of love. This version of the great Hungarian classic is based on the quintessential bowl of goulash soup, experienced on a recent trip to Hungary, at a farm in the countryside near Budapest. The cook (brilliant man) enriched his soup with quantities of whole garlic cloves. The result is *sweet* and luscious, *not strong*! I'd like to write it in neon letters across the sky. Don't be afraid! The soup has a gentle and subtle character and will comfort and sustain you – it will not smite you with vulgarity.

---

2 Spanish onions, peeled and
   coarsely chopped
10 fl oz/300 ml stock
2 tablespoons hot paprika or paprika
   paste (or use half hot, half sweet)
½ tablespoon lightly crushed
   caraway seeds
Peeled whole cloves from 1 head
   garlic

1 lb/480 g well-trimmed rump skirt
   steak, cut into 1-inch/2.5-cm
   cubes
4 pts/2.5 l stock
Salt to taste
1 lb/480 g all-purpose potatoes,
   peeled and diced into
   1-inch/2.5-cm cubes

---

1   Combine onions and stock in a heavy flameproof casserole that can be covered. Cover and bring to the boil. Boil for 3–5 minutes. Uncover and simmer until it is almost dry and the onions are starting to brown.

2   Remove from heat. Add paprika and caraway. Stir for a moment or two. Stir in the garlic and the beef.

3   Add stock and a bit of salt. Cover and simmer for 1½–2 hours, until the meat is almost tender. Remove from heat, cool and then refrigerate overnight.

4   Next day, scrape off and discard congealed fat. Bring the soup to a boil. Reduce heat, add potatoes and a bit more salt if needed, and simmer, covered, for 20–30 minutes, until the meat and potatoes are tender.

'What do you think? Young women of rank actually eat – you will never guess what – garlick! Our poor friend Lord Byron is quite corrupted by living among these people.'

Percy Bysshe Shelley, in a letter from Naples

RED PEPPER AND TOMATO BORSCHT

Makes 4 pts/2.5 l

What a heavenly brew; a really wild improvisation on a classic theme. The borscht fairly bursts with flavour, texture and nutrition. It freezes beautifully. A container pulled from the freezer, thawed and reheated in the microwave and served with good crusty bread makes a sumptuous meal.

2 large Spanish onions, chopped
1 small carrot, peeled and chopped
1 medium baking pototo, peeled and coarsely chopped
2½ pts/1.5 l stock
8 large red peppers, trimmed, ribbed, seeded and coarsely diced
Salt and freshly ground pepper to taste
5 shallots, coarsely chopped
Grated zest of half a small lemon
3 oz/90 g chopped sun-dried tomatoes
1 teaspoon red wine vinegar
8 fl oz/240 ml red wine
½ teaspoon allspice

1 large tin (1 lb 12 oz/840 g) plum tomatoes, drained and chopped
1 tablespoon sultanas
1 tablespoon brown sugar
1 tablespoon lemon juice
1 heaped tablespoon tomato paste
1 tablespoon chopped parsley
Purée from ½–1 large head Baked Garlic (see page 32)
1 small cabbage (8–10 oz/240– 300 g), cored, trimmed of tough outer leaves and shredded
Veal-Potato Balls (see page 160)
Fromage frais
Fresh dill fronds

1   Combine onions, carrot, potato and 4 fl oz/120 ml stock in a soup pot. Cover and bring to the boil. Reduce heat and simmer briskly for 3–4 minutes. Uncover and cook, stirring occasionally, until the liquid is gone, and the vegetables are browning. Stir in the peppers.

2   Pour in the remaining stock. Season with a bit of salt and pepper. Simmer, partially covered, for ½ hour, or until the vegetables are very tender. Set aside to cool.

3   While the soup is simmering, combine the shallots, lemon zest, sun-dried tomatoes, vinegar and wine in a frying pan. Cover and bring to the boil. Uncover and boil until the wine has evaporated. Cook, stirring, on moderate heat until the shallots are tender.

4   Remove from heat and add allspice. Stir to coat vegetables. Stir in the remaining ingredients except cabbage, Veal-Potato Balls, fromage frais and dill. Simmer, uncovered, until thick. Set aside.

5   Purée the cooled pepper mixture in the blender, in batches, and then push through a sieve. The pepper skins will be left behind. Discard them. Combine the sieved pepper mixture

and the tomato mixture in the soup pot. Add the cabbage. Thin with more broth if necessary. Simmer, partially covered, for 20 minutes, until the cabbage is almost tender.

6. Add the Veal-Potato Balls. Simmer, partially covered, for 10 minutes, to blend flavours and to finish the cabbage. Taste and adjust seasonings, adding salt, pepper, lemon juice and brown sugar, as needed. The soup should have a nice balance of sweet and sour. If possible, refrigerate for a day or so to mellow.

7. To serve, heat until piping hot. Serve in shallow soup bowls garnished with dollops of fromage frais and dill fronds.

♡ **FISH SOUP**

Makes 2½ pts/1.5 l

Excellent quality stock is essential to the success of this recipe. The soup has a delicate and haunting quality. Make it a main dish soup by adding 1 lb/480 g plaice fillets and 1 lb/480 g cod fillets (both of them skinned and cut into 1-inch/2.5-cm cubes) in step 6. Stir for 3–5 minutes until cooked through. Sprinkle with chopped parsley.

---

2 large heads garlic	1 pt/600 ml chicken stock
2 large baking potatoes	Cayenne pepper
Juice of ½–1 small lemon	Salt and freshly ground pepper
Salt to taste	Toasted French bread slices
4–5 tablespoons fromage frais	Raw garlic cloves
1 pt/600 ml fish stock	

---

1. Preheat oven to 400° F, 200° C, Gas Mark 6.
2. Wrap garlic heads in a sheet of foil, shiny side in. Wash potatoes, dry and pierce in several places with a thin skewer or fork. Bake both garlic and potatoes for 1–1½ hours until tender.
3. Scoop the potato flesh out of the skins (save the skins for another use, see page 210 or 308). Mash with a potato masher.
4. Squeeze the softened garlic into the potatoes. With an electric beater, beat the garlic and potatoes into a creamy mass. Beat in lemon juice and salt to taste and the fromage frais. Set aside in a non-reactive bowl.
5. Combine the stocks in a non-reactive pot. Bring to the boil. Boil for 3–5 minutes.
6. Ladle out ¾ pt/480 ml of stock. With a wire whisk, whisk the hot liquid into the potato-garlic mixture. Stir the mixture back into the soup. Stir over low heat until thoroughly amalgamated and hot. Add a pinch of cayenne pepper, salt and

101

freshly ground pepper to taste. Serve at once with toasted French bread slices that have been rubbed with raw garlic cloves.

🕐 ⧖ Use the microwave for steps 1 and 2 (see page 34).

♡ ❄ **BLACK BEAN SOUP**

Makes 3½ pts/2.1 l

A velvety purply-brown purée made from the noble black bean, the best – in my opinion – of all the dried pulses. It's worth searching for the beans (sometimes called turtle beans) in health food and wholefood stores.

---

1 lb/450 g soaked and cooked Black Beans (page 202)	*Steamed or boiled white rice (optional)*
2 pts/1.2 l stock	*Fromage frais*
Grated zest of 1 small orange	*A thinly sliced, peeled orange*
¼ pt/150 ml dry sherry	*Coriander leaves*
Juice of 1 small orange	

---

1   Combine beans, stock and orange zest in a saucepan. Simmer for 15 minutes. Cool.
2   In batches, purée the soup in a liquidizer. (Fill the container less than half full for each batch.) Then rub the purée through a sieve. Return to the saucepan.
3   Pour in the sherry and orange juice. Simmer for 10 minutes. Taste and adjust seasonings.
4   If you are using the rice, put a spoonful in the bottom of a warm soup bowl. Fill with soup. Put a dollop of fromage frais on the surface, and lay two orange slices on each side of the dollop. Sprinkle with coriander leaves and serve at once.

'Soups feed you
Beans for vitamins . . .
Soups that nourish
Make hope flourish
Beans for nutrition
Beans for ambition
The Best People are crazy about soups!
Beans are all the rage among the Higher Income Groups!'

From the opera *Paul Bunyan*: libretto,
W. H. Auden; score, Benjamin Britten

With Zest

A zester is one of the most useful little kitchen tools you can own. It has a plastic or wooden handle and a stainless steel blade with five tiny holes across the top. Scrape the blade across the surface of an unpeeled orange, lemon, or lime, and it will grate the aromatic zest into small slivers, leaving the bitter pith behind. Usually I like to zest the citrus fruit right over the saucepan or bowl so that the zest goes in, and some of the fragrant oils as well. (The oils add a lovely dimension of flavour, but the actual 'oiliness' is minuscule – it will not interfere with your low-fat regime.)

BEAN SOUP

Makes 3½ pts/2.1 l

This is a magnificent and sophisticated soup, full of intriguing textures and tastes floating around in perfect harmony. It has echoes of the culinary traditions of both Mexico and Thailand. Jalapeños are fiery Mexican peppers. Look for small tins of jalapeños in vinegar in delicatessens and some supermarkets. They are to be found where other Mexican foods (chilli, tortilla chips etc.) are found. The use of tinned beans makes the preparation of this soup quick and easy. Always rinse tinned beans before use so that a good proportion of their added salt is washed away.

---

1 tin (1 lb 12 oz/840 g) Italian tomatoes	2 tablespoons fresh parsley, coarsely chopped
1 small tin (4 oz/120 g) sliced jalapeños in vinegar	Several sprigs fresh coriander, coarsely chopped
1¾ pts/1 l stock	1 bunch spring onions, trimmed and sliced thin
3 tins (1 lb/480 g each) borlotti beans, drained and rinsed	1 large clove garlic, minced
1 rounded tablespoon tomato paste	4 tablespoons red wine vinegar
½ teaspoon dried oregano, crumbled	6 tablespoons water
	Juice of 1 lime
A few grinds of black pepper	6 tablespoons Parmesan cheese

---

1 Pour the tomatoes and their juices into a liquidizer. Add approximately ¼ of the jalapeños and ¼ of the jalapeño juice (use less if you want a tame soup, more if you pride yourself on your asbestos palate). Purée. Put the purée through a non-reactive sieve so that the seeds are left behind.

2 Pour the sieved mixture into a non-reactive soup pot. Add the

103

stock, beans, tomato paste, oregano and pepper. Simmer, uncovered for 20 minutes. Roughly mash some of the beans in the pot with a potato masher. (The recipe may be made in advance to this point. Cool and refrigerate until needed.)

3   Meanwhile, combine chopped parsley, chopped coriander, spring onions, garlic, vinegar and water in a small saucepan or frying pan. Boil, stirring occasionally until almost dry. Stir this mixture into the simmering bean soup.

4   Stir in the lime juice. Sprinkle on the Parmesan cheese. Stir gently until the cheese melts into the soup. Taste and add more lime juice, pepper or oregano to taste. If you feel it needs it, add a bit of salt, but it probably won't need much.

♡ ❄   **SPLIT PEA SOUP**

Makes 2½ pts/1.5 l

The baked garlic is optional in this hearty soup, but I strongly recommend that you try it; it gives a wonderful dimension to the pale green brew. The soup can be made in advance, but it will thicken dramatically in the refrigerator. Thin it with stock before reheating.

½ lb/225 g split peas, rinsed and picked over	*Purée from 1–2 heads baked garlic (optional) (page 32)*
2 baking potatoes peeled and cubed	*4 tablespoons Parmesan cheese*
3½ pts/2 l stock	*Salt*
1 large onion, chopped	

---

1   Combine peas, potatoes and 32 fl oz/960 ml stock in a saucepan. Bring to the boil, reduce heat and simmer briskly, partially covered, until peas and potatoes are tender, about 40 minutes. Cool slightly.

2   While the vegetables are simmering, sauté the onions in stock according to the Slim Cuisine method: combine onions and 4 fl oz/120 ml stock in a frying pan. Cover and bring to the boil. Uncover and boil for 5 minutes or so until the liquid has almost cooked away. Reduce heat and simmer until the onions are just about dry and beginning to stick and burn. Pour in a splash of stock and boil, stirring and scraping up the browned bits on the bottom of the frying pan.

3   When the peas and potatoes are tender, push them through a fine sieve or put them through a food mill and return them to the pot. Add the sautéed onions and the remaining stock and stir in the garlic purée, if used.

4   Simmer the soup for approximately 15 minutes. Add the cheese and stir gently until it melts into the soup. Taste and add a touch of salt if needed. Serve piping hot.

'Beautiful soup, so rich and green
Waiting in a hot tureen.'

Lewis Carroll, *Alice's Adventures in Wonderland*

♡ CHILLED CORN SOUP

Makes 3 pts/2 l

This recipe is adapted from the Roux brothers, my gastronomic heroes. I specify a frying pan, an odd utensil for soup. But you will find that the skimmed milk is less likely to scorch and overflow in a frying pan than in a saucepan.

1 small onion, halved and sliced into thin half-moons	Salt to taste
	Pinch nutmeg
4 fl oz/120 ml stock	Pinch paprika
12 oz/360 g sweet corn kernels	Snipped chives
28 fl oz/840 ml skimmed milk	

1   In a non-stick frying pan sauté the onion in the stock according to the Slim Cuisine technique (see page 24).
2   If the corn kernels are tinned, rinse and drain them. Add to the onion and stir. Pour in the milk, season with nutmeg and a bit of salt. Gently and slowly bring to the boil. Simmer for 5 minutes. Cool slightly.
3   Purée the mixture in the blender, then rub it through a sieve. Chill.
4   Serve with a sprinkling of paprika and chives on each bowlful.

Variation:

MEXICAN CORN SOUP

Add ground cumin, cayenne pepper and a pinch of crumbled dried oregano in Step 2. Omit the nutmeg. In Step 3 omit the paprika and chives. Garnish with chopped fresh coriander and a sprinkling of chilli powder.

JELLIED GAZPACHO

Serves 10

A trembling red jelly, studded with jewel-like bits of vegetables and herbs – fragrant, vivid, and exciting. Serve it unmoulded onto greens or creamy buttermilk, or – even better – spooned into clear glass bowls. It can be eaten with a spoon or spread onto savoury biscuits.

---

1 small and 1 large tin Italian plum tomatoes with juice (2 lb 10 oz/1,260 g in all)	1 clove garlic, crushed
4 teaspoons plain gelatine	2 tablespoons thinly sliced spring onions
6 oz/180 g tomato paste	½ yellow pepper, chopped
Juice of ½ lemon	¼ cucumber, peeled, seeded and chopped
2 fl oz/60 ml white wine vinegar	2 tablespoons parsley, chopped
Salt and pepper to taste	2 tinned plum tomatoes, seeded, well drained and chopped (in summer, use fresh tomatoes)
Dash of cayenne pepper (optional)	
1 teaspoon fresh oregano	
1 teaspoon fresh basil	

---

1 Liquidize the tomatoes, juice and all, then sieve them. You should end up with 1½ pts/900 ml of tomato juice. Save any extra for another use. Measure out 6 fl oz/180 ml and put into a non-reactive saucepan. Bring just to a simmer. Immediately remove from the heat.
2 Sprinkle the gelatine into the hot tomato juice. Stir well to dissolve. Add the remaining tomato juice, tomato paste, lemon juice, vinegar, salt, pepper and cayenne, if used. Stir very well. Let stand for an hour or so until the mixture is beginning to thicken.
3 Fold in the remaining ingredients. Pour the mixture into a mould, several small moulds or a large bowl. Cover and chill.
4 To serve, if you are using moulds, dip the bottom of each mould *very briefly* into warm water. Loosen the gelatine around the edges with a flexible palette knife. Unmould onto a bed of greens or onto a pool of buttermilk. Serve at once.

GAZPACHO

Makes 3 pts/1.8 l

This is a variation on Gazpacho, not at all the classic version. You will find it refreshing, herby and very beautiful, especially served in clear glass bowls.

2 tins (1 lb 12 oz/840 g each) Italian tomatoes	2 cloves garlic, minced
4 fresh ripe tomatoes, peeled and seeded	2 tablespoons chopped fresh parsley
Finely chopped fresh chilli peppers to taste, or chopped tinned chillies, or a mixture	2 tablespoons chopped fresh mint
	4 red peppers, or 2 red peppers and 2 yellow peppers, grilled (see page 31) and coarsely chopped
2 fl oz/60 ml red wine vinegar	

1   Drain the tinned tomatoes (save the juice). Chop the tinned and fresh tomatoes.
2   Combine all ingredients, including tomato juice, in a non-reactive bowl. Chill thoroughly.

🕐 Use tinned tomatoes only, and use tinned peppers.

❄ **BEETROOT BORSCHT**

Makes 4½ pts/2.7 l

Traditionally beetroot borscht is served cold, sometimes with a steaming hot potato nestled in the centre of each icy bowlful.

10 large beetroots, peeled and coarsely grated	3½ pts/2 l water
4 ripe tomatoes, peeled, seeded and chopped	2 fl oz/60 ml tomato paste
3 leeks, cleaned, trimmed and chopped (see note)	4 fl oz/120 ml lemon juice
	1½ oz/45 g sugar
	Salt to taste
	Fromage frais

1   Combine beets, tomatoes, leeks and water in a heavy pot that can be covered. Bring to the boil, reduce heat and simmer for 1 hour, partially covered.
2   Add tomato paste, lemon juice, sugar and salt. Simmer for an additional 30 minutes. Remove from heat.
3   Taste carefully and add additional lemon juice, sugar, or salt if necessary. The soup should be tart, but not unpleasantly so.
4   Cool, and then chill. Serve with a dollop of fromage frais on top of each serving.

Note: To trim leeks, cut off tip and 'beard'. Cut off and discard most of green portion, leaving just 1 inch/2.5 cm of green. With a sharp knife, slash through part of the white bulb and up through the remaining green portion. Wash leeks well under cold running

107

water, holding them apart at the slash to wash away sand. Then chop and proceed with the recipe.

♡ ✿ Substitute low-Calorie sweetener for the sugar. Add it after the soup has cooled.

'Cold soup is a very tricky thing and it is the rare hostess who can carry it off. More often than not the dinner guest is left with the impression that had he only come a little earlier he could have gotten it while it was still hot.'

Fran Lebowitz, *Metropolitan Life*

Main Dishes

'Cooking is like love. It should be entered into with abandon, or not at all.'

Harriet van Horne

Fish

'Fish dinners will make a man spring like a flea.'

Thomas Jordan

This section deals very specifically with techniques. There are countless ways of seasoning, saucing and serving fish. Once you learn the Slim Cuisine techniques of fish cookery, let your imagination run wild.

A fish dinner is my idea of culinary heaven. The delicacy of fish and its ability to 'marry' with a large spectrum of flavourful ingredients make finny creatures my first choice of main course for special dinner parties and celebration meals. A word of warning, however. When fish is overcooked or kept several days past its prime, it is fit for no one but a not-very-fastidious cat. Fish should be sparklingly fresh and *just* cooked so that it is moist, succulent and sweetly flavourful.

Secrets of Perfect Fish Cookery

To cook fish properly, cook it quickly. Do not 'cook until it flakes easily' as many recipes direct. Instead cook it until it turns opaque and just barely begins to flake. It should retain the faint sweet taste and moisture of the sea or stream. To achieve the proper effect, follow this foolproof rule of thumb developed by the Canadian Fisheries Board: With a ruler, measure the fish at its thickest point

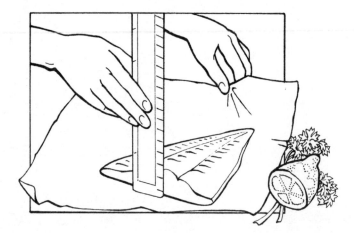

(see illustration). Cook the fish (under a grill, in the oven or in a frying pan) at high heat for 10 minutes per inch/2.5 cm thickness of fish. Thus if the fish is ½ inch/1.25 cm or less thick it will cook for 5 minutes, 1½ inch/3.75 cm for 15 minutes, and so on.

To Buy Fresh Fish

All the careful timing and exquisite seasoning in the world are useless when applied to old fish. Shop carefully and keep these points in mind:

1   If it smells fishy, forget it! Fish should have a faint, clean odour of the sea or the stream. Any trace of fishiness means old fish.
2   Fresh fish is firm. Poke it with your finger. If the flesh springs back it is fresh. If the dent remains, the fish is not for you.
3   A fish fillet should not shred or tear when held up. And fillets should never feel slimy.
4   Fish that has been stored improperly or too long develop sunken, milky, filmed eyes. Choose fish with bulging, bright, staring eyes, however unnerving that stare may be.
5   If the proprietor of the fish market does not allow you to poke, prod and smell the wares, consider finding another market.

Fish Facts

Fish makes a perfect main dish from a nutritional standpoint as well as a gastronomic one. Low in calories and sodium, high in protein and B vitamins, it is a dietitian's dream. The fat content of fish varies with the species, but even fattier fish is relatively low in calories, and fish fat is entirely different from animal fat. Recent scientific and medical studies in several different countries suggest that fish oils seem to have a protective effect on the heart. Frequent fish meals, coupled with an otherwise low-fat diet, may well help reduce the risk of heart disease.

Calorie Values for Boned Fish
(Calories per 3½ oz/100 g)

Cod	83	Lemon sole	91
Haddock	98	Salmon	197
Halibut	92	Brown trout	135
Plaice	93		

'My guest's nostrils swell out, a new light shines in his eyes and he goes after that fish as if he hadn't eaten a thing all day. He can't get over it. He praises it to the skies. He fills a glass with brandy and drinks a toast to the fish.'

Sholom Aleichem, *Tit for Tat*

Slim Cuisine Methods of Cooking Fish

Use no fats and oils and (it should go without saying) abandon all thoughts of deep frying. For the sake of good taste, avoid blanketing fish in thick tomato sauces, or excessive showerings of dried herbs. Keep it simple so that the fresh, vibrant taste of the fish itself shines through.

♡ ⊕   ## TO STEAM FISH IN PARCHMENT

Steaming fish *en papillote* (in paper packets) is a classic method that lends itself perfectly to Slim Cuisine. The fish steams in its own juices and emerges spectacularly succulent and luscious. Keep seasoning fresh and simple. For each piece of fish use a tablespoon of dry white wine, sherry or white vermouth, a tablespoon of lemon juice and a scattering of chopped fresh herbs. Try parsley, spring onion and minced fresh ginger; basil or mint and minced garlic; thyme, tarragon and slivered orange zest; coriander, lime juice and slivered lime zest; ginger, spring onions and soy sauce. Chopped or sliced mushrooms can be added too. Find combinations that please you and those you feed.

1   Use fish steaks, fillets, or small whole fish, such as trout, gutted and boned. (When using whole fish, remove the head and tail if desired. Some flavour will be lost with the head but you will be spared the baleful stare.) Rinse the fish and dry it on paper towels. With tweezers or a small pair of pliers, pull out any small bones that remain in the fillets or boneless whole fish.
2   With a ruler, measure the fish at its thickest point. (Be sure to measure its *depth* not its length!) Jot down the inches or centimetres of thickness.
3   For each piece of fish tear a piece of greaseproof paper large enough to enclose the piece generously. Place each portion of

fish on a piece of paper (fillets should be skin side down) near the bottom edge. Season with appropriate herbs, spices, citrus juice and spirits (see suggestions above). Fold the paper over the fish. The outer edges of the paper should be even. Crimp the paper closed over the fish as follows: fold down one corner; start a second fold so that it incorporates a bit of the first fold; continue folding and crimping all around until the fish is well secured and no steam or juice can escape. Make sure you leave space on top so that the paper does not touch the top surface of the fish.

Fold down one corner.

Start a second fold so that it incorporates a bit of the first fold.

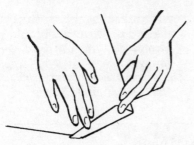

Continue folding and crimping all around until

the fish is well secured and no steam or juice can escape.

Make sure you leave space on top so that the paper does not touch the top surface of the fish.

113

4   Preheat the oven to 450° F, 230° C, Gas Mark 8. Place the fish packets, in one layer, on a baking sheet. Bake for 10 minutes per inch/2.5 cm thickness of fish (see page 110).
5   Give each diner a packet and a pair of scissors. When the packets are cut, the perfumed steam will imbue the air, delighting all present.

♡ ⊕   **PLAICE EN PAPILLOTE**

Serves 4

---

1 large Spanish onion, halved and
    sliced into paper-thin half moons
4 fl oz/120 ml stock
4 plaice fillets
Salt and freshly ground pepper to
    taste

2 tablespoons chopped fresh
    tarragon or 1 teaspoon dried
    tarragon
2 tablespoons chopped chives or
    thinly sliced spring onions

---

1   Preheat oven to 450° F, 230° C, Gas Mark 8.
2   Sauté the onion in stock according to the Slim Cuisine method (see page 24) until amber brown and meltingly tender.
3   Place each fillet on a square of greaseproof paper large enough to enclose it. Season each with salt and pepper, and top with an equal amount of herbs. Put some of the sautéed onions on top of each fillet.
4   Seal and cook according to the master recipe (see page 112). Serve at once.

♡ ⊕   **COD EN PAPILLOTE**

Serves 4

Here is a lovely fresh, simple way to cook cod in greaseproof-paper packets; just one example of how this method can produce a quick but extremely elegant main dish. Serve it with steamed new potatoes and a green salad tossed with one of the Slim Cuisine dressings (see page 284).

---

4 cod fillets, 4 oz/120 g each (choose
    fillets that are of equal thickness)
4 generous tablespoons chopped
    fresh parsley
4 generous tablespoons chopped
    fresh mint

4 tablespoons fresh lemon juice
4 tablespoons dry white vermouth
Salt and freshly ground pepper to
    taste

1 Preheat the oven to 450° F, 230° C, Gas Mark 8.
2 Measure the thickness of the cod fillets. Place each fillet on a sheet of greaseproof paper.
3 Sprinkle a tablespoon of parsley, mint, lemon juice, vermouth, and some salt and pepper over each fillet. Enclose the fillets in the paper according to the directions in the master recipe (see page 112).
4 Place the packets on a baking sheet and bake for 10 minutes per inch/2.5 cm thickness of fish. Serve at once, right from the packets.

STEAMED FISH BUNDLE

Serves 1

Fish can be baked in foil packets too. A foil packet takes longer to cook than a parchment one. This is an absolutely beautiful dish with its heaps of brilliantly coloured, lightly cooked vegetables surrounding the pearly, smoky fish. It was inspired by a dish sampled at one of my old haunts, the scintillating Legal Seafood in Cambridge, Massachusetts. This makes enough for one; prepare as many bundles as you wish. After 20 minutes, unwrap one bundle to check if the fish is done. (If it is, it will fall into moist flakes at the touch of a fork.) A piece of *fresh* haddock fillet, or even cod, may be substituted for the smoked haddock (don't use the kind of smoked haddock that has been dyed). If using *fresh* fillets, sprinkle with a tiny bit of salt before wrapping.

1 piece (4–5 oz/120–180 g) smoked haddock fillet	*2–3 small oyster or cultivated mushrooms, quartered*
1 small carrot, peeled and cut into thin sticks approximately 2 inches/5 cm long and ¼ inch/0.5 cm thick	*6 cherry tomatoes, halved*
	1 tablespoon chopped parsley
	1 tablespoon sliced spring onion
	1½ tablespoons fish, chicken, or vegetable stock
1 small courgette, thinly sliced	*1½ tablespoons dry vermouth*
½ red, ½ yellow pepper, peeled and cut into 2-inch/5-cm squares	*1 level tablespoon grated Parmesan cheese*
2–3 fresh shiitake mushrooms, trimmed of the stems and quartered	*Freshly ground pepper*

1 Preheat oven to 450° F, 230° C, Gas Mark 8.
2 Overlap two sheets of 12 × 16-inch/30 × 40-cm aluminium foil to form a 12 × 19-inch/30 × 48-cm rectangle. Put the fish, skin side down, in the centre. Arrange the carrots, courgettes, peppers and mushrooms around the fish in separate piles.

Place the cherry tomatoes, cut sides up, on the fish. Sprinkle on the parsley and green onion. Dribble on the stock and vermouth. Sprinkle with cheese. Grind on some black pepper. Fold the flaps of foil over and seal the top and edges to form a well-sealed, loose tent around the fish and vegetables.

3   Bake packet on the oven shelf for 20–25 minutes. When done, slash the foil along the bottom and slide fish and vegetables on to a warm plate.

♡   Omit cheese.

TO GRILL FISH

Years ago when I was visiting friends in Maine on the North East Coast of the United States, I learned to coat fish fillets with a thin layer of mayonnaise before grilling, to keep them beautifully moist. It works with Slim Cuisine mayonnaise too. For fish, I make the mayonnaise with a mixture of 2 parts yoghurt to 1 part Dijon mustard. In the grilling the coating turns fluffy, and the fish stays moist and pearly.

GRILLED PLAICE WITH MUSTARD

Serves 4

White wine	*2 tablespoons low-fat yoghurt*
4 plaice fillets	*Freshly ground pepper*
1 tablespoon Dijon mustard	

---

1   Preheat grill to its highest point.
2   Pour wine to a depth of ¹⁄₁₆ inch/0.15 cm into the grill pan.
3   Place the fillets in one layer in the pan. (They should not touch each other.)
4   Combine mustard, yoghurt and pepper. Spread evenly over each fillet.
5   Grill 4–5 inches/12 cm from the heat for 5 minutes. Serve at once.

♡ ⊕   ## TO OVEN-POACH FISH

1   Preheat the oven to 450° F, 230° C, Gas Mark 8.
2   With a ruler, measure the fish at its thickest point (be sure to measure its *depth* not its length!). Jot down the inches or centimetres of thickness.

3   Pour dry white wine or dry vermouth into a shallow baking dish to a depth of ¹⁄₁₆ inch/0.15 cm. Place the fish steaks or fish fillets (skin side down) in the wine in one layer (they should not touch each other). Season to taste or as indicated in the individual recipe. The seasoning suggestions for fish *en papillote* also apply to steamed fish and to poached fish. Cover each piece of fish with a lettuce leaf. (This keeps the fish from drying out.) Bake for 10 minutes per inch/2.5 cm thickness of fish. Discard lettuce leaves and serve at once.

SOLE WITH VERMOUTH

Makes 6 pieces

This is an exquisite dinner party dish. The preparation couldn't be easier. Use the freshest fish possible (never frozen fillets).

6 fillets of sole	Juice of 1 small lemon
Salt and freshly ground pepper to taste	¼ teaspoon dried thyme or 1 teaspoon chopped fresh thyme
4 fl oz/120 ml dry vermouth	2 tablespoons sliced spring onions
4 fl oz/120 ml Fish Stock (see page 22)	2 tablespoons chopped fresh parsley

1   Preheat oven to 400° F, 200° C, Gas Mark 6.
2   Trim fillets (freeze the trimmings for a future fish stock). Place fillets, skin side down, in one layer, in a shallow baking dish. Sprinkle with salt and pepper.
3   In a small non-reactive saucepan, combine vermouth, stock, lemon juice and thyme. Boil down until reduced by half. Pour over fish. Scatter on the spring onions and parsley.
4   Bake uncovered for 7–10 minutes, until opaque and cooked through. Serve at once, with rice, Wheat Pilaf (page 280), or steamed new potatoes.

TO OVEN-'FRY' FISH

126 Calories per 3½ oz/100 g (of cod)
0.6 g fat
(Traditional fried cod: 200 Calories per 3½ oz/100 g, 10.3 g fat)

1   Preheat oven to 500° F, 260° C, Gas Mark 9.
2   Choose haddock or cod fillets. With a ruler, measure the fillet at its thickest point. (Be sure to measure its *depth* not its length!) Jot down the inches or centimetres of thickness.

3   Dip one side of the fillets (not the skin side) into buttermilk or yoghurt, then dredge them in seasoned breadcrumbs. (Make your own. The packaged kind tend to be awful. Season them with salt and pepper and any herbs and spices you like.) The fish should be very well coated.

4   Place a rack on a flat baking sheet. Put the fillets, breaded side up, on the rack in one layer (they should not touch each other). Bake for 10 minutes per inch, 2.5 cm thickness. Serve at once with lemon wedges. This fish is particularly good on a bed of Helen's Terracotta Sauce (see page 234).

♡ ⊕   ## TO STEAM FISH FILLETS

Serves 4

Lettuce leaves	*3 tablespoons finely minced shallots*
4 fish fillets approximately 6 oz/	*or thinly sliced spring onions*
180 g each (white fish or salmon)	*2 tablespoons chopped fresh parsley*
2 tablespoons dry white wine or	*1 tablespoon chopped fresh herbs*
vermouth or 2 tablespoons fresh	*(tarragon, thyme, marjoram or*
lemon or lime juice	*chervil)*
	Salt and freshly ground pepper

---

1   Line a steamer rack with lettuce leaves. Arrange the fish fillets, skin side down, in one layer on the leaves. Sprinkle them evenly with all the remaining ingredients. Have water boiling in the bottom of the steamer.

2   Put the rack in the steamer, cover and steam the fish over boiling water for 10 minutes per inch/2.5 cm thickness. Serve at once.

Suggestions for Steamed, Poached or 'Fried' Fish

Serve the fish fillets on a bed of:
Remoulade Sauce (see page 304)
Tzatziki (see page 304)
Red or Yellow Pepper Sauce (see page 233), or coat the plate with half yellow pepper sauce, half red, before positioning the fish
Hungarian Green Sauce (see page 231)
Dill Pesto (see page 232)
Helen's Terracotta Sauce (see page 234)

♡ ASPARAGUS WITH PRAWN SAUCE

Serves 4

Asparagus and prawns go together like Ginger and Fred. This makes a stunning first course for a gala dinner, or a springtime main dish. For a main dish, you may want to increase the amount of asparagus. (As far as I'm concerned, no matter how much asparagus there is, it's never enough.)

2 lb/960 g thick asparagus	1 recipe 'Russian' Dressing (see
1 lb/480 g tiny shelled prawns	below)
	Chopped fresh parsley

1   Cut off the tough woody stems of the asparagus stalks. With a swivel-bladed peeler, peel the stalks from the stem up to the buds. Wash well under cold running water. Steam over boiling water until 'crisp-tender' (a stalk should bend just a little, when held up with tongs), 3–6 minutes. Rinse under cold water to stop cooking, drain and set aside until needed.

2   Spread the asparagus out on a plate. Fold together 'Russian' Dressing and prawns. Spoon the prawns and sauce over the asparagus stems. Sprinkle with parsley.

'Russian' Dressing

Makes approximately 6 fl oz/180 ml

This is based on an old-fashioned, very fattening American classic. The original contains mayonnaise; this version contains those invaluable Slim Cuisine staples, buttermilk and fromage frais. Use as a salad dressing or a sauce for cold peeled prawns.

3 fl oz/90 ml buttermilk	1 teaspoon grainy mustard – use
3 tablespoons fromage frais	New York Deli Mustard if
1½ tablespoons tomato paste	available (page 305)
1 tablespoon minced spring onions	¼ teaspoon Worcestershire sauce
1 tablespoon drained chopped capers	¼ teaspoon sugar – if you haven't
(optional)	used New York Deli Mustard
1 tablespoon minced parsley	

Whisk all ingredients together.

⏲ Use thin asparagus – they do not need to be peeled.

'Chowder for breakfast, and chowder for dinner, and chowder for supper, 'till you begin to look for fish-bones coming through your clothes.'

Herman Melville, *Moby Dick*

♡ ⊕ SMOKY FISH CHOWDER

Makes 4 pts/2.5 l

Serve as a main dish, with a big mixed green salad dressed with balsamic vinegar and plenty of crusty bread.

---

1 large onion, coarsely chopped
1⅕ pts/720 ml fish stock
2 fl oz/60 ml dry white wine
1 pt/600 ml skimmed milk
3 medium all-purpose potatoes,
*   steamed until almost tender,*
*   peeled and coarsely diced*
1 lb/480 g firm white fish fillets,
*   skinned and cut into*
*   1-inch/2.5-cm cubes*

1 lb/480 g smoked haddock,
*   skinned, boned and cut into*
*   1-inch/2.5-cm, cubes (use*
*   smoked haddock that has*
*   not been dyed)*
6 oz/180 g peeled, cooked, tiny
*   prawns*
Freshly ground pepper to taste
Freshly chopped parsley

---

1   Combine onion, ⅕ pt/120 ml stock and wine in a heavy-bottomed large pan. Cover and bring to the boil. Boil for 5 minutes. Uncover and boil until the onions are meltingly tender and beginning to brown.
2   Stir in remaining stock and milk. Bring to a simmer. Add potatoes and simmer gently for 3–5 minutes.
3   Stir in fish cubes. Barely simmer gently for 2–3 minutes. Stir in prawns and let heat through. Season with pepper and serve at once, sprinkled with fresh parsley.

♡ ❄ CALIFORNIA-STYLE CIOPPINO

Makes 5½ pts/3.5 l

A fully-fledged cioppino would contain lobster and clams in addition to the fish and shellfish listed here, but this slightly abbreviated version is just as delectable. The dish may be prepared with fish fillets only, if you can't find, or don't want, the prawns and mussels.

2 large Spanish onions, chopped
Approximately 1 pt/600 ml chicken
  stock, fish stock, or a
  combination
1 green or yellow pepper, seeded,
  peeled and chopped
2 cloves garlic, crushed
2 tins (14 oz/420 g each) chopped
  tomatoes
2 tablespoons tomato paste
12 fl oz/360 ml dry white wine
Salt and freshly ground pepper to
  taste

4 lb/2 kg firm white fish fillets (use
  a combination; choose from cod,
  halibut, haddock, sole, etc.)
  skinned and cut into
  1-inch/2.5-cm cubes
1 lb/480 g medium-sized prawns,
  shelled and de-veined
16–18 large fresh mussels,
  thoroughly scrubbed and
  de-bearded
2 tablespoons chopped fresh parsley
Croûtons (see below)
Red Pepper and Garlic Spread (see
  page 303)

1   Combine onions and 10 fl oz/300 ml stock in a large, heavy, non-reactive flameproof casserole that can be covered. Cover and bring to the boil. Boil for 5 minutes. Uncover, stir in pepper and garlic, and boil until the stock is almost gone and the onions are beginning to brown.
2   Add the tomatoes, tomato paste, wine, 12 fl oz/360 ml stock, salt and pepper to taste. Simmer, partially covered, for 25 minutes.
3   Uncover and add the fish. Cover tightly and simmer very gently for 3 minutes.
4   Uncover and add the prawns, mussels and parsley. Cover tightly and gently simmer for 3–5 minutes more, or until the mussels open. Discard any mussels that do not open. Sprinkle with parsley. Serve from the casserole. Pass Croûtons spread with the Red Pepper and Garlic Spread.

Croûtons

Slice a French baguette. Bake the slices on the oven rack at 300° F, 150° C, Gas Mark 2, until dried through but not browned.

Note: Leftovers reheat very successfully in the microwave.

🕐 Omit mussels – they seem to take forever to clean!

Meat

'Vegetables are interesting, but lack a sense of purpose when unaccompanied by a good cut of meat.'

Fran Lebowitz, *Metropolitan Life*

There is no need to cut out red meat, in fact it is wise not to. Meat is an excellent source of nutrition: high-quality protein, B vitamins, zinc and other important trace minerals, iron and more. In fact, the iron from meat is absorbed more readily into the body than the iron in any other foodstuff or iron supplement. Of course, meat is also a source of fat, much of it (although not all of it) saturated. So the trick is to eliminate as much of that fat as possible.

Here are the guidelines:

1 Buy the leanest meat possible. Goose skirt for instance, a paddle-shaped flat steak, is extremely lean and makes a wonderfully satisfying steak dinner. Beef fillet steak is lean, as is pork tenderloin. Always trim away all visible fat before cooking.

2 Rethink the *amount* of meat you eat at one meal. Serve plenty of vegetables and grains with smaller portions of meat. Do as the Chinese do, and make meat more of an accent than a main event. And there is certainly no need to eat meat every day. Eat poultry, fish, dairy and vegetarian meals as well.

3 Mince is a great favourite of mine. Some of the most comforting and delicious dishes in the world – meatballs, bolognese sauce, shepherd's pie, chilli con carne – are made with mince. Always buy *very* lean mince, whether it is beef, pork, lamb or

123

veal. The ideal is to buy a piece of extremely lean meat from the butcher and have him mince it.

4   Never brown mince in added fat. Use a non-stick frying pan and let it brown in its own juices. Then drain it very well in a colander. Even very lean meat will have rendered plenty of fat. After draining it well, spread it out on paper towels, cover with more paper towels, and blot. Blot out the frying pan. Then, when all possible fat has been removed, return the meat to the pan and proceed with the recipe.

5   Stews are disastrous when made from very lean meat. Use beef chuck, rump skirt or flank end brisket (see below), and trim off surrounding fat. Never brown the meat cubes in fat or oil when beginning a stew. Simply combine the ingredients and braise slowly and gently. During stewing, the meat cubes will have released lots of fat. Refrigerate the stew overnight, or quick chill the juices in the freezer. The fat will rise to the top and harden. Scrape off every speck and discard it.

Befriend Your Butcher

My sincere advice is to make friends with your butcher, although it can get out of hand. In Atlanta, Georgia, where I once lived, I looked a new butcher straight in the eye, smiled my sweetest smile, and asked a few earnest questions about beef brisket. Later, walking back to the car, there was the new butcher; he had flung off his apron and followed me to the car park. It was my fattest time, 15½ quivering stones (much too fat to squeeze my wedding ring on to my finger), and the butcher, riveted by my sincere gaze and thinking I was unattached and vastly beautiful, asked me out. Alas, it was a professional relationship I was after, to be conducted over the counter, involving learned exchanges about brisket, flank and tenderloin, resulting in the butcher tenderly wrapping choice cuts for my family's evening meal.

But still – it pays to court your butcher's good will. There are several cuts of beef not readily available at the supermarket that you should ask him to supply regularly for you.

1   **Goose skirt steak** (sometimes called flank skirt). A flat, *lean*, paddle-shaped, deeply flavoured cut of meat, perfect for grilling or pan frying.

2   **Rump skirt steak**. A fibrous, rich-in-gelatine cut, that makes excellent full-flavoured stews with copious juices.

3   **Brisket**. The butcher will have plenty of these, but for your purposes it must be cut as follows:

(a) boned;
(b) the point end separated from the smaller flank end and both pieces mercilessly trimmed of *every* scrap of fat. No matter how earnestly you explain this and how sincere your gaze, the butcher will not trim off enough fat. You will still need to do some additional trimming when you get home. The point end of the brisket makes a superb braised joint and the flank end is excellent cut into cubes and stewed.

❄ BRAISED BRISKET OF BEEF

Serves 6–8

Perfect for Sunday lunch. Make it ahead of time, and then devote yourself to the vegetables on the day. The gravy is spectacularly rich and deeply flavoured, and the meat is buttery tender. I'll wager that you have never tasted a joint of meat to rival this one for tenderness and flavour. See above for advice on buying and cooking brisket.

---

1 point cut brisket (about 4 lb/ 1.92 kg) trimmed of all fat
8 fl oz/240 ml beef or chicken stock
2 large Spanish onions, halved and sliced into thin half-moons
4 fl oz/120 ml red wine
2 fl oz/60 ml brandy
2 fl oz/60 ml tomato paste

Approximately 2 tablespoons sun-dried tomatoes, chopped (optional)
Salt and freshly ground pepper to taste
4 large garlic cloves, peeled and left whole
2 carrots, peeled and sliced
1 stalk celery with leaves, sliced
3 sprigs parsley

---

1   Preheat oven to 350° F, 180° C, Gas Mark 4.
2   In a large non-stick frying pan sear the brisket on both sides. When the meat is browned on both sides, put it on a plate and loosely cover it with foil.
3   Pour any fat drippings out of the frying pan and blot the pan with paper towels, but do not wipe off the browned bits. Pour 4 fl oz/120 ml stock into the frying pan. Add the onion. Cover and boil for 4–5 minutes. Uncover, turn down the heat and cook gently. When it is browned and almost tender, pour in the wine and brandy. Boil, scraping the pan with a wooden spoon to release all the browned bits. When the brandy has

cooked away, stir in the tomato paste and optional sun-dried tomatoes. Season with a bit of salt and freshly ground pepper. Scrape the mixture into a 9 × 13 × 2-inch/23 × 33 × 5-cm baking pan. Pour the remaining stock over the onion.

4   Season the meat on both sides with salt and pepper. Place the meat on the onion. Pour in any meat juices that have accumulated on the plate. Tuck the garlic, carrot and celery slices, and parsley around the meat. Cover the baking pan tightly with heavy-duty aluminium foil, shiny side down.

5   Place the baking dish in the oven for 1 hour. Reduce the oven temperature to 250° F, 120° C, Gas Mark 1, and bake for an additional 2–2½ hours, or until very tender.

6   When tender, remove the meat to a plate and cover to prevent it drying out. Let cool. Discard the parsley and celery. Pour the pan juices and remaining vegetables into a jug, add any juices that have accumulated under the meat, cool and refrigerate. When the meat has cooled, wrap well in cling film and refrigerate.

7   On the next day, skim any fat from the juices in the jug. Purée the vegetables and juices in the liquidizer. Then rub the purée through a sieve.

8   With a sharp carving knife, slice the meat thinly against the grain and arrange in a baking dish. Pour and spread some of the puréed sauce over the slices. Cover and refrigerate until serving time. To serve, reheat, covered, for 35–40 minutes in the oven at 325° F, 160° C, Gas Mark 3. Reheat the remaining puréed sauce in a saucepan and serve in a gravy boat.

❄ BEEF STEW

Makes 3½ pts/2.1 l

A good beef stew cannot be made with extra-lean meat. In the finished stew, cubes of such meat will be as dry as dust. Choose well-marbled slabs of chuck steak, rump skirt steak, or flank end brisket. This recipe shows you how to use the fat marbling in the meat to advantage. As the stew braises, the fat and the gelatine melt out of the meat leaving it very tender. Then all of the fat rendered from the meat is meticulously removed, leaving a rich, but low-fat gravy. I sent samples of this stew to a laboratory for analysis, to assure myself that the fat really was eliminated. Raw chuck braising steak contains 9.4 per cent fat, the finished recipe only 1.75!

3 lb/1,440 g very well trimmed chuck steak, rump skirt or flank end brisket, cut into ¾-inch/ 1.85-cm cubes
½ teaspoon dried thyme
1 bay leaf, crumbled
2 fl oz/60 ml brandy
12 fl oz/360 ml red wine
2 cloves garlic, crushed
16 fl oz/480 ml beef stock
3 carrots, peeled and sliced
3 onions, cut in half and sliced into thin half-moons

1 medium floury potato, peeled and cut into ½ inch/1.25 cm dice (King Edward potatoes work well here)
Salt and freshly ground pepper to taste
1 lb/480 g button mushrooms, quartered
4 fl oz/120 ml red wine
4 fl oz/120 ml chicken stock
1 tablespoon soy sauce

1   Combine the beef, thyme, bay leaf, brandy, wine and garlic in a plastic bag and close tightly. Allow to marinade for at least an hour, turning the bag occasionally. If you wish, refrigerate and leave overnight.

2   Preheat oven to 350° F, 180° C, Gas Mark 4.

3   Strain the marinade into a saucepan. Add beef stock. Boil until reduced by about ⅓. Skim off all foam and scum as it boils.

4   Combine the beef, carrots, onions, potato, salt and pepper in a heavy, non-reactive casserole. Cover tightly and bake for 2½ hours or until the beef is tender. Adjust the oven temperature down during the cooking time to maintain a gentle simmer. It must not boil.

5   Dump the stew into a sieve set over a large bowl. Cover the meat and vegetables well so that they do not dry out. Pour the juices into a glass jug and place in the freezer.

6   Put the mushrooms, wine, stock and soy sauce in a non-stick frying pan. Simmer until the mushrooms are almost tender and the liquid greatly reduced. Season to taste.

7   When the stew juices in the freezer are thoroughly chilled, the fat will have risen to the top and congealed on the surface. Scrape off and discard every bit of the fat. In the stew pot combine the defatted juices and the mushrooms with their juice. Bring to a boil. Stir in the meat and vegetables. Simmer for a few minutes for the flavours to blend.

8   Mash a few potato pieces against the side of the pot and then stir. The crushed potatoes will thicken the stew. Taste and adjust the seasonings to your liking. The stew may be refrigerated for a day or two before serving. The flavour improves.

❄ BEEF IN RED WINE

Makes 3½ pts/1.8 l

This is a simplified, low-fat, drastically Calorie-reduced version of *boeuf bourguignonne*.

---

3 large Spanish onions, chopped
18 fl oz/540 ml chicken stock
6 fl oz/180 ml dry red wine
1 lb/480 g mushrooms, quartered
Several dashes of soy sauce
½ teaspoon dried thyme
½ teaspoon dried tarragon

3 lb/1,440 g very well trimmed
   chuck steak, rump skirt or flank
   end brisket, cut in ¾-inch/
   1.9-cm cubes
1 tablespoon tomato paste
Salt and freshly ground pepper to
   taste
6 cloves garlic, halved

---

1   Preheat the oven to 350° F, 180° C, Gas Mark 4.
2   Combine onions and 12 fl oz/360 ml stock in a heavy non-reactive frying pan. Cover and boil for about 5 minutes. Uncover and simmer briskly until tender, browned, thick and syrupy. Raise the heat, pour in 2 fl oz/60 ml wine and boil until the alcohol has evaporated and the onions are a deep amber brown. Purée half the mixture. Combine puréed and unpuréed mixture. Set aside.
3   Combine the mushrooms, 6 fl oz/180 ml stock, 4 fl oz/120 ml wine, soy sauce and herbs in a heavy, non-reactive frying pan. Simmer briskly, stirring occasionally, until the mushrooms are tender and the liquid just about absorbed. Do not let the mushrooms scorch.
4   Combine the meat cubes with the mushrooms and onions in a baking dish. Add tomato paste, salt and pepper, and stir so that everything is well combined. Bury the garlic pieces in the stew. Bake in the oven, covered, for ½ an hour. Lower the heat to 300° F, 150° C, Gas Mark 2, and cook for another 2–2½ hours, or until the meat is very tender. Adjust oven temperature down if necessary, to keep stew at a very gentle simmer.
5   Drain, saving the juices. Cover the meat well to prevent it drying out. Chill the juices in the freezer until the fat rises to the top and hardens. Discard fat. Recombine meat and juices. Refrigerate or freeze until needed.

❄ BEEF CURRY

Makes 2½ pts/1.5 l

The thick curry sauce that blankets the beef comes from an onion spice purée; it has a rich texture and deep taste, although it contains no fat. The method is very unconventional, but the result is very curry-like.

---

3 large onions, coarsely chopped
Approximately 1 pt/600 ml chicken stock
1 teaspoon fresh ginger root, peeled and minced
2 cloves garlic, minced
1 teaspoon each: ground cumin, ground coriander, ground turmeric, sweet paprika or paprika paste, mild chilli powder

¼–½ teaspoon ground cayenne pepper
3 lb/1.5 kg very well trimmed rump skirt, or flank end brisket (see page 124), cut into ¾-inch/2-cm cubes
1 tablespoon tomato paste
Salt and freshly ground pepper to taste
1 teaspoon garam masala

---

1 Preheat the oven to 350° F, 180° C, Gas Mark 4.
2 Separate the segments of the onion pieces and spread them in a heavy frying pan. (Do *not* use a non-stick pan.) Add *no* liquid or fat. Heat the frying pan gently. Cook at moderate heat, without stirring, until the onions are sizzling and beginning to stick to the pan.
3 Stir in 10 fl oz/300 ml of stock and let it bubble up. Stir in the ginger, garlic and spices. Turn the heat down a bit and simmer, stirring frequently, until the mixture is very thick (not at all soupy), and the onions and spices are 'frying' in their own juices. Don't rush this step, it is essential that the spices should not have a raw harsh taste. Cook very gently for a few more minutes.
4 Scrape half of the onion-spice mixture into the container of the liquidizer. Purée. Pour the purée into a baking dish.
5 Stir in the unpuréed onion-spice mixture, the beef and tomato paste. Season to taste with salt and pepper.
6 Cover tightly and bake for 2–2½ hours until the meat is very tender. Adjust the oven temperature down during the cooking time to maintain a gentle simmer. It must not boil.
7 Dump the curry into a sieve or colander, over a large bowl. Put the meat into a bowl and cover well so that it does not dry out. Pour the juices into a glass jug. Chill overnight. The fat will rise to the surface and congeal. Discard every speck of fat.
8 Recombine meat and juices. Stir in garam masala. Simmer for 10–15 minutes. Serve with Basmati rice, Herb Sauce (use

coriander, page 285), a selection of vegetables and Curried Roast Potatoes.

✳ **STUFATINO**

Makes 2½ pts/1.5 l

Use a good wine (the alcohol cooks away) and you will have a rich, fragrant and satisfying Italian beef stew with quantities of gorgeous juices. I once served this to 180 ravenous obesity scientists at an obesity conference at Downing College in Cambridge. In their enthusiasm for this dish and other Slim Cuisine delicacies that my staff and I set on the buffet table, they almost devoured the casserole dishes and tablecloth as well. *No one* puts away prodigious quantities of food the way obesity scientists do.

---

2 onions, cut in half and sliced into
   thin half-moons
12 fl oz/360 ml stock
3 lb/1.5 kg well-trimmed rump
   skirt, or flank end brisket (see
   page 124), cut into
   1½-inch/4-cm cubes

4 cloves garlic, peeled but left whole
½ teaspoon dried rosemary
½ teaspoon dried marjoram
Salt and pepper to taste
2 tablespoons tomato paste
8 fl oz/240 ml Italian dry red wine

---

1   Preheat the oven to 300° F, 150° C, Gas Mark 2.
2   Combine onions and stock in an 8-inch/20-cm frying pan. Cover and bring to the boil. Boil for 5 minutes. Uncover. Reduce heat and simmer briskly until just about dry and beginning to stick a little bit.
3   Lower the heat. Toss and stir constantly with a wooden spoon until you smell a lovely, toasty, oniony aroma and the bottom of the pan is beginning to brown just a bit. Pour in a splash of dry wine or additional stock and turn the heat up again. Stir with the wooden spoon, scraping up all the browned bits.
4   Stir in beef, garlic, seasonings, tomato paste and wine. Add stock, if necessary, to just barely cover the contents of the pot. Cover tightly and cook in the oven for 2–3 hours until the meat is fork tender. Adjust the oven temperature down during this time so that the contents of the pot remain at a gentle simmer.
5   Dump the meat into a colander over a bowl. Pour the drained juices into a large jug. Put the meat into a bowl. Cover the meat and the jug and refrigerate overnight.
6   Next day, scrape off congealed fat from the juices in the jug.

Recombine the meat and juices. Reheat gently and serve with pasta, Polenta (page 215), or Mashed Potatoes (page 279).

❄ STEFADO OF BEEF

Makes approx 3 pts/2 l

Stefado of beef is the Greek entry into the beef stew sweepstakes. It has a beautiful balance of sweet and sour.

---

3 lb/1.5 kg well-trimmed rump skirt, or flank end brisket (page 124), cut into 1-inch/2.5-cm cubes	*1 teaspoon oregano, crumbled*
	1 teaspoon ground cinnamon
	1 teaspoon ground cumin
	½ teaspoon sugar
Approximately 3 tablespoons tomato paste	*4 fl oz/120 ml dry white wine*
	4 fl oz/120 ml red wine vinegar
2 tablespoons freshly chopped parsley	*24 tiny boiling onions, peeled*
	2 tablespoons additional freshly chopped parsley
Salt and pepper to taste	
1 bay leaf	

---

1   Preheat oven to 300° F, 150° C, Gas Mark 2.
2   Combine all ingredients except additional parsley. Mix very well.
3   Place in a heavy pot that can be covered. Cover tightly and simmer for 2 hours or until the meat is very tender, and the onions have almost disintegrated. Adjust oven temperature during cooking time so contents of pot remain at a simmer. Do not let it boil.
4   When tender, cool and refrigerate. Next day, discard congealed fat and reheat gently. Serve in a deep dish, garnished with parsley. Serve with rice, Wheat Pilaf (page 280), or Roast Potatoes (page 277).

❄ BEEF GOULASH

Makes 4½ pts/2.7 l

This is my family's favourite beef dish. I always have it in the freezer in individual servings. As you comfort yourself with this soul-warming stew, mull over the fact that peppers (including paprika), tomatoes and potatoes, those staples of Hungarian cookery, were gifts of the New World and did not hit Hungary until the Turks invaded, which is not that long ago in historic terms. The Magyars knew nothing about such ingredients.

131

5 large onions, peeled and coarsely chopped	3 cloves garlic, minced
12 fl oz/360 ml stock	3 lb/1.5 kg well-trimmed rump skirt, or flank end brisket (see page 124), cut into 1-inch/2.5-cm cubes
1½ tablespoons Hungarian paprika or Hungarian paprika paste	
2 large peppers (1 green, 1 yellow if possible), peeled and coarsely chopped	Salt and freshly ground pepper to taste
	3 heaped tablespoons tomato paste

1   Preheat oven to 350° F, 180° C, Gas Mark 4.
2   Combine onions and stock in a non-reactive flameproof casserole that can be covered. Cover and bring to the boil. Boil for 5 minutes. Uncover. Reduce heat and simmer briskly, stirring occasionally, until almost dry and beginning to brown a bit. Stir in paprika. Stir for a few seconds over *low* heat.
3   Add remaining ingredients, and stir well to combine. Place in oven and simmer for 2–3 hours, until the meat is very tender, in a savoury thick sauce. Cool and then refrigerate overnight. The next day, skim off fat. Serve the goulash in shallow soup plates. Serve Mashed Potatoes (page 279) or Roast Potatoes (page 277) on the side.

PEPPERED STEAK WITH MUSHROOM SAUCE

Serves 6

Goose skirt cooked this way is a snap to prepare, and can be served up in less than 30 minutes. Have the onions and mushrooms cooking in separate frying pans, then cook the steak. If you are in the habit of keeping Slim Cuisine Sautéed Mushrooms and 'Fried' Onions in the freezer, the job gets even easier. Any leftovers make one of the best sandwiches you have ever eaten. (Spread the bread with New York Deli Mustard, page 305.)

1 goose skirt steak, approximately 1½ lb/720 g	2 tablespoons chopped parsley
Freshly ground pepper to taste	Pinch or two of crumbled dried tarragon
Salt to taste	1 garlic clove, crushed
6 fl oz/180 ml red wine	Sautéed Mushrooms (page 29)
3 spring onions, trimmed and thinly sliced	'Fried' Onions (page 25)

1   Grind pepper over both sides of the meat and press it in. Let stand for 15 minutes.

2   Heat a heavy non-stick frying pan until moderately hot. Sear the meat on both sides. Use tongs to turn the meat.

3   Reduce the heat a bit and cook for 3–4 minutes on each side, until it feels springy, not mushy, when poked with your finger. Salt lightly on both sides. Remove to a warm plate, cover loosely with foil and keep warm.

4   Pour wine into the hot frying pan. While it fumes and sizzles, scrape up the brown bits with a wooden spoon or spatula. Stir in spring onions, herbs and garlic. When reduced and syrupy, stir in the Sautéed Mushrooms and their juices.

5   Pour in any juices that have accumulated under the steak. Slice the steak, thinly, against the grain.

6   Put a bed of 'Fried' Onions on a plate. Overlap the steak slices on the onions. Top with the mushroom sauce.

Goose Skirt Steak

Talk to your butcher. Smile at him. Reason with him. Ask him, most politely, to save the goose skirts for you. What a remarkable cut of meat: extremely lean, deeply flavourful, economical, and – if you cook it rare or medium-rare – very tender. Grill goose skirt or pan-sauté it without fat. Let it rest for 5–10 minutes for the juices to redistribute and then slice it thin, against the grain. Goose skirt satisfies steak cravings without guilt, and because of the way it is served – sliced thin and lavished with sautéed mushrooms or onions or a Slim Cuisine sauce – a little goes a long way.

GRILLED GOOSE SKIRT
STEAK

Serves 6

Goose skirt is the perfect cut of meat for outdoor grilling. On a charcoal grill it cooks in no time at all and feeds a lot of people happily on an economical amount of meat. One goose skirt (1½–2 lb/720–960 g) will feed six people or more, depending on the accompaniments. For a barbecue, marinate the steak (see marinade below). Depending on the intensity of flavour you want, marinate from 1 to 24 hours.

     Line your hibachi or charcoal grill with foil, shiny side up. This makes cleaning up easier and reflects heat. Never use a chemical starter on the charcoal; it will impart a revolting flavour to the meat. Use spills made from rolled-up paper. Start your fire at least 30 minutes before cooking time, and do not begin to cook until you have a good bed of glowing coals covered with a bed of white ash, and *no* flames.

Use tongs to turn the meat on the grill; a fork would make holes that allow delicious juices to drip away. A goose skirt steak should be cooked rare (red inside) or medium rare (pink) or it will not be tender. Make sure the meat is at room temperature, then cook it 4–5 minutes on each side for rare, 5–6 for medium rare. To check for doneness, poke it in the centre with your finger. If it feels very *soft* and mushy it is very rare, almost raw in fact. The firmer it gets, the more done. When it feels firmish but springy it is medium rare. As the steak cooks, brush it with marinade. If you just like the taste of good meat, don't bother with marinade, simply cover the steak with a good coating of freshly ground peppercorns.

When the meat is done, let it rest for 3 minutes, then slice it thinly, with a sharp knife, diagonally against the grain. Serve it with Browned Onions and New York Deli Mustard (page 305).

Marinade for Goose Skirt

3 tablespoons soy sauce	Salt and freshly ground pepper to
4 tablespoons lemon juice	taste
6 tablespoons tomato paste	3 tablespoons water
Pinch sugar	

'Four rare steaks please and hurry. We haven't eaten in five hundred and seventy-six thousand million years.'

Douglas Adams, *The Restaurant at the End of the Universe*

FIVE SPICE STEAK

Serves 6

Five spice powder is a fragrant Chinese mix of spices. Many supermarkets now stock it, but if you can't find it make your own with equal parts of ground cinnamon, fennel, star anise, cloves and ginger.

1 tablespoon ginger root, coarsely chopped	2 fl oz/60 ml reduced-salt Worcestershire sauce
4 large garlic cloves	½ tablespoon sugar
1½ teaspoons five spice powder	1 strip (3-inch/8-cm × 1-inch/ 2.5-cm) orange zest
16 fl oz/480 ml water	
4 fl oz/120 ml sherry	1 goose skirt steak (approx. 1 lb/ 480 g)

1   In a non-reactive pan, simmer all ingredients except steak for 15 minutes.
2   Put the steak in a shallow, non-reactive dish and pour marinade over it. Marinate for ½ hour or more, turning occasionally.
3   Preheat grill to highest setting. Cook steak 3 inches/7.6 cms from heat for 4–5 minutes each side (for rare).
4   Let meat rest for 3–4 minutes. Slice thinly against the grain and serve.

PEPPERED STEAK WITH SPICY MUSHROOM SAUCE

Serves 6

A zesty preparation for goose skirt. The mushroom sauce has echoes of both Mexico and New Orleans.

---

1 goose skirt	½ teaspoon dried oregano, crumbled
Freshly ground pepper to taste	2 tinned plum tomatoes, drained and chopped
Salt to taste	
1 medium onion, finely chopped	1 pt/600 ml stock
1 small carrot, finely chopped	Dash soy sauce
2 cloves garlic, minced	1 bay leaf
1 small stalk celery, finely chopped	½ lb/240 g mushrooms, quartered
1 tin (4 oz) mild green chillies, chopped (save the juices)	2–3 tablespoons fresh parsley, chopped

---

1   Grind pepper over both sides of the meat and press it in. Let stand for 15 minutes.
2   Heat a heavy, non-stick frying pan until moderately hot. Sear the meat on both sides. Use tongs to turn the meat.
3   Reduce heat a bit and cook for 3–4 minutes on each side. Salt lightly on both sides. Remove to a warm platter, cover loosely with foil, and keep warm.
4   Add the onion, carrot, garlic, celery, chillies, 1 teaspoon of chilli juice, oregano, tomatoes, half the stock, soy sauce, bay leaf and mushrooms to the pan. Boil, stirring and scraping the bottom of the pan until the vegetables are tender and the liquid greatly reduced. Add remaining stock. Bring to the boil and boil for 1 minute.
5   Return the meat and its accumulated meat juices to the pan and simmer, turning the beef with tongs as it cooks, for 1–2 minutes, to heat it through and cook it to your liking. To be tender the beef must remain rare, or medium rare.

6   Taste and adjust seasonings, adding a bit of salt if necessary or an extra dash of soy sauce. Discard the bay leaf. Slice the meat thinly against the grain and arrange on a warm platter. Pour the sauce over and serve at once.

Variations:

Sauté the steak (Steps 1–3) until rare or medium rare and then try one of the following:

STEAK AND MUSHROOMS

Serve the sautéed steak simply, with Sautéed Mushrooms (see page 29). Sauté the mushrooms in the pan in which you have cooked the beef.

STEAK PIZZAIOLA

Serve the sautéed steak with Tomato Sauce (see page 236).

STEAK WITH GARLIC-WINE SAUCE

When the steak has been sautéed, keep it warm. In the steak pan, boil 5 fl oz/150 ml each red wine and stock until reduced and syrupy. Add some dried crumbled thyme and tarragon if you like it. Stir in the purée of 1 head of baked garlic (see page 32). Season with salt, pepper and thyme. Slice the meat and pour the sauce over.

STEAK AND ONIONS

The eternal classic – serve the sautéed, sliced steak with Sweet and Sour Onions (see page 29) or Browned Onions (see page 26).

STUFFED GOOSE SKIRT STEAK

Serves 4

This looks like a conventional roasted joint of meat but, when sliced, reveals a beautiful pinwheel of vivid green spinach. It is also good served cold or at room temperature. Leftovers are delicious in sandwiches, with a bit of the cold sauce spread on bread.

16 fl oz/480 ml dry red wine
Juice and grated rind of ½ lemon
2 fl oz/60 ml reduced-salt
  Worcestershire sauce
1 dried bay leaf
4 cloves garlic, crushed
1 teaspoon fresh ginger, grated

1 goose skirt steak (approx. 1 lb/
  450 g) trimmed of any fat
1½ lb/675 g fresh spinach
Freshly ground pepper to taste
1 large Spanish onion, cut in half
  and sliced into thin half-moons

1 Preheat oven to 475° F, 240° C, Gas Mark 9.
2 Combine dry red wine, lemon juice and rind, Worcestershire sauce, bay leaf, garlic and ginger in a wide, shallow non-reactive dish.
3 Butterfly the steak as follows: slit it down the long end with a very sharp knife; cut it very carefully almost all the way through until you can open it flat like a book. Or better yet, have the butcher do this for you.
4 Marinade the steak in the wine mixture while you prepare the spinach. Wash the spinach well, stem it and tear it into shreds. Put it in a non-reactive saucepan, and stir it over moderate heat, until limp, but still bright green and fresh tasting. (It will cook in the water clinging to its leaves.) Drain well. Stir in 3 tablespoons of the marinade.
5 Remove steak from the marinade. Pour the marinade into a saucepan and boil until reduced by half.
6 Open out the skirt steak. Spread the spinach over the surface to within 1 inch/2.5 cm of the edges. Starting from a long edge, roll the beef like a swiss roll, into a long sausage-like shape. Tie the roll securely crosswise in several places with kitchen string.
7 Place the beef roll on a rack in a non-reactive baking pan that can be used on top of the stove as well as in the oven. Sprinkle it with a bit of salt and a generous amount of pepper. Scatter in the onion slices. Pour in the marinade. Roast for 10 minutes. Turn it after the first 5 minutes.
8 Reduce oven temperature to 350° F, 180° C, Gas Mark 4. Roast for 20 minutes more, turning it half-way through the roasting time.
9 Remove from oven. Put the beef on a platter, cover loosely with foil, and let rest for 15 minutes. Place the baking dish on the stove. Bring the pan juices to a boil. Boil until liquid is dark brown, thick and syrupy. Remove from the heat. Stir in any meat juices that have accumulated under the meat roll.
10 Remove and discard the string. Slice the meat thinly and serve, with the pan juices and the onion.

'To be put into the grave without ever enjoying a mouthful of good meat is inhuman.'

Bertolt Brecht, trans. Lee Baxendell, *To Eat of Meat Joyously*

CHINESE BEEF WITH ONIONS

Makes 1½ pts/900 ml

Switching to Slim Cuisine means ditching sesame oil, peanut oil and all the other oily essentials of Chinese cuisine. I was delighted to discover that stir-'frying' in stock can produce a very Chinese-tasting dish. As with most Chinese cookery, have everything diced, measured, sliced, crushed, etc., and laid out in logical order on your work surface. At the last minute, stir-fry furiously and serve at once.

---

1 goose skirt steak (about 1¼ lb/ 600 g), well trimmed
2 tablespoons teriyaki sauce
2 tablespoons dry sherry
1 tablespoon cornflour
2 thin slices peeled ginger root, minced

Approximately 8 fl oz/240 ml stock
1 large Spanish onion, cut in half and sliced into half-moons
2 cloves garlic, crushed
Chopped fresh parsley and coriander for garnish

---

1   With a very sharp carving knife, slice the steak on the diagonal, against the grain, into slices that are as thin as you can manage. Whisk together the teriyaki sauce, sherry and cornflour until the cornflour is dissolved. In a large bowl, with two spoons, toss the cornflour mixture with the beef, until the strips are well coated. Cover and set aside at room temperature for an hour.

2   Heat a large non-stick wok or frying pan. Pour in 2 fl oz/60 ml stock. When it boils furiously, dump in the meat. With two wooden paddles, constantly toss and turn the meat. Use the paddles to pull apart the strips as they cook. When they have lost their red raw look (about 2 minutes) scoop on to a plate. Cover loosely with foil and set aside.

3   Immediately pour 4 fl oz/120 ml of stock into the wok along with the onions and garlic. Stir once, cover and cook over high heat for 5 minutes. Uncover. Stir and cook over high heat until the onions are tender and surrounded by a scant, thick sauce.

4   Return the beef to the wok along with the meat juices that have accumulated. Season with a bit of salt if necessary. Stir together to mingle and heat through, about 1 minute. Heap on

to a plate and sprinkle with herbs. Serve at once, with steamed rice or Wheat Pilaf (page 280), Savoury Peppers (page 256) and Spicy Sprouts (page 257).

CHINESE BEEF WITH MUSHROOMS

Makes 1½ pts/900 ml

This is a variation on the previous recipe, with the added allure of the intense smoky taste of reconstituted dried Chinese mushrooms. The mushrooms are available in Chinese groceries and some supermarkets and delicatessens.

---

1 oz/30 g dried Chinese mushrooms
1 pt/600 ml warm water
1 goose skirt steak (about 1¼ lb/600 g)
2 tablespoons teriyaki sauce
2 tablespoons dry sherry
1 tablespoon cornflour
Approximately 8 fl oz/240 ml stock

1 fl oz/30 ml sherry
¼ lb/120 g button mushrooms, quartered
1 bunch (about 10) thin spring onions, trimmed and cut into 1½-inch/4-cm pieces
Chopped fresh parsley and coriander for garnish

---

1   Place mushrooms in a bowl. Pour on the warm water and let them soak for ½–1 hour. Drain through a coffee filter, reserving the liquid. Rinse the mushrooms under cold running water. Squeeze dry. Trim off and discard the stems, and cut each mushroom in half.

2   With a very sharp carving knife, slice the steak on the diagonal, against the grain, into slices that are as thin as you can manage. Whisk together the teriyaki sauce, sherry and cornflour until the cornflour is dissolved. In a large bowl, with two wooden spoons, toss the cornflour mixture with the beef, until the strips are well coated. Cover and set aside at room temperature for 1 hour.

3   Heat a large non-stick wok or frying pan. Pour in 2 fl oz/60 ml stock. When it boils furiously, dump in the meat. With two wooden paddles constantly toss and turn the meat. Use the paddles to pull apart the strips as they cook. When they have lost their red raw look (about 2 minutes) scoop on to a plate. Cover loosely with foil and set aside.

4   Immediately pour 2 fl oz/60 ml stock, 2 fl oz/60 ml of the mushroom liquid and 1 fl oz/30 ml sherry into the wok. Dump in the Chinese mushrooms and the button mushrooms. Stir and cook over high heat until the mushrooms are surrounded by a scant, thick sauce. Stir in the spring onions and cook for another 30–40 seconds.

5   Return the beef to the wok along with the meat juices that have accumulated. Season with a bit of salt if necessary. Stir together to mingle and heat through, about 1 minute. Heap on to a plate and sprinkle with herbs. Serve at once with rice or Wheat Pilaf (page 280).

BEEFSTEAK ON A BED OF ONIONS WITH RED PEPPER SAUCE

Serves 4

This is easy and spectacular; graphic proof that low-fat, low-Calorie food does not have to be dull and austere. Serve this to very special guests at a very special occasion. There is no need to babble about the low Calorie and fat levels. If you don't tell, no one will have an inkling that this is diet food.

---

8 centre-cut fillet steaks, each about ½ inch/1.25 cm thick
Freshly ground pepper
1 bunch trimmed, sliced spring onions
4 tablespoons fresh parsley, chopped

4 fl oz/120 ml dry red wine
1 batch Red Pepper Sauce (see page 233)
1 batch Browned Onions (see page 26), heated to sizzling point

---

1   Preheat the oven to 200° F, 100° C, Gas Mark 1.
2   Trim the steaks of any vestige of fat. Trim them into neat rounds.
3   Spread a sheet of greaseproof paper on your work surface. Sprinkle lavishly with freshly ground pepper. Place steaks on the paper. Grind lots more pepper on top of the steaks. Cover with another sheet of paper. With a kitchen mallet, gently pound the meat.
4   Heat a non-stick frying pan until hot. Place the steaks in the pan so that they are not touching each other. (Do in two batches if necessary.) Cook over high heat on one side for 2–3 minutes. Turn and cook on the second side for 2–3 minutes. At this point the steaks will be nicely browned on the outside and juicy and pink within. Remove with tongs to a platter and cover loosely with foil. Put them in the oven to keep warm.
5   Scrape the spring onions and parsley into the frying pan and pour in the wine. Boil, stirring and scraping with a wooden spatula to loosen all the browned bits, until almost all the liquid is gone. Reduce heat and stir in the red pepper sauce. Pour in any juices that have collected under the meat. Stir and cook for a few minutes.

140

6   Spread the browned onions out onto a warm platter. Overlap the steaks on the bed of onions. Pour a ribbon of pepper sauce down the length of the meat. Serve at once. Pass the rest of the sauce in a gravy boat.

Variations:

Use Pan-Sautéed Chicken Breasts (see page 172) or Steamed Fish Fillets (see page 118) instead of beef fillet.

Mince

I'd rather have mince than steak. When I'm hungry for 'home cooking', for something warm and comforting and evocative of happy childhood days, give me mince everytime. It's amazing the interesting things you can do with it. The following collection of recipes covers the UK, India, the USA, Italy, and the Middle East.

✳ ## CURRIED MINCE WITH POTATOES – KEEMA CURRY

Serves 6
179 Calories per serving
1.6 g fat
(Traditional keema curry: 448 Calories per serving, 28.8 g fat)

An Indian homestyle dish that sticks to the ribs. Make sure that your mince is very lean. Keema reheats well from both the refrigerator and the freezer. In fact, it improves with keeping.

---

2 medium onions cut into eighths	1 dried bay leaf, broken in half
20 fl oz/600 ml stock	1 green chilli, stemmed, seeded and
2 teaspoons fresh peeled ginger,	minced
minced	2 medium boiling potatoes, cut into
2 cloves garlic, minced	1-inch/2.5-cm dice
1 teaspoon ground cinnamon	3 tablespoons tomato paste
1 teaspoon ground coriander	Salt and freshly ground pepper to
Pinch ground cloves	taste
½ teaspoon cayenne pepper	1½ lb/720 g very lean minced beef
½ teaspoon ground allspice	1 tin (14 oz/420 g) chopped
6 whole green cardamom pods,	tomatoes
lightly crushed	1 teaspoon garam masala

---

1   Separate the segments of the onion pieces and spread them in a heavy, non-stick, frying pan. Add *no* liquid or fat. Heat the

141

frying pan gently. Cook at moderate heat, without stirring, for 7–10 minutes, until the onions are sizzling, speckled with dark amber, and beginning to stick to the pan.

2   Stir in 10 fl oz/300 ml of stock and let it bubble up, stirring up the browned deposits in the pan with a wooden spoon as it bubbles. Stir in the ginger, garlic, spices and chilli. Turn the heat down a bit and simmer, stirring frequently, until the mixture is very thick (not at all soupy), and the onions and spices are 'frying' in their own juices. Don't rush this step, as it is essential that the spices should not have a raw, harsh taste. Taste. Cook very gently for a few more minutes if necessary.

3   Toss the potatoes in the spice mixture until they are well coated. Stir in the tomato paste. Season to taste.

4   In another frying pan, cook the meat until it loses its red colour. Break it up with a wooden spoon as it cooks. Drain well in a colander. Spread out on paper towels and blot with more paper towels to eliminate even more fat. Stir the meat into the onion-potato mixture.

5   Stir in the remaining 10 oz/300 ml of stock and the tomatoes. Bring to the boil. Reduce heat and simmer briskly for about 30 minutes, uncovered, until the mixture is thick. Cover and simmer for 15 minutes more, until the potatoes are done. If at any time the mixture threatens to stick and burn stir in a bit more stock. Stir in the garam masala.

❄ CHILLI CON CARNE

Serves 6

This is a real Texas Chilli, with one difference – a real Texan would never stir the beans in with the meat, he would eat them on the side. If you wish, add chopped red, green and yellow peppers to the onions and spices in Step 2. It's not traditional, but it's good.

---

2 large onions, coarsely chopped
16 fl oz/480 ml stock
2 cloves garlic, crushed
2 tablespoons chilli powder
1 teaspoon ground cumin
1 teaspoon dried oregano, crumbled
1 teaspoon crushed chilli, optional
   (use depending on the strength
   of the chilli powder and your
   taste)

1½ lb/720 g very lean minced beef
4 tablespoons tomato paste
Salt and freshly ground pepper to
   taste
1 tin (15 oz/450 g) red kidney
   beans, drained and rinsed

---

1 Separate the segments of the onion pieces and spread them in a heavy, non-stick, frying pan. Add *no* liquid or fat. Heat the frying pan gently. Cook at moderate heat, without stirring, for 7–10 minutes, until the onions are sizzling, speckled with dark amber, and beginning to stick to the pan.

2 Stir in 10 fl oz/300 ml of stock and let it bubble up, stirring up the browned deposits in the pan with a wooden spoon as it bubbles. Stir in the garlic and spices. Turn the heat down a bit and simmer, stirring frequently, until the mixture is very thick (not at all soupy), and the onions and spices are 'frying' in their own juices. Don't rush this step, as it is essential that the spices should not have a raw, harsh taste. Taste. Cook very gently for a few more minutes if necessary.

3 In another non-stick frying pan, cook the meat until it loses its red colour. Break it up with a wooden spoon as it cooks. When the meat is thoroughly cooked, drain *very* well in a colander. Spread out on paper towels and blot with more paper towels to eliminate even more fat.

4 Combine the meat and the onion mixture. Stir in the tomato paste, the beans and enough remaining stock to just cover the contents of the pan. Add salt and pepper to taste. Bring to the simmer. Simmer, uncovered, until the mixture is thick, about ½ an hour.

⏲ ❄ BOLOGNESE SAUCE

Makes 2½ pts/1.5 l – serves 10
55 Calories per serving
0.4 g fat
(Traditional bolognese sauce: 208 Calories per serving, 16 g fat)

Everyone loves bolognese sauce. This version stretches a small amount of meat into a sumptuous amount of sauce. It's good on all types of pasta. Consider unusual shapes as well as the standard ones. My assistant served the sauce with couscous, and it was a wonderful combination. And at a buffet I attended, June Brown dispensed with pasta altogether and served it on a bed of braised carrot slices. Brilliant!

½ lb/226 g very lean minced beef
1 medium onion, chopped
2 large cloves of garlic, crushed
1 small red pepper, chopped
1 small yellow pepper, chopped

Salt and freshly ground pepper to taste
1 tablespoon chopped fresh oregano (¼ teaspoon dried)
1 tablespoon chopped fresh basil (¼ teaspoon dried)

*2 tins (1 lb/480 g each) chopped
     tomatoes
4 heaped tablespoons tomato paste
2-inch/5-cm piece of Parmesan
     cheese rind*

*½ lb/240 g button mushrooms,
     quartered
4 fl oz/120 ml dry red wine
4 fl oz/120 ml stock
Several dashes soy sauce*

1   Cook the beef and onion in a non-stick, heavy frying pan over
     medium heat. As it browns, break up any lumps with a
     wooden spoon. When the meat is almost browned, stir in the
     garlic and the peppers. Continue to stir and cook until the
     meat is completely cooked through and the onions are limp.
     Dump the mixture into a colander to drain away any fat.
     Spread it out on paper towels and blot with more paper
     towels. Return to the frying pan.
2   Add the chopped tomatoes, tomato paste, Parmesan rind,
     salt, pepper and herbs. Cover the frying pan and simmer for
     15 minutes.
3   Meanwhile, put the mushrooms, wine, stock and soy sauce
     into a non-reactive, non-stick heavy frying pan. Stir to com-
     bine everything very well. Simmer, stirring occasionally, until
     the liquid is almost gone. Let the mushrooms 'fry' gently in
     their own juices for a few moments. Do not let them scorch or
     stick. Add the mushrooms to the sauce.
4   Season the sauce to taste and simmer, partially covered, for
     approximately ten minutes more, until thick. The sauce may
     be refrigerated for a day or so or frozen. Serve with pasta, or as
     a filling for baked potatoes.

❄ SWEET AND SOUR STUFFED
CABBAGE

Makes approximately 20 cabbage rolls

Stuffed cabbage is always festive and heartwarming. Freezing the
cabbage first, then thawing it when needed, makes the cabbage
very easy to separate into individual leaves, and makes the leaves
flexible enough to wrap around the stuffing easily. The stuffing
and the sauce may be made a day or two in advance. Once
wrapped and in the oven, the cabbage rolls bake for 2 hours, but
totally unattended. As they bake, they fill the house with the
happiest of smells. Make the stuffed cabbage ahead of time and
refrigerate or freeze until needed. If you wish to cut the 2-hour
baking time short, steam the unstuffed cabbage leaves for about 3
minutes at the end of step 1. Then the stuffed rolls need to be baked

for only about 1 hour. But, personally, I'd rather have the ease of stuffing the leaves without the extra fiddling about of steaming.

1 large head frozen cabbage, thawed	*Stuffing (see below)*
(see note above)	*Tomato-Pepper Sauce (see below)*

1   Separate the cabbage into individual leaves. Place each leaf, curved side up, on your work surface. With a sharp paring knife, pare down the tough vein. Turn each leaf curved side down.

2   Fill each leaf with a tablespoon or so of stuffing. Fold the end over the stuffing, fold in the sides and roll into a neat parcel. Place each filled parcel in a baking dish, seam-side down. They should fill the dish in one layer.

3   Spread the sauce evenly over the cabbage rolls and let it run down the sides. The dish may be refrigerated at this point for a day or two.

4   Preheat oven to 350° F, 180° C, Gas Mark 4. Bake the cabbage, tightly covered, for 2 hours. Serve piping hot.

Stuffing

Makes 1½ pts/900 ml

1 large Spanish onion, chopped	*3 tablespoons tomato paste*
4 fl oz/120 ml red wine	*3 tablespoons sultanas soaked in*
1½ pts/900 ml stock	*2 fl oz/60 ml red wine*
1 yellow pepper, peeled and diced	*4 oz/120 g split red lentils, washed,*
½ teaspoon each dried tarragon,	*drained and picked over*
thyme and cinnamon	*½ lb/240 g very lean minced lamb,*
¼ teaspoon ground allspice	*sautéed, drained and blotted*
Pinch or 2 of ground cayenne	*Salt and freshly ground pepper to*
	taste

1   Spread the onion pieces in a large, heavy, non-reactive pan. Cook over high heat, without stirring, until they are sizzling and beginning to stick to the pan.

2   Pour in 4 fl oz/120 ml red wine. Boil, stirring and scraping up the browned bits in the pan, until the liquid is just about gone.

3   Add 3 fl oz/90 ml stock. Cover and boil for 5 minutes. Reduce heat. Stir in pepper. Pour in 2 fl oz/60 ml stock. Cover and simmer gently for 5–10 minutes.

4   Stir in the herbs, spices, tomato paste, sultanas and their wine, the lentils, the lamb and salt and pepper. Stir in 8 fl oz/240 ml stock. Cover and simmer for 20 minutes, uncovering to stir

occasionally. If it gets too dry and threatens to stick, add a bit more stock.

5 After 20 minutes, uncover and cook for 5–10 minutes more until the lentils are tender and the mixture is very thick.

Tomato-Pepper Sauce

Makes 2½ pts/1.5 l

---

2 red, 2 yellow peppers, grilled, peeled and coarsely chopped (substitute tinned red peppers if you are in a hurry)

12 ripe tomatoes, peeled, seeded, juiced and coarsely chopped (omit fresh tomatoes and increase the tinned tomatoes if you are in a hurry)

4 tins (14 oz/420 g each) chopped tomatoes

4 cloves garlic, minced

Salt and pepper to taste

Pinch of cayenne pepper

¼ teaspoon ground cumin

1 chilli pepper, minced (optional)

1½ tablespoons chopped fresh thyme

4 heaped tablespoons chopped parsley

1 tablesoon chopped fresh mint or basil

1 teaspoon fresh lemon or lime juice

½ teaspoon brown sugar

---

1 Combine all ingredients except herbs, citrus juice and sugar in a frying pan. Simmer uncovered for 30 minutes, until thickened.

2 Stir in fresh herbs, citrus juice and sugar. Simmer for 5 minutes more. Taste and adjust salt, pepper, sugar and citrus juice if necessary. It should have a good balance of sweet and sour.

Note: To prepare cabbage for stuffing, cut out the core several days in advance. Wrap the cored cabbage in clingfilm. Freeze. Thaw when needed.

'"Cool mountain water – and a stuffed cabbage. That's all I eat."
"Is stuffed cabbage allowed on your diet?"
"Who the hell cares if it's allowed! I love it!"'

Mel Brooks, *The 2013 Year Old Man*

❄ STUFFED PEPPERS

Makes 18 pieces

This was inspired by a beautiful dish of stuffed peppers served at Justin DeBlank's restaurant in London's Duke Street.

---

9 red peppers, cut in half (discard seeds and ribs) and peeled (use a swivel-bladed peeler, the microwave, or the grill – see page 30)
1 large Spanish onion, coarsely chopped
4 fl oz/120 ml dry red wine
5 fl oz/150 ml stock
2 medium carrots, peeled and diced
1 yellow pepper, peeled and diced
½ teaspoon each dried tarragon, dried thyme, ground cinnamon

¼ teaspoon ground allspice
Pinch or two of cayenne pepper
3 tablespoons tomato paste
3 tablespoons sultanas soaked in 2 fl oz/60 ml red wine
½ lb/240 g very lean minced beef, sautéed, drained and blotted
4 oz/120 g bulghur (cracked wheat), soaked for 30 minutes in water to cover and squeezed dry
Salt and freshly ground pepper to taste
Yoghurt Herb Sauce (see below)

---

1   Arrange peppers, cut sides up, in a shallow baking dish.
2   Spread onion pieces in a large, heavy, non-reactive frying pan. Cook over high heat, without stirring, for a minute or two, until they are sizzling and beginning to stick to the pan.
3   Pour in 4 fl oz/120 ml of red wine. Boil, stirring and scraping up the browned bits in the pan, until the liquid is just about gone.
4   Add 3 fl oz/90 ml of stock. Cover and boil for 5 minutes. Reduce heat.
5   Stir in carrots and yellow peppers. Pour in 2 fl oz/60 ml of stock. Cover and simmer gently for 5–10 minutes, until the carrots are tender but not at all mushy.
6   Uncover and stir in the herbs and spices. Cook gently, stirring, for a few moments. Stir in the tomato paste, the sultanas and their wine. Stir in the minced beef and the squeezed bulghur. Season to taste. Stir and cook for a minute or so.
7   Pile about 2 tablespoons of filling into each pepper half. Cover and refrigerate at this point if desired.
8   To serve, preheat the oven to 350° F, 180° C, Gas Mark 4. Cover the baking dish with foil, shiny side in. Bake for 30 minutes. Serve hot. Pass a jug of Yoghurt Herb Sauce.

Yoghurt Herb Sauce

Stir a generous handful of chopped fresh coriander, mint and parsley into non-fat yoghurt.

❄ SHEPHERD'S PIE

Serves 8
211 Calories per serving
3.2 g fat
(Traditional shepherd's pie 357 Calories, 23 g fat)

This pie is for a slim and healthy shepherd. Many changes can be rung on this familiar theme. See suggestions below.

---

2 lb/960 g lean minced lamb (beef or veal may be used as well)
3 onions, finely chopped
3 cloves garlic, minced
½ pt/300 ml stock
½ pt/300 ml dry red wine
1 tablespoon reduced-salt Worcestershire sauce
2 tablespoons tomato paste

Salt and freshly ground pepper to taste
Dash nutmeg
Well-seasoned mashed potatoes made from 2 lb/960 g potatoes and 4 fl oz/120 ml buttermilk (about 2 pts/1.2 l mashed potatoes)
6 tablespoons Parmesan cheese

---

1   Cook the lamb in a large non-stick frying pan, breaking up the lumps as it cooks. When the lamb is cooked through, drain it well in a colander. Spread it out on paper towels and blot it with more paper towels. Wash and dry the frying pan. Return the drained and blotted lamb to the pan.
2   Meanwhile, combine onion, garlic, 5 fl oz/150 ml stock and 5 fl oz/150 ml wine in a non-reactive frying pan. Simmer briskly, stirring occasionally until the onions are tender and the liquid is almost gone. Add this mixture to the drained lamb.
3   Stir in the Worcestershire sauce, tomato paste, salt and pepper. Stir in remaining stock and wine. Simmer uncovered for 20–30 minutes, stirring occasionally, until thick. Taste and adjust seasonings.
4   Spread the meat mixture in a gratin pan or in individual casseroles. Season the potatoes with nutmeg, and spread them over the meat. Sprinkle evenly with Parmesan cheese. At this point the pie may be covered tightly with cling film and refrigerated for up to 2 days. Bring to room temperature before proceeding.
5   Preheat oven to 375° F, 190° C, Gas Mark 5. Bake the pie uncovered, for 30–40 minutes, until browned and bubbly. Serve at once or cool, wrap tightly and freeze for a later meal. Reheat, covered, from the frozen state, either in the oven or the microwave.

Variations:

❄ MEXICAN-STYLE SHEPHERD'S PIE

Use beef, pork or a combination. When you cook the onions in Step 2, add 1 tablespoon chilli powder, 1 teaspoon crumbled dried oregano, ¼ teaspoon ground cinnamon, ½ teaspoon ground cumin, and ½ teaspoon crushed chillis. Omit the Worcestershire sauce in Step 3. Season the mashed potato with a pinch or 2 of ground cumin and ground cayenne.

❄ GREEK-STYLE SHEPHERD'S PIE

When you cook the onions in Step 2, add 1 teaspoon cinnamon and ½ teaspoon crumbled oregano. Omit the Worcestershire sauce in Step 3, but add the pulp of a baked aubergine (see page 37). Season the mashed potatoes with a pinch or two of cinnamon and some baked garlic purée (see page 32).

❄ HUNTER'S PIE

Serves 6

Venison is available in British markets from October to early April. It is lean as can be. During its short season try this delicate variation on the Shepherd's Pie theme.

1½ lb/720 g lean minced venison	*2 teaspoons lemon juice*
2 carrots, finely chopped	*1½ tablespoons tomato paste*
2 onions, finely chopped	*Salt and freshly ground pepper to*
3 cloves garlic, minced	*taste*
½ teaspoon dried thyme, crumbled	*Pinch cayenne pepper*
½ pt/300 ml dry red wine	*Well-seasoned mashed potatoes*
½ pt/300 ml stock	*made from 2 lb/960 g potatoes*
1 tablespoon cornflour	*and 4 fl oz/120 ml buttermilk*
2 tablespoons redcurrant jelly	*(see page 279)*
1 tablespoon reduced-salt	*4 tablespoons Parmesan cheese*
Worcestershire sauce	

1   Cook venison in a large non-stick frying pan until it has lost its redness. Break up the lumps with a wooden spoon as it cooks. When it is cooked, drain well in a colander to remove any rendered fat. Spread out on paper towels and blot it with more paper towels. Return the meat to the frying pan.

2   Meanwhile combine carrots, onion, garlic, thyme, 5 fl oz/ 150 ml wine and 5 fl oz/150 ml stock in a non-reactive frying

149

pan. Simmer briskly, stirring occasionally, until the vegetables are tender and the liquid is almost gone. Add this mixture to the venison.

3   Place cornflour, jelly, Worcestershire sauce, lemon juice and tomato paste in a liquidizer and blend. Stir the mixture into the venison. Stir in the remaining wine and stock. Season with salt, pepper and cayenne. Simmer uncovered for 20–30 minutes, until thick. Stir occasionally. Taste and adjust seasonings, adding salt, pepper, Worcestershire sauce or lemon juice to your taste.

4   Spread the meat mixture in a gratin pan or in individual casseroles. Spread the mashed potatoes over the meat. Sprinkle evenly with Parmesan cheese. At this point, the pie may be refrigerated for up to 2 days. Bring to room temperature before continuing.

5   Preheat oven to 375° F, 190° C, Gas Mark 5. Bake pie uncovered for 35–40 minutes, until browned and bubbly. Serve at once, or cool, cover tightly and freeze for a later meal. Reheat, covered, from the frozen state, either in the oven or the microwave.

❄ CURRIED SHEPHERD'S PIE

Serves 8

This is my all-time favourite shepherd's pie. I've made it many times and served it to the great and the near-great. Don't be afraid of the long list of ingredients – you are, basically, making your own curry powder with the long list of spices. The meat-aubergine mixture is at once hot, sweet and sour, and the potatoes are creamy and mellow with the taste of baked garlic.

2 large Spanish onions, coarsely chopped	1 tin (14 oz/420 g) chopped tomatoes
10 fl oz/300 ml of stock	4 oz/120 g raisins
1 teaspoon turmeric	4 tablespoons mango chutney
1 teaspoon cumin	1 tablespoon fresh lemon juice
1 teaspoon pure chilli powder	1 tablespoon Worcestershire sauce
1 teaspoon ground coriander	8 dried apricot halves, minced (use scissors)
1 teaspoon ground cardamoms	
1/4 teaspoon ground ginger	1 tablespoon tomato paste
1/4 teaspoon ground mustard	Mashed potatoes made with 7 large baking potatoes, salt, pepper and 8 fl oz/240 ml buttermilk (see page 279)
1/4 teaspoon ground cinnamon	
Pinch ground cloves, allspice and nutmeg	

Salt and freshly ground pepper to taste
3 cloves of garlic, minced
1½ lb/720 g lean minced lamb
Chopped pulp of 2 Baked
    Aubergines (page 37)
    approximately ¾ lb/360 g each

¼ teaspoon cayenne pepper
½ teaspoon garam masala
Purée from 1 head Baked Garlic
    (page 32)

---

1   Spread the onions out in a heavy frying pan. Add *no* liquid or fat. Heat the frying pan gently. Cook at moderate heat, without stirring, until the onions are sizzling, and beginning to stick to the pan.

2   Stir in the stock and let it bubble up, stirring up the browned deposits in the pan as it bubbles. Stir in the spices and the garlic. Turn down the heat and simmer, stirring frequently, until the mixture is very thick (not at all soupy) and the onions and spices are 'frying' in their own juices. Don't rush this step; it is essential that the spices do not have a harsh, raw taste. Taste. Cook very gently for a few more minutes if necessary. Scrape the mixture into a bowl.

3   In the same frying pan, cook the minced lamb over medium heat. As it browns, break up any lumps with a wooden spoon. When it is thoroughly cooked, drain *very* well in a colander set over a bowl. Discard the drained fat. Put the lamb and the onion mixture back into the frying pan.

4   Stir in the aubergine, tomatoes, raisins, chutney, lemon juice, Worcestershire sauce and apricots. Simmer for 30 minutes, stirring occasionally. Stir in the tomato paste and simmer for 5–10 minutes more, until thick. Taste and adjust seasonings. Spread the mixture into a gratin pan. Preheat oven to 375° F, 190° C, Gas Mark 5.

5   Season the potatoes with cayenne pepper, garam masala, Baked Garlic purée and salt and pepper. Taste and add more seasoning if needed. Spread the potatoes over the meat.

6   Bake for 40–50 minutes until brown and bubbling.

Alternative Topping

For a change, microwave or steam all-purpose unpeeled potatoes (about 5) until tender, but not falling apart. Slice ¼ inch/0.6 cm thick and overlap on the surface of the lamb mixture in the gratin pan. Pour over this custard topping:

151

5 egg whites
16 fl oz/480 ml skimmed milk
Salt and freshly ground pepper to
   taste

¼ teaspoon cayenne pepper
½ teaspoon garam masala

1   Preheat oven to 325° F, 170° C, Gas Mark 3.
2   Beat together the eggs, milk and seasonings. Pour evenly over
     the potatoes. Bake for 50–60 minutes, until browned and set.

✻   SHEPHERD'S PIE WITH LENTILS

Serves 8

My favourite shepherd's pies deviate from the norm: indeed they
often contain a rather eccentric assortment of ingredients. Here,
sultanas and red lentils stretch out a small amount of lamb and
make it absolutely irresistible.

1 large Spanish onion, chopped
4 fl oz/120 ml red wine
1½ pts/900 ml stock
2 medium carrots, peeled and diced
1 yellow pepper, peeled and diced
½ teaspoon each dried tarragon and
   thyme
¼ teaspoon each ground allspice
   and cinnamon
Pinch or two of ground cayenne
3 tablespoons tomato paste
1 tablespoon sultanas soaked in
   2 fl oz/60 ml red wine
4 oz/120 g split red lentils, washed,
   drained and picked over

½ lb/240 g very lean minced lamb,
   sautéed, drained and blotted
Salt and freshly ground pepper to
   taste

Potatoes (makes about
   2 pts/1.2 l mashed potatoes)
Well-seasoned mashed potatoes
   made from 2 lb/960 g potatoes,
   salt and pepper
Generous pinch allspice
Generous pinch cayenne pepper
4 fl oz/120 ml buttermilk
6 tablespoons Parmesan cheese

1   Spread the onion pieces in a large, heavy, non-reactive pan.
     Cook over high heat, without stirring, until they are sizzling
     and beginning to stick to the pan.
2   Pour in 4 fl oz/120 ml red wine. Boil, stirring and scraping up
     the browned bits in the pan, until the liquid is just about gone.
3   Add 3 fl oz/90 ml stock. Cover and boil for 5 minutes. Reduce
     heat. Stir in carrots and peppers. Pour in 2 fl oz/60 ml stock.
     Cover and simmer gently for 5–10 minutes, until the carrots
     are beginning to get tender.
4   Stir in the herbs, spices, tomato paste, sultanas and their wine,
     the lentils, the lamb and salt and pepper. Stir in 8 fl oz/240 ml
     stock. Cover and simmer for 20 minutes, uncovering to stir

occasionally. If it gets too dry and threatens to stick, add a bit more stock.

5   After 20 minutes, uncover and cook for 5–10 minutes more until the lentils are tender and the mixture is very thick.

6   Spread the lamb/vegetable mixture in a gratin pan. Season the potatoes with the allspice and cayenne pepper and beat in the buttermilk. Spread the potatoes over the meat mixture. Sprinkle evenly with Parmesan cheese. At this point the pie may be covered tightly with cling film and refrigerated for up to two days. Bring to room temperature before proceeding.

7   Preheat oven to 375° F, 190° C, Gas Mark 5. Bake the pie uncovered for 45–55 minutes until browned, puffed and bubbly. Serve at once, or cool, wrap tightly and freeze for a later meal. Reheat, covered, from the frozen state, either in the oven or the microwave.

HAMBURGERS

Makes 4 generous burgers
161 Calories per burger
2.5 g fat
(Traditional hamburger: 330 Calories, 23 g fat)

Imagine a huge hamburger – juicy and meaty – festooned with shreds of caramelized onions and doused in a thick, spicy red sauce, nestling between the halves of a wheaty bun. Sounds marvellous, but quite forbidden, doesn't it? Not to worry. The Slim Cuisine Burger is even juicier and more flavourful than the fattening original.

12 oz/360 g fine lean minced beef	1 (¾–1 lb/480 g) aubergine,
3 tablespoons crisp wholemeal	roasted, peeled and coarsely
breadcrumbs	chopped
1 scant tablespoon tomato paste	1–2 cloves garlic, minced
2 teaspoons low-fat fromage frais or	Salt and freshly ground pepper to
yoghurt	taste
2 tablespoons Parmesan cheese	2 tablespoons additional crisp
1 small onion, chopped fine	wholemeal breadcrumbs

1   Preheat the grill to its highest temperature. Place the grill shelf on its lowest position. Line the grill tray with foil, shiny side up. Place the grill rack on the tray.

2   Thoroughly mix together all ingredients except the additional breadcrumbs. Shape the mixture into 4 fat, oval cakes. Dredge them, on both sides, in the additional crumbs.

153

3   Grill on the rack in the lowest position for 3–4 minutes on each side, until crusty on the outside and medium rare within. (Cook more or less to your taste, but please don't incinerate them!)

4   Serve as they are, or in wholewheat buns with Browned Onions and Red Pepper Sauce. Or serve with a dollop of Pesto on each burger.

(L) [X] Prepare the aubergine in the microwave.

Meatballs

Tiny, succulent meatballs are delightful. Traditional meatballs are horrendously high in Calories and fat, but it is easy to remedy this. Slim Cuisine techniques result in meatballs that are much more delicate and refined than those made by the bad old methods. In fact, they are more like light and fluffy dumplings than meatballs. Instead of eggs (the yolk is extremely high fat), baked, puréed aubergine is combined with the minced meat. 'Wait!' I hear you exclaim. 'What about those of us who loathe aubergine?' Stay calm. There is no taste, no look, no evidence whatsoever of aubergine in the final cooked meatballs. The vegetable pulp imparts an exquisite lightness, but otherwise there is no sign of that pulp at all.

Instead of frying the meatballs in olive oil, butter or other highly unsuitable fat, Slim Cuisine calls for quick grilling, or sautéing in stock. The choice is yours and both methods will work beautifully for lamb, beef or pork. Traditional meatball recipes call for fairly high-fat minced meat. Obviously for these recipes you will use the leanest meat possible.

❅ GRILLED LAMB MEATBALLS

Makes 35 nut-sized meatballs
18 Calories per meatball
0.3 g fat
(Traditional meatballs: 88.2 calories per meatball, 5 g fat)

Good in Tomato Sauce, a lovely addition to pasta dishes, splendid with Steamed Asparagus and Red or Yellow Pepper Sauce (see page 245 or 233), or try them stuffed into pitta bread with Stir-'Fried' Peppers (see page 31) or Raita (see page 286).

1 lb/450 g lean minced lamb	2 tablespoons fresh chopped parsley
1 small aubergine (¾–1 lb/480g) baked and puréed or chopped fine (see page 37)	1 rounded tablespoon tomato paste
	Juice and grated rind of 1 small lemon
3 cloves garlic, minced	2 oz/50 g breadcrumbs
2 tablespoons fresh chopped mint (for a variation, substitute ½ tablespoon fennel seeds, or 1 tablespoon grated fresh ginger, or 2 tablespoons fresh chopped coriander)	Salt and freshly ground pepper to taste

1 Place minced lamb in a bowl. Add remaining ingredients. Mix with your hands until thoroughly amalgamated. Fry a tiny test piece (use no fat!) in a small, non-stick frying pan. Taste, then adjust seasonings in the meat mixture to your liking.

2 Preheat the grill to its highest setting.

3 With your hands roll small balls, each a little smaller than a walnut. You will have approximately 35 in all. Line the grill pan with foil, shiny side up. Put a rack on the grill pan. Place the meatballs on the rack.

4 When the grill is very hot, grill the meatballs, 1 inch/2.5 cm from the heat, for 5–7 minutes until browned on top and *just* cooked through (no need to turn them). Remove very gently using tongs and a spatula. Blot on paper towels to eliminate any faint trace of fat, and serve. The meatballs may be made in advance and refrigerated. To reheat, place them in a shallow frying pan with some warm stock. Simmer gently, covered, for 5–7 minutes. (Don't boil. The surface of the stock should barely move.) Fish out very gently with a slotted spoon.

🕐 ⬚ Prepare the aubergine in the microwave.

SAUTÉED VEAL MEATBALLS

Makes 35 meatballs

Elegant, delicate and exquisite. Sautéing in stock is more difficult and fussy than grilling, but it is worth the effort. Of course, you can grill these if you wish.

1 lb/450 g lean minced veal
1 small aubergine (¾–1 lb/450 g)
    baked and puréed or chopped fine
    (see page 37)
Garlic purée from 1 head of baked
    garlic (see page 32)
1 rounded tablespoon tomato paste
2 oz/50 g dry breadcrumbs

2 tablespoons chopped fresh parsley
Salt and freshly ground pepper to
    taste
Juice and grated rind of 1 small
    lemon
6 tablespoons freshly grated
    Parmesan cheese
Chicken stock

1   Combine all ingredients except chicken stock. Use your hands
    to mix it all gently but thoroughly. Fry a tiny piece in a
    non-stick frying pan (use no fat!) and taste. Adjust seasonings
    to your liking.
2   Form the mixture into balls that are a bit smaller than walnuts.
    Heat a large, heavy, non-stick frying pan. Pour in some stock
    to just film the bottom. Put in some veal balls. Do not crowd
    them. Do in several batches.
3   Let them get crusty, loosening with a spatula and turning with
    tongs so that they brown on all sides. (Be gentle, they are
    fragile.) When they are browned and crusty all over add a bit
    more stock and simmer for 2–3 minutes, turning them, until
    just cooked through. Blot on paper towels, then spread them
    in a wide, shallow dish. Repeat until all the meat is used. Add
    more stock as needed. When all the veal balls are done, cover
    well with cling film, and refrigerate until needed. (They may
    be prepared to this point three days ahead.)
4   To serve, pour ½ inch/1.25 cm of stock into a deep, non-stick
    frying pan. Add the veal balls in one layer. Cover and simmer
    for 10 minutes or so, until heated through.

Note: To grill the veal meatballs, follow the directions for grilling
the lamb meatballs with this difference: grill for 4 minutes, turn
very carefully (they are quite fragile) and grill for approximately
4 minutes on the second side.

🕐 ❄ Prepare the aubergine in the microwave.

❄ MEXICAN FRIJOL-ALBONDIGA CASSEROLE

Serves 6

Mexican baked beans with spicy meatballs. For a lively dinner
party serve this dish with Chilaquiles (see page 184), Steamed Rice,
and Lime-Cumin Courgettes (see page 258). Begin with Jellied
Gazpacho or Chilled Corn Soup and end with Mango Sorbet.

Beans

Makes 1¼ pts/750 ml

---

1 large onion, chopped	1 tin (1 lb/480 g) cannellini beans,
2 large cloves garlic, crushed	drained and rinsed
½ teaspoon dried oregano,	1 tin (1 lb/480 g) haricots blancs,
crumbled	drained and rinsed
½ teaspoon chilli powder	1 tinned green chilli, chopped
¾ teaspoon ground cumin	1 tin (1 lb/480 g) chopped tomatoes
6 fl oz/180 ml stock	2 tablespoons chopped parsley
1 teaspoon Dijon mustard	Salt to taste

---

1 In a large frying pan combine the onion, garlic, herbs and spices and stock. Boil until the mixture is almost dry.

2 Stir in the mustard, beans, chopped chilli, tomatoes, parsley and salt. Simmer gently, stirring occasionally, for 15–20 minutes until thick.

Albondigas

Makes 38 meatballs

---

1 lb/480 g very lean minced veal or	1 tablespoon fresh mint or
pork	coriander, chopped
Pulp from 1 (¾–1 lb/480 g) baked	½ teaspoon cumin
aubergine, peeled and chopped	Salt and freshly ground pepper to
(see page 37)	taste
2 spring onions, chopped	Juice and grated rind of ½ lime
2 oz/50 g dry wholewheat	1 tablespoon tomato paste
breadcrumbs	2 tinned green chillies, minced
	Several dashes tabasco sauce

---

1 Preheat grill. Line the grill tray with foil, shiny side up. Place the grill rack on the tray.

2 Combine all meatball ingredients in a bowl. Mix well with the hands until well blended. Fry a tiny piece in a small non-stick frying pan (use no fat!) and taste. Adjust seasonings to your taste.

3 Form the mixture into tiny balls, a little smaller than walnuts, and arrange on the grill rack. Grill close to the heat for four minutes on each side.

To Assemble

Stock
1 tablespoon Parmesan cheese

1 Preheat oven to 350° F, 180° C, Gas Mark 4.
2 Spread the beans on the bottom of a shallow baking dish. Add enough stock to make a slightly soupy mixture. Place albondigas on the bean mixture, pushing them in as you do so. Sprinkle the Parmesan cheese over everything. Cover the dish.
3 Bake for 30–35 minutes, until hot and bubbly.

❄ KOFTA CURRY

Serves 4 (31 meatballs)
148 Calories per serving
1.9 g fat
(Traditional kofta curry: 591 Calories per serving, 42.8 g fat)

Little meatballs, how I love them! Remember the Slim Cuisine technique of adding chopped, roasted aubergine to the meat. There will be no aubergine taste but the calories in each meatball will be reduced, and the meatballs will be tender and juicy even though the meat is very lean. Of all the curry recipes developed for this book, my tasters loved this one the best. It reheats well from both the refrigerator and the freezer.

Meatballs

2–3 cloves garlic, minced
Pulp from 1 baked aubergine (see page 37)
1 lb/480 g very lean ground lamb (lean beef can be used too, if desired)
½ teaspoon ground cinnamon

Pinch ground cloves
½ tablespoon fresh ginger root, finely grated
Salt to taste
2 tablespoons fresh coriander or parsley, chopped

Sauce

2 large onions, cut into eighths
16 fl oz/480 ml stock
2 cloves garlic, minced
½ teaspoon ground turmeric
½ teaspoon ground cinnamon

2 teaspoons ground coriander
Pinch cayenne pepper (or to taste)
3 tablespoons tomato paste
Salt to taste

1   Preheat the grill to its highest setting.
2   In a large bowl, combine the meatball ingredients. Mix with your hands until thoroughly amalgamated. Fry a tiny piece in a small frying pan (use no fat!) and taste. Adjust seasonings to your liking. Form the mixture into small balls, a little smaller than walnuts.
2   Line the grill tray with foil, shiny side up. Place a rack on the tray and arrange the meatballs on it. Grill, 1 inch/2.5 cm from the heat, for 5 minutes, until crusty brown on top. Set aside.
4   Separate the segments of the onion pieces. Spread them in a heavy, non-reactive frying pan. Add *no* liquid for fat. Heat the frying pan gently. Cook at moderate heat, without stirring, for 7–10 minutes, until the onions are sizzling, and beginning to stick to the pan.
5   Stir in 10 fl oz/300 ml of stock and let it bubble up, stirring up the browned deposits with a wooden spoon as it bubbles. Stir in the spices. Simmer gently, stirring all the while, until the mixture is very thick (not at all soupy). Don't rush this step, as it is essential that the spices cook properly. Taste the mixture. The spices should not have a raw, harsh taste. Cook very gently for a few more minutes if necessary.
6   Stir in the tomato paste and the remaining (6 fl oz) stock. Place the meatballs in this sauce. Simmer gently, covered, for 15–20 minutes, until the sauce is very thick and rich. Serve at once or cool and refrigerate until needed. This tastes good on the second or third day so do not hesitate to make in advance. Add more stock when reheating.

🕐 ✂ Prepare the aubergine in the microwave.

🕐 ❄   ## VEAL-POTATO BALLS

Makes approximately 50 meatballs

Serve veal-potato balls in Red Pepper and Tomato Borscht (page 100), or serve on toothpicks on a buffet with New York Deli Mustard (page 305) for dipping.

2 egg whites	*1 lb/480 g minced veal*
Grated zest of ½ small lemon	*3 oz/75 g mashed potatoes*
1 teaspoon chopped fresh dill	*2 tablespoons chopped fresh parsley*
½ teaspoon ground allspice	*1 tablespoon drained capers in*
Salt and a generous amount of	*vinegar, chopped*
freshly ground pepper to taste	*4 cloves garlic, minced*

1   Lightly beat the egg whites with the lemon zest, dill, allspice, salt and pepper. Add to the veal with the remaining ingredients. Combine well with your hands. Fry a tiny piece in a small non-stick frying pan and taste, then adjust seasonings to your liking.
2   Preheat the grill. Line the grill tray with foil, shiny side out.
3   Form the mixture into small balls, smaller than walnuts but a little larger than marbles.
4   Place the meatballs 1–2 inches/2.5–5 cm from the heat and grill for 2 minutes on one side and 3 minutes on the second side. Blot on paper towels.

❄ LAMB MEATBALLS FOR COUSCOUS

Makes approximately 35 meatballs

These spicy little morsels are perfect with Couscous with Vegetables (page 203) or on their own.

1 lb/480 g lean minced lamb	2 teaspoons ground cumin
1 small aubergine, baked, peeled and chopped fine (see page 37)	1 teaspoon ground coriander
	½ teaspoon ground cayenne
3 cloves garlic, crushed	2 oz/50 g wholemeal breadcrumbs
4 tablespoons chopped mint or parsley or a mixture	Salt and freshly ground pepper to taste
1 rounded tablespoon tomato paste	

1   Place minced lamb in a bowl. Add remaining ingredients. Mix with your hands until thoroughly amalgamated. Fry a tiny test piece (use no fat!) in a small, non-stick frying pan. Taste, then adjust seasonings in the meat to your liking.
2   Preheat the grill to its highest setting.
3   With your hands roll small balls, each a little smaller than a walnut. You will have approximately 35 in all. Line the grill pan with foil, shiny side up. Put a rack on the grill pan. Place the meatballs on the rack.
4   When the grill is very hot, grill the meatballs, 1 inch/2.5 cm from the heat, for 5–7 minutes, until browned on top and just cooked through (no need to turn them). Remove very gently, using tongs and a spatula. Blot on paper towels to eliminate any traces of fat, and serve. The meatballs may be made in advance and refrigerated. To reheat, place them in a shallow

frying pan with some warm stock. Simmer gently, covered, for 5–7 minutes. (Don't boil. The surface of the stock should barely move.) Fish out very gently with a slotted spoon.

🕐 ⊠ Bake the aubergine in the microwave.

❄ CHEESE STUFFED MEATBALLS

Makes 30 meatballs

Each meatball has a tender, gooey heart of melted Mozzarella cheese. These are excellent simmered in Tomato Sauce (page 236) for 30 minutes and served with pasta, Mashed Potatoes (page 279) or Polenta (page 215).

10 oz/300 g minced beef (very lean) *2 medium aubergines, baked, peeled* * and finely chopped (see page 37)* *2½ tablespoons brown breadcrumbs*	*3 tablespoons grated Parmesan* * cheese* *½ teaspoon herbes de Provence* *Salt and pepper to taste* *2½ oz/75 g Italian Mozzarella* * cheese*

1   Line a grill pan with foil, shiny side up. Put a rack on the grill pan. Preheat the grill to its highest setting.
2   Put the minced beef in a bowl. Add the aubergine, breadcrumbs, Parmesan cheese, herbs, salt and pepper. Mix very well with a fork or your hands. In a tiny frying pan, fry a tiny test piece, without using any fat. Taste and then adjust seasonings in the mixture to your liking.
3   Cut the Mozzarella cheese into 30 small pieces. Make the meatballs, enclosing a small piece of Mozzarella cheese in the centre of each. Roll each meatball thoroughly between the palms to enclose the Mozzarella cheese.
4   Arrange the meatballs on the grill rack. Grill for 3–5 minutes on one side, and 2–3 minutes on the second. Blot very well on paper towels.

🕐 ⊠ Bake the aubergine in the microwave.

MARJORIE HOEK'S 'TAMALE PIE' MEATBALLS

Makes approximately 24 meatballs

This recipe won first prize in a Slim Cuisine recipe contest. I loved it and so did all my helpers and testers. I was impressed with the spicing, which is *very* Mexican. Unsweetened chocolate is used as a seasoning in many Mexican savoury dishes; cocoa powder, of course, is a lower-fat form of chocolate. Cornmeal (maize meal) is available in many wholefood and speciality food stores. If you can't find fine cornmeal, polenta will do. Meatballs may not be elegant, but they can be quite marvellous. Serve it for a family dinner or as the centrepiece for a Mexican party buffet.

Meatball ingredients
1 lb/480 g very lean minced beef
2 oz/60 g fine cornmeal
1 egg
1 onion, finely chopped
1 teaspoon cumin
1 teaspoon paprika
1 teaspoon fat-reduced cocoa
   powder (see page 335)
1 teaspoon thyme, fresh if possible

½ teaspoon cayenne or 1 fresh
   chilli, finely chopped

Sauce ingredients
1 tin (14 oz/420 g) chopped
   tomatoes
8 fl oz/240 ml fresh, strained orange
   juice
Freshly ground black pepper to taste
Handful of chopped parsley

---

1   Preheat oven to 180° F, 350° C, Gas Mark 4.
2   Mix all ingredients with your hands. They should be thoroughly combined. Form into meatballs 1–1½ inches/2.5–4 cm in diameter. Place in one layer on a non-stick baking dish. Bake in the preheated oven until browned, 1½ hours or so.
3   Remove meatballs and blot on paper towels to eliminate rendered fat. Put the meatballs in a baking dish in one layer.
4   Combine sauce ingredients and pour over the meatballs. Return to the oven and bake uncovered until sauce is bubbly and tops of meatballs are well browned – about another 30 minutes. Sprinkle with parsley and serve.

ITALIAN SAUSAGE BALLS

Makes 35 sausage balls
25 Calories per sausage ball
0.2 g fat
(Traditional Italian sausage: 105 Calories per ounce, 8 g fat)

Sausage is a savoury mixture of minced pork and pork fat stuffed into animal intestine casings. The seasonings change with the type of sausage and the region of its birth: nutmeg and mace for German bratwurst; marjoram and garlic for Polish keilbasa; garlic and red pepper for Spanish chorizo; cinnamon, allspice and orange peel for Greek loukanika; sage and thyme for English butcher's sausage.

Use the technique for Slim Cuisine Meatballs to produce juicy, well-flavoured sausage meat without the fat. Pork is bred to be leaner and leaner these days. It should be no problem obtaining a lean piece at the butcher. Have him mince it for you. Or buy lean pork mince from the supermarket. Instead of stuffing the sausage mixture into casings, form it into balls and grill. Even though the meat is lean, it still has some fat in it, which drips off nicely in the grilling. This recipe is for one of my favourites; Italian sausage with crushed dried chillies and fennel seeds. Substitute any seasonings you like to produce *your* favourite sausages. And, if you wish, make your sausages with beef or veal, or a combination of meats.

---

1 lb/480 g minced lean pork
2–3 small aubergines (approx.
  ½ lb/240 g each) baked, skinned
  and puréed in the liquidizer (see
  page 37)
1 teaspoon fennel or anise seeds
¼ teaspoon crushed dried chillies

3 garlic cloves, crushed to a paste
  with a mallet
4 tablespoons parsley, finely
  chopped
3 tablespoons dry red wine
Salt and freshly ground pepper to
  taste

---

1   Combine all ingredients and mix very well until thoroughly amalgamated. Fry a tiny test piece (use no fat!) in a small, non-stick frying pan. Taste, then adjust seasonings in the meat mixture to your liking.

2   Preheat grill to its highest setting.

3   With your hands, roll small balls, each a little smaller than a walnut. Line the grill pan with foil, shiny side up. Put a rack on the grill pan. Place the sausage balls on the rack.

4   When the grill is very hot, grill the sausage balls, 1 inch/2.5 cm from the heat, for 5 minutes. Turn and grill for 2 minutes on the second side. Blot on paper towels to remove any trace of fat. Refrigerate until needed. Reheat in stock (see page 156).

    Prepare the aubergine in the microwave.

Sausage Ideas

Combine the Italian Sausages with Grilled or Stir-'Fried' Peppers (see page 256), Sautéed Mushrooms (see page 29) and Tomato Sauce (see page 236) and serve with pasta, or stuffed into crusty rolls. Italian Sausages in Tomato Sauce freeze very well.

Serve Sausage Balls with mashed potatoes and browned onions (see page 26).

Serve Sausage Balls with Sautéed Mushrooms (see page 29) and grilled tomatoes. What a breakfast!

'If there's an end
On which I'd spend
My last remaining cash
It's sausage, friend
It's sausage, friend,
It's sausage, friend, and mash.'

Sir A. P. Herbert

❄ AUBERGINE-SAUSAGE SAUCE FOR PASTA

Makes 3 pts/2 l

This is an interesting and delicious variant of Bolognese sauce. I learned it years ago from the proprietor of a New York Italian restaurant. The original version was very high in fat; this one is not, but it manages to surpass the original in taste.

Sausage ingredients
1 lb/480 g very lean minced pork
Finely chopped flesh of 3 Baked Aubergines (see page 37)
1 teapoon fennel or anise seeds
¼ teaspoon crushed dried chillies
3 garlic cloves, crushed to a paste with a mallet
4 tablespoons finely chopped fresh parsley
3 tablespoons dry red wine
Salt and freshly ground pepper to taste

Sauce ingredients
1 large Spanish onion, coarsely diced
1 red, 1 yellow pepper, cut into ½-inch/1.25-cm lengthwise strips, peeled
16 fl oz/480 ml tinned sieved tomatoes
4 large ripe summer tomatoes, peeled, seeded, juiced and chopped or 14 oz/420 g tinned chopped tomatoes
Chopped flesh of 2 additional Baked Aubergines (see page 37)
1 piece Parmesan rind

164

1   Combine the sausage ingredients in a large bowl and mix very well. Refrigerate, well covered, for a few hours. It can be kept, if necessary, for up to two days.
2   Combine sausage mix and chopped onion in a large, heavy frying pan. Cook, stirring, over moderate heat until the meat is thoroughly cooked and the onion is tender. Drain in a colander over a bowl. Blot the pan with paper towels.
3   When well drained, return to the pan. Stir in pepper strips. Stir and cook for about 3 minutes. Stir in remaining ingredients. Simmer, stirring occasionally, for 15 minutes or so, until the sauce is very thick and the peppers are tender. Serve tossed into freshly cooked pasta shells or rotini, or serve with Polenta (page 215).

❄   # SAUSAGE PATTIES

Makes 30–35 sausage patties

Sausage meat keeps for a day or two in the fridge, or you may want to form it into patties and freeze, to be used as needed. They make lovely breakfast sausages. (Please don't say that aubergine sounds peculiar as a breakfast ingredient. By now you know that baked aubergine is the secret ingredient in Slim Cuisine sausages and meatballs. It lessens the amount of meat in each sausage, provides juiciness and leaves *no* aubergine taste.) Or they are excellent surrounding that annual Christmas turkey.

---

1 lb/480 g lean minced pork
Chopped pulp of 1 Baked Aubergine
* (page 37)*
Salt and freshly ground pepper to
* taste*

1 teaspoon rubbed sage
¼ teaspoon allspice
Pinch of nutmeg

---

1   Combine all ingredients in a bowl. Use your hands to amalgamate it thoroughly. Fry a tiny test piece in a little frying pan (use no fat!) and taste. Adjust seasoning.
2   Line the grill tray with foil, shiny side up. Place a rack on the grill tray. Preheat the grill.
3   Form the sausage mixture into balls, a little smaller than walnuts. Flatten into plump patties. Place on grill rack.
4   Grill, close to the heat, for 2 minutes. Turn each one carefully, and grill for an additional 2–3 minutes. Blot on a layer of paper towels and serve.

🕐 ⊠ Bake the aubergine in the microwave.

VEAL SHANKS WITH WILD MUSHROOMS

Serves 6

Dried cèpes and morels can be purchased in many speciality food stores or the gourmet department of some supermarkets, but feel free to substitute if necessary. I have successfully used a mixture of fresh cultivated mushrooms and dried Chinese or Japanese shiitake mushrooms, available from Oriental food stores and some supermarkets. Sliced veal shank is sold in many supermarkets under the name 'osso buco' (hollow bone). One of the best things about this homely, warming dish is the gorgeous rich, thick gravy. Just the thing for an accompanying mound of mashed potatoes.

---

1 oz/30 g dried cèpes/porcini
1 oz/30 g dried morels
6 slices very well trimmed
* veal shank, each about*
* 1½ inches/4 cm thick*

12 fl oz/360 ml dry red wine
20 cloves garlic, peeled (optional)
½ lb/240 g fresh mushrooms,
* quartered*
Dash of soy sauce

---

1   Rinse the dried mushrooms briefly under cold running water, then soak them in warm water, to cover generously, for ½–1 hour. Strain the water through a cheesecloth-lined sieve or a coffee filter and reserve. Rinse the mushrooms under cold running water, and trim off and discard any tough stems.
2   Dry the veal. With a small sharp knife and a spoon cut and dig out the marrow from the hollow centre bone. Discard it. Brown the veal over a medium heat in a heavy-bottomed frying pan until lightly browned on both sides. Transfer to a plate.
3   Add 8 fl oz/240 ml of the red wine and 8 fl oz/240 ml of the mushroom-soaking liquid to the frying pan. Bring to the boil and let boil for 2 minutes, scraping the bottom of the pan with a wooden spoon or spatula. Reduce heat.
4   Return the veal shanks to the frying pan. Scatter in the garlic cloves. Season with salt and pepper to taste. Let simmer, covered, for about 20 minutes.
5   Meanwhile, put the fresh mushrooms and 4 fl oz/120 ml of dry red wine, a dash or two of soy sauce and 4 fl oz/120 ml of the mushroom-soaking liquid into a non-reactive, non-stick heavy frying pan. Stir to combine everything very well.
6   Simmer, stirring occasionally. At first the mushrooms will release a good deal of extra liquid. Continue simmering,

stirring occasionally until the liquid is almost gone. Let the mushrooms 'fry' gently in their own juices for a few moments. Do not let them scorch or stick. Stir in the soaked dried mushrooms.

7   When the veal shanks have cooked for 20 minutes, turn them over. Add enough of the mushroom-soaking liquid to barely cover the veal shanks and add the sautéed mushrooms to the frying pan. Cover and let the meat simmer for another 1½ hours or until it is meltingly tender and falling off the bones, and the liquid has cooked down to a thick, rich sauce. Baste with the pan juices occasionally.

8   Remove the veal and mushrooms to a serving plate, cover tightly and keep warm. Skim the fat from the sauce. Reheat briefly, then pour over the veal.

9   Serve at once.

PORK IN MUSTARD SAUCE

Makes 2½ pts/1.5 l

Pork tenderloin is one of the leanest cuts of meat of all. It cooks very quickly and yields elegant results.

---

2 well-trimmed pork tenderloins (approximately 12 oz/360 g each)	3 peppers (use both red and yellow), seeded, cut into strips approximately ½ inch/1.25 cm wide, 1½ inches/3.75 cm long, and peeled
Salt and freshly ground pepper to taste	2 cloves garlic, minced
2 large Spanish onions, cut into wedges (cut each peeled onion in sixteenths, then separate the petals)	2 rounded teaspoons grainy mustard
4 fl oz/120 ml stock	1 rounded teaspoon Dijon mustard
2 fl oz/60 ml white wine	2½ tablespoons fromage frais
	Pinch of cayenne pepper (optional)
	1 tablespoon freshly chopped parsley

---

1   Slice the pork tenderloins slightly on the diagonal into ½-inch/ 1.25-cm thick medallions.

2   Heat a large heavy-bottomed frying pan. When very hot, place a single layer of pork slices in the pan (they should not touch each other). Grind on some pepper. Let the pork slices brown (1–2 minutes). Then turn with tongs, sprinkle with salt, and brown for another minute or so on the second side. Remove to a plate and repeat until all the slices have been browned.

3   When all the pork slices are reposing on the plate, dump the onions, stock and wine into the frying pan. Let the liquid bubble up while you stir and scrape up the browned bits with a wooden spoon. Cover and cook on high heat for 2–3 minutes. Uncover, and add the peppers and garlic. Stir. Cover and cook for 4–5 minutes until the onions are cooked but retain a slight crispiness.

4   Add the mustards and stir to thoroughly coat the vegetables. Stir in 2 tablespoons of fromage frais and heat through. Do not boil.

5   Add pork slices and any accumulated meat juices. Sprinkle in cayenne. Stir and cook until the pork is heated through. Do not let the sauce boil. Add the additional ½ tablespoon of fromage frais. Stir well for a moment or so. Stir in parsley. Serve at once.

⊕   PORK MEDALLIONS ESTERHAZY

Serves 6

My version of the classic Hungarian dish is rich and filling; a perfect choice for a winter dinner party. The original royal Hungarian version was made with beef. If you wish, serve the sauce and vegetable garnish with lean beef fillet steaks, cooked rare either under the grill or in the pan (see page 133).

---

1 pork tenderloin, trimmed of all fat   *Esterhazy sauce (recipe follows)*
Salt and freshly ground pepper   *Garnish (recipe follows)*
8 fl oz/240 ml stock

---

1   Cut the pork into ¾-inch/1.9-cm slices. Sprinkle with salt and pepper.

2   Heat a heavy, non-stick frying pan until moderately hot. Sear the pork slices for 1–2 minutes on each side, until browned (do not crowd them). Pour in the stock, simmer, turning frequently, for approximately 5 minutes, until cooked through and tender. Transfer to a plate, cover loosely and keep warm.

3   Boil the stock for a few seconds, scraping the bottom of the pan with a wooden spatula. When the stock is thick and syrupy, reduce the heat and add the pork slices back to the pan. With tongs, turn a few times.

4   Arrange the pork on a warm platter. Stir the syrupy stock into the Esterhazy sauce. Pour some sauce over the pork. Top with the drained, hot vegetable garnish. Serve at once. Pass the rest of the sauce at the table.

♡ 🧸 ⊕   **ESTERHAZY SAUCE**

This is one of the most delicious sauces I know. Its richness is amazing, yet it contains virtually no fat. It may be made ahead of time and stored in the refrigerator. Bring to room temperature before proceeding with the recipe.

1 large onion, chopped	Salt and freshly ground pepper to
2 small carrots, peeled and chopped	taste
2 small parsnips, peeled and	Grated zest of 1 lemon
chopped	Juice of ½ a lemon
1 pt/600 ml stock	1 tablespoon Dijon mustard
1 dried bay leaf	4 fl oz/120 ml quark mixed with
	1½ fl oz/45 ml skimmed milk

1   Combine the vegetables with 4 fl oz/120 ml stock in a heavy frying pan. Cover and simmer briskly for 4–5 minutes. Uncover and simmer until the vegetables are almost tender and the liquid just about gone.

2   Add remaining stock, bay leaf, salt, pepper, lemon zest and lemon juice. Let simmer gently, uncovered, until the vegetables are very tender. Discard bay leaf. Cool slightly. Purée the mixture in a liquidizer with the mustard and the quark. Pour it into a saucepan.

3   Simmer gently for approximately 5 minutes. Taste and adjust seasonings. Remove from heat. Cover with a piece of cling film directly over the surface of the sauce and set aside until needed.

♡ 🧸 ⊕   **GARNISH**

This is good enough to serve as a vegetable accompaniment to other dishes on occasion, or use to top fish fillets *en papillote* (see page 112).

1 parsnip	8 fl oz/240 ml stock
1 carrot	Salt and freshly ground pepper to
1 stalk celery	taste

1   Scrape the vegetables and cut them into julienne. Combine with the stock and simmer briskly, stirring constantly, until tender, and the stock is thickened and reduced. Season to taste.

2   Set aside until needed.

POT ROAST LAMB

Serves 6–8

The pot roasting method of cooking a leg of lamb results in extremely tender meat, with the wonderful flavour of the marinade penetrating right to the bone.

---

4 cloves garlic, crushed
3 medium onions, finely chopped
4 fl oz/120 ml dry red wine
1 tin (14 oz/420 g) chopped
 tomatoes, sieved or liquidized
10–12 sun-dried tomatoes, coarsely
 chopped (optional)
Juice of 1 lemon
Grated zest of 1 lemon

1 teaspoon each of ground allspice,
 cinnamon, cumin
½ teaspoon caster sugar
1 teaspoon dried oregano, crumbled
1 very well trimmed leg of lamb –
 approximately 4 lb/2 kg (weight
 after fat has been trimmed)
Salt and pepper to taste

---

1   In a large, non-reactive vessel, combine all ingredients except salt and pepper and lamb. Add lamb and turn to coat with mixture. Cover. Refrigerate for up to two days. Before cooking, allow to return to room temperature.
2   Place lamb in a non-reactive roasting pan. Season with salt and freshly ground pepper. Pour the sauce over and around the meat. Cover very tightly with foil so that no steam can escape.
3   Roast at 350° F, 180° C, Gas Mark 4, for 2 hours. After 1 hour, uncover and baste. Re-cover tightly.
4   Remove lamb to a plate, cover loosely with foil and allow to rest while de-greasing the sauce.
5   Pour pan juices into a glass measuring jug and put into the freezer for 10–15 minutes. Remove and skim off the fat. Reheat. Slice the lamb and serve with the pan juices. If desired, the pan juices may be puréed in a liquidizer or pushed through a sieve.

Poultry

'There is no way of preparing a chicken which I don't like'

Marcella Hazan, *Marcella's Kitchen*

C hicken is famous for being low-fat and good for you, but it needs some help before it can live up to its reputation. Be ruthless with the chicken that you take home from the store. Pull off all the lumps of fat. (There will be several and they will be large.) Denude the bird of its fatty skin – all of it. Only then is the chicken ready for Slim Cuisine. The white meat is leaner than the dark, and each requires different handling.

Chicken Breasts

Skinless, boneless chicken breasts are perfect for a quick, elegant meal. When properly cooked, they have a remarkably creamy and delicate texture. If they are overcooked, however, they became stringy and dry. Many quality butchers and supermarkets carry chicken breasts from free-range birds that have been skinned, boned and split. When you get them home, meticulously trim away any traces of fat, gristle and skin. Under each chicken breast is a loose, narrow flap of flesh. Pull it off and save it for stir-fries, or chicken salad. The trimmed deflapped chicken breast is called the 'supreme' or the 'cutlet'. A 3½-oz/100-g chicken cutlet contains approximately 104 Calories and negligible fat. It is an excellent source of protein. It can be quickly pan-sautéed in a heavy non-stick frying pan and served with a delicate sauce. Sauté the chicken until it is just done, so that it is tender and plumply juicy.

171

PAN-SAUTÉED CHICKEN BREASTS

Heat a heavy, non-stick frying pan until moderately hot. Season the chicken with salt and pepper. Cook for 3 minutes on the skinned side, then carefully turn and cook on the second side, for approximately 3 minutes or until *just* cooked through (it will feel firm but a little springy when touched with your finger).

Chicken breasts prepared in this manner may be used with a variety of sauces, either hot or cold. Consider the following:

Yellow Pepper Sauce	(page 172)
Red Pepper Sauce	(page 233)
Beet Purée	(page 263)
Hungarian Green Sauce	(page 231)
Esterhazy Sauce	(page 169)
Tomato Sauce	(page 236)
Remoulade Sauce	(page 304)
Pesto	(page 231)

Or top the breasts with Sautéed Mushrooms (page 29) and shredded Mozzarella cheese. Grill for 1–2 minutes until the cheese is melted and bubbly.

Chicken Legs and Thighs

Unlike the breasts, the dark meat of chicken takes beautifully to slow, gentle braising. When cooked with flavoursome ingredients, the meat becomes succulent and comforting; perfect cold-weather fare. Before cooking the legs and thighs, remove and discard all skin and fat. For many braised dishes, consider cooking the dish the day before serving. Store it in the refrigerator. The next day, any fat in the sauce will have congealed. Spoon it out and discard it. Then reheat the casserole and serve. And remember that the meat from free-range birds is the most delicious.

CHICKEN WITH YELLOW PEPPER SAUCE

Makes 4 pieces

The rich, buttery yellow pepper sauce complements the juicy chicken cutlet very well. You will find the sauce useful in many other ways as well.

4 fl oz/120 ml dry white wine or dry
  vermouth
3 fl oz/90 ml tarragon wine vinegar
2 tablespoons minced shallots
½ teaspoon dried tarragon,
  crumbled

1 tablespoon chopped fresh parsley
6 yellow peppers, coarsely diced
½ pt/300 ml stock
Pinch of cayenne pepper
Salt and freshly ground pepper
4 chicken cutlets (see page 171)

1   Combine the first five ingredients in a small saucepan. Bring to the boil, reduce heat and simmer briskly until almost all the liquid has evaporated. Set aside.

2   Combine the peppers and stock in a deep, heavy frying pan. Bring to the boil. Cover, reduce heat and simmer for 20–30 minutes, until tender. Cool.

3   Purée the peppers in a liquidizer or food processor. Strain through a sieve or strainer, rubbing it through with a rubber spatula or a wooden spoon. The skins will be left behind. Discard them.

4   Put the purée in a saucepan. Simmer for a few minutes until it is thick enough to coat the back of a spoon. Stir in the tarragon infusion and season to taste with salt and pepper. This sauce may be prepared several days ahead and stored in the refrigerator until needed. Warm it while the chicken is cooking.

5   Heat a heavy, non-stick frying pan until moderately hot. Season the chicken with salt and pepper. Cook for 3 minutes on the skinned side, then carefully turn and cook on the second side for approximately 3 minutes or until *just* cooked through. (It will feel firm but a little springy when touched with your finger.) Place the chicken on a plate and cover loosely.

6   Stir any juices that have accumulated under the chicken into the hot yellow pepper sauce. Ladle a generous amount of the sauce onto warm dinner plates. Slice each chicken cutlet crosswise into ½-inch/1.25-cm slices. Overlap the slices from each cutlet on the puddle of sauce. Serve at once.

♡ ⊕ CHICKEN WITH RASPBERRIES

Makes 4 pieces

This is one of the most exciting chicken breast recipes I know. The garlic cloves are cooked and served like a vegetable. Use fresh, firm, unblemished bulbs. The manner of cooking ensures that they become tender and mild – not the slightest bit overpowering or 'garlicky'. If the thought of raspberries with garlic is just too shocking, omit the raspberry garnish (but not the raspberry juice –

173

it is essential to the goodness of the sauce). Although you have to thaw a package of frozen raspberries to get the little bit of juice needed, you can make a batch of Raspberry Sauce (see page 318) with the thawed berries for use in a dessert, later in the week.

16 large garlic cloves	4 chicken cutlets (see page 171)
1 teaspoon sugar	Salt and freshly ground pepper to
3½ tablespoons raspberry vinegar	taste
4 fl oz/120 ml water	Raspberry juice and a few
4 fl oz/120 ml chicken stock	raspberries for garnish

Note: Use thawed frozen raspberries for the garnish. Some of the juice will be used in Step 4 to augment the sauce.

1   Combine garlic, sugar, ½ tablespoon vinegar and ½ table-spoon water in a small saucepan. Bring to the boil. Reduce heat and simmer, uncovered, for about 3 minutes, until sugar dissolves. Increase the heat to a rapid simmer, cover, and let cook until the garlic is tender, and caramelized, and the liquid is just about gone, about 10 minutes.

2   Add the stock and the remaining vinegar and boil, uncovered, for another minute. Set aside.

3   Heat a heavy, non-stick frying pan until moderately hot. Season the chicken with salt and pepper. Cook for 3 minutes on the skinned side, then carefully turn and cook on the second side for approximately 3 minutes or until *just* cooked through. (The pieces will feel firm but a little springy when touched with your finger.) Place the chicken on a plate and cover loosely.

4   Add the sauce and the garlic to the frying pan. Bring to the boil, stirring and scraping with a wooden spoon as you do so. Add 1–2 tablespoons of juice from the thawed raspberries. After about a minute the sauce will be thick and syrupy. Remove from the heat. Taste and season with a tiny bit of salt and some pepper.

5   Pour any juices that have accumulated under the chicken into the sauce. Add the chicken and turn it to coat with the sauce. Arrange the chicken on a serving plate. Pour the sauce and the garlic over and around it. Place a few berries on each plate for garnish. Serve at once.

♡ ⊕ ❄ **CHICKEN CURRY**

Serves 6

This is an exquisite dish, excellent served warm, tepid or cool. It does not reheat well. The only tricky thing about the recipe is the timing. You want to catch the chicken at the exact moment of doneness, when it is creamy, tender and perfect.

6 skinless, boneless chicken breasts	½ bay leaf, finely crumbled
Juice of 1 large lemon	2 cloves garlic, minced
Salt to taste	2 medium onions, cut into eighths
1 teaspoon each: ground turmeric,	10 fl oz/300 ml stock
ground cumin, ground	4 fl oz/120 ml stock
coriander	2 tablespoons tomato paste
½ teaspoon each: caster sugar,	1 oz/30 g raisins
ground chillies, ground	3 tablespoons plain low-fat
cinnamon	yoghurt, at room temperature

1   Cut the chicken breasts crosswise into strips that are approximately 1 inch/2.5 cm wide. Each breast will yield about 5 strips. Put the strips in a bowl, squeeze the lemon juice over them, sprinkle with a bit of salt, and toss with two spoons to combine. Set aside.

2   Measure all the spices and herbs into a small bowl. Add the minced garlic.

3   Separate the segments of the onion pieces and spread them in a heavy, non-stick, frying pan. Add *no* liquid or fat. Heat the frying pan gently. Cook at moderate heat, without stirring, for 7–10 minutes, until the onions are sizzling, speckled with dark amber, and beginning to stick to the pan.

4   Stir in 10 fl oz/300 ml stock and let it bubble up, stirring up the browned deposits in the pan with a wooden spoon as it bubbles. Stir in the spices and garlic. Turn the heat down a bit and simmer, stirring frequently, until the mixture is very thick (not at all soupy), and the onions and spices are 'frying' in their own juices. Don't rush this step, as it is essential that the spices should not have a raw harsh taste. Taste. Cook very gently for a few more minutes if necessary.

5   Toss the chicken into the spicy onions in the frying pan. Stir and turn the chicken over low heat for 1 minute until everything is well combined. Stir in 4 fl oz/120 ml of stock and the tomato paste and raisins. Spread the mixture out evenly in the pan. Cover and cook over *lowest* heat for 4 minutes more.

6   Uncover. Add 2 tablespoons yoghurt. Stir over *low* heat for a few moments, until everything is amalgamated. Stir in the last

tablespoon of yoghurt and cook, stirring, for a moment or two more. Check the chicken for doneness. It should feel firm and springy, not soft and mushy. If you wish, cut into several pieces. You may even cut each strip in half. Each piece should be pearly white in the centre. Try to catch them when they are *just* done, at the moment they are turning from blush pink to creamy white. A minute or two of overcooking turns them tough and stringy. If they are not done yet, clap on the cover, turn off the heat and let them sit for a minute or two more. Stir everything up once more and serve warm or at room temperature.

CHICKEN WITH MANGO SAUCE

Serves 4

The ultimate dinner party dish, when you want to impress your guests. In fact you'll knock their socks off.

4 *chicken breasts of equal size, skinned but not boned*	4 *tablespoons mango chutney*
2 *large onions, cut in half and sliced into thin half-moons*	*Salt and freshly ground pepper to taste*
8 *fl oz/240 ml chicken stock*	*Pinch nutmeg*
2 *mangoes, peeled and chopped*	*Zest and juice of 1 lime*

1   Preheat oven to 350° F, 180° C, Gas Mark 4.
2   Sauté chicken breasts skinned side down, in a non-stick pan, until lightly browned. Set aside on a plate lined with paper towels. Blot well. Blot out any fat from the frying pan, but do not rub off any browned bits.
3   Put the onion and 3 fl oz/90 ml of stock in the pan. Cover and boil for 3–5 minutes. Uncover and stir, scraping up any browned bits in the pan. Stir in the mangoes, the chutney, and seasoning except the lime juice and zest. Simmer for 5 minutes.
4   Put the chicken, skinned side up, in a baking dish. Pour the mango mixture over the pieces. Cover and bake for 45 minutes or until the chicken is tender. Remove the chicken to a plate, cover loosely with foil and keep warm.
5   De-grease the pan juices. Purée them in the liquidizer. Correct seasonings. Pour over and around the chicken and serve at once.

BRAISED HONEY-MUSTARD CHICKEN

Makes 12 pieces

Serve this with rice to soak up the mustardy juices.

1½ tablespoons honey	*6 chicken legs, skinned*
Juice of ½ a lemon	*6 chicken thighs, skinned*
2 cloves garlic, minced	*Salt and freshly ground pepper to*
½ teaspoon soy sauce	* taste*
1–2 pinches cayenne pepper	*1 medium onion, coarsely chopped*
2 tablespoons Dijon mustard	

1 Preheat oven to 325° F, 170° C, Gas Mark 3.
2 In a small bowl, stir together the honey, lemon, garlic, soy sauce, cayenne pepper and mustard.
3 Season the chicken with salt and pepper. Put the chicken and onions in a casserole. Pour and scrape the mustard mixture over the chicken. Mix together very well so that the chicken and onions are coated with the sauce. Cover the baking dish with foil so that no steam can escape.
4 Bake for 1½ hours.

CHICKEN BRAISED WITH GARLIC

Makes 12 pieces
78 Calories per piece
1.5 g fat
(Traditional chicken braised with garlic: 166 Calories per piece, 2.8 g fat)

This is my low-fat version of a famous French classic. *Everyone* loves this dish, even confirmed garlic-haters. Slow, gentle cooking renders the usually pungent bulb sweet, mild and mysterious.

40 cloves garlic (see note)	*½ teaspoon allspice*
6 chicken legs, skinned	*¼ teaspoon cinnamon*
6 chicken thighs, skinned	*Pinch cayenne pepper*
2 medium onions, coarsely chopped	*Salt and freshly ground pepper to*
2 stalks celery, thinly sliced (save	* taste*
* the leaves)*	*2 fl oz/60 ml cognac*
2 tablespoons chopped fresh parsley	*3 fl oz/90 ml dry white vermouth*
1 teaspoon dried tarragon,	
* crumbled*	

1   Preheat oven to 325° F, 170° C, Gas Mark 3.
2   Place all ingredients in a deep, heavy pot that can be covered. Combine everything very well with your hands. Seal the pot very tightly with foil. Place the pot cover over the foil. The pot must be very well sealed so that no juices or steam can escape.
3   Bake for 1½ hours. Do not open the pot during this time.
4   Serve piping hot, with good crusty bread for mopping up the garlic and the juices. Open the pot at the table so that the diners get a blast of the wonderful fragrance that emerges as you open it.

Note: The garlic must be fresh and unblemished with no shrivelled cloves or green sprouts. If you wish, peel the garlic first, by parboiling the cloves for 3 minutes in water to cover, then slipping off the skins. If you are in a rush, however, throw in the garlic unpeeled. As it cooks, it will become a purée within its skin. Encourage diners to squeeze the purée out of the skin with their forks and spread it on bread. Garlic haters can ignore it completely, although they will be missing something marvellous if they do. Have a few empty plates on the table to receive the discarded garlic husks and the gnawed chicken bones. Both this and the preceding Honey-Mustard Chicken can be made a day ahead of time and reheated – the flavour will improve. Cook the dish for only 1¼ hours on the first day, cool and refrigerate. On the next day, scrape off the congealed fat, then reheat gently, covered, in the oven.

Variations:

Use the procedure in the preceding two recipes but try these combinations of ingredients:

Chicken Cacciatore: tomatoes, mushrooms, wine
Oreganato: lemon juice, oregano, onions, wine, garlic
Indian-Style: cardamom, cumin, coriander, cayenne, lemon juice and rind, onion, garlic, fresh coriander
American Barbecued: tomato purée, browned onions, cider vinegar, chillies, dash Worcestershire sauce, 1–2 pinches brown sugar

❄ CHICKEN IN ONION-TOMATO GRAVY

Makes 12 pieces

This homely chicken dish has an Indian accent. It is best made in advance so that the flavours mellow and the congealed fat can be removed the next day.

178

4 large onions
15 fl oz/450 ml stock
1 tablespoon minced fresh peeled
    ginger
4 cloves garlic, minced
1 teaspoon ground cumin
1 teaspoon ground coriander
½ teaspoon cayenne pepper (to
    taste)

1 pinch ground cloves
8 cardamom pods, lightly crushed
1 bay leaf, broken in half
2 cinnamon sticks, broken in halves
2 tins (14 oz/420 g each) chopped
    tomatoes
6 chicken legs, skinned
6 chicken thighs, skinned
Salt and pepper to taste

1   Separate the segments of the onion pieces and spread them in
    a heavy, non-stick, frying pan. Add *no* liquid or fat. Heat the
    frying pan gently. Cook at moderate heat, without stirring, for
    7–10 minutes, until the onions are sizzling, speckled with dark
    amber, and beginning to stick to the pan.

2   Stir in 10 fl oz/300 ml of stock and let it bubble up, stirring up
    the browned deposits in the pan with a wooden spoon as it
    bubbles. Stir in the ginger, garlic and spices. Turn the heat
    down a bit and simmer, stirring frequently, until the mixture is
    very thick (not at all soupy), and the onions and spices are
    'frying' in their own juices. Don't rush this step – it is essential
    that the spices should not have a raw harsh taste. Taste. Cook
    very gently for a few more minutes if necessary.

3   Stir the tomatoes into the onions. Set the pan aside.

4   Place the chicken thighs, skinned side down, in a non-stick
    frying pan. Heat gently until the chicken is sizzling. Do not
    add fat or oil! Brown the chicken thighs lightly on the skinned
    side, season with salt and pepper, turn and brown lightly on
    the other side. Blot them with paper towels, then place them,
    skinned side down, in one layer, on the tomato mixture.
    Repeat with the chicken legs. Place them between and over the
    thighs. Blot the pan with paper towels in order to mop up the
    rendered fat.

5   Pour the remaining stock into the frying pan and boil rapidly,
    until it is reduced by more than half. Stir and scrape up the
    browned bits on the bottom of the frying pan as it boils. Pour
    the stock over the chicken.

6   Bring the tomato-chicken mixture to the boil. Reduce heat,
    cover, and simmer for 20 minutes.

7   At the end of 20 minutes, turn and rearrange the chicken
    pieces in the pan. Cover and simmer until the chicken is done,
    20–30 minutes more.

8   Remove the chicken to a casserole or a platter. Cover loosely
    with foil so that it does not dry out. Tip the pan and skim as
    much fat as possible from the sauce. Boil the sauce for a few

minutes, until it is thick and pulpy. Recombine the chicken and sauce, cover, cool somewhat, and refrigerate.

9   The next day, scrape out the congealed fat and discard it. Reheat the chicken and sauce gently.

PIQUANT CHICKEN

Makes 8 pieces

I love this way of cooking chicken; it tastes so *fattening*! The mixture of yoghurt and mustard keeps the chicken meltingly tender and moist, but the taste is not at all yoghurty.

8 fl oz/240 ml yoghurt	*8 chicken thighs, skinned*
4 tablespoons Dijon mustard	*8 tablespoons wholemeal*
Salt and freshly ground pepper to	*breadcrumbs*
taste	

1   Mix together the yoghurt, mustard, salt and pepper.
2   Combine yoghurt mixture and chicken in a non-reactive dish that will hold them in one layer. Refrigerate for 12–24 hours.
3   Preheat oven to 375° F, 190° C, Gas Mark 5.
4   Line two baking trays with foil, shiny side up. Put a rack on each tray.
5   Put each piece of chicken, skinned side up, on the rack. They should be thoroughly coated with the yoghurt mixture. Sprinkle each piece with a tablespoon of crumbs.
6   Bake for 40–50 minutes, or until just done.

TANDOORI CHICKEN

Makes 8 pieces

This, like the previous Piquant Chicken, seems to please everyone. It can be served hot or cold, and makes a wonderful addition to a party buffet.

8 chicken drumsticks, skinned	*Pinch of ground cloves*
Salt and freshly ground pepper to	*¼ teaspoon ground cinnamon*
taste	*¼–½ teaspoon cayenne pepper*
1 tablespoon ground coriander	*12 fl oz/360 ml yoghurt*
1 teaspoon ground cumin	*6 cloves garlic, peeled and crushed*
1 teaspoon ground turmeric	*1 onion, chopped*
1 teaspoon garam masala	*1 piece ginger (1-inch/2.5-cm),*
¼ teaspoon nutmeg	*peeled and minced*

1   Slash each chicken drumstick in two places. Toss with salt and pepper. Set aside.
2   Combine remaining ingredients. Mix chicken with this mixture in a large bowl, cover, and allow to marinate in the refrigerator overnight.
3   Preheat oven to 350° F, 180° C, Gas Mark 4. Spread chicken pieces out in one layer in a shallow baking dish. Brush with some of the marinade. Cover tightly with foil. Bake for 30 minutes.
4   Uncover. Bake for 20–30 minutes more or until just done, but very moist. Remove from pan. Pour juices into a jug. Refrigerate the juices. Wipe out the baking dish. Heat the grill.
5   Arrange the chicken pieces in the dish in one layer. Grill about 3 inches/7 cm from the grilling element for approximately 2 minutes on each side, until nicely browned. Serve at once.
6   When the juices are cold, scrape out and discard hardened fat. Use the flavourful stock for sautéeing or soups.

CHICKEN VINDALOO

Makes 8 pieces
69 Calories per piece
1.5 g fat
(Traditional chicken vindaloo: 307 Calories per piece, 12 g fat)

Indian vindaloos are sour and spicy, and beautifully pungent.

2–3 tiny chilli peppers, thickly sliced	1 teaspoon whole cumin seeds
1 medium onion, cut into chunks	1 teaspoon whole coriander seeds
2 cloves garlic, lightly crushed	1 teaspoon turmeric
1 piece (2-inches/5-cm long) fresh ginger, peeled and cut into chunks	1 teaspoon whole mustard seeds
	2 tablespoons white vinegar
	8 chicken legs, skin and fat removed
	Salt to taste

1   Combine all ingredients except chicken and salt in the liquidizer. Purée the mixture, stopping to scrape down the sides of the container with a rubber spatula.
2   Slash each chicken leg in 2–3 places with a sharp knife. Toss the chicken and spice paste together. Allow to marinate for at least 1 hour.
3   Gently heat a heavy, non-stick frying pan that can hold the

pieces of chicken in one layer. When moderately hot, put in the chicken pieces and spice paste. Cook gently for 1–2 minutes, turning the chicken with tongs, until it has just lost its raw look. Do not brown it.

4   Turn the heat to the lowest point. Cover the pan tightly and cook for about 1 hour, or until the chicken is very tender. Turn the chicken every 15 minutes or so.

CHICKEN BHUNA

Makes 8 pieces
79 Calories per piece
1.9 g fat
(Traditional chicken bhuna: 323 Calories per piece, 12 g fat)

Eat this vibrant Indian dish at once, it does not hold well.

1 medium onion, chopped	1 teaspoon ground cumin
10 fl oz/300 ml stock	1 teaspoon chilli powder
2 cloves garlic, minced	Pinch cloves
1 teaspoon chopped fresh peeled	½ bay leaf, broken in half
ginger	1 tablespoon grated coconut
1 teaspoon turmeric	2–3 tablespoons tomato paste
½ teaspoon ground cinnamon	8 chicken thighs, skinned
½ teaspoon grated nutmeg	Chopped fresh coriander
½ teaspoon ground allspice	

1   Spread the onions in a heavy, non-stick, frying pan. Add *no* liquid or fat. Heat the frying pan gently. Cook at moderate heat, without stirring, for 7–10 minutes, until the onions are sizzling, speckled with dark amber, and beginning to stick to the pan.

2   Stir in 10 fl oz/300 ml of stock and let it bubble up, stirring up the browned deposits in the pan with a wooden spoon as it bubbles. Stir in the ginger, garlic and spices. Turn the heat down a bit and simmer, stirring frequently, until the mixture is very thick (not at all soupy), and the onions and spices are 'frying' in their own juices. Don't rush this step, it is essential that the spices should not have a raw harsh taste. Taste. Cook very gently for a few more minutes if necessary.

3   Stir in the coconut and tomato paste. Add the chicken and stir it around to coat it thoroughly with the spice mixture.

4   Cover and cook over the lowest possible heat for about 1 hour, until the chicken is very tender. Turn the pieces occasionally. Serve garnished with coriander.

182

OVEN-'FRIED' CHICKEN WITH CREAMY MINT DIPPING SAUCE

Makes 8 pieces of chicken
130 Calories per 'fried' chicken leg
2.4 g fat
(Traditional fried chicken: 232 Calories per piece, 7.3 g fat)

Oven-'frying' produces juicy, crispy crusted chicken that is prepared without a speck of oil or fat. The dipping sauce is Indian-inspired.

⅗ pt/360 ml plain yoghurt
6 oz/200 g breadcrumbs
Salt and freshly ground pepper to taste

4 chicken thighs, skinned
4 chicken legs, skinned
Dipping sauce (recipe follows)

---

1   Preheat oven to 400° F, 200° C, Gas Mark 6.
2   Pour the yoghurt into a wide, shallow bowl and set it on your work surface.
3   Season the breadcrumbs with salt and pepper. Spread crumbs out on a platter and place next to the yoghurt.
4   Place a wire rack over a baking sheet and set aside.
5   Dry the chicken pieces. Dip each piece into the yoghurt until thoroughly coated on both sides. Then roll each pieces in the crumbs, pressing the piece in so that the crumbs adhere. Each piece should be evenly coated.
6   Place the chicken on the wire rack. Bake for 40–45 minutes, or until just done.
7   To serve, place a piece of chicken on each of four small plates. Pour some sauce in a crescent on the bottom edge of each plate, around the chicken but not on it. Put the remaining pieces of chicken on a platter and pass the remaining sauce in a clear jug.

Note: If you don't use dairy produce with meat, dip the chicken into egg white instead of yoghurt and choose a vegetable purée sauce (see index) instead of the following one.

³⁄₅ pt/360 ml plain low-fat yoghurt
½ small onion, coarsely chopped
1 thin slice ginger root, peeled and
    chopped
1 teaspoon chopped fresh chillies (or
    more to taste)

Salt to taste
6 tablespoons fresh mint leaves
2 tablespoons fresh coriander
    (Chinese parsley) leaves
2 tablespoons fresh parsley leaves

Place all the ingredients in a blender or food processor. Flick the motor on and off until a thin, flecked green sauce is achieved. Serve at once.

POACHED CHICKEN

If you want to poach a chicken in a hurry, use this nifty technique taught to me by a Chinese friend.

1 chicken (2½ lb/1,125 g)
Boiling water (10 pts/6 l)

1   Bring the water to the boil in a deep pot.
2   Pull all excess fat from the chicken and wash well, inside and out, in cold water. Submerge the chicken in the boiling water. When the water returns to a full boil, cover and boil hard for 12 minutes (5 minutes per lb/480 g).
3   Remove the pot from the heat and let the chicken cool in the pot. (Do not leave it to cool at room temperature for more than 2 hours. It can, however, be refrigerated, pot, cooking liquid, and all, overnight.)
4   Remove it from the liquid. (It will still be quite warm so be careful.) Remove the skin. Pull the meat off the bones in large pieces. Discard all tendons and gristle. Tear the meat into chunks or shred it. Refrigerate in a shallow dish, moistened with a bit of stock and well covered with cling film until needed. Needless to say, this chicken is lovely in chicken salad. Or try it in Chilaquiles.

CHILAQUILES

Serves 6

This is an exciting, unusual and splendid recipe; a low-fat version of authentic Mexican home cooking. There are many versions, but they always involve layers of corn tortilla pieces and piquant sauce.

Sometimes meat or, as here, chicken is layered in too. The original versions are swimming in fat. I have used the recipe successfully with a smoked chicken, and if you are in a hurry you might want to use a ready-cooked chicken from the supermarket. Just be sure that you remove all skin and fat before using it. Corn tortillas are available in tins in many supermarkets and delicatessens. Reduce the amount of chilli peppers if you don't like spicy food.

1 pt/600 ml chicken stock	5 corn tortillas, baked in a 300° F,
1 large onion, chopped	150° C, Gas Mark 2 oven for
1 medium fresh chilli pepper, seeded	15–20 minutes, broken into
and coarsely diced	pieces (see page 308)
2 tiny fresh chilli peppers, diced	Meat from 1 (2–2½ lb/1.2 kg)
4 jalapeños tinned in vinegar,	poached chicken (see chicken
drained and coarsely diced	stock recipe or quick poached
2 tins (1 lb/480 g each) chopped	chicken recipe), shredded
tomatoes	6 oz/180 g part-skim Mozzarella
2 cloves garlic	cheese, shredded
Salt to taste	

1   In a heavy non-reactive frying pan, combine the onion in 4 fl oz/120 ml stock, cover and bring to the boil. Reduce heat and simmer for 5 minutes. Uncover, raise heat and simmer very briskly until almost all liquid has boiled away. Reduce heat and simmer gently until the liquid has gone and the onions are beginning to stick. Stir until they begin to toast and brown. Pour in a splash of stock and boil, stirring and scraping the browned bits on the bottom of the pan. Remove from the heat.

2   Place the chillies, jalapeños, tomatoes and garlic in the liquidizer. Blend to a smooth purée. Pour into the frying pan with the onions. Cook over low heat, stirring for a few minutes.

3   Add the remaining stock, and salt to taste, to the tomato mixture. Simmer, uncovered, for 35–45 minutes, until thick and pungent. At this point the sauce is almost hot enough to melt the frying pan. When it is mixed with the remaining ingredients, however, its piquancy will be somewhat diluted.

4   Preheat the oven to 350° F, 180° C, Gas Mark 4.

5   Layer ⅓ of the tortilla pieces, ⅓ of the sauce, ⅓ of the shredded chicken, and ⅓ of the cheese in a shallow non-reactive gratin dish or baking dish. Layer in the second ⅓ of tortilla pieces, sauce, chicken and cheese. Layer on the remaining tortilla pieces, the chicken, the cheese and the sauce.

6   Bake, uncovered, for 35 minutes until bubbly. Serve at once.

CHICKEN TARRAGON PIE

Serves 6

Here is a satisfying and interesting main course that uses both tender chicken meat and the Slim Cuisine onion-herb infusion. It is a sort of souffléd, savoury bread pudding. Serve with a salad of dark, leafy greens sprinkled with an interesting vinegar – balsamic, sherry or raspberry. The more interesting the vinegar, the less you will miss the olive oil. Because it contains high-fat eggs, make this pie only occasionally. If you do not have a poached chicken on hand, use the quick poached chicken recipe (see page 184) or buy a ready-cooked chicken from the supermarket. The recipe also works beautifully with a smoked chicken. Be sure to remove all skin and fat before using it.

---

6 oz/180 g stale bread torn into chunks
1 recipe onion-herb infusion (use tarragon as the herb, see page 27)
1 small poached or smoked chicken, shredded
2 oz/60 g part-skim Mozzarella, shredded

2 tablespoons grated Parmesan cheese
3 tablespoons chopped fresh parsley
3 eggs
4 fl oz/120 ml buttermilk
12 fl oz/360 ml skimmed milk
Salt, freshly ground pepper and cayenne pepper to taste

---

1 Preheat the oven to 350° F, 180° C, Gas Mark 4.
2 In a bowl, toss together the bread, the infusion, the chicken, the cheeses and the parsley. Spread this mixture in a 9 × 13-inch/23 × 33-cm shallow glass or ceramic baking dish.
3 Beat the eggs with the buttermilk. Gradually beat in the skimmed milk. Season with salt and peppers to taste. You will need very little salt because the infusion, the Parmesan and the peppers give plenty of flavour. Pour this mixture over the bread mixture. With a broad spatula or pancake turner, press the bread down into the liquid.
4 Bake for 40–45 minutes until puffed and set. A knife inserted near the centre should come out clean.

MOULDED CHICKEN SALAD

Serves 10
85 Calories per serving
0.4 g fat
(Traditional chicken salad: 234 Calories per serving, 18 g fat)

This is lovely as a luncheon dish or as a first course for a special dinner party. It makes a good sandwich filling too. Be sure that you season it well. It should not be bland.

Juice of 1 lemon	1 large stalk celery, finely minced
6 tablespoons chopped chives	2 poached chickens (use the poached
8 tablespoons chopped fresh dill	chicken left from making stock or
8 tablespoons chopped fresh parsley	see recipe for quick poached
⅕ pt/120 ml yoghurt or fromage	chicken, page 184)
frais cream cheese (see recipe)	Salt and freshly ground pepper to
Buttermilk	taste
Cayenne pepper	Watercress

1   Combine lemon juice, herbs, yoghurt cheese, 5 tablespoons buttermilk, cayenne pepper and celery in a large bowl.
2   Pull the chicken from the bones in chunks and shred it finely with your fingers. As you shred each chunk, stir it into the bowl. Discard every bit of fat, skin and gristle.
3   Stir in more buttermilk until the texture is creamy but not too loose. Season to taste with salt and freshly ground pepper and more cayenne if desired. The flavour should be very lively.
4   Tightly pack the mixture into a 1¼-pt/750-ml mould (heart-shaped is nice). Cover and refrigerate overnight. The mixture will taste quite yoghurty at first but it will mellow overnight until it tastes as if it were made with a lemony mayonnaise.
5   At serving time, loosen the mousse all round with a thin-bladed knife. Unmould onto a pretty serving plate. Garnish with watercress and serve.

CURRIED CHICKEN SALAD

Serves 10

This is an elegant, spicy version of the moulded chicken salad. It's a show-stopping buffet dish.

7 shallots, peeled and chopped	½ teaspoon ground chillies
8 oz/224 g sultanas	½ teaspoon ground allspice
4 fl oz/120 ml chicken stock	⅕ pt/120 ml yoghurt or fromage
4 fl oz/120 ml raspberry vinegar	frais cream cheese
2 teaspoons minced fresh ginger	Buttermilk
4 cloves garlic, minced	8 tablespoons chopped fresh parsley
1 teaspoon turmeric	1 large stalk celery, finely minced
2 teaspoons each: ground cumin,	2 poached chickens
ground coriander, ground	Salt, freshly ground pepper and
cinnamon	cayenne pepper to taste
¼ teaspoon ground cloves	Fresh coriander

1   Spread the shallot pieces in a heavy, non-stick frying pan. Add *no* liquid or fat. Heat the frying pan gently. Cook at moderate heat, without stirring, for 7–10 minutes, until the shallots are sizzling, speckled with dark amber, and beginning to stick to the pan.

2   Stir in the sultanas, stock, and raspberry vinegar and let it bubble up, stirring up the browned deposits in the pan with a wooden spoon as it bubbles. Stir in the ginger, garlic and spices. Turn the heat down a bit and simmer, stirring frequently, until the mixture is very thick (not at all soupy), and the shallots and spices are 'frying' in their own juices. Don't rush this step, it is essential that the spices should not have a raw harsh taste. Taste. Cook very gently for a few more minutes if necessary. Cool.

3   Combine the cooled mixture with the yoghurt, 5 tablespoons of buttermilk, parsley and celery in a large bowl.

4   Pull the chicken from the bones in chunks and shred each chunk into the bowl. Discard every bit of fat, skin and gristle.

5   Stir in more buttermilk until the texture is creamy but not too loose. Season with salt, freshly ground pepper and cayenne if you want it very spicy. Tightly pack the mixture into a mould as described in the previous recipe. Refrigerate overnight. At serving time, unmould on to a pretty plate and garnish with fresh coriander.

♡ ⊕   CHICKEN-BERRY SALAD

Serves 6

This is the most elegant of chicken salads. Serve it as a main dish at a light supper or a special luncheon. With its berries, creamy-textured chicken breast and light dressing, this salad is the essence of summer. Shredded poached chicken may be substituted for the chicken cutlets, or use smoked chicken.

---

6 chicken cutlets (see page 171)
1 lb/480 g mixed fresh berries (use blueberries, blackberries, strawberries, raspberries, whatever you can find)
½ lb/240 g seedless grapes

8 oz/240 g drained low-fat fromage frais
Juice of ½ small lemon
½ teaspoon mild honey
2 tablespoons buttermilk
Salt and freshly ground pepper to taste
Fresh mint leaves

---

1   Cook the chicken according to the pan-sauté method (see page 172).

2   Slice each chicken cutlet into crosswise wide slices on the diagonal. Overlap them on a pretty platter. Surround the chicken with the mixed berries and grapes.

3   Combine remaining ingredients except mint leaves. Pour a bit of dressing in a stripe down the centre of the chicken slices. Garnish with mint leaves. Serve the rest of the dressing separately.

CHICKEN PESTO POTATO SALAD

Make this main dish potato salad the star of an elegant summer buffet. Begin with Gazpacho (page 106) and conclude with Strawberries in Raspberry Sauce (page 319) and a cloud of fromage frais.

1 lb/480 g small new potatoes	4 fl oz/120 ml Slim Cuisine Pesto
1 lb/480 g boned and cubed smoked	(see page 231)
chicken	2 fl oz/60 ml buttermilk
1 red pepper, peeled and coarsely	Whole basil leaves
chopped	

1   Cut the potatoes into halves or quarters, depending on size. Do not peel. Steam over boiling water until cooked through but not mushy. Cool. When cool, cut into 1 inch/2.5 cm chunks.

2   Combine potatoes, chicken and peppers. Thin Pesto to dressing consistency with a bit of buttermilk. Toss the potato-chicken mixture with the Pesto. Serve on a plate, garnished with whole basil leaves.

♡ ORIENTAL CHICKEN SALAD

One of my best cold party buffet dishes. Don't add the mango until the last minute, or it will cause the chicken to develop a rubbery texture.

6 boned, skinned chicken breast	Salt and freshly ground pepper to
halves	taste
1 large onion, chopped	1 small red pepper, peeled and
2 cloves garlic, minced	chopped
A 1-inch/2.5-cm piece fresh ginger,	1 stalk celery, cut in half lengthwise
peeled and minced	and thinly sliced

Seeds of 5 cardamom pods
2 tablespoons soy sauce
2½ tablespoons dry sherry
2 tablespoons honey
3–4 fl oz/90–120 ml sherry, wine
  vinegar, or rice wine vinegar

1 mango, peeled and cubed

Garnish
1 sliced Granny Smith apple,
  rubbed with lemon juice
Fresh coriander or parsley

1   Preheat oven to 350° F, 180° C, Gas Mark 4.
2   Trim the chicken breasts of any bits of gristle and fat. Spread in one layer in a heavy, very shallow baking dish, skinned side up.
3   Combine onion, garlic, ginger, cardamom seeds, soy sauce, sherry and honey. Bring to the boil.
4   Pour this mixture evenly over the chicken. Cover tightly with foil. Bake for 30 minutes or until the chicken is *just* done.
5   Put the chicken in one layer on a plate. Cover loosely with cling film or foil. Pour and scrape the onions and juices into a saucepan.
6   Boil the juices until they are syrupy and the onions are amber and tender.
7   Cut the chicken into ½-inch/1.25-cm cubes. Sprinkle with the vinegar and toss together. Gently stir in the onion mixture. Season to taste with salt and pepper. Spread out in a shallow dish, cover and set aside.
8   Just before serving, stir in the pepper, celery and mango. Arrange attractively in a bowl or on a serving plate. Garnish with the apple slices and coriander or parsley. Serve at room temperature.

ROAST CHICKEN

Serves 3–4

Use a free-range chicken, a corn-fed one, or a Poulet Noir. The method of stuffing a savoury mixture under the breast skin produces a remarkably succulent and savoury bird. Discard the stuffing and the skin (too much fat) before serving.

1 3–3½ lb/1.5–1.75 kg chicken
4 tablespoons chopped parsley
4 cloves garlic, minced
1 small onion, minced
2 tablespoons chopped fresh
  rosemary

1 tablespoon Dijon mustard
1 tablespoon grated Parmesan
1 Spanish onion, cut in half and
  sliced into thick half-moons
Chicken stock
4 fl oz/120 ml white wine

1   Preheat oven to 375° F, 190° C, Gas Mark 5.
2   Loosen the skin on the chicken's breast. Combine remaining ingredients except Spanish onion, stock and wine. Spread this mixture over the breast, under the skin.
3   Spread out the Spanish onion slices in a roasting pan. Place a rack across the pan. Place the chicken, breast up, on the rack. Pour in 4 fl oz/120 ml stock and the wine.
4   Roast for 1¼–1½ hours, basting with the pan juices and additional stock, if necessary, every 15 minutes. Turn the chicken occasionally, so that it cooks evenly.
5   Remove the chicken from the roasting pan and allow to rest on a plate, loosely covered with foil. Thoroughly de-grease the pan juices.
6   Return the pan juices to the roasting pan and put the pan right on to the hob. Bring to the boil, scraping up the browned bits with a wooden spoon.
7   Discard the skin and the stuffing from the chicken. Serve the chicken with the pan juices.

LEMON ROASTED CHICKEN

Serves 4

This was inspired by a winning recipe in the *Daily Mail*'s Slim Cuisine recipe contest. I don't know which is better, the moist chicken meat, or the incredible gravy. Leftovers make superb sandwiches.

Juice of 1½ lemons	*1 medium (2½–3 lb/1–1.5 kg)*
1 teaspoon black pepper	*roasting chicken, trimmed of fat*
2 teaspoons cumin	*4–6 fl oz/120–180 ml dry white*
1 teaspoon paprika or paprika paste	*wine*

1   Mix the lemon juice with all the ingredients except chicken and wine. Make small incisions all over the chicken (except in the breast) and rub in the lemon mixture. Loosen the breast skin and rub the lemon mixture under the skin. Place the squeezed lemon halves in the chicken's cavity. Marinate overnight.
2   Next day, preheat the oven to 450° F, 230° C, Gas Mark 8. Place a rack across a flameproof shallow roasting pan. Place chicken on the rack and roast breast down for 15 minutes, breast up for approximately 45 minutes until just done.
3   Allow the chicken to rest on a plate, loosely covered with foil. Tilt the roasting pan, and prop it in the tilted position. With a large spoon, spoon out all fat (there will be plenty) and

discard. Put the roasting pan right on the hob, and turn the heat on full. Stir and scrape up the drippings and browned bits. Pour in 4–6 fl oz/120–180 ml dry white wine. Boil, stirring and scraping, until you have a dark, thick, rich sauce, and the alcohol has cooked away. Serve this powerful juice with the carved chicken.

♡ ⏰ CHICKEN LIVER KEBABS

Makes 10 small skewers

Chinese five-spice powder and chilli and garlic sauce are available in most supermarkets and delicatessens. This is a very delicate and attractive way to serve chicken livers. Remember, liver, although high in vitamins and minerals, is also high in cholesterol. Don't eat liver if your blood cholesterol level is high.

Marinade ingredients	Skewer ingredients
1 tablespoon teriyaki sauce	*1 lb/480 g chicken livers, trimmed*
¼ teaspoon five-spice powder	*and cut in halves*
Zest of ½ orange	*1 small red pepper, peeled and cut*
Freshly ground pepper to taste	*into 1-inch/2.5-cm squares*
2 tablespoons sherry	*1 small yellow pepper, peeled and*
1 teaspoon chilli and garlic sauce	*cut into 1-inch/2.5-cm squares*
	1 box cherry tomatoes

1   In a bowl, stir together teriyaki sauce, five-spice powder, orange zest, freshly ground pepper, sherry, and chilli and garlic sauce. Add the livers and stir well. Cover and leave to marinate at room temperature for 1 hour.

2   Preheat the grill to its highest point. Line the grill tray with foil, shiny side up, and place the rack on the grill tray.

3   Drain the livers and reserve the marinade. Using ten 4-inch/10-cm metal skewers, thread the chicken livers as follows: a pepper square, a liver half, a cherry tomato, a liver half, a pepper square, a liver half, a pepper square, a cherry tomato. Repeat until all the skewers are filled.

4   Grill, about 3 inches/8 cm from the heat, for 4–6 minutes altogether. Turn the skewers and baste with the marinade, using a pastry brush, about every 2 minutes. Do not overcook. The livers should be *just* cooked through and not dried out. Serve at once with rice, Kasha (see page 281), or Wheat Pilaf (see page 280).

♡ ROAST TURKEY

I turkeyed out years ago. It was Thanksgiving that did it. Year after year, late November arrived yet again, and with it the obligatory meal of the mythic big brown bird and its accompanying submythic vegetables. Ben Franklin campaigned for the turkey to be America's national bird. Had he succeeded, Americans would probably have spent the last 213 Novembers devouring roast eagle with all the trimmings, and I would have experienced an eagle crisis instead. Anyway, I serve shepherd's pie on Thanksgiving now. (Don't laugh. You haven't lived until you've tried my shepherd's pie – see page 153.) I found out that even though I opted out of the November turkey game, I was allowed to keep my citizenship. Indeed, except for this aberration I consider myself a good (though expatriate) American. But I digress. The point is that the British are caught in the turkey trap too, but it happens here in December. Turkeys are lean, but the fatty excesses that are committed upon them in the name of Christmas are appalling. Here is a delicious low-fat method of serving up the festive bird.

15–18 lb/7–8.5 kg free-range turkey	2 tablespoons chopped fresh rosemary
1 lemon	3 tablespoons Dijon mustard
4 tablespoons chopped fresh parsley	1 tablespoon grated Parmesan cheese
4 cloves minced garlic	6 Spanish onions
3 small onions, minced	Stock
	Cognac

---

1   Have the fresh turkey at room temperature. Remove giblets and use to make turkey stock. Save the liver for another use. Wash turkey inside and out and rub it inside with a cut lemon. Preheat oven to 325° F, 170° C, Gas Mark 3.

2   Loosen the skin on the turkey's breast. Combine parsley, garlic, minced onion, rosemary, Dijon mustard and Parmesan cheese. Spread the mixture over the breast, under the skin.

3   Stuff the large cavity of the bird with 3 large Spanish onions, quartered. Plug up opening with a ball of foil. Secure the neck flap of skin with a skewer. Secure the wings to the body with skewers. Do not truss legs. (The heat will penetrate to the thighs more efficiently if the legs are left free.)

4   Place turkey, breast down, on a rack in a roasting pan in the preheated oven. Put some stock and a small amount of cognac in the pan. Slice 3 onions into the pan. Roast, breast down, for a little more than half the cooking time. Then turn the breast

up for remainder of time. Baste the bird with stock and a bit of cognac every 20 minutes or so. Replenish stock as it evaporates. If the turkey browns too fast, drape it with clean cheesecloth and baste through the cloth.

5   When a thermometer inserted into the thickest part of the breast registers 170 to 175 degrees, the turkey is done. (Use an instant-read thermometer, if possible.) An overcooked bird is dry and tasteless, so check the temperature carefully. An 18 lb/8 kg bird will be done in about 4½ hours, but turkeys are unpredictable. Depend on your thermometer; use the clock only as a guide. When finished, let the turkey rest for 30 minutes.

6   While the bird is resting, pour the pan juices into a jug and place in the freezer so the fat rises to the top. Skim off *all* fat and pour the juices back into the roasting pan. Place the pan on the stove. Add a bit more stock if necessary and 4 fl oz/120 ml cognac. Boil down rapidly, stirring, and scraping up the browned bits. Strain the gravy or not, as you wish.

7   Discard the turkey skin (too much fat) and the stuffing under the skin (its purpose was to keep the breast meat moist and flavourful). Serve with the gravy and Chestnut Stuffing (see following recipe).

'The fact was, none of them cared for turkey. Still . . . it didn't seem right to serve anything else. It would just feel wrong.'

Anne Tyler, *The Accidental Tourist*

CHESTNUT STUFFING

To accompany a large roast turkey

It's best to bake this in a separate casserole, rather than in the cavity of the bird, so that it does not absorb an inordinate amount of fat. And the turkey will be juicier if roasted without stuffing.

Sausage Mix (see recipe below)
2 large onions, chopped
1 large tin (2 lb/960 g cooked, shelled) chestnuts, drained and rinsed
4 tablespoons chopped fresh parsley
1 teaspoon fresh thyme or ¼–½ teaspoon dried thyme

5 oz/150 g French bread, torn into pieces and toasted lightly in the oven
Approximately 4 fl oz/120 ml skimmed milk
Salt and pepper to taste
Pinch or two of cayenne pepper to taste

194

1 small Baked Aubergine, chopped fine (see page 37)	4 fl oz/120 ml cognac
1 rounded tablespoon tomato paste	8 fl oz/240 ml de-fatted turkey or chicken stock

1   Brown fresh Sausage Mix and onions in a heavy non-stick frying pan. Break up meat as it cooks. Drain off all fat.
2   Mash chestnuts and add to meat and onions. Add parsley, thyme, Baked Aubergine and tomato paste.
3   Moisten toasted bread with milk. Squeeze out excess. Place in a large bowl with chestnut mixture. Add salt, peppers and cognac and toss it all together. Taste and adjust seasonings. It should have a lively, peppery taste.
4   Put into a large gratin dish, pour in the stock, cover and bake at 325° F, 170° C, Gas Mark 3, for 1 hour. Uncover and bake for 1 additional hour.

Sausage Mix

1 lb/480 g lean minced veal	Juice and grated zest of ½ small lemon
1 small Baked Aubergine, chopped fine (see page 37)	6 tablespoons freshly grated Parmesan cheese
2 oz/50 g dry breadcrumbs	Salt and pepper to taste

Combine thoroughly.

BREAST OF DUCKLING À L'ORANGE

Serves 4

For duck lovers, this is as elegant and ducky as can be, without the quantities of fat usually found in duck preparations. Duck breast fillets are available all the year round in selected supermarkets throughout the UK. They are traditionally cooked medium rare (pink). Cooked this way, duck breast meat bears an uncanny resemblance to the finest beef steak.

4 duckling breast fillets	4 fl oz/120 ml fresh orange juice
¼ teaspoon ground cumin	4 fl oz/120 ml chicken or duck stock
¼ teaspoon ground ginger	2 fl oz/60 ml dry red wine
Freshly ground pepper	½ teaspoon red wine vinegar
Salt to taste	

1   Work your fingers between the duckling flesh and the skin. Gently and steadily pull the skin from each breast fillet. It

should strip right off. Use a sharp knife to help loosen it, should you hit a stubborn spot. Discard the skin and trim off and discard any fat and gristle on the fillets.

2   Combine the cumin and ginger. Sprinkle some of the spice mixture onto both sides of the duck breast fillets and rub it in. Sprinkle both sides of each fillet generously with freshly ground pepper and press it in. Set the fillets aside for 15 minutes.

3   Heat a heavy, non-stick frying pan until quite hot. It should be of a size to hold the fillets without letting them touch one another. When hot, salt the fillets lightly, and place them, skinned side up, in the pan. Cook for 3–4 minutes on each side, until medium rare (pink within). Use tongs to turn them. Test for the proper degree of doneness by poking them with your finger. If they feel mushy, they are very rare. If they feel firm, but springy, they are medium rare. If they feel quite firm with no springiness, they are well done and, in my opinion, overcooked.

4   Remove the fillets and blot gently with paper towels to remove any rendered fat. Put them on a warm platter, cover loosely with foil and set aside in a warm place. An oven set at its lowest point is perfect.

5   Gently blot the frying pan with paper towels, to remove any fat. Pour orange juice, stock, wine and wine vinegar into the pan. It will boil up furiously. Let it boil, stirring and scraping up the browned bits in the pan with a wooden spoon. When thickened and syrupy, remove from the heat. Stir in any juices that have accumulated under the fillets.

6   Slice each fillet into thin slices, on the diagonal, crosswise. Overlap them on warm plates. Pour the sauce over them. Serve at once.

Vegetarian

'An attachment à la Plato for a bashful young potato or a not too French French Bean'

W. S. Gilbert, *Patience*

A meal does not always have to be focused on meat, poultry or fish. Vegetables can easily be the star of a meal. There are vegetable recipes in other sections of the book as well that can be served as vegetarian main courses. Check the pasta and potato side dish sections in particular.

'Since he was not a man who easily showed his liking for people, he chose to cook them their favourite foods instead – the comfort foods that everyone turns to when he is feeling low.'

Ann Tyler, *Searching for Caleb*

❄ GRATIN OF RED BEANS, NEW ORLEANS STYLE

Serves 6

A colourful and spicy bean feast, to serve as a main dish or a vegetable accompaniment.

3 large onions, coarsely chopped	*1 tin (14 oz/420 g) chopped*
12 fl oz/360 ml stock	*tomatoes*
4 red peppers, peeled and coarsely	*1 bay leaf*
chopped	*Salt and freshly ground pepper to*
4 stalks celery, chopped	*taste*
½ teaspoon cumin	*4 fl oz/120 ml red wine*
½ teaspoon coriander	*2 tins (15 oz/450 g each) red kidney*
Pince of cayenne pepper	*beans, drained and rinsed*
½ teaspoon dried thyme	*2 tablespoons dry wholemeal*
¼ teaspoon dried oregano,	*breadcrumbs*
crumbled	*2 tablespoons grated Parmesan*
	cheese

1   Preheat oven to to 400° F, 200° C, Gas Mark 6.
2   Put the onions in a frying pan with 6 fl oz/180 ml of stock. Cover. Boil for 5 minutes. Uncover, reduce heat somewhat, and simmer until amber brown and beginning to stick to the pan.
3   Stir in the peppers, celery and a splash of stock. Stir and cook until the added vegetables are softened.
4   Stir in the cumin, coriander, cayenne pepper, thyme, oregano, tomatoes, bayleaf, salt and pepper and wine. Simmer, stirring occasionally, for 20–30 minutes, until thick and savoury.
5   Stir in the beans. Spread in a baking dish. Sprinkle with a mixture of the breadcrumbs and the grated cheese. (The recipe can be prepared to this point and refrigerated until needed.)
6   Bake the beans, uncovered, for 30 minutes, until bubbling and browned on top.

♡   Omit cheese.

♡ ⊕ ❄ **RAJMAA – RED KIDNEY**
BEANS

Makes 2 pts/1.2 l
Serves 8

This dish is adapted from a family recipe of Shashi Rattan. I have substituted the Slim Cuisine Curry technique for her traditional ones.

---

2 large onions, coarsely chopped
1 pt/600 ml vegetable stock
2 teaspoons minced ginger
1 clove garlic, crushed
½ teaspoon ground cumin
½ teaspoon ground cinnamon
½ teaspoon ground coriander
Dash of ground cloves and cayenne
1 bay leaf

4 green cardamom pods, lightly
    crushed
1 large tin tomatoes (1 lb 12 oz/
    840 g)
2 tins (15 oz/450 g each) well rinsed
    and drained kidney beans
Salt to taste
Chopped fresh coriander (optional)

---

1   Separate the segments of the onion pieces and spread them in a heavy, non-stick, frying pan. Add *no* liquid or fat. Heat the frying pan gently. Cook at moderate heat, without stirring, for 7–10 minutes, until the onions are sizzling, speckled with dark amber, and beginning to stick to the pan.
2   Stir in 10 fl oz/300 ml of stock and let it bubble up, stirring up the browned deposits in the pan with a wooden spoon as it bubbles. Stir in the ginger, garlic and spices. Turn the heat down a bit and simmer, stirring frequently, until the mixture is very thick (not at all soupy), and the onions and spices are 'frying' in their own juices. Don't rush this step, it is essential that the spices should not have a raw harsh taste. Taste. Cook very gently for a few more minutes if necessary.
3   Crush tomatoes with your hands and add them with their juices to the onions. Simmer for 3–4 minutes.
4   Add the beans, salt and remaining stock. Simmer briskly for 15–20 minutes until thick and savoury. Taste and adjust seasonings. Serve garnished with chopped coriander if desired.

BLACK BEAN CHILAQUILES

Serves 8

Chilaquiles are a sort of Mexican lasagne: tortilla pieces layered with sauce and cheese, and sometimes bits of poultry as well. There are many versions. If you don't want to bother soaking and cooking the dried beans, substitute 3 tins of red kidney beans. Traditionally, chilaquiles are made with tortilla pieces that have been deep fried. In my version, the tortillas are baked. Since baked tortillas are a compelling and healthy snack, as well as a component of chilaquiles, it pays to bake up a huge batch every once in a while, and store them in a biscuit tin until needed.

---

12 corn tortillas (see page 201)
1 onion, chopped
10 fl oz/300 ml stock
3 cloves garlic, crushed
½ teaspoon cayenne pepper
½ teaspoon ground cumin seed
½ teaspoon chilli powder
Black Beans (see recipe following)

16 fl oz/480 ml Tomato Sauce (see page 236), flavoured with cayenne and cumin
8 oz/240 g Mozzarella cheese, finely shredded
6 tablespoons Parmesan cheese
Chopped fresh coriander
Lime wedges

---

1   Preheat oven to 300° F, 150° C, Gas Mark 2.
2   Bake the tortillas directly on the oven shelf, for 15–20 minutes, turning once until crisp right through (they will break with a clean 'snap'). Break into coarse pieces and set aside.
3   Spread onion pieces out in a heavy frying pan. Cook over moderate heat, without stirring, until the onions are sizzling and beginning to stick to the pan. Stir in the stock and let it bubble up, stirring up the browned deposits in the pan with the wooden spoon as it bubbles. Stir in the garlic and spices. Turn the heat down and simmer, stirring frequently, until the mixture is thick (not at all soupy) and the onions and spices are 'frying' in their own juices. Don't rush this step, it is essential that the spices should not have a harsh raw taste.
4   Stir in the Black Beans and heat gently. Mash roughly, while still in the pan, with a potato masher. You want a rough lumpy mixture, not a smooth purée. Set aside. Set oven to 350° F, 180° C, Gas Mark 4.
5   In a gratin dish spread a layer of ⅓ of the tortilla pieces. Spread ⅓ of the Black Beans over the tortillas, and spread ⅓ of the Tomato Sauce over the Black Beans. Sprinkle with ⅓ of the cheeses. Repeat order. End with the remaining Tomato Sauce, Black Beans, tortillas, and cheeses.

6   Bake for 30 minutes, covered. Uncover and bake for 5–10 minutes more. Serve garnished with fresh coriander and lime wedges.

Tortillas

Tortillas are thin maize pancakes made from *masa* (lime-treated maize meal). I learned to make tortillas according to ancient tradition at the hacienda of an Aztec farming family in a remote Mexican town. Guadalupe, my hostess, lived in the hacienda that had been in her family for generations. She taught me to make tortillas as she makes them every day of her life; indeed, as all her female ancestors have done since before the conquest. For my tortilla lesson I knelt on the cold, hard floor of a stone-walled, high-ceilinged room next to the cow enclosure and pig pens. In front of me, a brisk fire of corn cobs and twigs blazed under a large clay griddle; to the side, a wet pile of *masa* waited on a tilted three-legged slab of volcanic rock. I was directed to pull off a lump of *masa*, flatten it into shape in a wooden tortilla press, pat it a few times, ease it on to the red-hot griddle, flip it over to bake the other side, then toss it into a napkin-lined basket. When Guadalupe did it, it seemed so simple: her movements were graceful and the whole process looked easy and languorous. But when I tried, it was not easy at all; the floor was punishingly hard, the griddle blisteringly hot and the tortilla press supremely uninterested in pressing the dough evenly for me. Guadalupe stood on the sidelines uttering commands, her mouth twitching in amusement at my awkwardness. Her tortillas were perfectly round, smooth, even discs. Mine were lopsided, uneven in thickness and uneven at the edges. How happy I am to tell you that these ornery but delicious things are available in tins. Just wield the tin opener, shake them out and toast in the oven. They do not, I hasten to add, begin to match the thinness, elegance and all-round excellence of Guadalupe's tortillas, but they sure are a convenience. And if you have a good Mexican or Latin American restaurant near your town, you may be able to buy fresh or frozen corn tortillas at a minimal price. I have done this successfully at Los Andes in Birmingham, Los Bandidos in Cambridge and Café Pacifico in London. It's certainly worth a try.

♡ ❄ **BLACK BEANS**

Makes 2½ pts/1.5 l

---

1 lb/480 g dried black beans, washed
    and picked over
3¼ pts/1,950 ml water
1 large Spanish onion, chopped
10 fl oz/300 ml stock
4 cloves garlic, peeled
½ teaspoon ground cumin

Pinch of ground cloves
¼ teaspoon ground allspice
½ teaspoon ground coriander
Pinch or two of cayenne pepper
3¼ pts/1.95 l stock
Freshly ground pepper to taste

---

1   In a cool part of the kitchen soak the beans overnight in 3¼ pts/1.95 l of water. On the next day, drain them.

2   Spread onion pieces on the bottom of a heavy saucepan. Heat until they sizzle and begin to stick to the pan. Pour in stock and stir in garlic and all seasonings. Simmer, stirring occasionally, until the mixture is thick and the onions and spices are 'frying' in their own juices. When the onions are tender, dump in the drained beans.

3   Stir in 3¼ pts/1.95 l stock. Cover and simmer for 1 hour.

4   Season to taste with salt and pepper. Simmer for an additional hour or more, until very tender. Taste and adjust seasonings.

❄ **VEGETARIAN CHILAQUILES**

Serves 6

Another variation on the 'Mexican lasagne' theme, this time with red and green peppers and plenty of sweet corn.

---

6 corn tortillas
1 large onion, chopped
1 red, 1 green pepper, peeled and
    chopped
1 chilli pepper, minced (a jalapeño
    chilli if possible)
6 fl oz/180 ml stock
1 teaspoon ground cumin
1 teaspoon ground coriander
Cayenne pepper to taste
½ teaspoon mild chilli powder
2 cloves garlic, crushed

3 tins (14 oz/420 g each) chopped
    tomatoes
Parmesan cheese rind
2 tablespoons tomato paste
Salt to taste
Pinch of sugar (optional)
12 oz/360 g frozen sweet corn (no
    need to thaw completely)
7 tablespoons grated Parmesan
    cheese
4 oz/120 g Mozzarella cheese,
    shredded

---

1   Preheat oven to 300° F, 150° C, Gas Mark 2.

2   Bake the tortillas directly on the oven shelf for 15–20 minutes,

turning once, until crisp right through. Break into coarse pieces and set aside.

3   Put the onion, peppers, chilli, stock, spices, and garlic in a heavy, non-reactive frying pan. Cover and bring to the boil. Boil for 5 minutes. Uncover, reduce heat and simmer for a few minutes more until the onion is tender and browned.

4   Stir in tomatoes and add cheese rind. Simmer, uncovered, for 20 minutes. Add tomato paste and simmer for 5 minutes. Add salt to taste, and a pinch of sugar if it is too acidic. Discard cheese rind. Set oven to 350° F, 180° C, Gas Mark 4.

5   In a shallow, non-reactive gratin dish or baking dish, layer ⅓ of the tortilla pieces, ⅓ of the sauce, ⅓ of the corn, ⅓ of the cheeses. Repeat twice.

6   Bake uncovered for 35 minutes, until bubbly. Serve at once.

♡ COUSCOUS WITH VEGETABLES

Makes 2 pts/1.2 l couscous, 3 pts/1.8 l vegetables

A fragrant vegetable curry surrounding a fluffy mound of couscous looks so pretty and tastes so good. To make this a gala party meal, add Lamb Meatballs (page 160), Piquant Chicken (page 180) and Stufatino (page 130), and arrange it all attractively on a huge plate.

Vegetable curry ingredients
1 large Spanish onion, coarsely
    chopped
24 fl oz/700 ml chicken stock
3 celery stalks, sliced into
    ½-inch/1.25-cm pieces
3 carrots, peeled and coarsely
    chopped
4 cloves garlic, minced
3 small turnips, peeled and coarsely
    chopped
1 red, 1 green, 1 yellow pepper,
    peeled and coarsely chopped
1 head fennel – trim off tough outer
    layer and slice into half-inch
    /1.25 cm pieces
1½ teaspoons ground cumin
¼ teaspoon allspice

½ teaspoon ground ginger
1 teaspoon ground turmeric
1½ teaspoons ground coriander
¼ teaspoon ground cayenne pepper
1 teaspoon paprika or paprika paste
1 lb/480 g courgettes, sliced into
    ½-inch/1.25-cm pieces
1 tin (15 oz/450 g) chick peas,
    drained
6 tablespoons fresh lemon juice
4 fl oz/120 ml chopped fresh parsley
2 fl oz/60 ml chopped fresh
    coriander

Couscous ingredients ♡ ⊕
¾ lb/360 g couscous
16 fl oz/480 ml boiling stock

---

1   Spread onion pieces out in a frying pan. Cook over moderate heat until the onions are sizzling and sticking to the pan. Stir in 10 fl oz/300 ml of stock and let it bubble up, stirring up the

browned deposits in the pan as it bubbles. Stir in celery, carrots, garlic, turnips, peppers, fennel and all spices. Turn the heat down a bit and simmer, stirring frequently until the mixture is thick (not at all soupy) and the vegetables and spices are 'frying' in their own juices.

2   Stir in the remaining vegetable curry ingredients, including the remaining 14 fl oz/420 ml stock. Season to taste with salt and freshly ground pepper. Simmer gently, covered, for 15 minutes.

3   Combine couscous with 16 fl oz/480 ml boiling stock in a large bowl. Let steep for 10–15 minutes, until the liquid is absorbed and the grains are tender. Fluff with a fork.

4   Serve the couscous in a mound on a large plate surrounded by the vegetables, or vice versa.

Omit chick peas. Substitute – if desired – drained, quartered artichoke hearts, or fresh cauliflower florets. Eat the curry without the couscous.

Couscous

Couscous, tiny grains of semolina, is available in cellophane packages in many supermarkets and wholefood shops. Most packaged couscous is pre-cooked; it only needs a brief steeping in hot liquid. The traditional method of cooking couscous involves at least two steamings in a special couscousière, and can take up to an hour, so the pre-cooked supermarket and wholefood store version is a great boon to busy cooks. Couscous purists sneer at the pre-cooked stuff, but I find it perfectly acceptable, and have used it as the focal point of many happy dinner parties. It also can be used to make a glorious pudding (see page 333).

'The Glaoui is one of the world's foremost manipulators of couscous balls. We watched him fascinated. He picks up a handful of the hot grain, tosses this in his palm without touching it with his fingers, and gently bounces it in the hollow of his hand until by some miracle it forms into a cohesive ball; this he then pops into his mouth, catching it on the fly. It was like watching a man with one hand make and eat golf balls.'

John Gunther, *Inside Africa*

VEGETARIAN CHILLI

Makes 3½ pts/2 l

Although I love good beef, I believe that my vegetarian chilli is better than any carnivore's chilli you might try. The faint-hearted may cut down on the amount of chilli powder, but if you use the full 5 tablespoons of *mild* I think you will find the dish not at all overpowering or incendiary.

---

4 oz/225 g bulghur
18 fl oz/540 ml vegetable stock,
   brought to the boil
1 Spanish onion, coarsely chopped
3 celery stalks, sliced ½ inch/
   1.25 cm thick
3 carrots, peeled and coarsely
   chopped
4 cloves garlic, minced
5 tablespoons chilli powder (half
   hot, half mild, or to taste)
2 teaspoons ground cumin
1 red pepper, peeled and coarsely
   chopped
1 yellow pepper, peeled and coarsely
   chopped

1 green pepper, peeled and coarsely
   chopped
2 tins (14 oz/420 g each) chopped
   tomatoes
1 tin (15 oz/450 g) red kidney
   beans, drained
1 tin (15 oz/450 g) chick peas,
   drained
1 large cauliflower, trimmed and
   cut into florets
Salt and freshly ground pepper to
   taste

Garnishes
Fromage frais
Grated Parmesan cheese
Chopped fresh coriander

---

1   Combine the bulghur and 8 fl oz/240 ml hot stock in a bowl. Cover and set aside.

2   Spread the onions out in a heavy frying pan. Cook over moderate heat, without stirring, for 7–10 minutes, until the onions are sizzling and beginning to stick to the pan. Stir in 10 fl oz/300 ml of stock and let it bubble up, stirring up the browned deposits in the pan with a wooden spoon as it bubbles. Stir in the celery, carrot, garlic, chilli powder, cumin and peppers. Turn the heat down a bit and simmer, stirring frequently, until the mixture is very thick (not at all soupy) and the vegetables and spices are 'frying' in their own juices. Don't rush this step, it is essential that the spices should not have a harsh, raw taste. Taste, and cook very gently for a few more minutes if necessary.

3   Stir in tomatoes, bulghur, kidney beans, chick peas, cauliflower and salt and pepper. Simmer for 30 minutes, until the mixture is thick and the cauliflower is tender, but not mushy. This chilli may be made a day in advance and reheated

gently at serving time. Serve with small bowls of the garnishes.

♡   Omit Parmesan cheese garnish.

♡ 🧸 ❄   BRAISED VEGETABLES

Makes 2 pts/1.2 l

This lovely stew is wonderful when baby artichokes appear in the markets. When they are out of season, substitute tinned artichoke hearts. If you also substitute tinned peppers for the fresh ones, this becomes a fast dish indeed.

1 large onion, coarsely chopped	1 red and 1 yellow pepper, peeled,
6 fl oz/180 ml stock	seeded and cut into
2 tablespoons lemon juice	½-inch/1.25-cm strips
8 baby artichokes	Salt and freshly ground pepper to
1 small tin Italian tomatoes,	taste
drained and crushed	1½ tablespoons chopped fresh
3 stalks celery, sliced	oregano
1 fennel bulb, trimmed and sliced	1½ tablespoons chopped fresh
½ lb/240 g mushrooms, quartered	parsley
	1½ tablespoons chopped fresh
	fennel leaves

1   Combine the onions, stock and lemon juice in a large, heavy, non-reactive frying pan. Cover and bring to the boil. Boil for 5 minutes. Uncover and simmer until the onions are amber brown and tender and the liquid is about gone.
2   Trim the artichokes: cut off stems, remove and discard tough outer leaves. Cut each in half. Stir the tomatoes and artichokes into the onion mixture. Simmer briskly, uncovered, for 10 minutes.
3   Stir in celery, fennel, mushrooms and peppers. Simmer uncovered, stirring occasionally, for about 30 minutes, until the vegetables are tender. If it gets too dry at any time, add a bit more stock.
4   Season with salt and pepper and stir in herbs.

🕐   . Substitute tinned artichoke hearts for the fresh ones and tinned peppers for the fresh peppers.

206

VEGETARIAN FONDUE

This is one of my favourite meals, for guests as well as just family. It's colourful, fun and unusual. Add protein by serving a starter that contains quark, yoghurt cheese, fromage frais, fish etc., (see the Starter chapter for ideas), or end with one of the buttermilk-based icecreams in the Dessert chapter. Choose your vegetables according to the season, and cook them carefully so that they are just done – flabby, mushy vegetables are unlovely things. Steaming is the best way to achieve perfection, both from a nutritional and culinary standpoint.

A selection of fresh vegetables, each steamed until just done. Consider:

Cauliflower	*(in florets)*
New potatoes	*(unpeeled)*
Broccoli	*(in florets)*
Small turnips	*(quartered)*
French beans	
Mangetout	
Asparagus	*(peeled and trimmed)*
Courgettes	*(cut into sticks)*
Sautéed whole button mushrooms	*(see page 29)*

A selection of hot and cold sauces. Consider:

Red Pepper Sauce	*Remoulade Sauce*
Yellow Pepper Sauce	*Tomato Sauce*
Beetroot Purée	*Pesto*
Hungarian Green Sauce	

If you decide you'd like to add meat, choose a meatball recipe (see page 155) and offer some as part of the selection. Arrange everything with colour, texture and shape in mind and, if you have small chafing dishes, use them to keep the warm sauces up to temperature. This is a convivial feast, perfect for a special celebration with good friends. If you have a microwave, you may facilitate the preparation by steaming the vegetables in advance. Let them cool, and then arrange them beautifully on individual plates. Cover tightly with cling film. At serving time, microwave each plate to heat the vegetables through. Do not let them overcook, however.

♡ ⚉ Serve the fondue without pesto.

Magical Mashed Spuds

There are few culinary therapies in the world as powerful as mashed potatoes. I mean this quite seriously. Starchy, high-carbohydrate foods are almost miraculous in their curative power. Recent fascinating research suggests that certain foods cause contentment and mood elevation by altering the amounts of key brain chemicals in much the same way as drugs used to treat severe depression. A chemical called serotonin must be present in the brain in proper amounts, or downward mood swings occur. Drugs in use for depression keep serotonin levels high by either retarding the body's removal of serotonin or promoting its build-up. The body makes serotonin from one of the components of dietary proteins: the amino acid tryptophan. Under ordinary circumstances, tryptophan has to compete with other amino acids to get into the brain. But when an individual ingests relatively more carbohydrate than protein, tryptophan has less competition getting in. When more tryptophan gets into the brain, more serotonin can be produced, and the individual feels calm and sleepy and much less anxious.

Personally, I find that an evening meal of mashed potatoes blankets me in a blissfully warm feeling of placid security. Don't *ever* think that potatoes are fattening and should be avoided. A medium potato contains about 90 fat-free Calories, and is bursting with vitamins A, C, B1, B6, niacin, not to mention iron, potassium and fibre. And a meal of potatoes leaves you feeling that you have dined well and copiously. Why not have a mashed potato evening every once in a while? Mound fluffy dollops of mashed spuds in a shallow soup plate (use your best pottery, the potatoes will taste even better). With a soup spoon, make a depression in the top of the mound. Fill the depression with something wonderful: Tomato-Broad Bean Ragoût, Mushroom Ragoût, 'Fried' Onions, Savoury Peppers – whatever sounds most seductively delicious at the time. Find a comfortable chair in a quiet corner, grab a large spoon and eat slowly and happily.

'Nothing like mashed potatoes when you are feeling blue. Nothing like getting into bed with a bowl of hot mashed potatoes.'

Nora Ephron, *Heartburn*

♡ MASHED POTATOES

Because life's trials and tribulations are eased by generous and frequent helpings of mashed spuds, quick methods of preparing them are desperately needed. Here are two suggestions.

1 Microwave ⊠

Choose large (½ lb/240 g each) baking potatoes. Prick them several times with a fork or thin skewer. Timing is as follows:

1 potato   – 7 minutes
2 potatoes – 11 minutes
3 potatoes – 16 minutes
4 potatoes – 20 minutes

When the time is up, use an oven glove to remove each potato from the oven. Squeeze the potato gently, then strip off the skin. Mash the potatoes with an old-fashioned masher, then – with an electric beater – beat in fromage frais, salt and freshly ground pepper.

2 Instant ⊕

I used to sneer at instant mashed potatoes, in fact I used to insist that you might as well eat the box and throw away the potatoes. I've changed my tune, but keep a few rules in mind.
1   Don't use the kind of instant potatoes that are made up of little pellets.
2   Don't use mashed potatoes that list salt, fat, or flavourings in the ingredients. (As of this writing, I find Waitrose brand and Mr. Mash instant potatoes to be excellent.)
3   Follow directions on the box as to amount of water. Ignore exhortations about knobs of butter or margarine. When the potatoes and water have been thoroughly mixed, beat in fromage frais until the potatoes are beautifully creamy. (I add almost a half carton of fromage frais for each large sachet of potatoes.) Season with salt and pepper.

(See page 279 in the Vegetable and Grain Side Dishes chapter for the traditional method of preparing old-fashioned mashed potatoes.)

PIPERADE POTATOES

Serves 6

Mashed potatoes mixed with herbed, sautéed vegetables make a lovely main dish, for nights when you want a meatless supper, but it's also good as an accompaniment to meat or poultry. When you are in a hurry, microwave your potatoes and use tinned peppers (see page 209), but Piperade Potatoes are at their best when prepared as the recipe is written.

---

3 large onions, cut in half and sliced into paper-thin half-moons
4 fl oz/120 ml stock
3 large cloves garlic, crushed
3 large bell peppers, cut in half lengthwise, sliced and peeled into thin strips (use 1 red, 1 green, 1 yellow if possible)
1 large tin (1 lb 12 oz/840 g) tomatoes, well drained, seeded and sliced into strips

Salt and freshly ground pepper to taste
¼ teaspoon dried oregano, crumbled
¼ teaspoon dried basil, crumbled
2 tablespoons chopped fresh parsley
4 large baking potatoes, baked
1 tablespoon grated Parmesan cheese

---

1   Combine the onions and 4 fl oz/120 ml stock in a wide, heavy, non-reactive frying pan. Cover and bring to the boil. Cook for 3–4 minutes. Uncover, turn heat down. Simmer briskly until onions are tender and amber brown. Use a splash more stock if needed to scrape up the browned bits on the bottom of the pan.
2   Add the garlic and peppers. Cook, stirring occasionally, until the peppers are tender. Stir in the tomatoes and herbs. Simmer, uncovered, until thick and saucy. Season to taste.
3   Preheat the oven to 400° F, 200° C, Gas Mark 6.
4   Perforate the potatoes and squeeze so the flesh surges up. Scoop into a bowl, mash well. Beat in the vegetable mixture. Taste and adjust seasoning. Spread into a shallow 9 × 13-inch/ 23 × 33-cm baking dish. Sprinkle evenly with cheese. (Save the potato skins for a special treat, see below.) Bake uncovered for ½ hour, until browned and bubbly.

♡ Omit cheese.

🕐 ✖ Microwave the potatoes and use tinned peppers.

Potato skins make a delectable snack. Cut them into strips and arrange on the grill tray. Sprinkle with Parmesan cheese and

freshly ground pepper. Grill for approximately 2 minutes, until the cheese is melted and the potato skins are crispy. Serve hot. Or save the skins for Potato Nachos (see page 308).

♡ Omit cheese; grill for 1–1½ minutes.

HUNGARIAN POTATO RAGOÛT

Makes 2 pts/1.2 l

Szekely goulash, that star of all Hungarian pork stews, works beautifully and deliciously with potatoes taking the place of the pork. Vegetarians should leave out the small amount of optional lean bacon, added at the end. If you wish, garnish each serving with a dollop of fromage frais. This is the sort of hearty cookery that comforts the deep corners of the soul.

---

1 jar sauerkraut
3 medium onions, halved and sliced
*   into thin half-moons*
3 cloves garlic, crushed
¼ teaspoon thyme
Approximately 12 fl oz/360 ml
*   stock*
2 fl oz/60 ml dry white vermouth
1½ tablespoons Hungarian sweet
*   paprika or paprika paste*

Pinch or two of cayenne pepper
1 tablespoon caraway seeds
1 tin (14 oz/420 g) chopped
*   tomatoes*
2 large all-purpose potatoes, halved
*   lengthwise and cut into*
*   ½-inch/1.25-cm chunks*
Salt and freshly ground pepper to
*   taste*
¼ lb/120 g lean, thin sliced bacon,
*   chopped (optional)*

---

1   Preheat the oven to 350° F, 180° C, Gas Mark 4.
2   Drain sauerkraut in a colander. Rinse well under cold water. Drain again and squeeze as dry as possible. Set aside.
3   Combine the onions, garlic, thyme, 4 fl oz/120 ml stock and the vermouth in a heavy non-reactive frying pan. Cover and simmer for 10 minutes. Uncover and cook over a moderate heat, stirring frequently, until the liquid is almost gone and the onions are browned.
4   Off the heat, stir in the paprika, cayenne pepper and caraway seeds. Stir for a few moments, until the onions are well coated with the paprika and it has lost its raw taste.
5   Toss in the tomatoes, the sauerkraut and the potatoes. Combine everything well. Dump the mixture into a non-reactive casserole. Season with salt and pepper and pour in stock to just barely cover the contents. Cover closely and bake for 1 hour.

6   Meanwhile, if you are using the bacon, gently sauté it, stirring, for a minute or so, in a non-stick frying pan. After the potatoes have cooked for 1 hour, scrape the bacon mixture into the casserole and gently stir in. Cover and bake for an additional ½ hour, or until the potatoes are tender.

♡   Omit bacon.

✳   ## POTATO STEFADO

Makes 3½ pts/2 l

A vegetarian version of the fragrant Greek beef stew on page 131

¾ lb/360 g mushrooms, halved or quartered, depending on size
3 large all-purpose potatoes, halved lengthwise and cut into 1½-inch/4-cm chunks
8 shallots, cut into quarters or eighths, depending on size
4 cloves garlic, crushed
1 large cauliflower, trimmed and broken into large florets
2 rounded tablespoons tomato paste
Salt and freshly ground pepper to taste

2 tablespoons chopped fresh parsley
1 bay leaf
1 teaspoon dried oregano
1 teaspoon ground cinnamon
1 teaspoon ground cumin
2 fl oz/60 ml red wine vinegar
Approximately 8 fl oz/240 ml stock

Garnish
Crumbled medium-fat feta cheese
Chopped parsley

---

1   Preheat oven to 350° F, 180° C, Gas Mark 4.
2   Combine all ingredients, except garnishes, in a non-reactive casserole that works on top of the stove as well as in the oven. Bring to the boil.
3   Cover tightly. Bake for 1–1¼ hours.
4   Garnish each serving with some feta and parsley.

♡   Omit the feta cheese.

♡ ⊕ ✳   ## POTATO-PEPPER STEW

Makes 3½ pts/2 l

Unsophisticated, filling and delicious. A huge bowlful is just the ticket at the end of a long day; you'll nourish both body and soul. If you wish, top each serving with a dollop of fromage frais.

3 large onions, coarsely chopped
3 cloves garlic, crushed
1 stalk celery, cut in half lengthwise
  and sliced
1 carrot, peeled and diced
Approximately 1½ pts/900 ml stock
6 medium 'all-purpose' (Willja
  work well) potatoes, unpeeled,
  diced into 1-inch/2.5-cm pieces

6 large red and/or yellow peppers,
  peeled and diced into
  1-inch/2.5-cm pieces
1 tin (14 oz/420 g) chopped Italian
  tomatoes
3 tablespoons chopped parsley
3 tablespoons chopped fresh basil
¼ teaspoon crushed dried chillies
  (or to taste)
Salt and pepper to taste

1   Combine onions, garlic, celery, carrot and 8 fl oz/240 ml of stock in a heavy, wide pot. Cover and boil for 5–10 minutes until tender and beginning to brown and stick to the pan. Uncover, stir and cook over moderate heat, adding a splash of stock as needed, and scraping up the browned bits, until the onions are amber brown, meltingly tender and syrupy.

2   Add the potatoes and peppers and stir until very well combined. Stir in all remaining ingredients. Pour in enough stock to almost cover the contents of the pot. Simmer, partially covered, stirring occasionally, until the potatoes are tender, about 30 minutes.

❄   # POTATO CHILLI

Makes 2 pts/1.2 l

Chilli con Patate is even better than Chilli con Carne; potatoes soak up seasonings so beautifully. This is the sort of good home cooking you'll find yourself making over and over again.

Approximately 12 fl oz/360 ml
  chicken or vegetable stock
3 large onions, halved and sliced
  into thin half-moons
2 cloves garlic, minced
1 teaspoon crumbled dried oregano
2 tablespoons chilli powder
1 teaspoon ground cumin
Cayenne pepper to taste

3 rounded tablespoons tomato paste
3 large all-purpose potatoes, halved
  and cut into 1½-inch/4-cm
  chunks
Salt and freshly ground pepper to
  taste
Grated Parmesan cheese
Fromage frais
Pepper Salad (recipe follows)

1   Preheat the oven to 350° F, 180° C, Gas Mark 4.
2   Combine 4 fl oz/120 ml of the stock with the onions and garlic

in a heavy frying pan. Cover and simmer briskly for 10 minutes.

3   Uncover and cook for 5–7 minutes, or until the onions are tender and browned and the liquid has cooked away. Stir in the oregano and spices. Stir over lowest heat until the onions are well coated with the spices, then blend in the tomato paste.

4   Toss the potatoes in the onion mixture. Season with salt and pepper. Pour in the remaining stock, and bring to a simmer, stirring. Scrape the mixture into a casserole. Cover and bake for 1–1¼ hours, or until the potatoes are tender and the sauce is very thick and rich. (This reheats well but you may have to add more stock.)

5   Serve in shallow soup bowls. Top each serving with a sprinkling of cheese, a dollop of fromage frais and a spoonful of Pepper Salad. Serve kidney beans on the side, if desired.

Pepper Salad

1 large green pepper, peeled and diced	1 tablespoon chopped fresh parsley
1 large red pepper, peeled and diced	½ tablespoon chopped fresh coriander
1 large yellow pepper, peeled and diced	Juice of 1 lime
3 thin spring onions, sliced	Salt to taste
	½ teaspoon sugar

Toss all the ingredients together in a bowl at least ½ hour before serving.

♡   Omit Parmesan cheese.

(·Ⱡ· ❄   # TURNIP-POTATO RATATOUILLE

Makes 2½ pts/1.5 l

Turnips and potatoes take the place of the traditional courgettes and aubergines in this main dish ratatouille.

2 medium onions, cut in half and sliced into paper-thin half-moons	3 ripe tomatoes, peeled, seeded, juiced and chopped (or substitute tinned)
6 fl oz/180 ml stock	
1 small red pepper, peeled and sliced	Salt and freshly ground pepper to taste
1 small yellow pepper, peeled and sliced	3 tablespoons shredded fresh basil or ¼ teaspoon crumbled dried basil

1 small green pepper, peeled and sliced	3 tablespoons chopped fresh parsley
3 cloves garlic, crushed	3 small waxy potatoes, coarsely diced
3 small turnips, peeled and coarsely diced	2 tablespoons grated Parmesan cheese

1   Combine the onions and 4 fl oz/120 ml stock in a frying pan. Cover and bring to the boil. Boil for 3–4 minutes.

2   Uncover and turn the heat down a bit. Simmer briskly, stirring, until the onions are tender and amber brown. Pour in a splash of additional stock and boil, stirring and scraping the browned bits on the bottom of the pan. Stir in the peppers and the garlic. Cook for a few minutes until the peppers lose their crispness.

3   Stir in turnips, tomatoes, seasonings and herbs. Cover and simmer very gently for 10 minutes. Add the potatoes, cover and simmer until the turnips and potatoes are tender. Spread the mixture in a gratin pan and sprinkle the surface with the cheese. At this point the dish may be refrigerated until serving time, for a day or two if necessary. In fact the flavour will improve. Bring to room temperature before proceeding.

4   Preheat the oven to 350° F, 180° C, Gas Mark 4. Bake the ratatouille, uncovered, until bubbling and lightly browned on top, about 20 minutes.

♡   Omit Parmesan cheese.

LAYERED POLENTA AND AUBERGINE

Serves 6

Polenta is coarse cornmeal; when added to boiling liquid and stirred over a modest flame, it cooks into a thick yellow corn porridge, the basis of countless comforting supper possibilities. Quick-cooking polenta, available in boxes from Italian delicatessens and many speciality food shops, cooks in 5 minutes. If you spoon the hot cooked polenta into a loaf tin, or into clean empty tins, and set it aside while you make a quick sauce, the polenta will be ready to be unmoulded, sliced and grilled (or simmered in the sauce) by the time the sauce is done. To me, an evening meal of polenta with a hearty sauce or ragoût is one of the happiest of culinary occasions. I put it right up there with mashed potato evenings.

34 fl oz/1 l stock or salted water
8 fl oz/240 ml quick-cooking polenta
(coarse maize meal)
1 large onion, coarsely chopped
1 red or yellow pepper, peeled and
coarsely chopped
2 cloves garlic, crushed
½ teaspoon dried basil
4 fl oz/120 ml stock
4 fl oz/120 ml dry red wine

2 tins (12 oz/360 g each) chopped
tomatoes
4–6 ripe tomatoes, peeled and
seeded
1 piece Parmesan rind
2–3 tablespoons tomato paste
4 tablespoons chopped fresh parsley
2 medium aubergines
6 tablespoons grated Parmesan
cheese

1   Bring 34 fl oz/1 l of stock or salted water to the boil. With a wire whisk, whisk in the polenta. (Whisk well so that the mixture does not form lumps.) Bring to the boil, immediately lower the heat, and cook on low heat, stirring (switch to a wooden spoon), for about 5 minutes until smooth and very thick. As it cooks, taste for seasonings and add salt if needed. Be careful it does not scorch. Pack into two clean round tins (the tins from the chopped tomatoes will do), cover with cling film and refrigerate.

2   Combine onion, pepper, garlic, basil, stock and wine. Cover and bring to the boil. Reduce heat and simmer for about 10 minutes. Uncover and continue cooking until vegetables are tender and the liquid is about gone. Stir in the tomatoes and Parmesan rind. Simmer for 15–20 minutes. Stir in tomato paste and parsley. Simmer for 5 minutes more. Season with salt and pepper. Remove the rind and set aside.

3   Pierce each aubergine several times with a thin skewer or fork. Put a paper towel on your microwave carousel and place aubergines on it. Microwave on high for 3 minutes, turning them once, after 1½ minutes. Remove from the oven and let stand for 3 minutes.

4   Slice the aubergine (unpeeled) into ½-inch/1.25-cm slices. Push or shake the polenta out of the tin (it will come out in a lovely, compact cylinder). The top of each cylinder will be crusty; take a thin slice off the top and discard. Slice the remainder approximately ½-inch/1.25-cm thick. Overlap alternating slices of polenta and aubergine in a shallow baking dish. Spread the sauce over them and sprinkle with the grated cheese. Bake at 350° F, 180° C, Gas Mark 4, for 30 minutes, or until hot and bubbly.

♡ Omit Parmesan cheese.

Variation I: Grilled Polenta with Herbed Onions or Intense Mushroom Ragoût ♡ ⊕

Polenta (see recipe above, step 1)
Herbed Onions (see page 218) or
   Intense Mushroom Ragoût (see
   page 219)

1   Line the grill tray with foil, shiny side out. Preheat the grill to its highest point.
2   In a saucepan, heat the Herbed Onions or Intense Mushroom Ragoût.
3   Shake the polenta out of the tins and slice. Place the polenta slices in a single layer on a non-stick baking sheet. Grill 6 inches/15 cm from the heat for approximately 6 minutes, until beginning to brown on top.
4   Mound the Herbed Onions or Intense Mushroom Ragoût on a serving dish. With a fish slice, carefully lift the polenta slices off the baking sheet. Overlap them around the onions or mushrooms and serve at once.

Variation II: Grilled Polenta with Tomato-Broad Bean Ragoût ⊕

Polenta (see main recipe, step 1)
Tomato-Broad Bean Ragoût (see
   page 218)

Thinly sliced Italian Mozzarella
   cheese
Freshly ground pepper to taste

1   Preheat the grill to its highest point.
2   Shake the polenta out of the tins. Slice the polenta and arrange in one layer on a non-stick baking sheet. Grill, 6 inches/15 cm from the heat, for approximately 6 minutes, until beginning to brown on top.
3   Spoon ragoût generously over the polenta rounds. Top each round with a slice of Mozzarella cheese. Sprinkle generously with freshly ground pepper. Grill, 3 inches/8 cm from the heat, for 3–4 minutes or until the cheese is melted, bubbly and speckled with brown. Lift slices off the sheet with a fish slice and place on plates. Or the polenta rounds can be placed in a baking dish in one layer. Spread the sauce over the polenta, and lay cheese slices over the top. Grill until bubbly and lightly browned. Serve from the baking dish.

♡   Omit cheese.

♡ ⊕ ❋ TOMATO-BROAD BEAN RAGOÛT

Makes approx. 4 pts/2.5 l

Tomato-broad bean ragoût can be eaten from a bowl as a thick soup, or it can accompany polenta or mashed potatoes. You may want to try it tossed with penne (pasta quills) as well.

2 large tins Italian plum tomatoes	Handful coarsely chopped sun-dried
Pinch or two dried crushed chillies	tomatoes (optional)
(optional)	1 tin (14 oz/420 g) broad beans
1 large tin (14 oz/420 g) pimientos	Freshly ground pepper to taste
(red peppers)	2–3 tablespoons tomato paste
1 piece Parmesan cheese rind	Chopped fresh parsley

1 Dump the plum tomatoes, juice and all, into a non-reactive saucepan. With a potato masher, roughly crush them. Sprinkle in the chillies.
2 Drain the liquid from the pimiento tin. With a pair of kitchen scissors, roughly chop up the pimientos, right in the tin. Dump them in with the tomatoes. Add the Parmesan rind and the sun-dried tomatoes, if you are using them. Bring to the boil.
3 Reduce heat and simmer for about 10 minutes. Add the drained broad beans and pepper and simmer for 10 minutes more, or until thick. Remove the Parmesan rind. Taste, and add a pinch of sugar if it seems too acidic. If you have some fresh parsley, stir in a handful of chopped leaves. Serve with Mashed Potatoes (page 279), jacket potatoes, Polenta (page 215), or pasta.

 Omit broad beans.

♡ 🐻 ⊕ ❋ HERBED ONIONS FOR POLENTA

Makes 1½ pts/900 ml

Braised onions with parsley, rosemary, fennel and a touch of red wine vinegar.

2 large cloves garlic, peeled	12 fl oz/360 ml stock
2 tablespoons fresh parsley	2 tablespoons red wine vinegar
½ tablespoon rosemary leaves	1 tablespoon tomato paste

½ teaspoon fennel seeds (optional)
4 large Spanish onions, peeled, cut
   in half and sliced into thin
   half-moons

3–4 fl oz/90–120 ml stock
Salt and freshly ground pepper to
   taste

---

1   Chop together the garlic, parsley, rosemary and optional fennel seeds. Set aside.
2   Combine the onions and 12 fl oz/360 ml stock in a deep, heavy, non-reactive frying pan that can be covered. Cover and bring to the boil. Boil for about 5–7 minutes. Uncover. Continue to cook, stirring occasionally, until the liquid is almost gone and the onions are beginning to brown and stick to the pan. Continue cooking for a moment or two. Pour in a splash of stock, and stir and scrape up the browned bits with a wooden spoon.
3   When the onions are amber brown and meltingly tender, stir in the garlic mixture. Stir together the wine vinegar, tomato paste and 3–4 fl oz/90–120 ml stock. Stir into the onions. Simmer, uncovered, for 5–10 minutes. Season to taste.

 ## INTENSE MUSHROOM RAGOÛT

Makes 2 pts/1.2 l

Dried mushrooms and their soaking juices add a new dimension to mushroom ragoût.

---

2 lb/960 g of mixed fresh
   mushrooms (look for fresh
   shiitake, chestnut and oyster
   mushrooms in addition to the
   ordinary cultivated ones; trim
   the tough stems from shiitakes
   before using them)
1 oz/30 g Reconstituted Dried
   Mushrooms (see below)

Freshly ground pepper to taste
Dash of teriyaki sauce
1 fl oz/30 ml medium sherry
2 fl oz/60 ml each stock and
   mushroom soaking water (see
   below)
1 fl oz/30 ml balsamic vinegar

---

1   Clean fresh mushrooms well, cut into quarters or eighths (depending on size) and combine with Reconstituted Dried Mushrooms, seasonings and liquids in a large, heavy, non-reactive frying pan.
2   Simmer, stirring occasionally. The mushrooms will exude a good deal of liquid. Continue cooking until the liquid is greatly reduced.

3   Cook, stirring, until the mushrooms are tender, and 'frying' in their syrupy sauce. Taste and correct seasonings.

Reconstituted Dried Mushrooms

---

1 oz/30 g dried cèpes/porcini

Rinse the dried mushrooms well under cold running water. Soak in hot water to cover generously for 1 hour. Strain the water through a double cheesecloth-lined sieve or a coffee filter, and reserve. Rinse the mushrooms under cold running water. Trim off and discard any tough stems. Chop the mushrooms coarsely. Use some of the filtered soaking water to cook the ragoût. Save the remainder for soups and sauce.

♡ 🐻 🕒 ❋ VEGETABLE GUMBO
Makes 5 pts/3 l

A thick, inelegant, extremely savoury vegetable stew with the consistency of a gumbo. Traditionally, gumbos are thickened with an oily dark roux, or with filé powder (powdered sassafras leaves), or both; this one gets its texture from baked aubergine and garlic. It is basically a pantry recipe, utilizing several excellent tinned and frozen products. Make it even quicker and more convenient to prepare by baking the aubergine and garlic in the microwave and substituting tinned pimientos for the fresh peppers. This concoction freezes very well.

---

2 large Spanish onions, cut in half and sliced into thin half-moons
10 fl oz/300 ml stock
¼ pt/150 ml dry red wine
2 red peppers, sliced into strips and peeled
2 yellow peppers, sliced into strips and peeled
1 teaspoon (or to taste) crushed dried chillies
1 large packet (2 lb/960 g) frozen sweetcorn kernels, partially thawed
1 large packet (2 lb/960 g) frozen button Brussels sprouts, partially thawed

3 tins (14 oz/420 g each) chopped tomatoes
Purée from 1 large head Baked Garlic (see page 32)
Chopped pulp from 2 Baked Aubergines (see page 37)
Salt and pepper to taste
4 rounded tablespoons tomato paste
1 tin artichoke hearts, drained and quartered
4–5 tablespoons chopped fresh parsley

---

1   Combine the onions and the stock in a large saucepan. Cover and bring to the boil. Uncover. Boil for approximately 5 minutes, until most of the liquid has cooked away. Reduce heat and simmer until just about dry and beginning to stick a little bit.
2   Lower the heat. Toss and stir constantly with a wooden spoon until you smell a lovely, toasty, oniony aroma and the bottom of the pan is beginning to brown just a bit. Pour in the wine and turn the heat up again. Stir with the wooden spoon, scraping up all the browned bits. When the liquid is gone, the onions should be meltingly tender and amber-coloured.
3   Stir in the peppers, crushed chillies, corn, sprouts, tomatoes, garlic, aubergine, salt and pepper. Simmer, uncovered, for 15 minutes.
4   Stir in the tomato paste and artichoke hearts. Simmer, uncovered, for 10–15 minutes longer. Stir in the parsley and adjust seasonings.

 Bake the aubergine and garlic in the microwave, and use tinned peppers.

BREAD AND CARAMELIZED ONION SOUFFLÉ

Serves 6–8

This is for people who find comfort in the gobs of melted cheese, the thick croûtons and the dark rich onions that are the glory of onion soup. Bread and onion soufflé is the soul of onion soup. It is, essentially, onion soup without the soup. Use the largest, sweetest Spanish onions that you can find. Leftovers reheat well in the microwave.

---

1 large garlic clove, split
4 large onions, peeled and trimmed
16 fl oz/480 ml stock
2 fl oz/60 ml dry vermouth
6 oz/180 g stale crusty French
  bread, cut into 1-inch/2.5-cm
  chunks

6 tablespoons Parmesan cheese
2 whole eggs plus 2 egg whites
16 fl oz/480 ml skimmed milk
Salt and freshly ground pepper to
  taste

---

1   Preheat the oven to 350° F, 180° C, Gas Mark 4.
2   Choose a shallow round or oval gratin dish. Rub it thoroughly with the cut sides of the garlic clove. Discard the garlic.

3   Cut onions in half. Slice into thin half-moons. Combine onions and 16 fl oz/480 ml of stock in a deep 10-inch/25-cm enamelled cast iron frying pan. Cover and bring to the boil. Reduce heat a bit and simmer briskly for 10 minutes.

4   Uncover the pot, raise the heat to medium, and cook, stirring occasionally, until the onions are amber brown. Pour in the vermouth and boil until the liquid cooks away, scraping the bottom of the pot with a wooden spoon all the while.

5   Toss the bread and onions together. Spread them in the gratin dish. Sprinkle on the grated cheese.

6   Beat the eggs and egg whites lightly together. Beat in the milk and salt and pepper. Pour the mixture evenly over the bread and cheese. Press the bread into the liquid with a spatula. Let stand for at least 1 hour. (The gratin may be covered and refrigerated overnight. On the next day bring it to room temperature before proceeding.)

7   Bake for 35–40 minutes, until set, puffed and golden. (A knife inserted near the centre will emerge clean.) If necessary, flash under the grill for a minute or two to brown the top. Serve at once.

FARMER'S OMELETTE

Serves 4

Eggs are low in calories, full of high-quality protein and a fine collection of vitamins and minerals, but the yolks are, alas, high fat. One egg, once in a while, won't hurt, but don't make a habit of it. Save this for an occasional special weekend breakfast.

1 *large baking potato, unpeeled, coarsely diced*	2–3 *tablespoons parsley, chopped*
1 *large onion, chopped*	3 *eggs*
3 *cloves garlic, crushed*	1 *egg white*
6–8 *fl oz/240 ml stock*	*Freshly ground pepper*
1–2 *fl oz/60 ml red wine (optional)*	2 *tablespoons grated Parmesan cheese*

1   Combine the potato, onion, garlic and stock in a frying pan. Bring to the boil, cover and boil for five minutes.

2   Uncover, reduce heat and simmer until the stock is almost gone and the vegetables are tender and beginning to brown. Pour in 1 oz/30 ml or so of wine or a splash of stock. Stir and scrape up browned bits. Transfer mixture to a large, non-stick omelette pan.

3   Preheat the grill. Beat the eggs and the egg white with parsley,

freshly ground pepper and Parmesan cheese. Pour over potato mixture. Let cook over medium heat without stirring for a few seconds until the eggs begin to set on the bottom.

4   With a flexible plastic spatula, lift the edges of the omelette away from the pan, and tilt the pan so that the uncooked egg flows beneath the cooked portion. Continue doing this all around the pan until the omelette is almost completely set, but soft and runny in the centre.

5   Place under the grill for 2–3 minutes to set and very lightly brown the top. Serve at once, in wedges, straight from the omelette pan.

Pasta and Sauces

'In the course of civilization's long and erratic march, no other discovery has done more than or possibly as much as pasta has to promote man's happiness.'

Marcella Hazan, *The Classic Italian Cookbook*

Slurping in the spaghetti (we never called it 'pasta' in those days) was one of the gastronomic glories of my American childhood. The long, luscious strands were inevitably buried under unsophisticated oceans of tomato sauce and there were always a few meatballs along to round things out nicely. Thinking of those comforting, sloppy meals of long ago makes me mistily nostalgic and ravenously hungry.

Here to assuage both physical and psychic hungers, are grown-up versions of those fondly remembered spaghetti feasts. Fat and Calories have been drastically cut, and ingredients and techniques have been upgraded to match the hard-won sophistication of adulthood, but these dishes still satisfy me (as they will you) in those cosy dim recesses of the soul that only *spaghetti* can reach.

Pasta Guidelines

For the sake of nutrient density, choose wholegrain pastas occasionally. In delicatessens and supermarkets, there is a gorgeous array of shapes and sizes from tiny wheels and shells to long, ribbon-like tagliatelle and flat, broad lasagne. If you grew up on white pasta and suspect that the wholewheat variety is pure stodge, you are in for a pleasant surprise. It is delicate in both taste and texture and its gentle brown colour is a lovely contrast to the brilliantly hued sauces into which it will be nestled. Cooking pasta perfectly is easy if you know the rules:

1   Bring plenty of lightly salted water to a rolling boil; at least 5 pts/3 l of water per lb/480 g of pasta. If you are stingy with the water, the pasta will be gummy.
2   When the water is violently boiling, add the pasta, stirring with a wooden spoon as you do so. Long pasta such as spaghetti, linguini, etc. should be separated with the spoon as it begins to cook.
3   Stir frequently as it boils so that the pieces do not clump together. *Never* put the lid on the pot!
4   Do not overcook your pasta or you will end up with mush. Cook it until it is *al dente* (to the tooth). In other words, the pasta should be slightly resistant to the bite. Not at all raw, of course, but not at all mushy either. Begin fishing out pieces to taste – test early enough to avoid overcooking. (Use the timing suggested on the package as a guideline only.)
5   Have a large colander waiting in the sink. When the pasta is *just* done, don't dawdle. Use oven gloves and extreme care. Drain it quickly into the colander, combine it with its sauce, and serve *at once*.

⊕ PASTA SHELLS ALFREDO

Serves 5
284 Calories per serving
2.6 g fat
(Traditional pasta Alfredo: 707 Calories per serving, 30 g fat)

Here is a dramatic example of the Calorie savings made possible by substituting dairy products. This supremely comforting dish is normally made with tons of butter and cream. Standard operating procedure for foodies in dire emotional straits (a recalcitrant lover, perhaps, or problems with the inland revenue) is to boil up some pasta shells, toss them hot and steaming into butter, double cream and grated Parmesan cheese, and to eat them blissfully with a large spoon. The consumption of this dish may cause your emotional troubles to fade temporarily into obscurity, but what does it do to your arteries and your avoirdupois? Nothing good! You will find the Slim Cuisine version of this comfort food just as delicious and even more comforting than the original. (You have the extra comfort of knowing that you are not harming your body.) This recipe may be multiplied or reduced as needed.

10 oz/300 g pasta shells (or use tagliatelle or fettuccini)	5 fl oz/150 ml skimmed milk, at room temperature
8 oz/240 g skimmed-milk quark, at room temperature	3 tablespoons freshly grated Parmesan cheese
	Freshly ground pepper to taste

1 Cook pasta to the *al dente* stage.
2 Meanwhile, scrape quark into a large, warm bowl. With a wooden spoon, beat in the skimmed milk and grated cheese.
3 Drain the pasta, and immediately toss it into the quark mixture. Grind in some pepper if desired, and serve at once.

Elegant Variation:

Toss some slivered smoked salmon into the pasta with the other ingredients, or add baked garlic purée (see page 32) and a handful of chopped fresh herbs (chives, parsley, basil).

⑤ PASTA WITH CREAMY FENNEL SAUCE

Serves 8

You will want to dive headfirst into this glorious bowl of pasta, and wallow. Why would anyone want to eat high-butterfat pasta dishes, when low-fat food can taste so outrageously good?

½ lb/240 g quark, at room temperature	3 peppers (1 each red, green, yellow), peeled and coarsely chopped
1 oz/30 g pine nuts	2 large cloves garlic, coarsely chopped
5 tablespoons grated Parmesan cheese	1 teaspoon dried tarragon, crumbled
Purée from 1–2 heads Baked Garlic (see page 32)	½ teaspoon dried thyme, crumbled
3 medium onions, coarsely chopped	Salt and freshly ground pepper to taste
8 oz/240 g white mushrooms, quartered	8 fl oz/240 ml stock
8 oz/240 g chestnut (brown) mushrooms, quartered	4 fl oz/120 ml red wine
1 head fennel, trimmed and sliced (cut each slice in half)	2 dashes soy sauce
	1 lb/480 g pasta quills
	4 fl oz/120 ml Tomato Sauce, unpuréed (see page 236)

1   Place quark, pine nuts, Parmesan cheese and Baked Garlic in the container of the food processor. Process until smooth and well blended. Set aside.
2   In a heavy, deep, non-reactive frying pan, combine the onions, stock, wine and soy sauce. Stir to combine very well. Bring to the boil. Simmer briskly, uncovered, stirring occasionally, until the vegetables are tender, and the liquid is greatly reduced and syrupy. Lower the heat a bit and cook gently, stirring occasionally, as the vegetables 'fry' in their own juices. When the liquid is almost gone, set aside.
3   Cook the quills in plenty of salted boiling water. Have a warm bowl ready. Warm the Tomato Sauce.
4   When the pasta is done, drain it well and toss it in the warm bowl with the cheese mixture. When the pasta is thoroughly coated, toss in the vegetable mixture and the Tomato Sauce. Rush to the table and serve *at once*.

PENNE WITH PESTO AND SMOKED CHICKEN

Serves 8

I invented this pasta dish for my mother-in-law when she came to visit. It was such a success that I made it again for my assistant's birthday lunch. Save this for very special occasions – it's glorious.

½ lb/225 g large mushrooms, cut into chunks
1 large red or yellow pepper, peeled and cut into pieces (see page 30)
1 onion, chopped
3 cloves garlic, chopped
6 fl oz/180 ml dry red wine
6 fl oz/180 ml stock
Dash or 2 soy sauce
1 tin (14 oz) chopped tomatoes
Piece Parmesan cheese rind
¼ teaspoon each: dried thyme, oregano, basil

1 tablespoon tomato paste
Salt and freshly ground pepper to taste
1 lb/480 g penne or pennoni (tubular, quill-shaped pasta)
8 oz/240 g mangetout, fresh, or frozen and thawed, destrung
4–6 oz/180 g smoked chicken, sliced thin and cut into ½-inch/1.25-cm pieces
4 fl oz/120 ml Slim Cuisine Pesto (see page 231)

---

1   Preheat the oven to its lowest point. Put a large serving bowl in the oven to keep warm.
2   Combine the mushrooms, pepper, onion, garlic, wine, stock and soy sauce in a heavy, non-reactive frying pan. Simmer

briskly, stirring occasionally, until the vegetables are tender and the liquid is thick and syrupy.

3   Stir in the tomatoes, Parmesan rind, herbs, tomato paste, salt and pepper. Simmer gently, uncovered, for 15 minutes. Stir occasionally.

4   Meanwhile, cook the penne or pennoni in plenty of boiling, salted water until *al dente*.

5   While the penne is cooking, put the mangetout into a sieve or strainer. Just before the penne is done, dip the sieve with the mangetout into the boiling pasta water. If the mangetout are frozen and thawed, leave in the boiling water for 2 seconds, if fresh for 10 seconds.

6   Drain the pasta in a colander. Pour it into the warm bowl. Immediately toss in the mangetout and the chicken. Toss with 2 spoons so that everything is well mixed. Remove the Parmesan rind and stir in the tomato–mushroom sauce. Toss well to distribute it. Toss in the pesto. Everything must be very well combined. Rush to the table and serve at once.

♡ ⊕ ❄ SPICY BEAN SAUCE FOR PASTA

Makes 2½ pts/1.5 l

Pasta is the ultimate fast food. With a good supply on hand, and a lavish choice of ingredients in the larder and freezer, lovely simple meals are always possible.

---

1 large Spanish onion, coarsely
   chopped
4 fl oz/120 ml stock
2 red peppers, peeled and coarsely
   chopped
2 stalks celery, sliced into
   ½-inch/1.25-cm pieces
2 fl oz/60 ml red wine
1 teaspoon ground cumin
1 teaspoon dried thyme
1 teaspoon dried tarragon
Pinch of cayenne pepper

½ teaspoon ground allspice
Garlic purée from Baked Garlic (see
   page 32), to taste (optional)
2 tins (14 oz/420 g each) chopped
   tomatoes
1 piece Parmesan rind
1 tin (15 oz/450 g) red kidney
   beans, drained and rinsed
1 tablespoon drained capers
Salt and freshly ground pepper to
   taste

---

1   Put the onion in a frying pan with 4 fl oz/120 ml of stock. Cover. Boil for 5 minutes. Uncover, reduce heat somewhat and simmer until amber brown and beginning to stick to the pan.

2   Stir in the peppers, celery and the red wine. Stir and cook until the added vegetables are softened. With your wooden spoon, scrape up the browned bits on the bottom of the pan as you stir.

3   Stir in herbs, spices, optional garlic, tomatoes and Parmesan rind. Simmer, uncovered, for 30 minutes or so, stirring occasionally, until thickened and savoury. Stir in the beans and the capers. Remove rind, then season to taste. Simmer for 5–10 minutes more. Serve over corkscrew pasta.

Note: To make a pasta-bean casserole, mix this sauce with cooked (al dente) pasta, either rotini or penne. Sprinkle the top with shredded Italian Mozzarella cheese and freshly grated Parmesan cheese. Bake until the cheese is melted and bubbly.

♡ ⊕   LEMONY PASTA SHELLS

Serves 1

When you want to whip up something in a hurry that is comforting yet low-Calorie, try this soothing pasta pilaff. (Broken-up angel hair pasta can be substituted for the shells, for an occasional change.) This amount makes a happy culinary indulgence for one, but you may comfort a companion or two, as well, by doubling or tripling the recipe. As a variation, try adding garlic purée from roasted garlic to the infusion. For a more substantial dish, add veal meatballs before the final simmering. (The meatball version is a great family pleaser.)

1 recipe Onion-Herb Infusion (see page 27)	*8 fl oz/240 ml boiling stock*
2 oz/60 g tiny pasta shells	*Freshly ground pepper to taste*
	Fresh lemon juice to taste

1   Heat the infusion in a pot. Toss the pasta with the infusion until it is well combined.

2   Stir in the hot stock and grind in some pepper. Cover and simmer over very low heat for 10–12 minutes or until the liquid is almost absorbed. (It will be just a bit soupy.)

3   Squeeze in the lemon juice (I like to use the juice of 1 small lemon), stir and serve at once.

'So what happens when we eat food? Well, the answer is that after the food is eaten, if it is rich in Calories and cream sauces and so on, we argue about the bill. Then after that we get fat. Then the fat gets deposited on women's hips, which causes more arguments, and in men's coronary arteries which ends arguments. There now, that wasn't very complex, was it?'

Robert Buckman, *Punch*

 ## HUNGARIAN GREEN SAUCE

Makes 1 pt/600 ml of sauce

The first time I made this delicate, pale green sauce, I was so pleased with myself that I walked around in a happy daze for the rest of the day. Serve the sauce with pasta, steamed fish, or Mushroom Ravioli (see page 75). Present it on a black, dark red, white or clear glass plate for maximum effect.

1½ lb/720 g green beans, trimmed	Pinch or two of cayenne pepper
5 shallots, halved and thinly sliced	2 fl oz/60 ml dry vermouth
1 large clove garlic, minced	6 fl oz/180 ml rich stock
1 teaspoon dried basil	4 oz/120 g quark
1 teaspoon sweet Hungarian paprika	Salt and freshly ground pepper to taste

1   Steam the green beans until very tender. Set aside.
2   Combine shallots, garlic, basil, paprika, cayenne pepper, vermouth and 2 fl oz/60 ml stock in a small frying pan. Boil, stirring occasionally, until the mixture is almost dry. Set aside.
3   Combine the beans, shallot infusion, remaining stock and quark in a liquidizer and purée.
4   Rub the purée through a sieve into a saucepan. Heat it gently. Taste and adjust seasonings.

Ⓢ ## PESTO

Makes 12 fl oz
9 Calories per teaspoon
0.4 g fat
(Traditional pesto: 31 Calories per teaspoon, 3 g fat)

Pesto is a vividly coloured and flavoured thick Italian basil sauce, almost a paste. It is very good served tossed into hot pasta. Traditionally, pesto is made with plenty of olive oil. I have eliminated the oil altogether. I love this lower-fat version of the pungent Italian sauce even more than the classic one. To serve it as a very elegant starter, cook some small pasta shells *al dente*. Drain, rinse in cold water and drain very well. With a small spoon, stuff each shell with pesto (it sounds fussy, but it is really very easy and very fast). Arrange on a bed of radicchio leaves.

---

7 tablespoons torn basil leaves
5 tablespoons roughly chopped
  parsley
5 tablespoons freshly grated
  Parmesan cheese
1 oz/30 g pine nuts

½ lb/240 g quark or fromage frais
  cream cheese (see page 39)
Purée from 2 heads of baked garlic
  (or, for a stronger taste, several
  cloves of raw garlic)
Salt and freshly ground pepper to
  taste

---

1   Combine all ingredients in the container of a food processor.
2   Process to a thick paste. Scrape into a bowl and refrigerate. If your quark is very fresh to begin with, the sauce will keep for a week.

Note: If fresh basil is unavailable, do not substitute dried. Make Parsley Pesto, Dill Pesto, or Spinach Pesto by substituting any of those greens for the elusive basil. If you use dill, omit the Parmesan. Dill Pesto is the perfect accompaniment to cold poached salmon.

More suggestions for Serving Pesto:

1   Fill poached mushroom caps (see page 74) with Pesto. Arrange on juicy, ripe, sliced summer tomatoes. Garnish with whole basil leaves.
2   Toss the Pesto with linguini, fettuccini or penne. Serve with Veal Meatballs (see page 156) or Italian Sausage Balls (see pages 163).
3   Toss fettuccini or linguini with both Pesto and Tomato Sauce (see page 236). Add Sautéed Mushrooms (see page 29) if you wish.
4   Serve Pesto with slices of smoked salmon or spread on smoked salmon sandwiches.
5   Serve pasta with Bolognese Sauce (see page 143). Put a good dollop of Pesto on top of each serving.

♡ 🐻 ❄️ **RED PEPPER SAUCE**

Makes 1½ pts/900 ml

This is a rich, crimson, thick pasta sauce with a vivid and lively taste. It packs a large flavour wallop with only 5 Calories per tablespoon! In addition to pasta, the sauce is lovely with steamed vegetables. For each serving, spoon some of the hot sauce in the centre of a white or clear glass plate. Surround with a neat mound of vegetables that have been steamed until they are crisp-tender. Try peeled, trimmed asparagus, cauliflower florets, trimmed spring onions or green beans. To turn this combination into a hearty main dish, add grilled meatballs (see page 155). If you want a smoky taste, grill the peppers (see page 31) instead of simmering them in stock.

---

10 red bell peppers, coarsely
   chopped
12 fl oz/360 ml stock
Salt, freshly ground black pepper
   and cayenne pepper to taste

Onion-Herb Infusion, using
   thyme, basil or tarragon (see
   page 27)

---

1   Combine the peppers and stock in a deep, heavy frying pan. Bring to the boil. Cover, reduce heat and simmer for 20–30 minutes until tender.
2   Season with salt and peppers. Cool.
3   Purée the mixture in a liquidizer or food processor. Strain though a sieve or strainer, rubbing it through with a rubber spatula or wooden spoon. The skins, which are tough, will be left behind. Discard them.
4   Put the purée into a saucepan. Stir in the infusion. Simmer for 30 minutes. Taste and adjust seasoning. This sauce will keep in the refrigerator for a week.

Variations:

♡ 🐻 **CREAMY RED PEPPER SAUCE**

Prepare sauce as before. Just before serving, stir in 3–4 tablespoons skimmed-milk quark. Stir and cook over low heat until smooth, creamy and heated through. Serve at once. This is particularly good with pasta.

♡ 🐻 ❄️ **TOMATO-PEPPER SAUCE**

Combine Red Pepper Sauce with Tomato Sauce (see page 236).

233

PASTA PRIMAVERA

Toss *al dente* pasta with Red Pepper Sauce; a tablespoon of chopped sun-dried tomatoes (optional, see page 49); Pesto (see page 231); Stir-'Fried' Courgettes in stock (see page 258); and Steamed Asparagus, cut into 1-inch/2.5-cm pieces. Rush, steaming hot, to the table.

HELEN'S TERRACOTTA SAUCE

Makes 1 pt/600 ml

I developed this sauce while my 3-year-old godson, Natty Bumpo, was staying with us. He and Helen Bray, his beloved nanny, helped to taste-test it during his three-week visit. The colour is a warm terracotta, the texture rough and chunky and the taste rich. Serve with pasta, fish, pan-sautéed chicken or steamed cauliflower.

1 lb mushrooms, quartered	¼ pt dry white wine
2 onions, chopped	2 dashes soy sauce
2 large red peppers, chopped	½ teaspoon dried tarragon
2 cloves garlic, crushed	½ teaspoon allspice
1 large carrot, peeled and coarsely grated	2 tablespoons tomato paste
Approx. 2 pts vegetable stock	Salt and freshly ground pepper to taste

1   Combine mushrooms, onions, peppers, garlic, carrot, 8 fl oz/ 300 ml stock, wine, soy sauce, tarragon and allspice in a large, non-stick frying pan. Stir to combine very well. Bring to the boil, reduce heat somewhat, and simmer briskly until the vegetables are tender and the liquid is greatly reduced and syrupy. Lower the heat and let the vegetables 'fry' in their own juices, stirring occasionally.

2   Stir in the tomato paste. Season with salt and pepper. Cool slightly.

3   Purée the mixture in a liquidizer or food processor. Push half of the purée through a non-reactive sieve. Combine the sieved and unsieved mixtures. Refrigerate until needed.

4   To reheat, pour into a saucepan and thin with 2–3 tablespoons stock or water. Simmer gently, stirring occasionally. Be *very* careful because the sauce is thick and is prone to violent, volcanic bubbling.

Pasta Pronto

Pasta suppers are fun. They provide plenty of scope for exuberant improvisation and they can often be prepared in less than half an hour. When you have worked late and are ready for a sumptuous and comforting meal, although you haven't had the time to plan for it, think of pasta. Put the water on to boil and choose your pasta type from the selection you are sure to have in the larder. Then open the fridge and explore. Some of the most fascinating pasta sauces are born of a good leftover rummage. My favourite? Leftover Chilli Con Carne (see page 142), Tomato Sauce (see page 236) and Sautéed Mushrooms (see page 29) combined in a saucepan with a handful of raisins and a few pine nuts. Let it simmer gently while the pasta (penne works well) cooks. When the penne is done, toss with the improvised sauce and hey presto! Pasta al Picadillo.

♡ LEMON CREAM SAUCE

Makes 16 fl oz/480 ml

A delicate pasta sauce with a fresh, lemony taste. Drain the fromage frais in a cheesecloth-lined sieve for a few hours before using it in this recipe. To elevate this to ambrosia, toss in some slivered smoked salmon.

1/5 pt/120 ml water	2 tablespoons buttermilk, at room
Grated rind of 1/2 lemon	temperature
4 tablespoons fresh lemon juice	2/5 pt/240 ml drained low-fat
Salt and freshly ground pepper to	fromage frais, at room
taste	temperature

1   Combine water, lemon rind, lemon juice, salt and pepper in a small frying pan or saucepan. Boil, uncovered, until reduced to about 4 tablespoons. Cool.
2   Beat the lemon infusion and the buttermilk into the fromage frais. (This may be made a few days in advance and stored in the refrigerator. The flavour will intensify.) Bring to room temperature before using. Toss into hot, freshly cooked spaghetti, tagliatelle or shells.

♡ 🐻 ⊕ ❄ TOMATO SAUCE

Makes 1½ pts/900 ml
19 Calories per 4 fl oz/120 ml serving
0.0 g fat
(Traditional tomato sauce: 156 Calories per serving, 7.7 g fat)

If you think it is impossible to make a good tomato sauce without olive oil or butter, think again! This is fast, easy to make and lovely on pasta, or pizza. Sautéed chopped red and yellow peppers and sautéed mushrooms (see page 29) may be added. It freezes very well.

---

3 shallots, finely chopped
2 cloves garlic, peeled and crushed
Pinch cayenne pepper
6 fl oz/180 ml stock
6 fl oz/180 ml dry red wine, white wine or vermouth
1 tablespoon chopped fresh parsley

1 tablespoon each chopped fresh basil, thyme and oregano or ¼ teaspoon each dried basil, thyme and oregano
3 tins (14 oz/420 g each) chopped tomatoes
Parmesan cheese rind
Salt and freshly ground pepper to taste
2 tablespoons tomato paste

---

1   Combine shallots, garlic, cayenne, stock, wine and herbs in a heavy frying pan. Bring to the boil. Reduce heat and simmer briskly until almost all the liquid has been evaporated. Season to taste.

2   Stir in the drained tomatoes (you may crush them with your hands), Parmesan rind, salt and pepper. Simmer, partially covered, for 15 minutes. Stir in the tomato paste and simmer for 5 minutes more. Taste and adjust seasonings. Discard the Parmesan rind. Serve with pasta or on pizza, or try it spooned into jacket potatoes.

Variation:
🐻 SHAWM'S SMOOTH TOMATO SAUCE

My son loves homemade tomato sauce, but hates lumps in his food. Should you have such a family member or friend, let this sauce cool somewhat, and then purée it in the liquidizer. Rub it through a non-reactive sieve. It's convenient to make this sauce in bulk, and then store it in small tubs in the freezer.

'The Colonel did the cooking, and tomatoes kept creeping into everything, which gave him delusions of persecution.'

Dorothy Parker, *Mrs Hofstedder on Josephine St.*

236

HERBED AUBERGINE SAUCE

Makes 1 pt/600 ml

A hearty, spicy sauce that is particularly good tossed with penne, ziti or rotelli.

---

2 aubergines, approx. ½ lb/240 g each, baked (see page 37)

5 shallots, peeled, halved and thinly sliced

½–1 tablespoon fennel seeds

1 tablespoon rosemary leaves, crumbled

1 teaspoon crushed chillies (or to taste)

4 fl oz/120 ml dry red wine

10 fl oz/300 ml chicken or vegetable stock

4 peppers, 2 yellow and 2 red, peeled and cut into thin strips (see page 256)

1 tin (14 oz/420 g) chopped Italian tomatoes

1–2 tablespoons roasted garlic purée (see page 32)

1 tablespoon tomato paste

Salt and freshly ground pepper to taste

1 piece Parmesan rind

---

1   Peel the aubergines and cut them in half. Discard any seeds that seem large and tough. Chop the flesh coarsely. Set aside.
2   In a frying pan, combine the shallots, fennel seeds and rosemary, chillies, wine and 4 fl oz/120 ml of stock. Boil briskly, stirring frequently, until almost dry. Add this mixture to the aubergine.
3   Heat 2 fl oz/60 ml of stock in the frying pan in which you cooked the shallot mixture. When very hot, dump in the peppers. Stir-'fry' until the liquid is almost gone. Scrape the peppers in with the aubergine.
4   Combine with the remaining ingredients, including the remaining stock. Simmer for 10–15 minutes until thick and savoury. Taste and adjust seasonings. Serve with pasta or as a filling for jacket potatoes or potato cases (see page 308) or use as a filling in a vegetarian lasagne.

Microwave the garlic and aubergine, and use tinned peppers.

Variation:
CREAMY AUBERGINE SAUCE

Stir in some skimmed-milk quark and heat gently.

More Pasta Ideas

For a quick and delicious meal try any of the following tossed with the pasta of your choice.

♡ Any vegetable (or combination of several vegetables) trimmed, cut up and stir-'fried' in a combination of stock and wine. Add chopped herbs and some Slim Cuisine Sautéed Onions if you wish.

♡ Sautéed Mushrooms, alone or sautéed with peeled chopped yellow and red peppers and onions (see page 29).

♡ Tzatziki (see page 304).

♡ Room-temperature yoghurt mixed with salt and pepper and chopped fresh herbs. Add a clove or two of crushed garlic marinated in a bit of white wine vinegar if desired.

♡ Room-temperature low-fat cottage cheese or quark thinned a bit with skimmed milk, seasoned with ground cinnamon, caraway seeds or poppy seeds. If desired, add some thinly sliced cabbage stir-'fried' in stock until just barely tender.

Hummus (see page 302).

♡ Salsa (see page 269).

♡ Tomato Sauce (see page 236) to which you have added drained, flaked tuna in brine, crushed raw garlic or baked garlic purée, a few capers and a handful of chopped parsley. Add a dash or two of tabasco sauce.

♡ Tomato Sauce in which you have simmered stock-sautéed slivered carrots, cooked kidney beans, chick peas and chopped parsley.

♡ Browned Onions (see page 26) and Stir-'Fried' Peppers (see page 256).

♡ Mustard Cream (see page 270).

Pesto, Tomato Sauce, Italian Sweet and Sour Courgettes (see page 259) and Sautéed Mushrooms.

❄ ## LASAGNE

Serves 8
294 Calories per serving
6 g fat
(Traditional lasagne: 2,136 Calories per serving)

The tastiest lasagne is made with a bolognese sauce that is based on crumbled Italian sausage meat. The sausage is a combination of pork shoulder, anise seed and crushed chillies. It's delicious but distressingly high in fat. Here I have eliminated the high fat level, but kept the unique Italian sausage taste.

1 recipe Bolognese Sauce (see page 143)	1 lb/480 g low-fat quark
3 small baked aubergines, peeled, seeded (if the seeds are large) and chopped (see page 30)	4 oz/120 g Mozzarella cheese, shredded
½–1 tablespoon anise or fennel seeds	5 fl oz/150 ml skimmed milk
1–2 good pinches crushed dried chillies	10 tablespoons Parmesan cheese
	10 fl oz/300 ml stock
	5 oz/150 g lasagne sheets, green or white (the kind that need no precooking)

1   Make the Bolognese sauce, adding the chopped flesh of the aubergine, the anise seeds and the crushed chillies before simmering the sauce. It should be well seasoned.
2   In a bowl, stir together the quark, Mozzarella cheese, milk and 7 tablespoons Parmesan cheese.
3   Preheat the oven to 400° F, 200° C, Gas Mark 6.
4   Warm the stock. Pour 5 fl oz/150 ml of the stock in a 9-inch/ 23-cm square, 2½-inch/6.25-cm deep non-reactive baking dish. Pour the rest of the warm stock into a shallow dish.
5   Place a single layer of lasagne sheets in the stock in the baking dish. (Turn them to wet them thoroughly with the stock.)
6   Cover with ⅓ of the Bolognese sauce. Spread half the cheese mixture over the sauce. Dip some lasagne sheets into the warm stock in the shallow dish, turning them to wet them thoroughly. Spread in an even layer over the cheese.
7   Repeat, making another layer of sauce, cheese and lasagne sheets.
8   Top with the remaining sauce and an even sprinkling of the remaining Parmesan cheese.
9   Place a baking sheet on the oven floor to catch splatters and ease cleaning up. Bake the lasagne, uncovered, in the lower half of the oven for 1 hour. Let stand for 15 minutes before serving.

❅   **CHICKEN LASAGNE**

Serves 8 generously

I love the spice and herb combination in this dish: allspice, tarragon and a hint of soy sauce. Chicken Lasagne is delicious with a chicken that you poach yourself, a ready-cooked chicken from the super-market, or a smoked chicken.

5 peppers (mixed yellow and green) peeled and chopped (see page 256)	Shredded or diced meat from 1 small (2–2½ lb) poached or smoked chicken. (Make sure all fat, gristle and skin is discarded.)
3 medium onions, finely chopped	
2 cloves garlic, minced	
1 lb/480 g mushrooms, quartered	1 lb/480 g skimmed-milk quark
1 pt/600 ml stock	3 oz/90 g part-skimmed Mozzarella cheese, shredded
4 fl oz/120 ml dry white wine	
2 dashes soy sauce	5 tablespoons grated Parmesan cheese
½ teaspoon allspice	
½ teaspoon dried tarragon	4 fl oz/120 ml skimmed milk
Freshly ground pepper to taste	7 oz lasagne sheets (the kind that need no pre-cooking)
2 tablespoons tomato paste	

1   Combine peppers, onions, garlic, mushrooms, 8 oz/300 ml stock, wine, soy sauce and seasonings in a large, non-stick frying pan. Stir to combine very well. Bring to the boil. Simmer briskly until the vegetables are tender and the liquid is greatly reduced and syrupy. Lower the heat a bit and cook gently, stirring occasionally, while the vegetables 'fry' in their own juices.

2   When the mixture is very thick and not at all soupy, stir in the tomato paste. Remove from the heat and stir in the chicken. Taste and adjust the seasonings. Set aside.

3   Stir together the quark, Mozzarella cheese, 3 tablespoons of Parmesan cheese and the milk. Set aside.

4   Choose a shallow, non-reactive 9-inch/23-cm-square baking dish. Pour 4 fl oz/120 ml of warm stock into the dish. Pour 3 oz/90 ml of warm stock into an extra shallow dish and keep it at hand.

5   Put an even layer of uncooked lasagne sheets in the shallow baking dish, turning them to wet them thoroughly. Cover with half the chicken mixture.

6   Dip more lasagne sheets in the stock in the extra dish, turning them to wet them. Put an even layer of the wet sheets over the chicken mixture. Cover with half the quark mixture.

7   Dip more lasagne sheets in the extra stock and put them in an even layer over the quark. Spread over the remaining chicken mixture. Spread the remaining quark mixture on top, mixing it in with the chicken mixture as you spread. Sprinkle 2 table-spoons of grated Parmesan evenly over the top. Pour 4 fl oz/ 120 ml of stock evenly over the baking dish, letting it flow down the sides.

8   Bake at 400° F, 200° C, Gas Mark 6, for 45 minutes until browned and bubbly, and almost all the liquid is absorbed. Put the baking dish on a rack and let it sit for 15 minutes before cutting and serving. The rest of the liquid will be absorbed and the lasagne will cut nicely into neat squares.

The lasagne may be refrigerated for several days or frozen. If desired, cut into serving pieces and freeze in small dishes, covered in cling film.

❄ VEGETARIAN LASAGNE

Serves 6

Lasagne is no longer considered sophisticated, but watch the faces of your guests light up with joy when you ferry one – hot, steamy and odorous – to the table.

½ lb/240 g thinly julienned carrots
½ lb/240 g thinly julienned peeled
red peppers
1 lb/480 g mushrooms, quartered
2 large onions, chopped
8 fl oz/240 ml dry white wine
18 fl oz/540 ml vegetable stock
Several dashes soy sauce
1½ teaspoons dried tarragon
½ teaspoon ground allspice
2 tablespoons tomato paste
2 tablespoons chopped parsley
Salt and freshly ground pepper to
taste

1½ lb/720 g spinach, washed,
stemmed and torn into strips, or
1½ lb/720 g frozen chopped
spinach
1 lb/480 g low-fat quark
5–6 oz/150–180 g medium-fat
Mozzarella cheese, shredded
6 tablespoons grated Parmesan
cheese
5 tablespoons skimmed milk
5 oz/150 g lasagne sheets (the type
that need no pre-cooking)

---

1   Combine the carrots, peppers, mushrooms, onions, wine, 8 fl oz/240 ml of stock, soy sauce, tarragon and ¼ teaspoon allspice in a heavy, deep, non-reactive frying pan. Simmer briskly, stirring occasionally, until the mixture is thick and the vegetables are tender. Stir in the tomato paste and parsley. Season with salt and pepper.
2   Cook the spinach in the water clinging to its leaves, until it is just limp. Drain and squeeze as dry as possible. If frozen spinach is being used, just drain it and squeeze as dry as possible. Season the spinach with a bit of salt and pepper and ¼ teaspoon allspice.
3   Mix together the quark, the Mozzarella cheese, 4 tablespoons of Parmesan cheese and the skimmed milk.

4   Pour 3–4 fl oz/90–120 ml of warm stock on to the surface of a non-reactive 8½–10-inch/21.5 × 25-cm baking dish. Pour 2–3 fl oz/90–120 ml of additional warm stock in a shallow dish and keep it at hand. Place a single layer of lasagne in the 8½ × 10-inch/21.5 × 25-cm baking dish. Turn to thoroughly wet them with the stock. Spread the spinach over the lasagne layer. Dip more lasagne in the warm stock you have kept at hand and put on an even layer on the spinach.

5   Spread the cheese mixture on the lasagne. Dip more lasagne in the stock and put on an even layer over the cheese. Spread half the vegetable mixture on the layer, top with more wet lasagne. Spread on the remaining vegetables. Spread the remaining cheese over the top, mixing it in with the vegetables as you spread. Sprinkle evenly with 2 tablespoons of Parmesan cheese. Pour 4 fl oz/120 ml of stock evenly over the baking dish, letting it seep down.

6   Bake, covered, at 400° F, 200° C, Gas Mark 6, for 30 minutes. Uncover and bake for 10–15 minutes more, until browned and bubbly and the stock has been absorbed.

❄   # LARDER LASAGNE

Serves 6

This vegetarian dish is easily made from larder and freezer staples, yet the result is quite good. It can be made ahead and refrigerated for a day if desired – in fact the flavour improves under these circumstances.

---

1 bag (1 lb/480 g) frozen ratatouille vegetables (do not thaw)
Approx. 2 pts/1,200 ml stock
3 large Spanish onions, cut in half and sliced into thin half-moons
3 cloves garlic, crushed
4 tablespoons tomato paste
2 tablespoons chopped parsley
1 tablespoon fresh thyme (¼ teaspoon dried)
1 tablespoon chopped fresh basil (¼ teaspoon dried)
1 tablespoon fresh oregano (¼ teaspoon dried)

Salt, freshly ground pepper and cayenne pepper to taste
Approx. ¼ lb/120 g lasagne sheets (the kind that need no precooking)
¾ lb/360 g low-fat quark
5 tablespoons skimmed milk
Freshly grated nutmeg to taste
5 oz/150 g shredded low-fat Mozzarella cheese
7 tablespoons grated Parmesan cheese

1   Combine the *frozen* vegetables and 8 fl oz/240 ml stock in a deep heavy non-reactive frying pan. Bring to the boil, reduce heat and simmer, covered, for about 15 minutes.

2   Stir, and simmer, uncovered, for 15 minutes more.

3   Meanwhile, sauté the onions and garlic in ⅖ pt/240 ml stock according to the Slim Cuisine technique. When they are meltingly tender and amber brown, set aside.

4   Stir the sautéed onions, the tomato paste and the herbs and spices into the ratatouille mixture. Simmer, stirring occasionally for an additional 15 minutes until thick. If during this time it becomes too dry, and begins to stick, add a bit more stock.

5   Preheat the oven to 400° F, 200° C, Gas Mark 6.

6   Pour 3–4 fl oz/120 ml of stock onto the surface of a non-reactive 9×13-inch/23×33-cm baking dish. Place a layer of lasagne sheets in the stock. Turn them to thoroughly wet them with stock.

7   Mix together the quark, milk, nutmeg, Mozzarella cheese and 4 tablespoons of Parmesan.

8   Spread half the ratatouille over the pasta. Spread half the cheese mixture over the ratatouille. Top with another layer of pasta.

9   Spread on an even layer of the remaining ratatouille. Spread the remaining cheese over this, mixing it in with the ratatouille as you spread. Sprinkle evenly with the last 2 tablespoons of Parmesan. Pour 4–5 fl oz/150 ml of stock over the top. (The baking dish can be refrigerated at this point for baking on the following day.) Bring to room temperature before baking.

10   Bake, uncovered, for 35 minutes.

Vegetable and Grain Side Dishes

'Even today, well-brought up English girls are taught by their mothers to boil all veggies for at least a month and a half, just in case one of the dinner guests turns up without his teeth.'

Calvin Trillin, *Third Helpings*

S team your vegetables, sauté them, stir-'fry', bake or braise them, but *please* don't boil them to death. Boiling robs them of many nutrients, and causes small children to utter loud retching noises when presented with a plate of the miserably flabby things. What a glorious profusion of vegetables can be found in British markets as the seasons change. From the humble roots to slim, elegant asparagus, from familiar sprouts to exotic fennel, from celery to celery root – experiment, taste, revel in the variety.

♡ 🐻 **STEAMED ASPARAGUS**

Please take the time to peel your asparagus before cooking it – what a difference it makes! This asparagus is so good that in season I often eat a large platter for dinner all by itself. Believe me, it is worth the peeling. If you want to get fancy, serve this asparagus as a first course with Red or Yellow Pepper Sauce (see page 233). Put a puddle of the sauce on a pretty plate, and surround the puddle with the beautiful green stalks. For a main course, add Veal Meatballs.

Fresh asparagus stalks, washed

---

1   Cut off the tough woody bottom portion of each stalk. With a swivel-bladed vegetable peeler, peel each stalk from the bottom up to the buds. If you are not going to cook them at once, stand them in a glass of water as if they were a bunch of flowers.
2   Place the stalks in a steamer basket. Steam over boiling water for 3–7 minutes (depending on size) until crisp-tender. To test, pull out one stalk with tongs. Hold it up. It should just bend a *little* bit.

Use thin asparagus; it needs no peeling.

 ## STIR-'FRIED' ASPARAGUS

Fresh asparagus stalks, washed	*Pinch thyme and tarragon*
3–4 fl oz/120 ml stock	*Salt and freshly ground pepper to*
½ lime	*taste*

---

1   Trim and peel the asparagus (see previous recipe) and cut into 1-inch/2.5-cm lengths. Heat 3–4 fl oz/120 ml of stock in a non-reactive wok or frying pan. Throw in the asparagus and toss and turn in the hot stock for about 2 minutes (use two wooden spoons or spatulas).
2   Squeeze in the juice of ½ a lime, add a pinch each of thyme and tarragon and salt and freshly ground pepper to taste. Keep stir-frying for a few more moments, until crisp-tender (more crisp than tender). Serve at once.

Use thin asparagus; it needs no peeling.

STEAMED BROCCOLI

Broccoli is so awful when boiled until flabby. Try it steamed briefly and rejoice in its special taste and texture.

1   Wash the head of broccoli very well. Split it into single stalks. Cut off and discard the tough ends. Peel the stalks up to the flowers with a paring knife.
2   Spread the broccoli evenly in a steamer. If you love garlic,

246

sprinkle some chopped cloves of this over the broccoli. Cover and steam over boiling water for 5–7 minutes until crisp-tender (test with a cake tester or a tooth pick). Serve at once with wedges of lemon or lime.

3   If the broccoli is to be served cold, refresh under running cold water to stop the cooking and set the vivid green colour.

Variation:

Cut the florets off the stalks. Save the stalks to serve on the next day. Steam the florets for 3–4 minutes over boiling water. Serve hot or cold, with lemon juice or reduced stock (see page 253).

To serve the stalks, peel them and slice ¼-inch thick and steam until tender or stir-'fry' in a small amount of stock and lemon juice until crisp-tender (see page 258 for stir-'fry' procedures).

 CREAMED SPINACH

Serves 4

4 oz/120 g low-fat quark at room temperature	Salt and pepper to taste
	Pinch nutmeg
2–3 tablespoons skimmed milk, at room temperature	1 lb/480 g spinach, very well washed, stemmed and cut into strips
Purée from 1 head roasted garlic	

1   Stir together the quark and milk. Stir in the garlic, salt, pepper and nutmeg.
2   Put the spinach into a large, non-reactive pot. Cook, stirring, in the water that clings to its leaves, until limp and greatly reduced in volume but still bright green. Drain in a colander.
3   Fold the spinach and the quark mixture together. Serve at once.

Buy pre-washed spinach. Roast garlic in the microwave.

DUXELLES

Makes 1 pt/600 ml

Duxelles is a kind of mushroom hash, with a very intense mushroom taste. It is useful in all sorts of preparations, so it pays to make it in quantity and store it in the refrigerator or freezer. At its most basic, try it spread thickly on bread, or stirred into sauces or soups. Better still, try it in Baked Potatoes (see page 268) or in

247

Ravioli (see page 75). For the most intense mushroom flavour use a combination of types of fresh mushrooms. I use shiitakes, trimmed of their tough stems, chestnut mushrooms, oyster mushrooms and the usual cultivated ones.

1½ lb/720 g mixed mushrooms, cleaned well	1 teaspoon dried tarragon, crumbled
8 fl oz/240 ml vegetable stock	Salt and freshly ground pepper to taste
4 fl oz/120 ml sherry	
Several dashes soy sauce	

1   Chop the mushrooms very, very finely. This is best done in a food processor if you have one. Quarter the mushrooms and put them into the food processor bowl. Pulse on and off until very finely chopped. You will need to do this in 2 or more batches.

2   Empty all the chopped mushrooms into a deep, non-reactive frying pan. Add the stock, sherry, soy sauce and tarragon. Stir it all up. The mushrooms will be barely moistened but it doesn't matter.

3   Cook over moderate heat, stirring occasionally until the mushrooms have rendered quite a bit of liquid. Turn the heat up a bit and simmer briskly, stirring occasionally until the mushrooms are very dark, very thick and quite dry. Season to taste. Store in the refrigerator until needed.

'Free! Free at last! His mouth watered at the thought of the meals he was going to have in the next few days. Potatoes and Martinis and warm buttered rolls and all the other forbidden foods.'

Robert Silverberg, *The Iron Chancellor*

♡ ⊕ ❄ MUSHROOM RAGOÛT

Serve this mushroom-lover's special as a vegetable side dish or as a starter. The more kinds of mushrooms you can find, the nicer this will be.

A variety of fresh mushrooms (look for fresh shiitake, chestnut and oyster mushrooms in addition to the ordinary cultivated ones; trim the tough stems from shiitakes before using them)
Freshly ground pepper to taste

Dash of soy sauce
Dry sherry or dry vermouth
Stock
Purée from roasted garlic (optional)
Toast Cups (recipe follows)
  (optional)

1   Clean mushrooms well, cut into quarters or eighths (depending on size) and combine with seasonings and liquids in a large non-stick frying pan.
2   Cook briskly until the liquid in the pan is greatly reduced.
3   Stir in the garlic purée. Cook, stirring, for a minute or so more, until the mushrooms are tender, and in a syrupy sauce. Taste and correct seasonings.
4   Spoon individual servings of the ragoût into toast cups and serve at once.

🐻 Serve the ragoût without the toast cups.

TOAST CUPS

Use a non-stick patty tin (or muffin tin) and a thin-sliced loaf of bread. Trim the crusts from each slice of bread. Roll over each slice with a rolling pin. Gently fit each slice into one of the cups of the tin. Bake at 400° F, 200° C, Gas Mark 6, for 10–15 minutes until lightly browned.

Variation:
♡ 🐻 ⊕ MUSHROOM SALAD

As a lower-calorie alternative, add some good wine vinegar (optional) to the finished ragoût and serve in lettuce cups or chicory leaves.

A Vegetable Selection

Lavishness is one of the best aspects of Slim Cuisine. With the fat density gone, Calories are low, and some foods can be eaten in vast quantities with no fear of bulging out of one's clothes the next day. Vegetables fall into this category. With no butter, oil, or margarine used in their preparation, vegetables are extremely low in Calories yet they are high in vitamins, minerals and fibre. Not only *can* you eat large quantities, you *should*. Large and frequent helpings of vegetables are important to your nutritional well-being. Slim Cuisine techniques make them a pleasure to eat; your psychological well-being will benefit as well.

For a special dinner party, serve Braised Brisket of Beef (page 125) and a vast selection of vegetables. Include Sautéed Mushrooms, 'Fried' Onions, Sautéed Spring Onions or Braised Leeks, Stir-'Fried' Peppers or Savoury Peppers, Stir-'Fried' Courgettes or Baked Courgettes, Spicy Sprouts, Braised Fennel and Roast Potatoes. These vegetables, arranged on a large plate, make a wonderfully tempting edible mosaic; one that guests will dig into with a feeling of delighted exhilaration. *All* the vegetables on the plate can be prepared ahead of time, some as early as two days ahead. The onions, peppers and mushrooms may be prepared weeks ahead and frozen.

'Your exploration of food should be governed by infinite curiosity. Fling open the gastronomic gates . . .'

Dana Kaye, *The Travelling Woman*

♡ ⏱ ❄ BRAISED MUSHROOMS

Serve as a vegetable accompaniment or a starter. It works well on a buffet at a drinks party. Because the soy sauce is salty, you won't want to add any salt as you cook the mushrooms.

---

3 lb/1,440 g button mushrooms, cleaned

16 fl oz/480 ml salt-free vegetable or chicken stock

4 fl oz/120 ml dry sherry

4 tablespoons soy sauce

1 tablespoon sugar

2 large cloves garlic, peeled and crushed

2 thin slices ginger root, peeled and chopped

---

1   Place the mushrooms in a deep, heavy non-reactive pot. Add all remaining ingredients.
2   Bring to the boil. Reduce heat to a brisk simmer and cook, uncovered, stirring occasionally, until the mushrooms are deep mahogany brown and the liquid is greatly reduced.
3   With a slotted spoon, remove the mushrooms to a bowl. Boil the remaining liquid until reduced by half. Pour over the mushrooms. Serve hot or at room temperature. If they are to be part of a buffet, have cocktail picks nearby for spearing.

♡ 🧸 ❄   **BRAISED CARROTS**

Carrots braised in fresh citrus juices until tender make a good addition to Sunday lunch or a holiday dinner.

Large carrots, peeled and cut in half lengthwise	1-inch/2.5-cm piece each lemon zest and orange zest
Stock	2–3 large cloves garlic, peeled and halved
Juice of 1 large orange	Salt and freshly ground pepper to taste
Juice of ½ large lemon	

1   Preheat oven to 400° F, 200° C, Gas Mark 6.
2   Arrange carrots, in one layer, in a shallow baking dish. Pour in stock to a depth of a little less than ½ inch/1.25 cm. Pour the juices over the carrots and scatter in the lemon and orange zest and the garlic. Season lightly with salt and generously with freshly ground pepper. Cover the dish with foil, shiny side in.
3   Bake for 45 minutes. Uncover and bake for 15 minutes more. By then the carrots should be tender, and the liquid gone. Serve at once, or refrigerate or freeze until needed. Reheat in the microwave or conventional oven. Add a bit of stock first.

'One of the greatest luxuries in dining is to be able to command plenty of good vegetables well served up.'

Thomas Walker, *The Art of Dining*

❆ BRAISED LEEKS

Makes 12 pieces

12 leeks	*4 fl oz/120 ml stock*
Freshly ground pepper	*3 tablespoons Parmesan cheese*

1 Preheat oven to 350° F, 180° C, Gas Mark 4.
2 Trim off 'beard' and all but ¼-inch/0.6-cm of green portion of leeks. (Save greens for stock.) Clean the leeks well. Arrange them in one layer in a baking dish and pour the stock over them. Sprinkle with the cheese and pepper.
3 Bake uncovered for 30–45 minutes, turning the leeks once during this time. They are done when they are tender, and the stock has cooked down to a glaze.

♡ ❀ Omit cheese.

♡ ❆ BRAISED SHALLOTS

Makes 1 pt/600 ml

These shallots are meant to be served as a chutney or a relish. They go very well with Grilled Goose Skirt Steak (page 133) or Hamburgers (page 154).

2 tablespoons golden raisins	*Grated zest of ½ lemon*
8 fl oz/240 ml dry red wine	*Salt and freshly ground pepper*
12 fl oz/360 ml stock	*Juice of ½ lemon (to taste)*
1½ lb/720 g shallots, peeled and	
halved (substitute thinly sliced	
onions when shallots are	
unavailable)	

1 Combine the raisins and wine in a small bowl. Set aside.
2 Pour 4 fl oz/120 ml stock into a heavy non-reactive frying pan. Add shallots. Cook over medium heat, shaking the pan frequently, until the shallots are lightly browned and the stock has almost cooked away.
3 Add the remaining stock, the wine, raisins, lemon zest and salt and pepper. Cook, partially covered, for 30 minutes, until the shallots are very tender. Squeeze in the lemon juice. Serve cold.

 Omit raisins.

❄ BRAISED FENNEL

Serves 4

Fennel looks a lot like celery and tastes like mild liquorice. Braised fennel is very good as a companion to meats, or as part of a vegetable dinner.

---

*2 bulbs fennel, trimmed and cut
    in half lengthwise, then each
    half cut into wedges approx.
    ½-inch/1.25-cm wide*
Freshly ground pepper

4 fl oz/120 ml stock
3 tablespoons Parmesan cheese

---

1   Preheat oven to 350° F, 180° C, Gas Mark 4.
2   Arrange fennel in one layer (cut side down) in a baking dish. Pour over 4 fl oz/120 ml stock. Season with pepper. Sprinkle evenly with 3 tablespoons Parmesan cheese.
3   Bake uncovered for 45 minutes. The fennel will become meltingly tender and the stock will have cooked almost completely away, leaving a rich glaze. Serve at once.

♡ 🐻   Omit cheese.

Seasoning Vegetables

Melted butter or margarine are the classic toppings for steamed vegetables. I lived for many years in the American South where vegetables are seasoned with bacon or fatback. In the Mediterranean countries the vegetables glisten with a coating of olive oil. None of these are appropriate to the Slim Cuisine regime. What to do?

Try this. Boil good-quality vegetable or chicken stock until greatly reduced and syrupy. Toss with the vegetables. Even better, mix the stock with dry red or white wine, dry vermouth, or dry sherry, interesting wine vinegar, or lemon or lime juice, and then boil down until syrupy. Add herbs or spices before you boil, but season with salt, to taste, *after* the boiling, or it will be much too salty.

BRAISED CAULIFLOWER
WITH FENNEL SEEDS

Serves 4

This is a sensational vegetable dish with enough interesting play of flavours to make it the star of a meal. It can be served hot or cold, but I like it best at room temperature, when all the splendid flavour seems to explode in the mouth. It is not a visually beautiful dish, so line a bowl with curly lettuce leaves, and spoon in the cauliflower, then garnish with parsley.

---

1 large clove garlic, peeled
2 tablespoons fresh parsley
1 tablespoon rosemary leaves
½–1 tablespoon fennel seeds
½ pt/300 ml browned onions or sautéed onions (see page 24)
2 tablespoons red wine vinegar

1 large or 2 small cauliflowers, broken into florets
6 fl oz/180 ml stock
1 heaped tablespoon tomato paste
Salt and freshly ground pepper to taste
Chopped parsley

---

1   Chop together the garlic, parsley, rosemary and fennel. Set aside.
2   Place the browned onions in a deep, heavy frying pan. Heat until the onions begin to sizzle and stick to the frying pan. Pour in the wine vinegar and boil, stirring and scraping up the browned bits with a wooden spoon.
3   When the liquid is almost gone, stir in the garlic mixture. Add the cauliflower. Toss everything together until it is well combined.
4   Whisk together the stock and the tomato paste. Season with salt and pepper. Pour over the cauliflower and stir again. Bring to the boil, cover, reduce heat and simmer until the cauliflower is very tender but not disintegrating (about ½ hour in all). Cool to room temperature and serve. Garnish liberally with chopped parsley. This may be prepared 1–2 days ahead, in fact the flavour will improve. Store in the refrigerator. Bring to room temperature before serving. Add the parsley garnish just before serving.

CAULIFLOWER AND PEPPERS

Serves 4

The ivory-white cauliflower pieces, studded with crimson pepper strips, look so pretty, and the tastes and textures of the two vegetables play against each other very well.

1 large cauliflower, trimmed and separated into florets	6 fl oz/180 ml stock
	1 clove garlic, minced
2 large red peppers, seeded, ribbed and cut into their natural sections	½ teaspoon cumin seeds
	Salt and freshly ground pepper to taste

1   Steam the cauliflower over boiling water, until partially cooked, about 3 minutes. Refresh under cold water and set aside.
2   With a swivel-bladed vegetable peeler, peel each pepper piece. Cut the peppers into strips about ½ inch/1.25 cm wide.
3   Heat half the stock in a heavy frying pan. When it begins to bubble, stir in the garlic and peppers. Stir and toss with two wooden spoons until the peppers are almost crisp tender and the liquid is almost gone. Lower heat and let the peppers 'fry' gently in their own juices as you stir them. When they are very tender, stir in the cauliflower.
4   Sprinkle in the cumin and stir well. Pour in the remaining stock. Cover and simmer until the cauliflower is tender but not mushy. Season to taste.

Substitute tinned peppers for the fresh ones.

STIR-'FRIED' CAULIFLOWER

Serves 4

Cauliflower is very good steamed until crisp-tender. It is even better stir-'fried' in stock.

1 large head cauliflower	1 clove garlic, minced (optional)
6 fl oz/180 ml stock	Salt and freshly ground pepper to taste
Dash of fresh lemon juice	

1   Cut off and discard the tough end of the cauliflower stalk. Discard the leaves. Separate the cauliflower in florets.

2   Pour the stock and lemon juice into a wide, heavy, non-reactive frying pan or wok. Heat to simmering. Toss in the cauliflower, optional garlic, and salt and pepper, cover and simmer for 3 minutes.
3   Uncover. Turn the heat to high. Stir and toss the florets in the boiling stock until the stock is almost gone and the cauliflower is crisp-tender. Serve at once.

♡ 🧸 ❄ STIR-'FRIED' PEPPERS

Peeling the peppers sounds tedious, but it is not much more difficult than peeling a carrot, and the textural difference between a peeled and unpeeled pepper is a big one. And without the skin, the peppers, when cooked in stock, produce a thick and delicious sauce. They are much more digestible when peeled, too. This is a very rich-tasting, colourful and soul-satisfying vegetable dish, well worth the peeling time. Eat it as a vegetable accompaniment, try it tossed into pasta, or serve it as a sauce with Goose Skirt Steak (see page 133) or Pan-Sautéed Chicken Breasts (see page 172).

3 red peppers	*6 fl oz/180 ml stock*
3 yellow peppers	*Freshly ground pepper to taste*

1   Cut the peppers in half, lengthwise. Remove the stem, the seeds and the ribs. Cut the halves into their natural sections.
2   Peel each pepper piece with a swivel-bladed vegetable peeler. Cut each piece into strips about ½ inch/1.25 cm wide.
3   Heat the stock in a heavy frying pan. When very hot, toss in the peppers and grind in some black pepper. With two wooden spoons, toss and turn the peppers in the hot stock until the liquid has cooked down considerably. Turn down the heat a bit and 'fry' them for a few minutes in their own juices, until they are very tender, and the pepper juices have formed a thick sauce. Serve at once with their delicious juices, or serve at room temperature. This dish may be made in advance and rewarmed later or the next day.

♡ 🧸 ❄ SAVOURY PEPPERS

Makes 2 pts/1.2 l

This is a sumptuous Slim Cuisine stir-'fry'. Turn it into a pretty first course by tossing in some tiny cooked peeled prawns at the very end. Add a teaspoon of chopped drained capers as well.

6–8 red peppers	2 fl oz/60 ml sherry
4–5 cloves garlic, peeled and coarsely diced	Splash of balsamic vinegar (optional)
4 fl oz/120 ml vegetable stock	Freshly ground pepper to taste

1   Stem and seed peppers, cut into ½-inch/1.25-cm wide strips. Peel each strip with a swivel-bladed vegetable peeler.
2   Combine peppers and remaining ingredients in a heavy, non-reactive frying pan. Bring to the boil. Cook, stirring occasionally, until the peppers are tender and the liquid is greatly reduced. Continue to stir and cook – the peppers and garlic chunks will be 'frying' in their own juices – until the peppers are in a thick, syrupy, scant sauce. Serve at once, or cool for a later time.

♡ ❀ ⊕   **SPICY SPROUTS**

Brown rice wine vinegar, soy sauce, and chilli and garlic paste are available in most supermarkets. If you don't want to gussy up your sprouts with such tastes, leave them out by all means.

1 large bag (2 lb/960 g) frozen baby Brussels sprouts	1 teaspoon brown rice wine vinegar
12 fl oz/360 ml stock	½ teaspoon soy sauce
Freshly ground pepper and crushed dried chilli to taste	½ teaspoon chilli and garlic paste

1   Place the still-frozen sprouts, stock and peppers in a wide, heavy, non-reactive frying pan. Cover and cook over high heat until the stock comes to the boil.
2   Uncover and cook, stirring, until the sprouts are thawed and just barely warm. They should still be crunchy.
3   Drain well and return liquid to the pan. Stir in remaining ingredients. Boil rapidly until greatly reduced.
4   Return sprouts to the pan. Stir and cook gently until the sprouts are tender, hot and glazed. Taste and adjust seasonings.

This may be prepared a few days ahead of time and stored in the refrigerator. The sprouts are as delicious cold as hot.

♡ 🐻 ⊕ ❄ SAUTÉED SPRING ONIONS

Imagine trying to cook without onions! The mind boggles. Slim, elegant spring onions are usually sliced and used as a garnish or salad ingredient, but they make a delectable vegetable, cooked whole, in quantity. Make plenty of these, they are moreish, to say the least.

Thin spring onions
Stock

---

1   Trim the onions of their 'beard' and of all but 1–2 inches/ 2.5–5 cm of their green.
2   Heat ¼ inch/0.6 cm of stock in a heavy, wide frying pan. Arrange the spring onions in the pan in one layer. Cook over high heat, turning the onions occasionally with tongs, until the onions are tender and bathed in a syrupy glaze. Serve at once.

Variation: Gratin of Spring Onions

Place the sautéed spring onions in a shallow baking dish and, with a rubber spatula, scrape the glaze over them. The onions should be lying in one direction, and in one layer. Sprinkle with a small amount of Parmesan cheese and drizzle with a small amount of stock. Bake at 350° F, 180° C, Gas Mark 5, until heated through and the cheese has melted, 15–20 minutes.

♡ 🐻 ⊕ ❄ STIR-'FRIED' COURGETTES WITH LIME AND CUMIN

Serves 6

This recipe is a prime example of how to stir-'fry', without oil. Try leftovers served cold with a sprinkling of interesting wine vinegar.

6–8 small courgettes	*Salt and freshly ground pepper to*
4 fl oz/120 ml stock	*taste*
Generous pinch of ground cumin	*Juice of 1 lime*

---

1   Wash and trim the courgettes but do not peel them. Cut them in half and then into strips about 2 inches/5 cm long and ½ inch/1.25 cm wide.

2   Pour the stock into a heavy, non-reactive frying pan. Bring to the boil.

3   Dump in the courgettes. Grind in a generous amount of pepper, and sprinkle in the cumin. With two wooden spoons, constantly toss and turn the vegetables over high heat until they are crisp-tender, and the stock has cooked down to almost nothing. Squeeze in the lime juice, season lightly with salt to taste and let the courgettes stir-'fry' for a minute or so in their own juices. Serve at once.

Variations:

♡ 🧸 🕐 ❄ STIR-'FRIED' COURGETTES WITH GARLIC AND GINGER

Mince a clove of garlic and a thin slice of peeled ginger root. Put them in the frying pan with the stock and 1 fl oz/30 ml dry sherry and let boil for a few seconds before dumping in the courgettes. Omit the pepper and the lime juice. If desired, sprinkle with some chopped fresh coriander before serving.

🕐 ❄ ITALIAN SWEET AND SOUR COURGETTES

Add 3 cloves of minced garlic to the stock and let boil for a few seconds. Dump in the courgettes, freshly ground pepper, 2 tablespoons each of raisins, drained, rinsed capers, and pine kernels, and the juice of 1 lime. Just before serving, stir in some finely chopped parsley. Serve hot or cold.

 Omit the raisins and pine kernels.

♡ 🧸 ❄ BAKED COURGETTES, ITALIAN STYLE

Makes 1½ pts/900 ml

Courgettes, zucchini, green summer squash; whatever you call them, they are wonderful simmered in a thick tomato sauce. If you are feeling self-indulgent, add a handful of sun-dried tomatoes.

1 large onion, coarsely chopped
1–2 large cloves garlic, coarsely
  chopped
6 fl oz/180 ml dry red wine
6 fl oz/180 ml stock
Handful sun-dried tomatoes,
  chopped (optional)
Generous pinch oregano
Salt and freshly ground pepper to
  taste

2 tins (14 oz/420 g each) chopped
  Italian tomatoes
1 piece Parmesan rind
3 tablespoons tomato paste
8 medium courgettes, sliced
  ½ inch/1.25 cm thick
2 tablespoons chopped fresh parsley
A scattering of shredded fresh basil
  leaves

1   Combine onions, garlic, wine, stock, sun-dried tomatoes and oregano in a heavy non-reactive frying pan. Cover and bring to the boil. Reduce heat and simmer briskly until almost all the liquid has been evaporated. Uncover, and cook gently, letting the onions and tomatoes 'fry' in their own juices. Season to taste.

2   Stir in the chopped tomatoes, Parmesan rind, salt and pepper. Simmer, partially covered, for 15 minutes. Stir in the tomato paste and simmer for 5 minutes more. Taste and adjust seasonings. Discard the Parmesan rind.

3   Stir in courgettes. Bake, uncovered, at 350° F, 180° C, Gas Mark 4, for 30–40 minutes, until the courgettes are tender. Stir occasionally during this time. Garnish with herbs and serve.

♡ 🐻 ❄ **WHIPPED SWEDES**

I *love* swedes; I even loved them back home in the States, where they are known as rutabagas – an ungainly name if ever there was one.

1 large Spanish onion, chopped
6 fl oz/180 ml stock
Splash or two of medium sherry
1 large packet frozen diced swedes
2 tablespoons stock
4–6 fl oz/120–180 ml buttermilk

Purée from 1 head Baked Garlic
  (optional, see page 32)
Salt and pepper
½–1 teaspoon crumbled dried
  rosemary
Crushed chilli peppers to taste
  (optional)

1   Preheat oven to 350° F, 180° C, Gas Mark 4.

2   Combine onions, and 6 fl oz/180 ml stock in a heavy frying pan. Cover and bring to the boil. Boil rapidly for 5–7 minutes, until the onions are almost dry and beginning to brown.

Uncover. Continue to cook, stirring, until the onions are sticking and browning. Pour in a splash of sherry, stir and scrape up the browned bits. When the onions are tender and amber brown, remove from the heat and set aside.

3   Defrost frozen swedes with 2 tablespoons stock in the microwave.

4   Place defrosted swedes with their liquid in a food processor. Add remaining ingredients, including sautéed onions. Process until very smooth.

5   Spread the mixture into a gratin dish, cover, and bake for 30 minutes, until hot and bubbly.

❄ Ⓢ PURÉE OF SWEDE, TURNIP AND WHITE BEANS

One of my favourite vegetarian meals consists of this purée, Intense Mushroom Ragoût (page 219) and Creamy Spinach (page 247).

---

3 carrots, chopped	2 tins (14 oz/420 g each) white
1 large onion, chopped	kidney beans (cannellini beans),
2 stalks celery, chopped	drained
3 cloves garlic, crushed	5 oz/150 g frozen diced swede,
1 bay leaf	thawed, cooked according to
1 teaspoon herbes de Provence,	packet directions
crumbled	6 fl oz/180 ml fromage frais
12 fl oz/360 ml stock	Salt and freshly ground pepper to
5 medium turnips, peeled and	taste
chopped	2 tablespoons grated Parmesan
	cheese

---

1   Combine carrots, onion, celery, garlic, bay leaf, herbes de Provence and 6 fl oz/180 ml stock in a large heavy-bottomed frying pan. Cover and bring to the boil. Reduce heat and simmer for 15–20 minutes until vegetables are tender. Uncover, raise heat, and cook until the liquid has evaporated and the vegetables are browning.

2   Stir in the turnips and the remaining stock. Cover and simmer until all vegetables are tender, about 15 minutes. Add beans.

3   Cook, uncovered, for 5 minutes more, until all the liquid is gone. Discard bay leaf. Season with salt and pepper.

4   Purée the vegetable mixture in the food processor. Process in the swede and the fromage frais. Correct seasonings.

5   Preheat oven to 400° F, 200° C, Gas Mark 6. Spread the vegetable purée in a gratin pan. Sprinkle with cheese. Bake uncovered for 30 minutes, until hot, bubbly and brown.

This freezes very well. Prepare the recipe as far as step 4, then cool and freeze. Bake from the frozen state at 400° F, 200° C, Gas Mark 6, covered for 30 minutes, uncovered for 30 minutes, or cook from the frozen state in the microwave (approximately 6 minutes on high), then flash under a hot grill to brown the top.

♡ Omit Parmesan cheese.

GRATIN OF BAKED VEGETABLES

Serves 6

Warming, comforting and an attractive, glowing orange. The gratin freezes very well, and, when frozen, reheats beautifully in the microwave.

---

5 white turnips, peeled
6 medium carrots, peeled
Purée from one head baked garlic
  (see page 32)
2–3 tablespoons buttermilk

Salt and freshly ground pepper to
  taste
4 tablespoons freshly grated
  Parmesan cheese

---

1   Preheat the oven to 425° F, 220° C, Gas Mark 7.
2   Loosely wrap the whole turnips in foil, shiny side in, crimping the package well so that no steam escapes. Wrap the carrots in similar fashion. Bake for 1 hour in the preheated oven, until the vegetables are very tender.
3   Unwrap. Trim stem and root ends. Place the turnips in a bowl and mash them with a potato masher. Scrape into the bowl of a food processor. Cut the trimmed carrots into chunks. Add to the turnips. Add the garlic purée.
4   Process the vegetables until they are smooth. Add buttermilk and process until blended. Season to taste.
5   Scrape the mixture into a small non-reactive gratin dish or shallow baking dish. Smooth the top and sprinkle with Parmesan. (The dish may be prepared ahead of time to this point. Refrigerate, well covered, until needed. It will keep for up to two days. Bring to room temperature before proceeding.)
6   Reduce oven temperature to 350° F, 180° C, Gas Mark 4. Bake uncovered for 30–45 minutes until browned on top and thoroughly hot.

♡ 🧸 Omit Parmesan cheese.

Variations:

Parsnips or swedes may be substituted for the carrots or turnips. Potatoes may be added, although with potatoes, do not use a food processor. Purée by pushing through a sieve or a food mill. Seasonings may be varied as well. Try ground allspice, cinnamon, cumin or mace.

♡ 🐻 ❄️ **Baked Beetroot**

Make the most of beetroots by baking them. No other cooking method brings out their sweetness and flavour as well, and the texture will be very good indeed. Trim the greens away, and wrap the whole, unpeeled beetroots in heavy-duty foil, shiny side in (3–4 beetroots may go in one package). Bake at 400° F, 200° C, Gas Mark 6, for 1–2 hours, until tender. (Timing depends on age and size.) Use a skewer for testing doneness. The skewer should go in easily but the beetroots should not be mushy. Cool, then trim and slip off the skins. Serve sliced with a sauce of 2–3 parts yoghurt to one part Dijon mustard (less mustard if you don't like spicy food) mixed with a clove of crushed garlic, that has marinated for a few minutes in a little bit of wine vinegar. Season with salt, freshly ground pepper and a pinch or two of sugar.

 ⊞ ⊕ *To microwave large beetroots:*

Trim the beetroot and wrap each in microwave-safe cling film. Microwave at full power for 15 minutes (1 beetroot) or 20 minutes (6 beetroots). Turn them over and microwave for another 15 minutes (1 root) or 20 minutes (2 roots).

> 'As for beetroots, their excuse for being is the fine colour they add to pale dishes.'
>
> Alice B. Toklas, *The Alice B. Toklas Cookbook*

♡ 🐻 ⑤ **BEETROOT PURÉE**

Makes 1 pt/600 ml sauce

Ruby red and textural, this is an unusual and interesting purée. Serve it mounded in poached button mushrooms (see page 74) or spoon dollops onto the wide ends of chicory leaves. Or serve it as a spread on black bread, with smoked salmon if you're feeling luxurious. The mushroom and chicory versions make a visually stunning party dish, especially if they are arranged on a black plate. I like to keep this purée for snacking. It makes a dandy between-meal nibble.

---

2 lb/960 g baked beetroots (see page 263), or use ready-cooked beetroots from the supermarket (if they are very vinegary, omit the amount of vinegar in the recipe)	8 tablespoons fromage frais 1–2 cloves garlic Salt and freshly ground pepper 1½–2 tablespoons wine vinegar

---

1   Slip the skins off the beetroots and allow them to cool. Cut into chunks.
2   Combine the cooled beetroots and all remaining ingredients in the food processor. Process until puréed (the texture will remain somewhat rough). Taste and adjust seasonings – it should be quite peppery with a nice balance of sweet and sour. Chill.

Variation:

Stir in grated, squeezed dry, horseradish instead of garlic.

   Bake beetroot in the microwave.

VEGETABLE BHAJI

Serves 6

This Bhaji packs lots of nutrition into a very low-calorie, low-fat dish. The sauce is a thick and rich purée of onions, peppers, mushrooms and carrots. Serve the Bhaji with Raita (see page 286) and Basmati Rice for a wonderfully satisfying main dish, or serve it as part of an array of curries. I have also served it tossed into pasta.

---

2 large onions, cut into eighths Approx. 1 pt/600 ml stock 2 cloves garlic, crushed 1½ teaspoons ground cumin 1½ teaspoons ground coriander ½ teaspoon allspice ½ teaspoon ground turmeric ½ teaspoon ground ginger	¾ lb/360 g mushrooms, quartered 1 tablespoon tomato paste 2 medium boiling potatoes, peeled and cut into 1½-inch/3.75-cm pieces 1 large cauliflower, trimmed and broken into large florets ½ large lemon

---

¼ teaspoon cayenne pepper (or to
taste)
1 small red and 1 small yellow
pepper, chopped
3 carrots, peeled and coarsely
chopped

Salt to taste
½ lb/240 g French beans, trimmed
and cut into 1½-inch/3.75-cm
lengths

1   Separate the segments of the onion pieces and spread them in
    a heavy, non-stick frying pan. Add *no* liquid or fat. Heat the
    frying pan gently. Cook at moderate heat, without stirring, for
    7–10 minutes, until the onions are sizzling, speckled with dark
    amber, and beginning to stick to the pan.
2   Stir in 10 fl oz/300 ml of stock and let it bubble up, stirring up
    the browned deposits in the pan with a wooden spoon as it
    bubbles. Stir in the garlic, spices, peppers, carrots and
    mushrooms. Turn the heat down a bit and simmer, stirring
    frequently, until the mixture is very thick (not at all soupy),
    and the vegetables and spices are 'frying' in their own juices.
    Don't rush this step – it is essential that the spices should not
    have a raw harsh taste. Cook very gently for a few more
    minutes. Stir in the tomato paste.
3   Purée half the mixture in a liquidizer and push it through a
    sieve. Combine the puréed and unpuréed mixture in the pan.
4   Add the potatoes and cauliflower to the pan. Toss everything
    together very well. Pour in stock to reach about ⅓ of the way
    up the sides of the pan. Squeeze the juice of ½ lemon over the
    contents of the pan. Season with salt. Bring to the boil.
5   Reduce heat, cover the pan and simmer for 15 minutes. Stir in
    beans and continue simmering for 5 minutes more or until all
    the vegetables are tender.

Note: This reheats very well. If you plan to cook ahead, under-
cook the Bhaji slightly so that the vegetables do not turn to mush
when they are reheated.

❄   ## VEGETABLE STUFFED
    ## PEPPERS

Makes 12 pieces

Don't grumble about the extra work of peeling the peppers. When
peeled, their delicious juices mingle with the stock and tomato
paste to form a splendid sauce. And the texture of the peeled
peppers is very special.

Several dashes soy sauce
4 fl oz/120 ml stock
2 fl oz/60 ml sherry
2 cloves garlic, crushed
8 oz/225 g coarsely grated, peeled raw carrot
8 oz/225 g coarsely grated, peeled white turnip
4 oz/112 g coarsely grated onion
4 oz/112 g coarsely grated, unpeeled all-purpose potato
4 oz/112 g pine nuts
4 oz/112 g raisins, soaked in 4 fl oz/120 ml dry sherry for 15 minutes

Salt and freshly ground pepper to taste
¼ teaspoon grated nutmeg
6 large red or yellow peppers, halved lengthwise, seeded and peeled with a swivel-bladed peeler, or in the microwave (see page 30)
2 tablespoons grated Parmesan cheese
8 fl oz/240 ml stock
2 fl oz/60 ml tomato paste

1 Preheat oven to 350° F, 180° C, Gas Mark 4.
2 Heat soy sauce, stock and sherry in a large frying pan. Add vegetables and toss until tender but not at all mushy, and the liquid is almost gone.
3 Stir in nuts, drained raisins, salt, pepper and nutmeg. Set aside.
4 Arrange the peppers, peeled side down, in one or two baking dishes. Fill each half with an equal amount of vegetable mixture. Sprinkle each with 1 teaspoon Parmesan cheese.
5 Whisk together the remaining ingredients. Pour around the peppers. Cover the dish with foil and bake for 1 hour.

♡ Omit pine nuts and Parmesan cheese.

 Omit pine nuts, Parmesan cheese and raisins.

GREEN BEAN SOUFFLÉ

Serves 6

This is an easy soufflé: impressive and unusual as a first course, or as an accompaniment to meat or poultry.

1 lb/480 g frozen green beans
5 shallots or onions, halved and thinly sliced
1 large clove garlic, minced
1 teaspoon dried basil
1 teaspoon sweet Hungarian paprika or paprika paste
Pinch or two of cayenne pepper

2 fl oz/60 ml dry vermouth
6 fl oz/180 ml rich stock
Salt and freshly ground pepper to taste
4 oz/120 g quark
2 tablespoons Parmesan cheese
8 egg whites, at room temperature
Pinch of cream of tartar

1   Steam the green beans until very tender. Set aside.
2   Combine shallots, garlic, basil, paprika, cayenne pepper, ver-
     mouth and 2 fl oz/60 ml of stock in a small frying pan. Boil,
     stirring occasionally, until the mixture is almost dry. Set aside.
3   Combine the beans, shallot infusion, remaining stock and
     quark in the container of a liquidizer, and purée.
4   Rub the purée through a sieve into a saucepan. Heat it very
     gently. Taste and adjust seasonings. (It should be quite
     peppery.) Cool.
5   Stir Parmesan cheese into the cooled mixture.
6   Beat egg whites in an electric mixer on slow speed. Add pinch
     of cream of tartar and beat on the highest speed until the
     whites hold firm peaks.
7   Gently fold the whites into the green bean mixture.
8   Spoon the green bean mixture into a soufflé dish. Cook on the
     middle shelf of the oven for 40 minutes, until puffed and firm.
     (Remove the rack above before baking.) Serve at once.

♡ ❄   **SPICY LENTILS**

Makes 3.5 pts/2 l

This makes *a lot* of lentils, but it freezes or refrigerates well and
tastes so good upon reheating. If you wish, dilute the leftovers
with plenty of stock to make a delicious soup.

2 large onions, cut into eighths	*Cayenne pepper to taste*
3 pts/1.8 l stock	*1 lb/480 g brown lentils, washed*
1 tablespoon minced fresh ginger	*and picked over*
1 clove garlic, minced	*Salt*
1 teaspoon ground cinnamon	*2 large limes*
1 teaspoon ground coriander	*Chopped fresh coriander (optional)*

1   Separate the segments of the onion pieces and spread them in
     a heavy, non-stick frying pan. Add *no* liquid or fat. Heat the
     frying pan gently. Cook at moderate heat, without stirring, for
     7–10 minutes, until the onions are sizzling, speckled with dark
     amber, and beginning to stick to the pan.
2   Stir in 10 fl oz/300 ml of stock and let it bubble up, stirring up
     the browned deposits in the pan with a wooden spoon as it
     bubbles. Stir in the ginger, garlic and spices. Turn the heat
     down a bit and simmer, stirring frequently, until the mixture is
     very thick (not at all soupy), and the onions and spices are
     'frying' in their own juices. Don't rush this step, as it is

essential that the spices should not have a raw, harsh taste. Taste. Cook very gently for a few more minutes if necessary.

3   Add in the lentils. Stir so that they are coated with the onions and spices. Add some salt. Cut the limes in half. Squeeze the juice into the lentils. Add the squeezed halves to the pan. Pour in 2 pts/1,200 ml of stock.

4   Simmer, uncovered, for 10 minutes. Skim off foam as it comes to the surface.

5   Cover and simmer gently, stirring occasionally, for 45–50 minutes. Add more stock during this time as needed.

6   Taste the lentils. If they are not quite tender, add more stock and simmer for 15–20 minutes, until completely tender and the mixture is hot. Taste and add more salt and lime juice if necessary. Serve hot, garnished with coriander if desired.

♡   **BAKED POTATOES**

Jacket potatoes are comforting, sustaining and deeply satisfying. I've always thought that they were much too good to be relegated to the status of a mere accompaniment. For a fun, informal and easy dinner, try serving a big napkin-lined basket of jacket potatoes, surrounded by an array of bowls containing all those things that go so delectably well in the potatoes. Remember, the potatoes themselves are low-fat, low-Calorie and high-nutrition. When stuffing the potatoes, beware of wicked things like butter, soured cream and high-fat cheeses. Instead try a dollop of yoghurt or fromage frais, a splash of buttermilk, a modest shower of freshly grated Parmesan cheese, a squeeze of lemon juice, a scattering of herbs, a mound of Duxelles (see page 270), a deluge of homemade Salsa (see page 269) or a dab or so of Dijon mustard. Whatever you do, don't neglect to eat the skin. It is chock-full of nutrients, and the contrast of crunchy skin against tender flesh is part of what makes a jacket potato so special.

Large, unblemished baking potatoes	*King Edwards to a very floury*
(try Wiljas or King Edwards if	*texture. Both are very good for*
you can find them. Wiljas bake	*the soul)*
to a very creamy texture and	

---

1   Preheat the oven to 425° F, 220° C, Gas Mark 7.

2   Scrub the potatoes and pierce them in several places with a thin skewer or the prongs of a fork. Never wrap the potatoes in foil, or they will steam rather than bake.

3   Bake directly on the oven shelf for about 1¼ hours or until the

potatoes yield softly to a gentle squeeze. (Arm yourself with an ovenglove before you squeeze!)

4   Split the potatoes by perforating them lengthwise and breadthwise with the prongs of a fork and squeezing, so that the tender potato flesh comes surging up. Sprinkle on a tiny bit of salt and a generous grinding of fresh black pepper and you have one of the earth's great foods at its simplest. Or serve with the accompaniments suggested above.

Note: Baked potatoes make the most wonderful mashed potatoes. Scoop out the potato flesh (and save the skins for a private nibble). Put the potatoes through a ricer or, for a homelier (and much easier) effect, mash with a potato masher. With a wooden spoon, beat some buttermilk into the hot potatoes. Season with a touch of salt and plenty of freshly ground pepper.

 ## SALSA FOR BAKED POTATOES

Makes ⅘ pt/480 ml

This cold Mexican sauce spooned into steaming hot jacket potatoes is very good indeed. I also like to toss the cold Salsa with hot pasta. It makes a ravishing 'hot as summer, cold as winter' effect.

---

2 large tins (1 lb 12 oz/784 g each) Italian tomatoes (or use peeled and seeded fresh tomatoes in the summer when 'real' tomatoes are available)	2 fl oz/60 ml red wine vinegar
	2 cloves garlic, minced
	2 tablespoons chopped fresh parsley
	1 tablespoon chopped fresh coriander
Finely chopped fresh chilli peppers, to taste, or chopped tinned chillies or a mixture	

---

1   Drain the tomatoes and chop them (save the juice for soups).
2   Combine all ingredients in a non-reactive bowl. Chill.

Note: To turn this into a cold soup, use the tomato liquid as well. If you wish, add chopped baked peppers (see page 30).

DUXELLES CREAM FOR BAKED POTATOES

1 recipe Duxelles (mushroom 'hash', see page 247)	½ lb/240 g quark 2–3 tablespoons buttermilk

Stir the Duxelles into the quark. Beat in the buttermilk.

MUSTARD CREAM FOR BAKED POTATOES

2 tablespoons buttermilk ¼ lb/120 g yoghurt cheese (see page 39)	2 tablespoons Dijon mustard 1 tablespoon chopped fresh parsley 1 tablespoon chopped fresh chives

Combine all ingredients in a processor and process until perfectly smooth. Failing a processor, beat with a wooden spoon.

BORSCHT POTATOES

One of the classic ways to serve Borscht (Russian beetroot soup) is cold, with a steaming-hot, floury potato in it. The hot/cold contrast is marvellous. I have reversed the classic. It is still quite marvellous.

Large baked potatoes Beetroot Purée (see page 263)	Dill fronds (optional)

1   With a fork, perforate the hot potatoes lengthwise and breadthwise and squeeze open.
2   Pile a generous dollop of cold Beetroot Purée on each potato. Top each with a dill frond. Serve at once.

STUFFED POTATOES

Serves 2–4

Serve these as a main course with Braised Mushrooms (page 250) and Chinese-Style Cabbage Salad (page 288) or Tomato-Basil Salad (page 289) or serve as an accompaniment to Peppered Steak (page 132). Serve 2–3 halves per person as a main course, 1–2 as an accompaniment. This recipe works beautifully with King Edward potatoes.

1 large head garlic	4 tablespoons grated Parmesan
2 large baking potatoes	cheese
4 oz/112 g quark	Salt and freshly ground pepper to
Approx. 6 fl oz/180 ml buttermilk	taste
	Cayenne pepper to taste

1   Preheat the oven to 400° F, 200° C, Gas Mark 6.
2   Prepare the garlic heads for baking (page 32). Place the foil-wrapped garlic in the oven. Bake for ¾–1 hour.
3   Pierce the potatoes in several places with a skewer or fork. Let them bake directly on the oven shelf for 1–1¼ hours, while the garlic bakes.
4   Meanwhile, beat together the remaining ingredients. When the garlic is done squeeze the softened garlic pulp into the cheese mixture.
5   When the potatoes are done, cut them in half lengthwise. Scoop the potato flesh into a bowl. Be very careful to leave the potato shells intact. Mash the potatoes with a masher. With a wooden spoon, beat in the cheese-garlic mixture. Beat in more buttermilk, if necessary, to make a very creamy mixture. Adjust seasonings.
6   Pile the potato mixture into the potato shells. Place them in a baking dish. (The recipe may be prepared up to this point and refrigerated. Bring back to room temperature before continuing.)
7   Place the baking dish in the hot oven. Bake for 10–15 minutes. If they have not browned lightly on the top at this point, put briefly under the grill. Serve at once.

♡   Omit Parmesan cheese.

'No-one has feared developing leprosy from eating French Fries . . . but we all know that Fries make us fat (or fatter), cause blemishes, induce indigestion, nourish ulcers, and make havoc of cholesterol counts. Yet everybody keeps stuffing them down . . . the greasier and more awful the better.'

James Villas, *Esquire* Magazine

 # POTATO CASES

Potato Cases are perfect if you are craving crisps or chips. They are crunchy and just right for potato-snack needs. If you wish, cut them in quarters instead of halves. They will bake faster, and be more like finger food.

1   Preheat the oven to 400° F, 220° C, Gas Mark 7.
2   Scrub the potatoes and halve them lengthwise.
3   With a teaspoon or a melon-baller, scoop out the insides, leaving a shell about ¼ inch/0.6 cm thick. Save the scraps for another use (see note).
4   Bake directly on the oven rack for 25–35 minutes, until golden brown and very crisp. Serve at once – as they are; with dips; or filled with a savoury mixture.

Note: Don't you dare throw the potato scraps away. Use them to make a wonderful gratin. It may be made at once, refrigerated, and reheated at a later date.

Potato Scrap Gratin

1   Scoop the potatoes right into a saucepan and add enough stock to barely cover. Season with a bit of salt and plenty of pepper. If you wish you may add a bit of grated nutmeg or a pinch of ground cumin and cayenne pepper. Simmer covered until tender. Do not drain.
2   Mash roughly (just to chop up the pieces, not to purée them) right in the pot, with a potato masher. Spread into a gratin dish. Dribble on a bit of skimmed milk, and sprinkle with some Parmesan. Bake, in a hot oven, uncovered, for 50–60 minutes, until bubbly and well browned on top. Serve at once, or refrigerate for reheating in a day to two.

POTATO GRATIN

Serves 8

This gratin is a symphony of texture and taste. The starch in the potatoes, the flavourful stock and the grated cheese form a thick, creamy sauce that binds the tender potato slices under a crusty top – sheer heaven!

1 large clove garlic	*Salt and freshly ground pepper*
4 large unpeeled baking potatoes	*⅗ pt/360 ml of vegetable or chicken*
4 tablespoons freshly grated	*stock*
Parmesan cheese	

1   Preheat the oven to 400° F, 200° C, Gas Mark 6.
2   Peel the garlic clove and split it. Rub a 9 × 13-inch/23 × 33-cm oval gratin dish with the split sides of the garlic.

3   Slice the potatoes paper-thin. Do not soak them in water at any time. Slice just before using.
4   Layer ⅓ of the potato slices in the gratin dish and sprinkle evenly with Parmesan cheese, salt and pepper. Pour ⅓ of the stock over the potatoes.
5   Repeat twice more. With a broad spatula, press the top layer down into the liquid.
6   Bake in the preheated oven for approximately 1½ hours until the potatoes are tender, the liquid has cooked down to a thick sauce and the top is brown and crusty.

  Omit cheese.

Note: The gratin can be made the morning or the day before and reheated in a microwave or a 375° F, 190° C, Gas Mark 5, oven.

Variations:

1   Layer Browned Onions (see page 26) with the potatoes, cheese and stock. Cook as directed.
2   Mix 1 tablespoon Dijon mustard with 4 oz/120 ml whisky. Stir in the stock. Proceed and bake as directed.
3   Layer Sautéed Mushrooms (see page 29) with the potatoes. For pure luxury, add soaked, drained, dried mushrooms and use some of the strained mushroom liquor for part of the stock.

GRATIN OF BAKED POTATOES, ONIONS AND GARLIC

Serves 8

I invented this dish for a book I wrote a few years ago, *Comfort Food*. I have cut out the high-fat ingredients of the original recipe, but it is still one of the most comforting recipes I know.

---

4 large baking potatoes, baked and mashed (save skins for another use)
Purée from 2 large heads of baked garlic (see page 32)
2 large Spanish onions, baked and puréed (see page 38)
Salt and freshly ground pepper to taste

2–3 tablespoons buttermilk
4–5 tablespoons freshly grated Parmesan cheese
1 tablespoon instant dried skimmed-milk powder
3 tablespoons stock

---

1   Preheat oven to 325° F, 170° C, Gas Mark 3.

2   Combine the potato, garlic, onions, salt and pepper. Beat with a wooden spoon. Beat in the buttermilk.
3   Scrape the mixture into a gratin dish. Smooth the top and sprinkle with the cheese. (The recipe may be prepared in advance to this stage and refrigerated, covered, for a few days. Bring to room temperature before proceeding.) Whisk together the milk powder and the stock. Dribble the mixture evenly over the top of the potatoes. Bake uncovered for 35–45 minutes, until brown, bubbly and thoroughly hot. Serve at once. (This is very exciting when it is cold, too.)

♡   Omit cheese.

'If you have formed the habit of checking on every new diet that comes along, you will find that mercifully, they all blur together, leaving you with only one definite piece of information: french-fried potatoes are out.'

Jean Kerr, *Please Don't Eat the Daisies*

♡   **CHIPS**

173 Calories for chips from 1 large (8 oz) potato
0.2 g fat
(Traditional chips: 270 Calories per 8-oz potato, 13 g fat)

Why deprive yourself of crisps or chips? You can feast on these compelling munchies to your heart's content, if you use no fat. They are actually superior to the usual fat-laden kind, because as you munch, you taste *potato*, not a mouthful of grease and salt. The Potatoes may be sliced thick (½ inch/1.25 cm) or thin ¼ inch/ 0.6 cm). The thin ones will be crisp and crunchy like crisps, the thicker ones will be brown and crunchy on the outside, and floury-tender within, like chips. This recipe works very well with large Maris Pipers.

Baking potatoes	Warm stock

1   Preheat the oven to 425° F, 220° C, Gas Mark 7.
2   Don't bother to peel the potatoes. Cut them crosswise into ¼–½ inch/0.6–1.25-cm slices. Cut each slice in half.
3   Put a little bit of warm stock in a large bowl along with the potatoes and stir them around well with your hands so that they are coated with the warm stock.
4   You will need one or two flat baking sheets with non-stick

coating. Spread the potatoes on the sheet(s) in one layer. Put them in the oven and leave them for ½ an hour.

5   Pull the potatoes out and with a spatula gently turn them. Bake in the oven for approximately another 5–15 minutes. (The timing depends on the thickness of the slices.) By this time they should be browned, crunchy and puffed. Serve at once. (These may be sprinkled with a bit of salt if desired, but I find they don't really need it.)

'Fire officers in Cambridgeshire want to banish chip pans from the county's kitchens. Grill it or bake it, but don't deep-fry it – that is the message from the Fire and Rescue Service.'

Cambridge Evening News

♡ ⊠   **QUICKER CHIPS**

Serves 1 male teenager, or 3–4 normal people

I am constantly updating, revising and improving this perennial family favourite. Here is the up-to-the-minute version, quicker than the previous one. I hope one day to be able to remove a spud from the larder, eye it sternly and utter '"Fry" yourself!', and it will immediately form itself into perfect grease-free chips. Until that unlikely time, this is the quickest and best I can do. I promise, these chips will amaze you. I can't make them often enough for my family.

---

2 large baking potatoes,	*Salt (optional)*
approximately 12 oz/360 g each	

---

1   Preheat oven to 400° F, 200° C, Gas Mark 6.
2   Scrub the potatoes but do not peel them. Pierce them in several places with a fork or thin skewer. Line the microwave carousel with a paper towel.
3   Place potatoes on the carousel. Microwave at full power for 6 minutes, turning the potatoes over after 3 minutes.
4   Remove the potatoes from the oven and allow to stand for 5 minutes.
5   With a sharp knife, cut each potato lengthwise into ¼–½-inch/ 0.6–1.25-cm thick strips. Arrange in one layer on one or two *non-stick* baking trays. Bake for approximately 20–30 minutes, turning the potatoes with tongs approximately half-way

through, and shaking the tray every once in a while so that they do not stick. When they are beautifully browned and a bit puffy, they are done. Salt lightly if desired and serve.

♡ ⏲ **PAN-'FRIED' POTATOES WITH ONIONS**

Serves 2

---

1 large Spanish onion	*Salt and freshly ground pepper to*
Approximately 8 fl oz/240 ml stock	*taste*
8 small new potatoes, unpeeled	

---

1   Cut the onion into quarters. Slice each quarter crosswise into ½ inch/1.25 cm chunks.
2   Spread the onion chunks evenly over the bottom of a heavy non-reactive frying pan. Heat until sizzling and beginning to stick to the bottom of the pan.
3   While the onions are cooking, cut the new potatoes in half lengthwise, then slice crosswise into ¼-inch/0.6-cm thick slices.
4   When the onions are sizzling and sticking, stir in 2 fl oz/60 ml of stock. Let it fume and foam and boil up, stirring up the browned bits in the frying pan as it does so. Boil, stirring, until just about dry.
5   Stir in most of the remaining stock. Stir in potatoes. Reduce heat to simmering.
6   Cover and allow to simmer gently for approximately 10 minutes.
7   Uncover and test a potato. If not yet tender, add a bit more stock, re-cover and simmer until tender but not falling apart.
8   Uncover, raise heat and cook, turning the potatoes occasionally, until they are browned. Season to taste and serve at once.

'"He eats French fries," she says and sinks into the kitchen chair to Weep Her Heart Out once and for all. "He goes after school with Melvyn Weiner and stuffs himself with French-fried potatoes."'

Philip Roth, *Portnoy's Complaint*

276

♡ ROAST POTATOES

The better the stock, the better the roast potatoes. If you have any dripping left from a roast chicken (with the fat skimmed off, of course) try using it for roasting the potatoes instead of using plain stock.

Stock	Salt and freshly ground pepper
Small whole new potatoes, or medium-sized potatoes, halved or quartered	

1 Preheat oven to 400° F, 200° C, Gas Mark 6.
2 Pour stock into a shallow baking dish to a depth of about ¼ inch/0.6 cm. Put the potatoes in the dish in one layer. Season with salt and pepper, and stir them around.
3 Bake uncovered for 40–50 minutes, shaking the pan and stirring occasionally. When they are browned and tender, they are done. (Pour a bit more stock into the dish as necessary during cooking.)

'"I haven't eaten potatoes for twenty-five years," said Frank in a far-off brooding tone. . . .
    The potatoes were brought. Not all the perfumes of Araby smelt so sweet. They ate them with their fingers.'

W. Somerset Maugham, *The Three Fat Women of Antibes*

♡ ROAST POTATOES WITH ROASTED GARLIC AND ONION

Serves 4

Melting tenderness and superb flavour with no fat at all. As they bake, the kitchen is filled with the most tantalizing aroma.

1 head fresh, firm garlic	Approx. 6 fl oz/180 ml stock
3 medium onions, halved and sliced into thin half-moons	Salt and freshly ground pepper to taste
8 medium new potatoes, unpeeled and cut in half	

1 Preheat oven to 400° F, 200° C, Gas Mark 6.
2 Separate the head of garlic into cloves. Hit each clove smartly with a kitchen mallet. Remove and discard the skin. Scatter the

crushed cloves and the onion slices on the bottom of a baking dish that will hold the halved potatoes in one layer.

3   Place the halved potatoes, cut sides down, on the bed of garlic and onions. Pour in stock to come about ¼ up the sides of the dish. Sprinkle salt and pepper evenly over all.

4   Bake uncovered for 1 hour, until the potatoes are tender, the onions beginning to brown and the liquid about gone. Serve piping hot. Encourage diners to mash the garlic, onion and potatoes together if they wish.

♡ CURRIED ROAST POTATOES

Serves 4 as an accompaniment

With plenty of Raita (see page 286) these would make a good meal. No meat is needed.

1 large onion, cut in half and each half cut into eighths	*½ teaspoon ground cayenne pepper*
Approx. 15 fl oz/450 ml stock	*1 clove garlic, crushed*
1 thin slice ginger, minced	*Salt and pepper to taste*
1 teaspoon ground coriander	*4 medium potatoes, unpeeled and quartered*
1 teaspoon ground cumin	*Wedges of fresh lime*

1   Separate the segments of the onion pieces and spread them in a heavy, non-stick frying pan. Add *no* liquid or fat. Heat the frying pan gently. Cook at moderate heat, without stirring, for 7–10 minutes, until the onions are sizzling, speckled with dark amber, and beginning to stick to the pan.

2   Stir in 10 fl oz/300 ml of stock and let it bubble up, stirring up the browned deposits in the pan with a wooden spoon as it bubbles. Stir in the ginger, garlic and spices. Turn the heat down a bit and simmer, stirring frequently, until the mixture is very thick (not at all soupy), and the onions and spices are 'frying' in their own juices. Don't rush this step – it is essential that the spices should not have a raw, harsh taste. Taste. Cook very gently for a few more minutes if necessary.

3   Toss the potatoes into the mixture. Stir to combine everything very well. Scrape the potatoes and spices into a shallow baking dish that can hold them in one layer. Add the remaining stock.

4   Bake for 1 hour, stirring occasionally and adding a bit more stock as needed, until the potatoes are tender. The finished dish should be dry. Serve hot with wedges of lime.

MASHED POTATOES

Nothing helps you drift into serene calm faster than a steaming bowlful of this magical food. Conventionally prepared, the mashed spuds are usually loaded with cream and butter, producing sensual pleasure as you eat, followed by guilt and fat the next day. Let's keep the sensual pleasure and eliminate the guilt and fat.

To make perfect mashed potatoes, choose large baking potatoes. They have a floury texture when cooked, and mash up into a fluffy, ethereal cloud. Avoid waxy boiling potatoes; they become a sticky mass when mashed. Boil the baking potatoes, in a covered pot of salted water to generously cover, until very tender but *not* falling apart. You will obtain the best results as far as taste and nutrition are concerned if the potatoes are boiled whole and unpeeled; but, if you are in a hurry, they may be peeled and quartered before boiling.

When the potatoes are tender, drain them in a colander. (If you love to bake bread, save the potato liquid. It is excellent for bread dough.) If the potatoes are whole and unpeeled, grasp with an oven glove and scrape off the skins with a table knife. Quarter them and return to the pot. If they were already peeled and quartered, simply return them to the pot directly after draining.

Cover the pot and shake it over low heat to toss the potatoes as they dry. For exceptionally fluffy, airy mashed potatoes, force them through a ricer into a warm bowl. For homelier, denser potatoes, use a potato masher, and mash them right in the pan over very low heat. Work the potatoes well with the masher. It is alright to leave in a lump or two, to prove that these are *real* mashed potatoes, but watch out for rampant lumpiness or they will be awful. Don't be tempted to use your food processor; you'll end up with a gluey mess.

When the potatoes are mashed or riced, season to taste with salt and pepper. (For a really interesting if unconventional taste, add a bit of ground cumin and cayenne pepper too.) With a wooden spoon, beat in a liberal amount of room-temperature buttermilk until they look creamy and luxurious. A bit of freshly grated Parmesan cheese can be beaten in too if you wish.

♡ Omit the Parmesan cheese.

Variations:

1   Add one of the following vegetables to mashed potatoes (steam or bake the vegetables and use an equal weight of the vegetable and of potatoes):

Mashed swedes
Mashed parsnips
Mashed turnips
Mashed carrots
Mashed celeriac

2   Or stir in:
Browned onions (see page 26)
Puréed, baked onion (see page 38)
Baked garlic purée (see page 32)
Medium-fat creamy goat cheese
Chopped chives

3   Or, for a delectable potato experience, fill a bowl with mashed potatoes. Make a well in the potatoes with the back of a dessert spoon. Fill the well with Sautéed Mushrooms, or Mushroom Ragoût (see page 249).

4   Or make a Mashed Potato Gratin: Mash the potatoes, beat in plenty of buttermilk and a bit of Parmesan, season with salt, freshly ground black pepper, a sprinkle of cayenne pepper and a couple of pinches of ground cumin. Spread in a gratin dish. Dribble a bit of skimmed milk evenly over the surface and sprinkle with some Parmesan. (It may be made in advance to this point and refrigerated. Bring to room temperature before proceeding.) Bake at 400° F, 200° C, Gas Mark 6, for ¾–1 hour until puffed with a golden crust.

♡   **WHEAT PILAF**

Makes approximately 2 pts/1.2 l

Bulghur is available in wholefood shops, and most supermarkets as well. It is made from dried wheat berries that have been parched, steamed and crushed. Bulghur is chock full of fibre, and vitamin E, and has a gloriously nutty taste and texture. It complements many main dishes beautifully; try it with Chinese Beef (page 138) instead of the more obvious rice or try it with Chicken Liver Kebabs (page 192) or any stew.

1 Spanish onion, coarsely chopped	*8 fl oz/240 ml bulghur*
½ pt/300 ml stock	*½ pt/300 ml fresh strained orange*
½ teaspoon ground coriander	*juice*
½ teaspoon ground cumin	*Salt and freshly ground pepper to*
2 cloves garlic, minced	*taste*
Grated zest from ½ large orange	*Chopped fresh coriander (optional)*

1   Spread onion pieces in a heavy frying pan that can be covered. Heat gently. Cook at a moderate heat for a few minutes until the onions begin to sizzle and stick to the pan.
2   Stir in 4 fl oz/120 ml stock and let it bubble up as you stir and scrape up any browned bits. Stir in the spices and garlic. Simmer until the mixture is very thick and the onions are 'frying' in their own juices. Zest the ½ orange right over the onions so that the zest goes in with some oils. Add the bulghur and stir until everything is well combined. Bring the remaining stock to the boil with the orange juice and add it to the wheat. Season with salt and pepper.
3   Cover the pan and simmer over lowest heat for about 20 minutes, until the bulghur is tender but not mushy, and all the liquid is absorbed. Fluff with a fork. To serve, mound on a warm plate or spoon into a warm bowl. Garnish with coriander.

♡ KASHA WITH MUSHROOMS

Makes 2 pts/1.2 l

Kasha is roasted buckwheat groats, available in many wholefood stores. I urge you to try kasha, and some of the other grains discussed in this collection. If you like rice, you'll *love* kasha, couscous, bulghur (cracked wheat) and polenta. They add important fibre and vitamin E (one of the fat-soluble vitamins) to your diet, but – as important – they are delicious, easy to eat, a wonderful complement to all sorts of dishes, and each one of them is a serenity-producing food. My recipe for kasha is a classic one, except for the omission of egg yolks, and butter or chicken fat. It may be prepared without the dried mushrooms if desired; in that case use 16 fl oz/480 ml stock in step 6.

½ oz/15 g dried mushrooms (look for cèpes or the Italian counterpart, porcini)	1 Spanish onion, coarsely chopped
	4 fl oz/120 ml stock
	2 egg whites, lightly beaten
½ lb/240 g fresh mushrooms, coarsely chopped	8 fl oz/240 ml kasha (roasted buckwheat groats)
2 fl oz/60 ml stock	8 fl oz/240 ml stock
2 fl oz/60 ml dry sherry	Salt and freshly ground pepper to taste
Generous dash of soy sauce	

---

1   Rinse the dried mushrooms well under cold running water. Soak in hot water to cover generously for at least an hour. Strain the water through a coffee filter, or a double cheese-

cloth-lined sieve, and reserve. Briefly rinse the soaked mushrooms once more under cold water. Trim off and discard any tough stems. Coarsely chop the dried mushrooms.

2   Combine the soaked mushrooms, the fresh mushrooms, 2 fl oz/60 ml stock, the sherry and the soy sauce in a heavy non-reactive frying pan. Simmer briskly, stirring occasionally, until the liquid is almost gone, and the mushrooms are 'frying' in their own juices. Set aside.

3   Combine the onions and 4 fl oz/120 ml of stock in a heavy non-reactive frying pan. Cover and bring to the boil. Reduce heat a bit, and let simmer briskly for 5–7 minutes or until almost dry. Uncover and cook until beginning to stick and brown. Pour in a splash or two of stock and stir and scrape until the onions are beautifully brown, syrupy and tender. Add to the mushrooms.

4   Stir the egg white into the kasha. Mix until the grains are well coated with the egg.

5   Heat a large, heavy frying pan. With a wooden spoon or paddle stir the kasha in the pan, over moderate heat, until each grain is dry and separate. It will give off an appetizingly toasty aroma. This should take about 5 minutes. Scrape the kasha into a large pot that can be covered.

6   Combine the 8 fl oz/240 ml stock with 8 fl oz/240 ml reserved mushroom liquid, and bring to the boil.

7   Stir the boiling liquid into the kasha. Cover the pot and simmer over the lowest heat for 30 minutes. Remove from the heat, uncover and drape a clean tea towel over the pot. Re-cover and let stand for 5–10 minutes, until the liquid is absorbed and the kasha is fluffy and tender, with each grain separate.

8   Mix kasha, onions and mushrooms.

Note: This may be prepared in advance and reheated in the microwave or conventional oven. To make the classic and beloved Russian-Jewish dish kasha varnishkas, mix equal amounts of this kasha with freshly boiled and drained bowtie-shaped pasta.

Salads and Dressings

'Following her is Leonid, a young student who is too shy to speak to Natasha but places a mixed green salad on her doorstep every night.'

Woody Allen, *Without Feathers*

Salads often seduce dieters into outrageous over-indulgence. Although everyone knows that salads are perfect for chronic Calorie counters, it is easy to forget that lashings of thick, oily dressings, fried croûtons and the like are the antithesis of diet food. Leave off the densely calorific components, and salads can be a dieter's salvation. And by replacing the sludgy, oil-laden dressings with delicate, low-fat ones, the salads will be aesthetically much more pleasing.

General Guidelines for Salad Dressings

Use the Slim Cuisine 'mayonnaise' dressings (see page 40) or drain low-fat fromage frais or yoghurt for an hour in a cheese-cloth-lined sieve. Mix it with a splash of freshly squeezed lemon or orange juice or wine vinegar.

To this basic mixture may be added minced raw garlic or roasted garlic purée, chopped fresh herbs, ground spices, grated citrus zest, grated fresh ginger, minced shallots or spring onion, a dash of soy sauce or Worcestershire (look for reduced-salt Worcestershire in wholefood shops), Dijon mustard, a few dashes of Tabasco sauce, minced capers, a dab of tomato paste (for a

'Russian' dressing) or grated horseradish. Choose the flavouring to complement the salad.

For a creamy, zesty dressing, try mixing 2–3 parts of drained low-fat yoghurt to one part Dijon mustard with a splash or two of interesting vinegar (balsamic, raspberry, sherry, herb, etc.). In fact, the more interesting vinegars, particularly sherry and balsamic, make good dressings all by themselves.

If you love to eat salad in restaurants, order them without dressings. Carry a small jar of your own dressing and apply it discreetly.

♡ CREAMY SALAD DRESSING

Salads are full of fibre, low-fat, low-Calorie, vitamin- and mineral-packed veggies, and, alas, usually drenched in horrifically high-fat dressings. How nice to know that you can have your salad cream minus the fat by using Slim Cuisine 'mayonnaise' as a base.

Wine vinegar (use as interesting a vinegar as you can find and afford. Sherry, balsamic or raspberry vinegars are excellent. White wine tarragon vinegar works nicely too)	*Buttermilk* *'Mayonnaise' (see page 40)*

Whisk the vinegar and a bit of buttermilk into the 'mayonnaise' in a thin stream until the consistency of single cream.

Vary this dressing to your taste with garlic, herbs, spices, etc. A specific example follows.

♡ ⑤ CREAMY HERB SALAD DRESSING

Makes 8 fl oz/240 ml dressing

Try this variation of the previous recipe on a special tossed salad – for instance, green and red lettuces tossed with chicory leaves, strips of red and yellow pepper, watercress and orange segments.

⅕ pt/120 ml yoghurt cream cheese	*2 cloves crushed garlic (optional)*
4 tablespoons buttermilk	*⅛ pt/75 ml fresh basil leaves*
1–2 tablespoons Dijon mustard	*Salt and freshly ground pepper to*
1½ tablespoons sherry vinegar	*taste*

1   Combine all the ingredients in the container of a food processor.
2   Process until smooth. Scrape into a jar, cover tightly and refrigerate until needed.

CREAMY MUSTARD HERB DRESSING

Makes 12 fl oz/360 ml

A lovely salad cream for all sorts of salads. To use as a mayonnaise-type sandwich spread, omit the buttermilk.

4 fl oz/120 ml quark	*1 teaspoon Dijon mustard or New*
4 fl oz/120 ml fromage frais	*York Deli Mustard (page 305)*
4 fl oz/120 ml buttermilk	*1 tablespoon freshly chopped*
Dash Worcestershire sauce	*parsley*
	Freshly ground pepper to taste

Whisk all ingredients together. Refrigerate.

♡ BRUSSELS SPROUTS IN DILL PESTO

Serves 6

For a change, instead of serving good old sprouts, plainly steamed, try them cold, folded into a creamy, dill-flecked sauce. The sprouts and the yoghurt-herb paste may be prepared in advance. Add the fromage frais and combine everything just before serving, or the dish will become watery.

1 large bag frozen button Brussels	*3 tablespoons fromage frais*
sprouts (do not thaw)	*1 tablespoon raspberry vinegar, or*
8 tablespoons snipped dill leaves	*wine vinegar*
5 tablespoons roughly chopped	*Salt and freshly ground pepper to*
parsley	*taste*
¼ lb/120 g yoghurt cheese (see	*Red lettuce or radicchio*
page 39)	*Watercress*

1   Steam the frozen sprouts over boiling water for 7–10 minutes, until cooked through but still a bit crunchy. Rinse under cold running water, drain well and chill.
2   Combine the dill, parsley and yoghurt cheese in the container

of a food processor. Process to a thick paste. Stir in the fromage blanc and vinegar.
3 Combine the dill sauce and the sprouts. Season to taste.
4 Serve on red lettuce or radicchio. Garnish with watercress.

CUCUMBER RAITA

Makes approximately 1 pt/600 ml

Always serve a cooling Raita (yoghurt salad) with your curries. Here are my favourites.

---

1 pt/600 ml low-fat yoghurt	*Chopped fresh parsley*
1 large cucumber, peeled, halved	*Chopped fresh coriander*
and seeded	*Thinly sliced spring onions (green*
Salt and freshly ground pepper to	*and white portions)*
taste	*Chilli powder (optional)*

---

1 Dump yoghurt into a bowl.
2 Grate the cucumber into the yoghurt.
3 Stir to combine. Season to taste with salt and pepper. Garnish generously with parsley, coriander and spring onions. Sprinkle on chilli powder if desired. Serve at once as an accompaniment to curries.

Variation:

Mix plenty of chopped fresh mint with yoghurt. Omit the cucumbers and the coriander.

MARINADED CUCUMBER SALAD

Serves 6

A low-fat version of a classic Hungarian salad. The creamy variation on these cucumbers is especially good with grilled skirt steak or roasted chicken. Serve it on the same plate as the meat, so that the meat juices mingle with the salad.

---

2 large cucumbers, peeled	*½ teaspoon Hungarian paprika*
Salt	*Freshly ground pepper*
3 tablespoons white wine vinegar	*1 small clove garlic, crushed*
3 tablespoons cold water	*(optional)*
½ teaspoon caster sugar	

---

1   Slice the cucumber thinly into a colander. Toss lightly with salt. Let drain for ½ hour. Rinse and blot dry on paper towels.
2   Meanwhile, whisk together the vinegar, water, sugar, ¼ teaspoon of paprika, pepper and garlic. Mix this into the rinsed drained cucumbers. Chill for an hour or so before serving. Just before serving, sprinkle the remaining paprika over the top of the salad.

♡ Creamy Variation

After mixing the cucumbers with the dressing, blend in 8 fl oz/ 240 ml of low-fat fromage frais. Chill, sprinkle with paprika and serve.

COLE SLAW

Serves 8

There are infinite versions of cole slaw. Mine is extremely colourful and full of texture and contrasting flavour. If you own a food processor, the grating and slicing is child's play. This is particularly good for a buffet, a barbecue or a picnic.

½ small head red cabbage	⅕ pt/120 ml grated white radish
½ small head white cabbage	2 tablespoons drained yoghurt (see page 39)
3 small carrots, grated	
1 medium red pepper, cut into very thin strips	3–4 tablespoons buttermilk
	1 tablespoon German mustard
1 medium yellow pepper, cut into very thin strips	1 tablespoon white wine vinegar
	2 small cloves garlic
2 stalks celery, sliced thin	1 tablespoon chopped parsley
½ head fennel, trimmed and sliced thin	Salt and freshly ground pepper to taste

1   Cut the core out of the cabbage halves and trim away the tough outer leaves. With a chef's knife or with the slicing disk (*not* the grating disk) of a food processor, slice it into thin slices. Combine the cabbage with the rest of the vegetables.
2   Combine the remaining ingredients in the liquidizer. Blend until smooth. Toss this dressing with the vegetables. Let marinate for at least an hour before serving.

♡ CHINESE-STYLE CABBAGE SALAD

Serves 4

This is an approximation of the cabbage salad my friend Frank Ma used to serve me at his Chinese restaurant in Atlanta, Georgia. I have adapted it somewhat but the salad still has the authentic Chinese taste.

¾ lb/360 g green cabbage, shredded	*1 teaspoon sugar*
2 large carrots, shredded	*1 small clove garlic, crushed*
4 tablespoons fresh lime or lemon	*Cayenne pepper to taste*
juice	*1 tablespoon soy sauce*

1 Combine cabbage and carrots in a large bowl.
2 Whisk together the remaining ingredients. Toss into the vegetables. Toss the salad with 2 spoons so that the cabbage is well coated with the dressing. Let stand for at least 15 minutes, stirring occasionally.

♡ FENNEL-PEPPER SALAD

Serves 4

The liquorice crunchiness of fennel makes this salad exceptionally pleasing. Serve it as a separate course, either before or after the main dish.

1 medium head fennel, trimmed of tough outer layer and core, and sliced thin (save feathery leaves)	*1 tablespoon capers, drained and rinsed*
1 small red pepper, sliced thin	*2 large cloves garlic*
1 small yellow pepper, sliced thin	*1 small bunch fresh parsley* -
¼ lb/120 g button mushrooms, cleaned well and sliced thin	*2 fl oz/60 ml Slim Cuisine 'mayonnaise'*
	1–2 tablespoons buttermilk
	1 tablespoon wine vinegar

1 Combine the fennel, peppers, mushrooms and capers in a bowl.
2 Finely chop together the garlic and parsley. Toss it, along with the feathery fennel leaves, into the vegetables.
3 Whisk together the mayonnaise, buttermilk and vinegar. Toss the dressing with the salad, or pass it in a clear glass jug. Serve at once.

♡ 🐻 🕐 TOMATO-BASIL SALAD

Tomato and basil form a heavenly culinary alliance. Make the most of this duo during the summer, when both are in glorious profusion. For a more substantial salad, alternate slices of tomato with slices of Italian part-skim Mozzarella cheese.

Ripe tomatoes
Basil leaves, torn into shreds
Salt and freshly ground pepper

Sherry vinegar or other good, mild
  wine vinegar

---

1   Neatly cut the stem out of the tomatoes. Slice them from stem to stern. Arrange the slices on a plate. Sprinkle lightly with salt and pepper.
2   Scatter the shredded basil over the tomatoes. Sprinkle on a modest amount of vinegar. Let stand for 10 minutes before serving.

♡ ORANGE WATERCRESS SALAD

This is a beautiful and refreshing salad, perfect for warm weather. Reckon on ½ an orange per person, a few sprigs of watercress and a teaspoon of dressing. For a stunning presentation, arrange the salad on clear glass plates.

Juicy, seedless oranges
Watercress (wash and shake dry)
Low-fat yoghurt, drained for about
  1 hour

Freshly ground pepper
½ teaspoon grated orange rind
Pinch ground cumin

---

1   On a cutting board, slice the oranges thinly. With a paring knife, neatly remove the rind and white pith from each slice. Do not wipe away the orange juice that collects on the board.
2   Overlap the orange slices on half of a clear glass plate. Fan out the watercress on the lower half. Stir the orange juice that has collected on the cutting board into the drained yoghurt along with the pepper, orange rind and cumin. Either serve the dressing in a clear glass jug along with the salad, or pour a thin stripe of dressing down the centre of each row of orange slices, and serve the rest separately.

MANGO AND TOMATO SALAD

Serves 4

If the mango is ripe, and the tomatoes are *real* tomatoes, not those pathetic impostors often found in supermarkets, this salad will scintillate. Serve it as a separate course.

1 mango	*Dressing (see below)*
6 small tomatoes, sliced	

1   With a sharp knife slice straight down on the mango, slicing it through, but missing the large flat centre stone to which quite a bit of mango flesh clings. Repeat on the other side of the stone.
2   Carefully peel the skin from both halves. Slice each half thinly to produce long strips of mango and set aside.
3   Peel the skin from the mango flesh around the stone and put the flesh in a small bowl along with any juices and set aside to use in the dressing.
4   Arrange the tomato slices in two rows around the perimeter of a pretty dish. Fill the centre with overlapping mango slices. Pass the dressing separately.

Dressing

2 tablespoons fromage frais	*Pinch of dry mustard*
2 tablespoons wine vinegar	*Excess mango flesh and juice (see*
1 tablespoon buttermilk	*above)*
Dash of Worcestershire sauce	*Pinch or two of brown sugar, to*
	taste

Whisk together all ingredients except the excess mango and the sugar. Put them in the container of the liquidizer together with the mango flesh and juice. Blend until perfectly smooth. Taste and blend in a pinch or two of brown sugar if necessary. Refrigerate until needed.

MARINATED PEPPERS

Makes 2 pts/1.2 l

One of the best marinated vegetable dishes I know, and perfect for an elegant picnic.

6 large peppers (a combination of red, yellow and orange) cut into ¾ inch/2 cm strips and peeled	2 fl oz/60 ml balsamic vinegar 1 tablespoon caster sugar Salt to taste (be very sparing)

1   Place the pepper strips in a shallow dish.
2   Combine the vinegar and sugar and stir to dissolve the sugar. Pour the mixture over the peppers and toss well. Sprinkle with a modest amount of salt.
3   Refrigerate for at least 12 hours. Shake the dish or stir the peppers, when you think of it. Serve cold.

♡ 🧸 🕐 MARINATED CARROTS

Makes 1 pt/600 ml

Devotees of Slim Cuisine soon become carrot fiends; the beautiful orange root is so crisp, sweet and good tasting, and you can eat all you want. In some cultures, some form of sliced carrots are always eaten for luck at the New Year, because the slices resemble golden coins.

1 lb/480 g carrots, peeled and sliced ¼ inch/0.6 cm thick 3 cloves garlic, very coarsely chopped ⅕ pt/120 ml wine vinegar ¼ teaspoon ground cumin	Pinch or two of ground cayenne (or to taste) Pinch or two of cinnamon Pinch or two of allspice Salt and freshly ground pepper to taste 2 tablespoons chopped parsley

1   Steam the carrots and garlic over boiling water for 5–10 minutes until the carrots are crisp-tender. Cool under cold running water and drain well.
2   While the carrots are steaming, combine the vinegar with the ground spices. Shake well.
3   Toss together the carrots, vinegar mixture and parsley. Refrigerate until needed. Serve cold or at room temperature.

♡   NEW YORK POTATO SALAD

Serves 10
123 Calories per serving
0.3 g fat
(Traditional potato salad: 273 Calories per serving, 18 g fat)

One of my favourite potato salads is New York Jewish delicatessen style. It is made with baking potatoes that mash up a bit when chopped. When mixed with the dressing they mash even more, so that the final texture is compellingly smooth and creamy. In fact, it is almost a mashed potato salad. Make it for a crowd, or store it in the refrigerator to nibble at through the week. It gets better each day.

3 lb/1,440 g baking potatoes	1 teaspoon sugar
2 small carrots, peeled	Salt to taste
1 small celery stalk	6 fl oz/180 ml Slim Cuisine
1 red pepper, peeled	'mayonnaise' (see note)
1 yellow pepper, peeled	

1   Put potatoes in enough lightly salted water to cover gener-
    ously and boil until tender. Drain and cool for a few minutes
    (they should still be warm when the dressing is added to
    them).
2   Grate 1 carrot, the celery and half of each pepper.
3   With a table knife, scrape the skins off the still-warm potatoes.
    Place the potatoes on a chopping board. With a hand chopper
    or a chef's knife, chop them. As you chop, they will mash
    slightly. Put them in a bowl.
4   Squeeze any accumulated liquid out of the grated vegetables.
    Add the vegetables to the potatoes. Sprinkle with sugar and
    salt. Mix lightly.
5   With a wooden spoon, fold in the mayonnaise. As you do so,
    the potatoes will mash even more. When well combined,
    refrigerate until serving time.
6   To serve, mound the salad on a platter. Chop the remaining
    pepper and grate the carrot. Garnish the salad all around its
    perimeter with the vegetables.

Note: Follow directions for Slim Cuisine 'mayonnaise' with this
difference: use half low-fat yoghurt and half low-fat fromage frais.

♡ ⊕   **SPICY POTATO SALAD**

Serves 6

Cold potatoes don't have to nestle under a mantle of that evil
ointment – mayonnaise. Egg yolks and oil . . . I ask you! You might
as well trowel it on your hips and have done with it. Try this
creamy, herby, spicy dressing instead.

1½ lb/720 g boiling potatoes, unpeeled, steamed until tender but not mushy	½ small red pepper, peeled and diced
2 tablespoons fresh lime juice	½ small green pepper, peeled and diced
1 teaspoon soy sauce	½ small yellow pepper, peeled and diced
¼ teaspoon cayenne pepper	
½ teaspoon cumin	Salt and freshly ground pepper to taste
1 teaspoon caraway seeds	
2 stalks celery, diced	Dressing (see below)
1 carrot, coarsely grated	

1   Cool the potatoes to lukewarm. Cut into 1-inch/2.5-cm cubes. Toss with the lime juice, soy sauce and spices.
2   Gently combine potatoes with the remaining ingredients. Chill.

'Shall we go to Schrafft's . . . where they have mayonnaise in fiascos?'

E. B. White, *Across the Street and Into the Grill*

Dressing

3 tablespoons yoghurt	1 tablespoon snipped chives
1 tablespoon buttermilk	1 tablespoon chopped parsley
3 spring onions, trimmed and sliced thin	

Combine thoroughly.

♡ ⊕   CHICK PEA-POTATO SALAD

Serves 8

This is a lively potato salad. The chick peas and potatoes complement each other so the quality of protein is high and, of course, the yoghurt adds still more good protein. As a result the salad would be excellent as part of a vegetarian meal.

1 lb/480 g boiling potatoes	3 spring onions, trimmed and sliced thinly
1 tin chick peas	
2 tablespoons fresh lime juice	2 tablespoons chopped fresh parsley
1 teaspoon soy sauce	3 tablespoons drained yoghurt
½ teaspoon ground cumin	1 tablespoon buttermilk
¼ teaspoon cayenne pepper (much less if you don't like things spicy)	

1 Steam the potatoes until tender but not mushy. Cut into ½-inch/1.25-cm cubes while still warm.
2 Drain and rinse the chick peas. Combine them in a bowl with the potatoes. Stir together the lime juice, soy sauce and spices. Add to the potatoes. Toss gently with 2 spoons so that they absorb the liquid. Stir in the spring onions and parsley.
3 Stir together the yoghurt and buttermilk. Gently fold the mixture into the potatoes.

♡ **ONION-TOMATO RELISH**

Makes approximately 12 fl oz/360 ml

A vibrant sweet and sour relish that is a perfect addition to barbecues and picnics.

---

4 oz/120 g raisins
4 fl oz/120 ml dark rum
20 large cloves garlic, peeled and sliced
6 fl oz/180 ml stock
1½ lb/720 g frozen pearl onions, unthawed

6 fl oz/180 ml apple juice
1 tin (1 lb/480 g) chopped Italian tomatoes
Salt and freshly ground pepper to taste

---

1 Combine the raisins and rum in a small bowl. Set aside.
2 Combine the garlic and 4 fl oz/120 ml stock in a large, heavy non-reactive frying pan. Boil, uncovered, until the stock is thick and syrupy and the garlic is very tender.
3 Add the frozen onions and 3 fl oz/90 ml apple juice. Simmer briskly, uncovered, until the mixture is almost dry and the onions are beginning to brown. Add the remaining apple juice and continue cooking, shaking the pan occasionally until the onions are browned and glazed.
4 Add a splash of stock. Simmer, shaking the frying pan for a few minutes until the onions are deeply and evenly browned.
5 Stir in the tomatoes, salt and pepper. Stir in the raisins and the rum. Simmer gently, covered, for 40 minutes, until the mixture is very thick and the onions are very tender. Uncover to stir occasionally. Add a bit of stock if the mixture gets thick too early and threatens to burn.
6 Store in the refrigerator. Serve at room temperature.

♡ # TABOULI

Serves 8

Tabouli is a salad of herbs, tomatoes and grain. The colourful mixture is extraordinarily refreshing. The success of the dish depends on the tomatoes; they must be ripe and bursting with flavour. Tabouli goes very well with grilled fish, chicken or meat, or with lamb meatballs. And it makes a pretty addition to a salad buffet. Bulghur is available in most wholefood stores.

---

8 oz/240 g cracked wheat (bulghur)
4 fl oz/120 ml fresh lemon juice
2 bunches parsley, stemmed and
  finely chopped
1 bunch spring onions, trimmed
  and finely chopped

1 bunch fresh mint, finely chopped
2 lb/960 g skinned (see page 48) ripe
  tomatoes (squeeze out seeds and
  juice) chopped
Salt and freshly ground pepper to
  taste

---

1   Soak the wheat in cold water to cover. Use a large bowl as it will expand a great deal. After 30 minutes, squeeze the grains with your hands to drain them and place in a clean bowl.
2   Stir in the lemon juice, and all remaining ingredients. Mix well. Let sit for at least 1 hour before serving.

Snacks and Sandwiches

'So we'll just investigate the icebox as we have done so oft at midnight . . . and all that it will be, I do assure you, will be something swift and quick and ready, something instant and felicitous, and quite delicate and dainty – just a snack!'

Thomas Wolfe, *Of Time and the River*

It's the cravings and snackings and in-between munchings that get you into trouble. Little crispy fried things scoffed down in frightening quantity; butter- and mayonnaise-smeared sandwiches overstuffed with fatty meats; oily, sausage-festooned pizzas; 'fun' foods, but so bad for your weight maintenance and your health. Apply Slim Cuisine techniques to your snacking, and you can still have fun. After all, a sandwich is one of the friendliest edible objects in the world. There's something about two pieces of bread slapped together with interesting (and sometimes eccentric) ingredients that can cheer up the dourest snacker. Why deprive yourself? And why miss out on crispy little munchies, on pizza, on nachos? Read on.

Slim Sandwiches

Legend has it that the Fourth Earl of Sandwich, unwilling to leave the gaming table although quite hungry, invented a portable meal. Did he have any inkling of the culinary revolution he was setting in motion? How could he envisage baked beans on toast, chip butties, stuffed pittas, bagels and cream cheese, hamburgers, ham and swiss, hot dogs, peanut butter and jelly? That impromptu eighteenth-century portable meal, and all its twentieth-century guises, now bears the Earl's name. There is no other meal that offers such a contrast of flavours and textures in a single bite. In fact, a sandwich makes a happy occasion. Two pieces of bread and an interesting filling can add glamour to any lunch box, and cheer a gloomy mood. In your quest for great sandwiches, don't fall into the butter and mayonnaise trap. Spread your sandwiches with quark or any of the quark spreads from this collection. Try Red Pepper and Garlic Spread, Pesto, Chive Spread – even 'Russian' Dressing (substitute quark for the fromage frais and cut down on the buttermilk).

For your sandwiches use a good wholegrain sliced bakery loaf that has some character, a crusty rye or a moist black bread.

Sliced chicken (roasted, smoked or poached)
Tomatoes
Pesto

Tzatziki
Smoked salmon
♡ *Sliced Cucumber*
Dill pesto
♡ *Liptauer cheese*
Sliced turkey

Sliced brisket (page 125)
Deli mustard (page 305)
♡ *Tonnato*
Roasted peppers
♡ *Russian dressing*
Coleslaw
Sliced chicken

Hummus
Sliced tomatoes
Chopped parsley

Lamb meatballs or kofta curry
Raita (cucumber or mint)

Served in pitta bread pockets

Italian sausage balls
Tomato sauce
Stir-'fried' or grilled peppers
Served in pitta bread pockets or rolls
♡ *Dill chicken salad*
Sliced tomatoes
♡ *Lemon chicken (page 191)*
Chive spread (page 303)
♡ *Curried chicken salad*
Chopped fresh coriander
Sliced mango

Peppered goose skirt steak slices
Browned onions or sweet and sour onions
Mustard
♡ *Pan-sautéed chicken cutlet*
Stir-'fried' peppers

SLIM REUBEN

Sliced smoked chicken
Rinsed and drained sauerkraut
Thinly sliced Mozzarella

Slim Cuisine Russian dressing

Toast this sandwich in a sandwich toaster.

♡ ## CLUB SANDWICH

Slim Cuisine 'mayonnaise'
Smoked chicken
Sliced tomato
Lettuce

Toast the bread first

SUMMER SANDWICH

Tomatoes
Quark or thinly-sliced Mozzarella
Fresh basil and chopped garlic

A light sprinkling of excellent wine
vinegar (optional)

LUXURIOUS SUMMER SANDWICH

Chop together fresh basil, fresh garlic and Parmesan cheese, and put this mixture on one slice of wholegrain bread. Top with sliced ripe tomatoes and thin slices of Mozzarella. Spread the top piece of bread with sun-dried tomatoes that have been soaked in stock, drained and chopped. Toast this sandwich in a sandwich toaster.

PIZZA SANDWICH

Thinly sliced Mozzarella cheese
Tomato sauce
Crumbled dried oregano
Add if desired:
Crumbled dried chilli peppers

A spoonful of sautéed mushrooms
(see page 29)
A few slices of peeled red and yellow
peppers

Toast this sandwich in a sandwich toaster

299

♡ VEGETARIAN SANDWICH 1

Beetroot Purée (see page 263) or Beetroots in Mustard Sauce (see page 263)	*Watercress*

♡ VEGETARIAN SANDWICH 2

Chopped fresh spinach (raw) Sliced mushrooms (raw)	*Dijon mustard mixed with yoghurt*

Use black bread for this sandwich

GOOD SPREADS FOR HONEST BREAD

These are marvellous on slices of toasted granary or rye bread.

Garlic spread (quark mixed with baked garlic purée and a touch of finely grated Parmesan. Vary with grated nutmeg, chopped fresh herbs, or chopped chives or spring onions)	*Beetroot Purée (see page 263) Duxelles (see page 247)*

⊕ ELLE GALE'S SARDINE FISH CREAM

Makes ⅖ pt/240 ml

This is best with the goat's milk curd cheese from Beck Farm, Elle's place in Histon, near Cambridge, but it's also good with quark, or any other low-fat curd cheese. Mash together 4 oz/120 g quark or other low-fat curd cheese with the contents of a 4-oz/120-g tin of sardines in tomato sauce (check the label and make sure it contains no oil). Stir in 2 teaspoons chopped chives; 2 spring onions, chopped; 3 drops reduced-salt Worcestershire sauce; 1 teaspoon lemon juice; salt and pepper to taste.

♡ LIPTAUER CHEESE

Conventionally, this Hungarian cheese spread is made with full fat cheese and soured cream. My version has approximately ⅓ the Calories of the original, yet there is virtually no difference in taste. Will fill five coeur à la creme moulds.

---

1 carton (1 lb 1½ oz) skimmed milk quark
3 fl oz/90 ml buttermilk
1 tablespoon sweet Hungarian paprika or paprika paste

Salt and freshly ground pepper to taste
2 teaspoons caraway seeds
Several dashes of Tabasco sauce
1 teaspoon chopped capers

---

1   Combine all ingredients in a bowl. Beat to a smooth paste.
2   This may be served in coeur à la crème moulds (perforated heart-shaped moulds). Line the moulds with damp cheesecloth leaving an overhang. Scrape an equal portion of the mixture into each mould. Fold up the overhang to cover. Place the moulds, perforated side down, on a rack placed on a baking sheet. Refrigerate overnight to drain. Unmould, arrange attractively on a bed of greens and serve.
3   If you do not have any coeur à la creme moulds, scrape the mixture into a colander lined with damp cheesecloth, and let drain overnight. Serve with thin-sliced wholemeal bread or with slices of cucumber and courgette. Spread the mixture on the bread or vegetable slices

Another serving suggestion: Mound the mixture into halved seeded and ribbed red, yellow, green or purple peppers. Serve with crudités for dipping. (Crudités are raw vegetables, cut into bite-sized pieces. Try cauliflower, broccoli, courgette, cucumber, carrot, turnip, radishes etc.)

Vary this recipe with different ingredients. Try roasted garlic purée and chopped chives; finely chopped mushrooms simmered in stock until tender and dry, seasoned with a touch of nutmeg and cayenne pepper; puréed roasted red pepper with a squeeze of lemon juice . . . The possibilities are endless!

⑤ TONNATO SAUCE

Makes ¾ pt/450 ml
25 Calories per tablespoon
0.1 g fat
(Traditional tonnato sauce: 73 Calories per tablespoon, 2.6 g fat)

Tonnato is an Italian tuna mayonnaise and one of my favourite cold sauces. It is traditionally served on slices of roasted veal or turkey breast. It is good as a first course with lightly steamed, chilled vegetables. It is also heavenly spread on toast.

½ pt/300 ml yoghurt cheese or fromage frais (see page 39)
Purée from 1 head baked garlic (see page 32)
2 tins (7 oz/210 g each) of tuna packed in brine, very well drained

Juice of ½ lemon
2 teaspoons capers
Salt and freshly ground pepper to taste

1   Combine all the ingredients in the container of a food processor, and process until very smooth. Scrape into a crock or bowl and refrigerate for at least a day. (The sauce will keep for a week and improve in flavour each day.)
2   Serve as a sauce or dip with crudités or lightly steamed vegetables.

HUMMUS

Makes 1 pt/600 ml
23 Calories per tablespoon
0.4 g fat
(Traditional hummus: 48 Calories per tablespoon, 1.4 g fat)

A low-fat version of a classic Middle Eastern chick pea spread. The texture is rich and unctuous.

1½ tablespoons sesame seeds
2 tins (15½ oz/465 g each) of chick peas, drained (reserve ¼ to ⅓ of the liquid from one tin)

Purée from 1 head roasted garlic or 2–3 large raw garlic cloves
Juice of 2 large lemons

1   Toast the sesame seeds in a small heavy frying pan. Stir them constantly and do not allow them to scorch.
2   Place the sesame seeds in a liquidizer and process until they are pulverized.
3   Add all the remaining ingredients including ¼ of one tin of the chick pea liquid. Process until very smooth and creamy; the consistency of mashed potatoes. Add a little more of the chick pea liquid if the mixture is too thick and add a bit more lemon juice if you prefer a sharper taste. Serve as a sandwich spread, or a dip with toasted pitta bread wedges and raw vegetables.

Variations:

1   Mix hummus with an equal amount of quark and use as a filling for baked potatoes or potato cases (see page 271).
2   Thin with chicken or vegetable stock to a sauce-like consistency, and toss with hot pasta.

♡   **RED PEPPER AND GARLIC SPREAD**

Makes 16 fl oz/480 ml

I devised this while trying to work out a substitute for rouille, the red pepper and garlic mayonnaise of the South of France. If you want a really strong garlicky taste, add a crushed clove or two of fresh garlic, but I prefer the mellow and subtle character of the whole roasted bulb.

Purée from 1 head Baked Garlic (see   *Several dashes Tabasco sauce*
* page 32)*   *1 lb/480 g quark*
1 large tin pimientos (red peppers),
* drained*

Combine all ingredients in a liquidizer or food processor and blend until smooth. Serve as a dip, a spread, a filling for Vegetable Canapés (page 73), or an accompaniment to fish soups and stews.

⏲   Roast garlic in the microwave.

♡ ⏲ Ⓢ   **CHIVE SPREAD**

Makes 6 fl oz/180 ml

A prime example of how quark can be used to make excellent rich-tasting spreads for bread. To turn this into a garlic spread, substitute Baked Garlic purée (page 32) for the chives. The chive spread is particularly good on split bagels or brown bread, topped with slices of smoked salmon.

---

1 box (7 oz/210 g) quark
1 bunch fresh chives

---

1   Scrape the quark into the bowl of a food processor. With scissors, snip the chives over the bowl, so the pieces fall in.
2   Process until the quark is very smooth, creamy and green-

flecked. Scrape into a ramekin or small bowl, cover with cling film and refrigerate until needed.

♡ ## TZATZIKI

Makes approx. ⅘ pt/500 ml as a dip, 1⅕ pt/750 ml as a sauce
15 Calories per tablespoon
0.1 g fat
(Traditional Tzatziki: 30 Calories per tablespoon, 2 g fat)

Serve this zesty Greek mixture as a dip with toasted pitta bread triangles, or as a sauce for steamed or grilled fish or grilled lean meat (Goose Skirt Steak, page 133, for instance.) The meat juices mingling with the cold Tzatziki are absolutely delicious.

1¾ pts/1 l skimmed milk yoghurt	2 large cloves garlic, minced
2 large cucumbers	1½ teaspoons white wine vinegar
Salt	Freshly ground pepper to taste

1   Drain the yoghurt for 24 hours (as described in the yoghurt cheese recipe) if you want to serve the Tzatziki as a dip. To serve it as a sauce, drain it for 6–7 hours only.
2   Peel the cucumbers. Cut them in half lengthwise. Use a teaspoon to scrape out the seeds. Discard them. Grate the cucumbers into a colander. Salt them and allow to drain for ½ hour. This draws out their bitterness.
3   Place the minced garlic and vinegar in a small bowl and allow to marinate while the cucumbers are draining.
4   Rinse the drained cucumbers, squeeze them as dry as possible and blot them on paper towels. Place in the bowl with the marinated garlic. Add the drained yoghurt and a few gridings of fresh pepper and stir. Serve at once or store in the refrigerator. It will keep for several days, and improve in flavour each day.

♡ ## REMOULADE SAUCE

Makes approx. 2 pt/1.2 l sauce

This sauce is versatile as a dip, a sandwich spread or a sauce for julienned celeriac, cold poached chicken, steamed prawns or very lean, rare cold beef.

2 pts/1.2 l Slim Cuisine
   'mayonnaise' made from
   yoghurt or fromage frais or a
   mixture of both (see page 40)
2 teaspoons Dijon mustard
4 tablespoons capers, rinsed
4 tablespoons chopped cornichons
   (small, sour gherkins)

4 tablespoons chopped fresh parsley
1 teaspoon paprika
6 spring onions, chopped, green
   and white parts
Few drops Tabasco sauce
½ tablespoon dried tarragon,
   crumbled

Mix all the ingredients together with a wire whisk. Allow to ripen
in the refrigerator for at least 1 hour before using.

Ⓢ NEW YORK DELI MUSTARD

Makes 8 fl oz/240 ml

Home-made mustard is habit-forming. Once you've tried it, you
will want to have a jar in the fridge always. It's good as a sandwich
spread, a dip, or a sauce.

5 level tablespoons dry mustard
1 tablespoon mustard seeds
4 fl oz/120 ml warm water
8 fl oz/240 ml cider vinegar
1 large garlic clove, peeled and
   crushed

2 tablespoons dark brown sugar
1 teaspoon salt
¼ teaspoon ground ginger
¼ teaspoon ground allspice
¼ teaspoon ground cinnamon

1   Whisk together the dry mustard, mustard seeds and 4 fl oz/
    120 ml warm water in a heavy non-reactive saucepan. Set
    aside.
2   In a second non-reactive saucepan, combine all the remaining
    ingredients. Bring to the boil, reduce the heat and simmer
    gently for 5 minutes. Let cool for 2 or 3 minutes. Whisk the
    spiced vinegar into the mustard.
3   Bring to a simmer and simmer very gently, stirring frequently,
    for 10 minutes; it should just bubble gently around the edges.
    With a rubber spatula, scrape the mixture into a bowl. Let
    stand for 2 hours.
4   Scrape the mustard into the container of a food processor.
    Process to a grainy purée.
5   Scrape the mustard into a jar. Cover and allow to mellow
    overnight at room temperature. Store in the refrigerator.

'There was often no money at all and we existed on dry bread rubbed with garlic . . . As a change we had bread smeared with mustard, when there was any mustard.'

Theodora FitzGibbon, *With Love*

⊕ CHEESE ON TOAST

Lightly toast a piece of rye bread. Halve a clove of garlic. Rub the hot toast with the garlic. Cover the toast thinly with sliced Mozzarella cheese. Grill for 2–3 minutes until melted and speckled with brown. Sprinkle lightly with Hungarian paprika. Devour at once.

'Many the long night I've dreamed of cheese – toasted, mostly.'

Robert Louis Stevenson, *Treasure Island*

⊕ PIZZA

Pizza, with its gooey cheese and spicy sauce, may not be elegant, but it is one of the most satisfying dishes in the world. Happily, it is also one of the healthiest, if you avoid additions such as sausage, ham and other fatty meats.

When you are eating pizza out, (at one of the wonderful Pizza Express restaurants, for example,) specify that your pizza be prepared with no oil and no salt. The pizza will still be sumptuous, yet your Slim Cuisine regime will stay intact.

It's fun to make pizza at home and easy too if you begin with pitta bread as your base. Leave the pitta as it is or, to cut the calories even more, split each pitta into two rounds. Place the pitta on the grill tray (if they are split, place them smooth side down). Smear with Slim Cuisine Tomato Sauce (see page 236) and top with thin slices of part-skimmed Mozzarella cheese. Use the Italian brands that come packed in water. If you wish, top the tomato sauce with Sautéed Mushrooms, Browned Onions, Sliced Meatballs, or Stir-'Fried' Peppers (see page 256) before laying on the cheese. Sprinkle on a little oregano. Have the grill set to its highest heat and place the grill tray in the lowest position. Grill for 3–4 minutes until the cheese is nicely gooey and runny. Eat with pleasure and no guilt at all.

CORN TORTILLAS AND TORTILLA CHIPS

Tortilla chips, sometimes called nacho chips (totopos in Mexico) are very popular as snack food. They are compelling munchies on their own, or as paddles for dips. Alas, they are always fried and often oversalted too. If you can find tortillas in your supermarket or local deli, you can make your own healthy tortilla chips; no frying and only as much salt as you want. Look for wide, flat cans of corn tortillas. Bake as many tortillas as you like, in one layer, on the shelf of your oven at 300° F, 150° C, Gas Mark 2, for 15–20 minutes until crisp. Remove and break into eighths. (Alternatively, for neater pieces, cut the tortillas in quarters or eighths with scissors *before* baking. Spread the pieces directly on the oven shelf.) Sprinkle with a bit of salt, or chilli powder, paprika, cumin, whatever you like. Or leave unseasoned, so that the pure and heady maize taste comes through. Store in an airtight biscuit tin. Eat as they are, use with dips, or consider one of the following:

TOSTADAS

1   Spread *whole* baked tortillas with Chilli con Carne (see page 142) and sprinkle with shredded Mozzarella. Grill for 1–2 minutes, to melt the cheese. Serve at once.
2   Spread the whole baked tortilla with mashed, cooked beans (black beans or kidney beans) that have been seasoned with salt, ground cumin and chilli powder. Sprinkle with shredded Mozzarella. Grill as above. Serve at once.
3   Spread with mashed beans (see 2, above) that have been thinned with a bit of stock and gently warmed. Top with crisp, shredded lettuce, a dollop of fromage frais, and finely chopped red and yellow peppers.

NACHOS AL CARBON

Break the baked tortillas into quarters (or cut them into quarters with scissors before you bake them). Spread in one layer on a baking tray or ovenproof platter. Put a dollop of mashed beans (see above) on each. Top each with a slice of Peppered Goose Skirt Steak, with or without the Mushroom Sauce (see page 132). Top with shredded Mozzarella. Grill for 1 minute to melt the cheese. Add a dab of fromage frais and some Salsa if you wish (see page 269). Place the tray in the middle of the table and let everyone grab and munch.

NACHOS

Nachos – little corn chips topped with tomatoes and cheese – are
irresistible. I defy you to eat just one. (Or just two, for that matter.)
These compelling morsels make great party food.

Tortillas (see page 307)
Tomato Sauce (page 236) or
    Tomato-Pepper Sauce (see page
    233)*
Italian Mozzarella cheese, cut into
    strips

Dried oregano
Freshly ground pepper
Fresh coriander leaves (optional)
Fromage frais

---

1   Preheat oven to 300° F, 150° C, Gas Mark 2.
2   Bake tortillas directly on the oven shelf, turning once, for
15–20 minutes until crisp right through. (Test by breaking
one. It should break with a crisp 'snap'.) Break each tortilla
into eighths. They will keep, in a covered tin, for months (if
you hide them). Preheat the grill.
3   Spread the tortilla chips, in one layer, on a foil-lined baking
sheet. Put a dollop of sauce on each. Top with a strip of
Mozzarella cheese. Sprinkle on some oregano (rub it between
your fingertips), and grind on some pepper.
4   Grill, about 3 inches/8 cm from the heat, until the cheese is
melted, approximately 3 minutes. Transfer the nachos to a
plate and garnish with coriander leaves if desired. Serve at
once. Pass a bowl of fromage frais so that each diner may
garnish each nacho with a dollop.

Variation I: Potato Skin Nachos

When you have scooped out baked jacket potatoes in order to make
Mashed Potatoes (see page 279), *do not throw the skins away!* Save
them, wrapped in foil in the fridge, until the snack urge strikes,
then make Potato Skin Nachos. Cut the skins into 2 inch/5 cm
squares. Place in one layer, skin-side down, on a foil-lined baking
tray. Grill, 3 inches/8 cm from the heat, for 30–40 seconds, to crisp a
bit. Then spoon a dollop of sauce on each, top with a strip of
Mozzarella, sprinkle with oregano and cook and serve as above.

⊕ Variation II: Tortilla Pizzas

My 17-year-old son Shawm, the teenage pizza monster, invented
this method. Open a tin of tortillas. Insert two into the toaster slots.
Toast until crisp through. (Watch it – they should not brown or
burn. It won't take very long. Underestimate the time and then

push them back down if necessary. Timing depends on your particular toaster.) Place the whole, crisp tortillas on a foil-lined baking tray. Sprinkle with shredded Mozzarella. Grill for approximately 3 minutes. Serve at once.

Sweet Things and Drinks

'Mrs Mayfair gorged herself on three desserts and kept saying "Just a sliver, that's all. Just a sliver!" when the chocolate cake went round.

"Poor Henrietta", Mrs Prescott said, watching her enormous sister-in-law spooning down ice cream. "It's that psychosomatic hunger they're always talking about. Makes her eat so."'

Sylvia Plath, *The Day Mr Prescott Died*

You've heard it a thousand times: puddings and sweets are evil, they will rot your teeth, pad your hips and probably initiate moral disintegration. Don't believe it! I have a wonderful surprise for you: a whole clutch of indulgent and flossy desserts that will contribute not an iota to the decay of your teeth, your litheness or your good character. These sweets are all visual knockouts, as well as delicious. Some are 'nouvelle' in character, others endearingly old-fashioned, but each will end a meal with a flourish.

Dessert Guidelines

1   Desserts should always be considered a significant and important component of a meal, not a cholesterol-, fat- and Calorie-laden 'reward' for finishing all your vegetables. Plan your

311

desserts so that they contribute valuable nutrients along with their Calories. Worthless Calories are a Slim Cuisine no-no.

2   A little bit of sugar every once in a while will not hurt. Just remember that sugar should always be a light seasoning to be used by the sprinkle; not a major ingredient to be used by the handful. NutraSweet (Canderel) is extremely low in Calories and has no aftertaste. It can be used in recipes that do not call for high heat. (When heated, the sweetness in NutraSweet dissipates.) Whichever you choose, use it in moderation. It is a good idea to alternate sweeteners, so that you do not overload on one or the other. If you decide to substitute sugar for NutraSweet in any of these recipes, you will be adding 34 Calories per tablespoonful of sugar to the Calorie count of the finished dish.

3   High-quality unsweetened frozen fruits and berries are available in exhilarating profusion in supermarkets, and in freezer stores (like Bejam). Keep your freezer stocked at all times with a good variety. Many splendid, nutritious desserts can be made in minutes with a generous supply at hand. Also keep on hand a selection of low-fat dairy products: yoghurt, fromage frais, buttermilk, skimmed milk, etc.

'Cecily (sweetly):   Sugar?
Gwendolyn (superciliously):   No, thank you. Sugar is not
                        fashionable any more.'

Oscar Wilde *The Importance of Being Earnest*

Icecreams and Sorbets

Slim Cuisine icecreams are so creamy, so vividly fruity and outrageously voluptuous that you will feel delightful pangs of guilt as you polish off a large serving. Not to worry. They are nutrient-dense and Calorie-shy. It's okay to indulge. Make them, serve them and eat them. They do not store well. (These recipes can be halved, if desired.) Use these ideas as guidelines and invent your own versions.

♡ ⊕ ⑤　**BANANA ICECREAM**

Makes approximately 1¾ pts/1 l

4 bananas, peeled, cut into chunks, and frozen (they should be frozen so that you have separate pieces, not a large frozen mass)	*½ teaspoon vanilla essence* *3–4 tablespoons NutraSweet/Canderel* *5 fl oz/150 ml buttermilk*

1　Place the frozen banana chunks in the container of the food processor. Add the vanilla, sweetener and half the buttermilk.
2　Turn on the processor and let it run for a few moments. Then, while it is running, pour in the remaining buttermilk in a thin, steady stream. Let the machine run until the mixture is beautifully smooth and creamy. Spoon into bowls and serve at once.

BANANA GINGER ICECREAM

As for Banana Icecream, but omit vanilla essence. Add a scant teaspoon of grated fresh ginger and, if you wish, a splash of dark rum.

'I doubt whether the world holds for anyone a more soul-stirring surprise than the first adventure with ice cream.'

Heywood Broun, *Seeing Things at Night*

♡ ⊕ ⑤　**RASPBERRY ICECREAM**

Makes approximately 1¼ pts/750 ml

12 oz/360 g packet frozen raspberries (unsweetened) *6–8 fl oz/180–240 ml cold buttermilk*	*4–5 tablespoons NutraSweet/Canderel*

1　Do not thaw the berries. Dump them, still frozen, into the bowl of a food processor or liquidizer. Pour in half of the buttermilk and sprinkle in the sweetener.
2　Turn on the machine. Process for a few seconds, stopping to scrape down the sides if necessary.
3　With the machine running, pour in the remaining buttermilk. Process until the mixture forms a super-creamy ice cream. Spoon into clear glass goblets and serve at once.

313

Variations:

1 Strawberry Icecream. Substitute frozen stawberries for the raspberries.
2 Strawberry-Orange Icecream. Add the pulp, juice and grated zest of an orange to the berries in Step 1.
3 Apple Icecream. Substitute frozen apple pieces and a frozen banana cut into chunks for the raspberries. Add a sprinkling of cinnamon.

Slim Cuisine Icecream

As an American, I was born with an icecream gene, the way the English are born with a tea gene, and the French with a champagne gene. In America, the butterfat level of icecream is sky high, and every supermarket has endless aisles of freezer cases, overflowing with 'designer' icecreams: elegant packaging, enough butterfat to choke a brontosaurus and vividly intense flavours. To make things even more outrageous, many of the supermarkets (foodie seduction markets, really) are open 24 hours a day, *every day in the year*. When one is overcome by an ice cream attack, even at 3.00 a.m., it can be satisfied in minutes. A pint of macadamia nut-chocolate chip, two spoons and thou beside me in the bed, . . . Paradise indeed. When I moved to England almost five years ago, the 24-hour seduction markets with their compelling freezer cabinets were far away. And I had foresworn butterfat anyway. What to do about those cravings? My solution to the icecream dilemma has reached the status of legend. The Slim Cuisine icecream recipes from *Slim Cuisine I* get fan letters. For instance: 'The banana icecream is terrific! Couldn't believe how rich and creamy it was', or 'I have honestly never tasted any icecream more delicious', and 'Every time that I make your icecream, I thank you out loud and so do my family and friends. It's unbelievable!!!! and you are a heroine.' It is an instant technique, so if *you* get an icecream attack at 3.00 a.m., pull out the frozen fruit, dump it in the food processor, pour in the buttermilk and presto!, the best cold comfort in the world.

♡ ⊕ Ⓢ **BLUEBERRY ICECREAM**

Serves 6

For this brilliantly coloured icecream, squirrel away blueberries in the freezer. In season, buy them in profusion, freeze them flat on trays, then transfer to plastic bags. Blueberries are usually sweet enough – but you may need the barest sprinkle of sweetener.

---

12 oz/360 g frozen blueberries　　　*NutraSweet (Canderel) (optional)*
6–8 fl oz/240 ml cold buttermilk

1　Do not thaw the berries. Dump them, still frozen, into the bowl of a processor or liquidizer. Pour in half of the buttermilk.
2　Turn on the machine. Process for a few seconds, stopping to scrape down the sides if necessary. Taste. Add a bit of Canderel if needed. Pour in the remaining buttermilk. Process until the mixture forms a super-creamy icecream. Spoon into clear glass goblets and serve *at once*.

More Icecream Ideas:

Frozen peaches flavoured with almond or vanilla essence, or try combinations: pineapple/orange; raspberry/melon; banana/strawberry.

♡ ⊕ Ⓢ　**PINEAPPLE SORBET**

For this wonderfully refreshing recipe you need frozen pineapple cubes. Buy ripe pineapples, peel and cube them, discarding the tough core, and freeze the cubes flat on baking trays. When thoroughly frozen, transfer to plastic bags. When you want to make sorbet, remove the amount you need. If the cubes have frozen together in the bag, so that you have a solid mass, drop the bag on the floor a few times to separate them.

Frozen pineapple cubes　　　*A splash or two of dark rum*

1　Place the frozen pineapple cubes and the rum in the container of the food processor. Turn the machine on. It will rattle and clatter and leap all over the counter. Steady it and allow it to run, stopping occasionally to scrape down the sides with a rubber spatula, until it is of a sorbet consistency. Serve at once.

'Tastes and odours can never be described unless they are comparable with known tastes and odours and the mango is unique and completely superior. It may be peeled and eaten out of hand, gnawing at last on the great pit; it may be cut daintily and served just so.'

Marjorie Kinnan Rawlings, *Cross Creek*

♡ ⊕ ⑤　**MANGO SORBET**

You haven't lived until you've tasted Mango Sorbet. Use it as a stunning finish to an elegant dinner, or serve it for a private indulgence. The mango cubes can be frozen months ahead of time. (Make sure that you use really ripe mangoes.) The sorbet itself must be prepared just before serving. It's very easy and very quick. Simply excuse yourself, retire to the food processor, whip it up, and serve it forth proudly. Your guests will admire your talent and ingenuity.

Frozen mango cubes (see below)　　*A sprinkle of NutraSweet and a*
A splash or 2 of dark rum (optional)　　*tablespoon of buttermilk, if*
　　　　　　　　　　　　　　　　　　necessary

1　With a sharp knife slice down on each whole mango as if you were slicing it in half, but try to miss the large flat centre stone. Slice down again on the other side of the stone. You will now have 2 half mangoes and the flat centre stone to which quite a bit of mango flesh clings.

2　With a small, sharp paring knife score each mango half lengthwise and crosswise, cutting all the way to, but not through, the skin. Push out the skin as if you were pushing the half mango inside out. The mango flesh will stand out in cubes. Slice these cubes off the skin.

3　With the knife, remove the skin from the mango flesh remaining on the stone. Slice the flesh off the stone. Spread all the mango cubes and pieces on a flat tray and freeze. When frozen solid, transfer to plastic bags. Pull out the bags when you are ready to make the sorbet. If the cubes have frozen together in the bag, so that you have a solid mass, drop it on the floor a few times.

4　To make the sorbet, place the frozen mango cubes and the optional rum in the container of a food processor. Turn the machine on. It will rattle and clatter all over the counter. Steady it and allow it to run, stopping occasionally to scrape down the sides with a rubber spatula. It will seem quite splintery at first. Taste for sweetness. If necessary, add a sprinkling of NutraSweet, but if the mangoes were really ripe it probably won't be necessary. Continue processing and if the mango does not seem to be coming to sorbet consistency add 1–2 tablespoons (no more) of buttermilk. When the mixture reaches a very smooth sorbet consistency, place several small balls of the sorbet on each plate. Garnish with mint leaves. (In the summer, a scattering of raspberries, blackberries and other berries can be arranged on the plate as well.)

Variation:

This recipe works very well with ripe cantaloupe too. Remove the melon flesh with a teaspoon or a melon baller and freeze the pieces flat, then transfer to plastic bags.

'One of those musty fragrant, deep-ribbed cantaloupes, chilled to the heart now, in all their pink-flesh taste and ripeness . . . or a bowl of those red raspberries, most luscious and most rich.'

Thomas Wolfe, *Time and the River*

♡ **SLIM 'WHIPPED CREAM'**

In summer months seasonal fruits or berries with a creamy topping make an elegant, hard-to-improve finale to a meal. Here is the simplest (and one of the best). Quickly and gently rinse some strawberries in a colander under running water. Shake dry. Put them, in a bowl, on the table. Give everyone a small bowl of fromage frais and an even smaller bowl of dark brown sugar (1 tablespoon or less). Let everyone pick up a berry by its green top, dip it into the fromage frais, then into sugar. Eating these delectable morsels is pure summer pleasure. If you want to get a bit more elegant, try the following topping for fresh berries or sliced peaches, or whatever you like – it's *better* than whipped cream.

---

8 fl oz/240 ml fromage frais	Pinch of salt
¼ teaspoon vanilla essence	2 tablespoons sugar
2 egg whites, at room temperature	

---

1 Mix together the fromage frais and vanilla.
2 In a spotlessly clean bowl, with a wire whip, beat the egg whites with the salt until they are foamy. Add sugar, a little at

a time, and continue beating until the egg whites are shiny and hold firm peaks.

3   Fold the beaten egg whites into the fromage frais.

♡   # RASPBERRY SAUCE

Makes 16 fl oz/480 ml

This is a basic dessert sauce, useful in myriad ways. It can top icecreams, or be swirled into fromage frais or yoghurt to create a fruit fool, or served as a dipping sauce for fresh whole strawberries.

---

2 boxes (12 oz/360 g each) frozen   *NutraSweet (Canderel) to taste*
   raspberries, thawed and drained

---

1   Purée the berries in the liquidizer.
2   Pour into a sieve and rub through. Discard the seeds.
3   Stir in sweetener (2–3 tablespoons) to taste. Refrigerate until needed.

⊕   Thaw berries in the microwave.

Variations:

Substitute other fruit – frozen blackcurrants, strawberries or blackberries – for the raspberries. Sweeten to taste. The Blackcurrant Sauce is wonderful enough to serve as a pudding all by itself (or perhaps topped with a dollop of low-fat fromage frais).

♡ ⊕   # MANGO SAUCE

Place cubed, fresh, ripe mango (see Mango Sorbet, page 316, for procedure) into the jar of the liquidizer. Purée until perfectly smooth. To end a summer meal on a sublime note, pour a puddle of Mango Sauce on each dessert plate. Heap a generous serving of raspberries on each puddle. Top with a cloud of Slim Cuisine 'Whipped Cream' (see page 317). When raspberries are out of season, substitute peeled, sliced kiwi fruit.

♡ **STRAWBERRIES ON RED
AND WHITE SAUCE**

This very beautiful dessert would make a perfect ending to a special dinner party. The presentation is inspired by *nouvelle cuisine*, the Calories are minimal.

Fresh, ripe strawberries	*Buttermilk*
Raspberry sauce (see page 318)	*Mint leaves*

1 Hull the strawberries.
2 Use clear glass plates if possible. Pour some raspberry sauce on one half of the plate. Pour some buttermilk on the other half.
3 Place strawberries in a row down the dividing line. Garnish with fresh mint leaves.

♡ ⊕ **STRAWBERRIES IN
RASPBERRY SAUCE**

Serve each diner a heap of fresh strawberries, a puddle of Raspberry Sauce (see opposite) and a cloud of low-fat fromage frais. The drill is to pick up a berry by its green stem, dip it in the puddle, dabble it in the cloud, and pop it in the mouth. If you and someone you love share this berry feast, pop them into each other's mouths. Sheer heaven!

Variation: Strawberry Fondue

Serve each diner a bowl of whole strawberries with the stems still on, a bowl of fromage frais, a bowl of Chocolate Cream Sauce (page 335), and a bowl of Raspberry Sauce (page 318), then allow your guests to dip and nibble at will.

> 'To get back to the sublime, one will always dine on lucullan dishes, but as if Lucullus had rounded up a new type of health food; melons from the Pace gardens, wild strawberries gathered from the slopes of the Dardanelles; raspberries as big as crabapples . . .'
>
> Anita Loos, *The Italians Have a Word for It*

'Now you can eat all the pudding you want and not end up like one.'

David Gelef, *Punch*

CRUNCHY BANANAS ON RED AND WHITE SAUCE

Serves 4

Kids love this, and adults won't complain either. The buttermilk, combined with the sauce, tastes deceptively rich and creamy.

1 rounded tablespoon low-fat fromage frais or yoghurt	1 heaped tablespoon dry wholewheat breadcrumbs
½ tablespoon ground, toasted, skinned hazelnuts	2 bananas
	Buttermilk
	Strawberry Sauce (see page 318)

1 Preheat the grill to its highest point. Line the grill pan with foil, shiny side up. Place a rack on the pan.
2 Put the fromage frais on a plate. Mix the nuts and crumbs on another plate.
3 Cut each banana in half lengthwise. Cut each half into 5 pieces.
4 Dip the top side of each banana piece in the fromage frais. Then dredge it in the crumbs. Place on the grill rack crumbed side up.
5 Grill on the lowest shelf for 3–4 minutes, until crispy on top.
6 Pour some strawberry sauce on half the surface of a small plate. Pour some buttermilk on the other half. Place 5 banana pieces down the centre. Serve at once.

♡ Omit hazelnuts.

♡ # ALMOND CURD WITH BLACKCURRANT SAUCE

Serves 6

I borrowed the Almond Curd from Chinese Cuisine, and added a dollop of fragrant Blackcurrant Sauce. The combination is stunning and deeply soothing.

1 sachet gelatine
12 fl oz/360 ml hot water
12 fl oz/360 ml skimmed milk
½ teaspoon pure almond essence

¼ teaspoon pure vanilla essence
6 tablespoons Canderel
   (NutraSweet)
Blackcurrant Sauce (see page 318)

1   Mix the gelatine into the hot water. Stir until thoroughly dissolved. Stir in milk, and almond and vanilla essences. Cool to room temperature.
2   When cooled, add the sweetener. Stir until it is dissolved.
3   Pour the mixture into a shallow 2-pt/1,200-ml baking pan and chill for several hours, or overnight, until set.
4   To serve, spoon into shallow goblets. Top with a dollop of Blackcurrant Sauce.

♡   # TROPICAL FRUIT JELLY

Serves 6

A refreshing jelly, evocative of sunshine both in taste and colour. It is a very soft jelly, not at all rubbery, so serve it in bowls, rather than trying to mould it. Passion fruit is ripe when it is wrinkled and wizened looking; mango when it is soft to the touch and fragrant. It is impossible to say how much sweetener will be needed; it depends on the fruit and juices, so taste as you go.

24 fl oz/720 ml fresh orange juice
2 fl oz/60 ml lime juice
2 tablespoons plain gelatine

Approx. 4 tablespoons Canderel
   (NutraSweet)
4 passion fruit
2 ripe mangoes

1   In a saucepan combine 4 fl oz/120 ml of orange juice with the lime juice. Sprinkle the gelatine over the juices. Stir over low heat until warm and dissolved. Do not let it come to a simmer.
2   Pour the remaining orange juice into a bowl. Stir in the gelatine mixture. Taste and add a tablespoon or so of sweetener if the juice is particularly acid. If the orange juice is sweet, you may need no sweetener at all, or only a sprinkle. Chill the mixture for an hour or so, until thickened but not set.
3   Meanwhile cut the passion fruit in half, and scoop the pulp, seeds and all, into the liquidizer container. Cut the mangoes in half (over a bowl, to catch the juices) and scoop out the flesh (see page 316 for procedure). Add mango flesh and juices to the liquidizer. Purée briefly. Push through a non-reactive sieve to eliminate the passion fruit seeds.

4   Thoroughly stir the puréed mixture into the thickened juice. Test and add sweetener to taste. Stir thoroughly to dissolve.
5   Return to the refrigerator for another hour or so, until set. Serve spooned into glass goblets.

Variation:

Omit the passion fruit and use only mangoes, if desired. Instead of puréeing them, process them until they are finely chopped. Stir into the jelly in Step 4.

♡ ⑤   GINGER LIME MOUSSE

Serves 6

This mousse is exquisitely subtle and fragrant. Serve it to your gastronome friends as a finale to a very special dinner party. It's the sort of thing that should be eaten slowly and lingeringly so that every nuance can be savoured.

---

4 fl oz/120 ml water
2 rounded tablespoons grated fresh
*   ginger root*
Grated zest of 1 lime
Juice of 1 lime
1 sachet gelatine

6 tablespoons NutraSweet
*   (Canderel)*
16 fl oz/480 ml low-fat fromage
frais
8 fl oz/240 ml buttermilk

---

1   Combine the water, ginger and lime zest in a saucepan. Simmer for 5 minutes. Stir in the lime juice. Remove from the heat. Stir in the gelatine.
2   Cool to room temperature.
3   When cooled, strain the mixture, pressing down on the solids to extract their flavour. Stir the sweetener into the strained mixture until it is dissolved.
4   Place the fromage frais and the sweetened mixture into the container of the food processor, or liquidizer. Process until perfectly smooth. While the machine is running, pour in the buttermilk in a steady stream.
5   Pour and scrape the mixture into an attractive serving dish or into 6 individual glass goblets. Chill for several hours or overnight.

BLACKBERRY GRATIN

Serves 8

This old-fashioned, juicy-purple fruit pudding is one of my all-time favourites. Because it uses frozen berries, it can be enjoyed all the year round. A summertime recipe for fruit gratin, using fresh berries, follows. I like to serve this lukewarm, but it's good at room temperature as well, and it's good cold. And leftovers served right from the fridge make a splendid breakfast.

1 lb/480 g frozen blackberries, thawed	*1 tablespoon ground toasted skinned hazelnuts*
2 rounded tablespoons brown sugar	*½ pt/300 ml low-fat fromage frais*
2 tablespoons dry coarse wholewheat breadcrumbs	

1   Preheat the grill to its highest point.
2   Thoroughly mix the thawed berries with one tablespoon of brown sugar, the crumbs and the ground nuts. Spread the mixture into a non-reactive, oval or round 1-pt/600-ml gratin dish.
3   Spread the fromage frais smoothly and evenly over the berries. Sprinkle the top with the remaining tablespoon of brown sugar.
4   Grill not too close to the heating element or flame for 4–5 minutes, until the mixture is bubbly and the sugar caramelized. Allow to cool slightly. Spoon into glass bowls and serve.

FRESH BERRY GRATIN

Use whole raspberries, whole blueberries, halved strawberries, etc. The berries and part of the fromage frais remain cool, but the topping becomes hot and bubbly. It is a most pleasing contrast.

Berries	*Brown sugar*
Fromage frais	

1   Preheat grill.
2   Spread the berries in a gratin dish.
3   Spread fromage frais evenly over the berries. Sprinkle evenly with 1–2 tablespoons dark brown sugar.
4   Grill close to the heating element for 1 minute, until the sugar is melted and bubbly. Serve *at once*.

♡ ORANGE CREAM JELLY

Makes 25 fl oz/750 ml

For Easter, chill the orange jelly and chocolate jelly in bunny moulds, and unmould on to meringue nests.

---

25 fl oz/750 ml strained, freshly
squeezed orange juice
2 sachets gelatine

2–3 tablespoons caster sugar
6–7 tablespoons fromage frais

---

1   Pour 4 fl oz/120 ml orange juice into a saucepan. Sprinkle in the gelatine. Stir over low heat until warm and dissolved. Do not let it come to a simmer. Stir in sugar and let dissolve.
2   Pour in the remaining juice. Chill until thickened and almost set.
3   Scrape into a cold bowl and whip until fluffy and perfectly smooth with an electric beater. Thoroughly beat in the fromage frais. Everything must be well amalgamated. Pour into a mould and chill overnight. Unmould and serve.

♡ ORANGES WITH ORANGE BRANDY

I like to make this beautiful dessert with a combination of blood oranges and ordinary ones. What a radiant and refreshing way to end a meal!

Oranges, 2 per person
Orange liqueur (Cointreau or
Grand Marnier)

Candied Peel (optional, see below)
Fromage frais
Brown sugar

---

1   Peel the oranges over a bowl to catch the juices. Peel so that the zest and the bitter pith come away. (If you are making the Candied Peel, use a zester to remove the zest. Cut away the pith with a knife, and discard.)
2   On a cutting board, slice the oranges about ¼ inch/0.6 cm thick.
3   Overlap the slices on pretty glass plates (two oranges per plate). Pour the juices from the bowl and the cutting board evenly over the slices. Pour ½ tablespoon of orange liqueur over each plate of slices and scatter on a bit of peel.
4   Set aside until needed. Centre a dollop of fromage frais on each arrangement of slices, and sprinkle each dollop with ¼ teaspoon brown sugar. Serve at once.

Candied Peel

Julienned zest of 2–4 oranges	*2 fl oz/60 ml water*
2 fl oz/60 ml orange liqueur	
(Cointreau or Grand Marnier)	

1   Combine zest, orange liqueur and water in a small non-reactive frying pan. Bring to a slow simmer.
2   Simmer very slowly, stirring occasionally, until all the liquid is evaporated. Spread out on greaseproof paper to cool. Refrigerate until needed.

🕐 Omit peel.

FRUIT COMPÔTE

Makes 1 pt/600 ml

As good for breakfast as for dessert.

4 tablespoons sultanas	*½ cinnamon stick*
1 lb/480 g mixed dried fruit (dried	*Juice and grated zest of 1 lemon*
apricots, apples, figs, prunes,	*Fromage frais, yoghurt, or Lemon*
pears)	*Cream Sauce (see following*
8 fl oz/240 ml dry white wine	*recipe)*
1½ oz/45 g caster sugar	

1   Combine the raisins, fruit, 8 fl oz/240 ml water, and the wine, in a baking dish. Allow to soak for 1 hour.
2   Preheat the oven to 350° F, 180° C, Gas Mark 4.
3   At the end of the hour, stir in the sugar, cinnamon stick, and lemon juice and zest. Cover the dish and bake for 1 hour. Serve warm or cold with fromage frais, yoghurt, or Lemon Cream Sauce.

🕐 LEMON CREAM SAUCE

Approximately ½ pt/300 ml sauce

The perfect topping for dried fruit compôte, or for fresh fruit salads.

⅕ pt/120 ml water	*2 tablespoons buttermilk*
Grated zest of ½ lemon	*⅖ pt/240 ml drained fromage frais*
4 tablespoons fresh lemon juice	*½–1 tablespoon honey*

1   Combine water, lemon zest and lemon juice in a small saucepan. Boil, uncovered, until reduced to about 4 tablespoons. Cool.
2   Beat the lemon infusion and buttermilk into the fromage frais. Beat in the honey. Store in the refrigerator until needed.

POACHED PEARS IN HONEYED RED WINE

Serves 6

Pears poached in wine take on a beautiful red-purple glow. I love the way they look standing on white plates in a pool of their sauce.

---

1 pt/600 ml red wine   *Juice from 1 lemon*
1 teaspoon vanilla essence   *¼ teaspoon cinnamon*
3 tablespoons honey   *6 ripe but firm pears*
Grated zest from ½ lemon

---

1   Preheat oven to 375° F, 190° C, Gas Mark 5.
2   Combine wine, vanilla, honey, all the lemon zest, half the lemon juice, and cinnamon, in a non-reactive pot. Bring to the boil, stirring occasionally. Reduce heat, partially cover, and simmer for 15 minutes.
3   Have ready a bowl of water to which you have added the remaining lemon juice. Peel the pears, but leave them whole. As they are peeled, drop them in the bowl of water. When all are peeled, put them in a baking dish. Pour the wine mixture over them. Cover and bake for 30–45 minutes, until tender but not mushy. Baste the pears occasionally. Cool, then refrigerate. They will keep for days. Serve cold.

CHERRIES IN HONEYED CREAM

Serves 4

Fruit in the freezer and fromage frais in the fridge should be facts of your kitchen life. Never be without them. What is life, after all, without pudding? Look for the frozen cherries in frozen food shops such as Bejam.

---

1 package frozen dark cherries   *6 fl oz/180 ml fromage frais*
1½ tablespoons honey   *1 teaspoon brown sugar*
½ teaspoon vanilla essence

---

1 Thaw the cherries until their juices begin to flow, but they are still icy cold. Arrange an equal amount of cherries and their juices in each of 4 glass bowls.
2 While the cherries are thawing, gently fold the honey and vanilla into the fromage frais.
3 Pour the fromage frais evenly over each serving of cherries. Sprinkle each evenly with ¼ teaspoon of brown sugar. Let it stand for 5 minutes before serving.

🕐 ⊠ Thaw cherries in the microwave.

♡ Omit honey – substitute low-Calorie sweetener if desired.

PRUNES IN LEMON SAUCE

Makes 10 fl oz/300 ml

Mention prunes in the United States, and everyone snickers and looks vaguely embarrassed. Somehow prunes have become associated with geriatric diets and 'regularity', and no one wants to admit their lusciousness and versatility. Go figure it out!

½ lb/240 g large prunes	20 fl oz/600 ml strong lemon
1 piece (2 inches/5 cm long)	verbena tea
cinnamon stick	½–1 tablespoon sugar
	1 small lemon

1 Put the prunes and cinnamon stick in a saucepan. Pour in tea and bring to the boil. Reduce heat and simmer, covered, for 15 minutes.
2 Uncover and stir in sugar, and the juice of ½ lemon. Slice the other ½ lemon and add the slices. Simmer, uncovered, for 10–15 minutes more. If a lot of juices remain, drain the prunes and boil the juices for 5 minutes. Re-combine. Serve warm or cold, with yoghurt or fromage frais if desired.

BRÛLÉE OF CARAMELIZED BANANAS

Serves 12

The more I experiment with very low-fat cookery, the more amazed and delighted I am. Both these banana puddings are so over-the-top delicious, they taste almost decadent. Both may be served hot or cold, but the soufflé is definitely at its best (and most dramatic) when hot and inflated. And both puddings may be served with Raspberry Sauce (page 318) or Blackcurrant Sauce (page 318).

Banana base ingredients
6 large bananas, ripe but firm
Juice of ½ lime
Juice of ½ large lemon
3 fl oz/90 ml fresh orange juice
1½ tablespoons orange liqueur or
dark rum
1 rounded tablespoon dark brown
sugar

Topping ingredients
1½ very ripe bananas, peeled and
sliced

Few drops lemon juice
½ teaspoon vanilla essence
½ teaspoon orange liqueur or dark
rum
4 egg whites, at room temperature
Pinch of cream of tartar
¾ pt/480 ml fromage frais, in a
large bowl
½ tablespoon dry wholemeal
breadcrumbs
½ tablespoon brown sugar

1 Prepare base: Preheat the grill to its highest setting.
2 Peel the bananas and cut in half lengthwise, then cut each half in half crosswise.
3 Put the juices and liqueur in a shallow baking dish or gratin dish that can hold the bananas in one layer. Turn the bananas in the juice, then arrange them in one layer, cut side down. Sprinkle evenly with the sugar.
4 Grill, 3 inches/8 cm from the heat, for 5 minutes, or until the bananas are well browned on top. Drain liquid into a small frying pan. Arrange the bananas, cut side down, in an attractive gratin dish. Boil the drained juices rapidly until very thick and syrupy. Be careful not to scorch them. Pour and scrape over the bananas. Set aside.
5 Prepare brûlée topping: purée the very ripe bananas in the liquidizer with the lemon juice, vanilla and the liqueur. The mixture should be very smooth.
6 In a spotlessly clean bowl, with an electric mixer, beat the egg whites until they are foamy. Add a pinch of cream of tartar and beat until they hold soft peaks.
7 Continue beating, adding the puréed banana a bit at a time. Stop and scrape down the sides of the bowl occasionally. When all the puréed banana has been added and the egg whites are creamy, greatly expanded, and hold firm peaks, scrape them into the bowl of fromage frais.
8 With a large rubber spatula, fold the egg whites and fromage frais together, turning the bowl as you fold. Spread this mixture over the grilled bananas in the gratin dish, swirling it into decorative peaks. Sprinkle evenly with the breadcrumbs and sugar.
9 Grill, 3 inches/8 cm from the heat, for 3–4 minutes, until browned. Serve at once, or chill and serve later.

328

Variation: Soufflé of Caramelized Bananas

Prepare the grilled banana base as outlined in the previous recipe.

Topping ingredients	4 egg whites, at room temperature
3 large very ripe bananas	Pinch of cream of tartar
Juice of ½ lemon	2 tablespoons fromage frais
½ teaspoon each vanilla essence and	½ tablespoon each brown sugar,
orange liqueur or dark rum	dry wholemeal breadcrumbs

---

1 Preheat the oven to 350° F, 180° C, Gas Mark 4.
2 Purée the bananas with the lemon juice, vanilla and orange liqueur or rum in the liquidizer.
3 In an impeccably clean bowl, with an impeccably clean electric beater, beat the egg whites until foamy. Add cream of tartar and beat until the egg whites hold soft peaks.
4 Add puréed bananas a little at a time as you beat. Stop occasionally to scrape down the sides. When all the puréed bananas have been added and the egg whites have greatly expanded, are creamy and hold firm peaks, stop beating.
5 Spoon the fromage frais over the beaten whites. With a rubber spatula, gently scrape the fromage frais over the surface of the whites in a thin layer. With the spatula, gently fold the layer of fromage frais into the whites.
6 Spread the mixture evenly over the grilled bananas. Sprinkle evenly with sugar and breadcrumbs. Bake (give it plenty of head room) for approximately 15 minutes, until dramatically puffed, and the juices are starting to bubble up through the soufflé topping. Serve *at once*, to gasps of delight.

'But there is something missing in any cuisine that asks us to think of a banana as a portion of potassium. There is something skewed about an eating regimen designed to do the most for every part of your body except the tip of your tongue.'

Ellen Goodman, *Washington Post*

FRENCH TOAST

Serves 6

In the United States, French toast is eaten as a festive breakfast (almost all breakfasts are festive in the US) with lashings of pure maple syrup. It also makes a lovely pudding, or a teatime treat. I have edited out the cream and butter of the traditional version, but the texture is still voluptuously custardy.

6 oz/180 g 1–2-day-old bakery
  white bread
3 eggs
2 egg whites
16 fl oz/480 ml skimmed milk

Pinch of nutmeg (optional)
Pinch of salt
Caster sugar or icing sugar
  (optional)

1   Slice bread. Cut each slice in half. Neatly arrange slices, overlapping, in an 8 inch/20 cm square, 1–2 inch/2–5 cm deep baking dish.
2   Beat the eggs and whites. Gently beat in milk, nutmeg and salt. Pour the mixture over the bread. Use a broad spatula to push the bread into the liquid. Be careful not to break up the bread. Cover the dish and refrigerate overnight.
3   Remove the dish from the refrigerator and let it stand while you preheat the oven to 350° F, 180° C, Gas Mark 4. Put the kettle on to boil.
4   Choose a baking dish larger than the one with the bread. Put it in the preheated oven. Put the bread dish in the larger dish. Pour boiling water in the larger dish to come about halfway up the sides of the smaller dish. Bake for 30–40 minutes, until puffed and firm. (A knife inserted near the centre will emerge clean.)
5   Serve at once with a sprinkling of caster sugar or a small sifting of icing sugar on each serving, if desired.

BREAD PUDDING

Serves 6

Talk about voluptuous custard! This is VC to the max. Bread pudding is nursery food's finest expression. *Everyone* loves this, indeed, some may weep a nostalgic tear or two on to their plates.

6 oz/180 g 1–2-day-old unsliced
  bakery white bread
3 eggs
2 egg whites
3½–4 tablespoons caster sugar

16 fl oz/480 ml skimmed milk
1 teaspoon vanilla essence
Pinch or two of cinnamon
  (optional)

1   Cut bread into ¾–1-inch/2–2.5-cm chunks. Put them in an 8-inch/20-cm square, 1–2-inch/2.5–5-cm deep baking dish.
2   Beat the eggs and whites with the sugar. Gently beat in the milk and flavourings. Pour the mixture over the bread. Use a broad spatula to push the bread into the liquid. Stir it all up,

but be careful not to break up the bread. Cover the dish and refrigerate for several hours (or overnight).

3   Remove the dish from the refrigerator, and let stand at room temperature while you preheat the oven to 350° F, 180° C, Gas Mark 4. Put the kettle on to boil.

4   Choose a baking dish larger than the one with the bread. Put it in the preheated oven. Put the bread dish in the larger dish. Pour boiling water in the larger dish to come about halfway up the sides of the smaller dish. Bake for 30–40 minutes, until puffed and firm. (A knife inserted near the centre will emerge clean.)

5   Cool the bread pudding on a rack. Serve warm or at room temperature.

CHOCOLATE BREAD PUDDING

Serves 6

Bread pudding, cocoa and dried fruit *put together!* Who could ask for anything more?

6 oz/180 g unsliced bakery wholemeal bread	4½–5 tablespoons dark brown sugar
3 tablespoons sultanas	1 tablespoon sifted unsweetened
7 dried figs or pitted prunes, chopped coarsely	fat-reduced cocoa (see page 335)
	¼ teaspoon ground cinnamon
5 egg whites	1 teaspoon vanilla essence
	16 fl oz/480 ml skimmed milk

1   Cut the bread into ¾–1-inch/2–2.5-cm chunks. Spread them out in an 8-inch/20-cm square, 1½–2-inch (4–5-cm) deep baking dish with the sultanas and prunes.

2   Beat the egg whites with the sugar. Sprinkle in the cocoa and flavourings. Beat to blend. Gently beat in the milk. Pour the mixture over the bread. Use a broad spatula to push the bread into the liquid. Stir it all up, but be careful not to break up the bread. Cover the dish and refrigerate for several hours (or overnight).

3   Remove the dish from the refrigerator, and let stand at room temperature while you preheat the oven to 350° F, 180° C, Gas Mark 4. Put the kettle on to boil.

4   Choose a baking dish larger than the one with the bread. Put it in the preheated oven. Put the bread dish in the large dish. Pour boiling water in the larger dish to come about halfway up

the sides of the smaller dish. Bake for 30–40 minutes, until puffed and firm.

5   Cool the bread pudding on a rack. Serve warm or at room temperature.

BREAD PUDDING WITH MINCEMEAT

Serves 6

I developed this for the BBC's *Daytime Live* as a Slim Cuisine substitute for Easter's hot cross buns.

6 oz/180 g 1–2-day-old unsliced bakery white bread	1 teaspoon vanilla essence
4 eggs	Pinch or two of cinnamon or mixed spice
3½–4 tablespoons caster sugar	6 oz/180 g Slim Cuisine Mincemeat
16 fl oz/480 g skimmed milk	(see following recipe)

1   Cut bread into ¾–1-inch/2–2.5-cm chunks. Put them in an 8-inch/20-cm square, 1–2-inch/2.5–5-cm deep baking dish.

2   Beat the eggs with the sugar. Beat in the milk and flavourings. Stir in the fruit mix. Pour the mixture over the bread. Use a broad spatula to push the bread into the liquid. Stir it all up, but be careful not to break up the bread. Cover the dish and refrigerate for several hours (or overnight).

3   Remove the dish from the refrigerator, and let stand at room temperature while you preheat the oven to 350° F, 180° C, Gas Mark 4. Put the kettle on to boil.

4   Choose a baking dish larger than the one with the bread. Put it in the preheated oven. Put the bread dish in the larger dish. Pour boiling water in the larger dish to come about halfway up the sides of the smaller dish. Bake for 30–40 minutes, until puffed and firm. (A knife inserted near the centre will emerge clean.)

5   Cool the bread pudding on a rack. Serve warm or at room temperature.

⏲ � Ⓢ
SLIM CUISINE
MINCEMEAT

Makes 2½ pts/1.5 l

---

1 packet (18 oz/500 g) cake fruit
(finely minced mixed dried
fruit); the mix you choose should
include sultanas, currants,
orange and lemon peel
1 packet (9 oz/250 g) dried apricots,
coarsely chopped (use scissors)

1 packet (5 oz/125 g) dried apple
chunks, coarsely chopped (use
scissors)
½ teaspoon each ground cinnamon,
allspice and nutmeg
2 fl oz/60 ml each medium sherry
and brandy
4 fl oz/120 ml water

---

1   Combine all ingredients and mix well.
2   Pour into a 4-pt/2,400-ml soufflé dish. Cover with cling film.
     Pierce the cling film and microwave on high for 4 minutes,
     stirring once halfway through.

Note: This mixture will keep, well covered in the refrigerator, for
months. It improves with age.

Mince pies. Use the mixture inside filo pastry triangles. See page
76 for instructions for using filo.

SEMOLINA PUDDING –
COLD VERSION

Makes 1⅕ pts/720 ml

Semolina pudding is one of those nursery dishes that induce
tranquillity. It is hard to decide which is better, the cold version or
the warm one. It is probably the one you are eating at the time.

---

9 oz/270 g couscous
16 fl oz/480 ml skimmed milk
3 oz/90 g caster sugar
1 cinnamon stick

1 tablespoon plain gelatine
⅕ pt/120 ml warm water
14 fl oz/420 ml fromage frais

---

1   Combine couscous, milk, sugar and cinnamon stick in a
     heavy-bottomed saucepan. Whisk together well. Slowly bring
     to the boil, stirring very frequently. Do not let it scorch.
2   Turn heat to its lowest point and simmer for about 5 minutes,
     stirring frequently, until thick and cooked. Remove from heat
     and let it rest for 5 minutes.

3   While the couscous is resting, dissolve the gelatine in the warm water.
4   Stir the gelatine thoroughly into the semolina. Discard the cinnamon stick. Cool the mixture to room temperature.
5   Thoroughly fold in the fromage frais. Pour into a glass bowl. Chill for several hours or overnight.

SEMOLINA PUDDING – WARM VERSION

Makes 1⅕ pts/720 ml

When you need gentleness, love, warm understanding and something soft and sweet to cry into, this is your pudding. Or make it for a good friend who is going through a difficult patch.

9 oz/270 g couscous	*1 cinnamon stick*
16 fl oz/480 ml skimmed milk	*14 fl oz/420 ml fromage frais, at*
3 oz/90 g caster sugar	*room temperature*

1   Combine couscous, milk, sugar and cinnamon stick in a heavy-bottomed saucepan. Whisk together well. Slowly bring to the boil, stirring very frequently. Do not let it scorch.
2   Turn heat to its lowest point and simmer for about 5 minutes, stirring frequently, until thick and cooked. Remove from heat and let it rest for 15 minutes.
3   Fold in the fromage frais. Serve at once.

Variations

1   Both the warm and cold version may be served with Chocolate Cream Sauce (see below) or Raspberry Sauce (page 318).
2   Serve the warm version with a spoonful of jam (see Plum Jam, page 343) stirred in. This version makes a super breakfast, when you want to start the day in a relaxed way. But if you have to be tough and hard for the work jungle, choose another breakfast. This one will turn you into an adorable and sweet pussycat for hours.

A Note to Chocoholics

Unsweetened cocoa powder is a form of chocolate with some of the cocoa butter removed. Not, alas, all the cocoa butter; cocoa powder is not fat-free. At about 22% fat, for most cocoa powders it is a slightly lower-fat form of chocolate. Some people (I am one) consider chocolate one of life's essentials. It has a dark, erotic quality that speaks to the emotions as well as the tastebuds. It is possible, I am delighted to say, to obtain a truly low-fat cocoa powder (12%). Although the fat has been drastically reduced, there is no loss of taste or quality. See the Mail Order Guide (page 345) for information. You will find my Slim Cuisine chocolate creations intensely chocolaty; they are therapeutic but not for bingeing. Eat them occasionally, but don't overdo it.

CHOCOLATE CREAM SAUCE

Makes 1¼ pts/750 ml

Don't ever feel sorry for yourself because you are living on a low-fat diet. Make this sauce occasionally. Should self-pity threaten to overcome you, rush to the kitchen and whip up a batch of Banana Icecream (page 313). Pour some of this sauce into a large goblet. Scoop in some Banana Icecream. Pour a bit of Raspberry Sauce on top (page 318), and crumble on a Chocolate Meringue (page 337). Eat with a large spoon while grinning foolishly.

---

16 fl oz/480 ml skimmed milk
4 tablespoons caster sugar
2 tablespoon cornflour
1 teaspoon vanilla essence
1½ tablespoons orange liqueur
  (Grand Marnier or Cointreau)

3–4 tablespoons unsweetened
  fat-reduced cocoa powder, sieved
  (see below)
½ large orange
4 fl oz/120 ml fromage frais

---

1 Pour 12 fl oz/360 ml milk into a heavy non-stick pan. Heat very gently. Add sugar and stir over low heat until dissolved.
2 Stir together the cornflour with 4 fl oz/120 ml cold milk. Stir into the hot milk-sugar mixture. Stir and cook over low heat until thick. Continue cooking and stirring for 1–2 minutes more. Stir in the vanilla and orange liqueur. Scrape into a large bowl.
3 Off the heat, stir in the cocoa powder gradually. When it is well incorporated, zest the orange right over the bowl so that

the zest and some of the orange oil go into the mixture. Let cool until barely warm.

4   Fold the fromage frais into the chocolate mixture. Scrape into a bowl. Chill with a piece of cling film directly on the surface to prevent a skin forming.

'No sooner had he wiped the whipped cream from his lips before a plate mountain-high in ice cream, bristling with macaroons, was thrust before him.'

John Anthony West, *Gladys's Gregory*

MILK CHOCOLATE JELLY

Makes 25 fl oz/750 ml

Both the chocolate jelly and orange jelly (page 324) can be un-moulded on to a Meringue Pie Shell (page 337) and surrounded by satsuma or mandarin sections, strawberries and raspberries; or they can be chilled in a bowl until set and then spooned into small meringue shells. If spooning into small meringue shells, use only 1 sachet gelatine in the recipe. Try orange jelly in chocolate mering-ue, and chocolate jelly in white meringue. One more suggestion: if you unmould the jelly on to a Meringue Pie Shell, try surrounding it with *frozen* raspberries and cherries. As they thaw, their juices are released and the meringue turns gooey (the chocolate meringue becomes fudgy). It's quite impossibly delicious and satisfying on a very basic level.

2 sachets gelatine	*12 fl oz/360 ml skimmed milk*
12 fl oz/360 ml hot water	*3 tablespoons fat-reduced cocoa (see*
8 tablespoons caster sugar	*page 335) sifted*
½ teaspoon vanilla essence	*6–7 tablespoons fromage frais*

1   Mix the gelatine into the hot water. Stir until thoroughly dissolved. Stir in sugar and let it dissolve. Stir in vanilla, milk and cocoa. Chill until the mixture is thickened and almost completely set.

2   Scrape into a cold bowl and whip with an electric mixer until fluffy and very smooth. Thoroughly beat in the fromage frais. Everything must be very well amalgamated. Pour into a mould and chill overnight until totally set. Unmould and serve.

CHOCOLATE MERINGUES

Makes 100

These delightfully crunchy little morsels work out at about 10 Calories each. The chocolate taste is very intense.

---

3 egg whites, at room temperature
Pinch of cream of tartar and salt
5 oz/150 g sugar

1 teaspoon vanilla essence
4 tablespoons fat-reduced cocoa,
(see page 335) sifted

---

1   Preheat oven to 225° F, 110° C, Gas Mark 1.
2   Beat egg whites with cream of tartar and salt until foamy. Increase speed. Beat, adding sugar, 1–2 tablespoons at a time, until shiny and stiff and firm peaks hold. Fold in vanilla and cocoa.
3   Line two baking sheets with greaseproof paper. Drop batter on sheets by the half teaspoonful, 1 inch/2.5 cm apart. Bake for 45 minutes. (To make small nests, make a dent in each dollop of batter with a spoon before baking.)
4   Turn oven off. Leave in the oven for at least 3 hours. (They may stay in overnight.) Do not open the door until the time is up.

Variation I: White Meringues

Follow the above recipe but omit the cocoa. The meringue mixture – chocolate or white – can be made into free form shapes, or piped through a pastry bag in order to make bunnies, etc.

Variation II: Meringue Pie Shell

Use a rubber spatula to scrape the meringue mixture into an ungreased 9-inch/23-cm pie pan (do not use one with a detachable bottom), and smooth it over the bottom and up the sides. Bake for 1 hour and cool as above. The shell will have a wonderfully fudgy texture.

Airy Pleasures

Soufflés are dramatic, gossamer creations, although the thought of making one fills many novice cooks with fear and trembling. A soufflé's spectacular appearance – and the blissful sighs that greet it as it emerges from the kitchen in all its airy glory – make soufflé cookery very gratifying indeed. Ignore all the stories you have heard about their unpredictability and their penchant for collapsing from the vibrations of a footstep. Soufflés are really very easy to produce.

I must also tell you to ignore most of the usual rules of soufflé cookery. Traditionally, they are made with an egg yolk-enriched base. Egg yolks contain fat and the base is usually a thick white sauce – rich in butter and cream. To bring the fat level even higher, the soufflé dish is always liberally buttered or oiled.

I had a glorious time breaking all the rules, and I've come up with some beauties. They rise to spectacular heights, they taste *intensely* of their main ingredient, and – although they collapse if left to stand, as do all soufflés – they do not collapse as pathetically as do traditional ones. Should there be any leftover soufflé (you may have to hide it in an opaque plastic container and label it 'tripes in prune sauce'), it is delicious served (cut into wedges) on the next day, with no apologies needed. It will be a lovely, spongy pudding.

Here are a few helpful soufflé hints:

1   Beaten egg whites folded into a fruit base (or combined with cocoa, page 335) cause the soufflé's magical rise in the oven. The eggs should be beaten with a wire whip (an electric mixer with a wire whip attachment is the ideal) in an immaculately clean bowl. The slightest trace of grease (luckily, there will be no grease in *your* kitchen) or egg yolk will prevent the egg whites from expanding. Have the egg whites at room temperature; cold egg whites will not whip up to maximum volume.

2   Always be sure that there is no oven shelf above the soufflé. These beauties really rise, and you may open the oven to find your soufflé has left its dish and is hanging from the upper shelf. Give it plenty of head room.

3   A baking soufflé is not as temperamental as you might imagine. You may walk around the kitchen, and even talk out loud while it is baking. I wouldn't dance the fandango in front of the oven, however.

4   Bake it until it has risen impressively and a thin skewer inserted near the centre comes out *almost* clean. Or – if you prefer a very firm soufflé – when the skewer emerges clean.

5   Have everyone seated and ready. Serve *at once*.

'The words people use for a Chartres or a Mozart,
He's using to praise a soufflé.'

Judith Viorst, *The Gourmet*

Ⓢ BANANA SOUFFLÉ
Serves 4–6

3 medium-sized ripe bananas	Pinch of cream of tartar
1 tablespoon dark rum	Approximately 2 tablespoons sugar
½ teaspoon nutmeg	(less if the bananas are very
½ teaspoon cinnamon	sweet)
1 scant tablespoon lemon juice	½ teaspoon vanilla
8 egg whites, at room temperature	

1   Preheat oven to 350° F, 180° C, Gas Mark 4.
2   Cut bananas into thick slices. Purée with the rum, the spices
    and the lemon juice in a food processor or blender. Scrape into
    a large bowl.
3   Beat egg whites in an electric mixer on medium speed until
    foamy. Add cream of tartar and beat on highest speed, adding
    sugar a little at a time, until the sugar is dissolved and the
    whites are shiny and thick and hold firm peaks. Fold in the
    vanilla.
4   Gently fold the whites into the banana mixture.
5   Spoon the banana mixture into a 5½–6pt/3,300–3,600-ml
    soufflé dish. Cook on the middle shelf of the oven for 30–35
    minutes. (Remove the top shelf first.) Serve at once.

Note: If you wish to gild the lily, serve with Chocolate Cream
Sauce (page 335), or Raspberry Sauce (page 318).

Ⓢ MANGO SOUFFLÉ
Serves 4–6

3 large ripe mangoes, peeled, pitted	2 fl oz/60 ml water
and chopped	3 tablespoons dark rum
1½ teaspoons lime juice	2 tablespoons sugar
2 tablespoons cornflour	8 egg whites, at room temperature

1   Purée mangoes and lime juice in the food processor.
2   Combine cornflour and water and whisk until a smooth paste.

3   Stir into the mango mixture. Bring to the boil. Reduce heat and simmer for 4–5 minutes, until very thick.
4   Stir in rum and 1 tablespoon sugar and cook for 1 minute more. Scrape into a large bowl and leave to cool.
5   Beat egg whites in an electric mixer on medium speed until foamy. Add remaining sugar, a little at a time, while beating on highest speed, until the sugar is dissolved and the whites are shiny and thick and hold firm peaks.
6   Gently fold the whites into the mango mixture.
7   Spoon the mango mixture into a 5½–6-pt (3,300–3,600-ml) soufflé dish. Cook on the middle shelf of the oven for 35–40 minutes. (Remove the top shelf first.) Serve at once.

CHOCOLATE SOUFFLÉ

Serves 6

I would not be worthy of my mission in life if I were not able to come up with a decadent-tasting chocolate dessert like this every once in a while. Ignore rumours you may have heard about carob being a good substitute for chocolate. As far as I'm concerned, carob is an abomination on the face of the earth. This is the *real thing*. Eat it and weep.

---

9 tablespoons caster sugar
9 tablespoons unsweetened,
    fat-reduced cocoa (see page 335)

9 egg whites, at room temperature
Pinch of cream of tartar
1½ teaspoons of vanilla
1½ teaspoons dark rum

---

1   Preheat the oven to 350° F, 180° C, Gas Mark 4.
2   Sift together all of the sugar except about 2 tablespoons with all of the cocoa. Set aside.
3   In an electric mixer beat the egg whites with the cream of tartar until foamy. At highest speed, continue beating, adding the 2 tablespoons of plain sugar a little at a time, until the whites hold stiff peaks.
4   With a rubber spatula, fold the sugar-cocoa mixture into the beaten whites. Fold in the vanilla and rum.
5   Pile the egg white mixture into a 5½–6-pt/3,300–3,600-ml soufflé dish. Bake in the centre of the oven (remove the top shelf) for 30–40 minutes. *Serve at once.* (Pass a jug of Raspberry Sauce, page 318, if desired.)

Variation: Fudgy Chocolate Torte

To make a chocolate cake follow the recipe above but use a 10-inch/25-cm non-stick flan tin instead of a soufflé dish and bake for 20–30 minutes. (A skewer inserted near the middle should emerge not quite clean.) Remove from the oven and let the tin cool on a rack. Serve wedges of this dense torte on pools of Raspberry Sauce (page 318), topped with Chocolate Cream Sauce (page 335), and garnished with a few raspberries.

'. . . the Chocolate Elite – the select millions who like chocolate in all its infinite variety, using ''like'' as in ''I like to breathe.'''

Sandra Boynton, *Chocolate the Consuming Passion*

♡⊕ CAPPUCCINO

Cappuccino – strong coffee topped with frothy steamed milk – is usually made with full-fat milk or half cream. Even if you have no cappuccino machine to steam the milk and you don't touch whole milk or cream, you can still make a beautifully frothy, creamy mug of cappuccino at home. You need good coffee, a microwave, a liquidizer and skimmed milk.

Skimmed milk
Filtered coffee, made from dark
  roasted coffee beans

Fat-reduced cocoa powder (see page
  335)

---

1   Bring the milk just to the boil. (The microwave is perfect for this.) Pour some of the milk into the liquidizer container and cover. (Fill it a little less than half, or you may splash and burn yourself, and make a terrible mess.) Turn the machine on; wait a moment, then carefully lift up a tiny corner of the lid on the side away from you so that some air gets in. *Be careful* – stand back and avert your face slightly. Blend on high for 50–60 seconds. Pour the milk into a jug. Repeat until all milk has been whipped.
2   Fill coffee cup or mugs ½–⅔ full. Top up with milk, including some of the froth. With a tea strainer, sift a tiny bit of cocoa on to each mugful. Serve at once.

341

CELEBRATION PUNCH

Makes 9½ pts/5.7 l/55 punch cup servings

I devised this party drink when the *Daytime Live* folks asked me to develop a festive non-alcoholic drink for the last show of the season.

---

*3 pts/1,800 ml strong lemon
   verbena tea*
2½ pts/1,500 ml cranberry juice
*2½/1,500 ml low-Calorie American
   dry ginger ale*

*1½ pts/900 ml low-Calorie
   sparkling lemonade*
Strawberry ice cubes (see below)

Combine all ingredients, except ice cubes. Serve the punch ice-cold. Add the strawberry ice cubes at the last minute.

Note: This recipe can be scaled down if desired.

Strawberry Ice Cubes

Quarter fresh strawberries. Put a quarter berry in each compartment of ice cube trays. Fill with water and freeze.

🕐 Omit strawberry ice cubes.

🕐 ALCOHOL-FREE SANGRIA

Makes 7 pts/4 l

Just the thing for picnics and barbecues. It tastes quite alcoholic. You may find that people become slightly tipsy through the power of suggestion, if you don't tell how innocent the drink is.

---

*16 fl oz/500 ml chilled fresh orange
   juice*
*1 box (36 fl oz/1 litre chilled
   cranberry juice*

2 limes
*1 pt/600 ml sparkling mineral
   water*

---

1   In a jug, stir together the orange and cranberry juices. Halve the limes, and squeeze in their juice. Drop the squeezed lime halves into the jug. Refrigerate.
2   Pour in the water just before serving.

PLUM JAM

Approximately ½ pt/300 ml

This is an easy and fresh-tasting almost instant plum jam, that will brighten the breakfast table, or make a simple pudding stirred into fromage frais. With good bread, and jam like this, why would you want to grease things up with butter or margarine?

1 lb/480 ml chunked, unpeeled plums (golden, red, or purple)	*Approximately 1 tablespoon sugar* *Lemon juice (optional)*

1   Mash the plums with a potato masher, until they are a lumpy purée. Spread the purée in a shallow dish and sprinkle with sugar. Let sit for 30 minutes.
2   Stir and taste. Add a squirt of lemon juice, if the taste needs sharpening. Serve spread on toast.

STRAWBERRY CREAM FOR BREAKFAST OR TEA

This is a splendid substitute for butter, Devonshire cream or whipped cream and strawberry jam. Spread it on scones, bread or toast for an unbelievably delicious low-Calorie snack. It tastes indulgent and luxurious, but contains just a fraction of the Calories of real cream and jam.

Very ripe (or overripe) strawberries
Skimmed-milk quark

Mash the strawberries with a fork. With a wooden spoon, beat the strawberries into the quark. Scrape into a bowl or crock, cover with cling film and refrigerate for a few hours for the flavours to blend. This will keep for several days and improve in flavour each day.

APRICOT JAM

Makes 1⅕ pts/720 ml

1 lb/480 g dried apricots	*2 tablespoons brandy*

1   Put the apricots in a heavy saucepan. Add water to generously cover. Bring to simmer.

2   Cook over low heat, stirring frequently, until the apricots lose their shape and cook into a lumpy mass. This will take anything from 15 minutes to 1 hour, depending on the fruit.

3   Stir in the brandy and a few more ounces of water. Cook for a few more minutes, stirring, until the mixture is very thick. Be careful not to scorch the mixture. Cool.

4   Taste. If the mixture is too tart, stir in a bit of Canderel or sugar. If too sweet, stir in a few drops of fresh lemon juice. Scrape the mixture into a crock or bowl. Cover tightly and refrigerate. It will keep for weeks.

APRICOT CREAM

Fold together equal parts of Apricot Jam and low-fat fromage frais. If desired, sprinkle each portion with a few toasted pine kernels.

Mail Order Guide

Write or telephone for a price list.

Anton's Delicatessen
101 Hare Lane
Claygate
Esher
Surrey
KT10 0QX

Tel: 0372 62306

Tinned tortillas
Mexican specialities
American specialities
Balsamic vinegar
Dry pack sun-dried tomatoes

Books for Cooks
4 Blenheim Crescent
London
W11 1NN

Tel: 01 221 1992

Dry pack sun-dried tomatoes

Culpeper Limited
Hadstock Road
Linton
Cambridgeshire
CB1 6NJ

Tel: 0223 894054

Californian dry pack sun-dried
tomatoes, no added salt

Italian Taste
32 Abbeygate Street
Bury St Edmunds
Suffolk

Tel: 0284 752605

Dry pack sun-dried tomatoes
Balsamic vinegar
Quick-cooking polenta
Dried mushrooms

Health Craze
Cromwell Court
115 Earls Court Road
London
SW5
Tel: 01 244 7784

Vegetable stock powders and pastes including Friggs Vegetale and Healthrite stock paste
Pulses and dried beans, including black beans

Parsons Trading Ltd
Orion House
Gray's Place
Slough
Berkshire
SL2 5AF
Tel: 0753 26196

Excellent quality fat-reduced cocoa powder

Index

347

349

351